Alexander Fleming
The Man and the Myth

Dr R. G. Macfarlane, CBE, is Emeritus Professor of Clinical Pathology in the University of Oxford, a Fellow of the Royal Society, a Quondam Fellow of All Souls College, Oxford, and President of the Haemophilia Society.

His career has been in hospital clinical pathology, teaching and research in London and Oxford, apart from a post in bacteriology at the Wellcome Laboratories in 1939–41 and service in the RAMC in 1944–45 to work on gas gangrene in battle casualties with a mobile bacteriological laboratory in Normandy and N.W. Europe. Since he was a student at St Bartholomew's Hospital in 1931 his main interest has been in haemophilia and the mechanism of blood clotting. This led, in 1953, to the introduction of a therapy that, for the first time, allowed haemophilia patients safely to undergo major surgery. From 1959–67 he was Director of a unit set up in Oxford by the Medical Research Council to carry this work forward.

Gwyn Macfarlane is the author of many scientific papers and of books including *Howard Florey: The Making of a Great Scientist*.

D1102143

Alexander Fleming

The Man and the Myth

———

Gwyn Macfarlane

Oxford   New York

OXFORD UNIVERSITY PRESS

1985

Oxford University Press, Walton Street, Oxford OX2 6DP

London New York Toronto
Delhi Bombay Calcutta Madras Karachi
Kuala Lumpur Singapore Hong Kong Tokyo
Nairobi Dar es Salaam Cape Town
Melbourne Auckland

and associated companies in
Beirut Berlin Ibadan Mexico City Nicosia

Oxford is a trade mark of Oxford University Press

First published 1984 by Chatto & Windus
First issued as an Oxford University Press paperback 1985

British Library Cataloguing in Publication Data
Macfarlane, Gwyn
Alexander Fleming: the man and the myth.
1. Fleming, Sir Alexander
2. Bacteriologists—Great Britain—Biography
3. Penicillin—History
I. Title
616'.014'0924 QR31.F5
ISBN 0-19-281884-8

Printed in Great Britain by
Richard Clay (The Chaucer Press) Ltd.
Bungay, Suffolk

Preface

If the subject of this biography needs no introduction – the name Alexander Fleming must be one of the most famous in the world – the book itself needs an explanation. So much has been written about Fleming already: at least seven biographies in Britain alone, including the official one by André Maurois; descriptions of his life and achievements in scores of books on penicillin, and in literally hundreds of newspaper and magazine articles. Why then should one add to an overflowing bibliography?

The first answer is that almost all these biographical accounts tell the same story, and this book will present a significantly different one. In the familiar picture, Fleming is the altruistic hero of a rags-to-riches romance, the poor farmer's son from Ayrshire who became a brilliant bacteriologist and who struggled to achieve, not riches for himself, but the gift to the world of penicillin and the greatest single advance in medical history. Since much of the framework of this popular story is factually correct, how can a different version be justified? The answer lies in the point of view, the angle from which the facts are seen and interpreted.

Almost all Fleming's biographers have been writers without medical or scientific training. They have tried to extract for non-medical readers a personal, human drama from what is, in reality, a scientific drama. In this way much that is true and exciting has been lost and the gaps have been filled by fanciful distortions or pure inventions to give an appearance of credibility. That this is only an appearance becomes obvious to anyone who studies the details of Fleming's scientific work. As a scientist he is extremely interesting. As a person he was less so, and the literary efforts to create hidden motives and depths of character are misdirected and misleading.

A sad consequence of this romantic approach has been the obliteration of real mysteries. One such mystery surrounds the discovery of penicillin itself. How did it happen? In the popular version a stray mould landed on one of Fleming's culture plates and destroyed the germs. At once his genius for observation and deduction revealed to him both the phenomenon and its immense importance. And there the story of the discovery ends – just where it should begin. Closer examination reveals a series of chance events of almost unbelievable improbability. How pale is the fiction beside the fact!

A second mystery is the failure to develop penicillin during the twelve years that followed its discovery. Some writers have virtually ignored this – in one recent biography, for example, these years are covered in only twenty-nine lines. Others have imagined an epic struggle by Fleming against impossible odds. André Maurois writes: 'There is something deeply moving in the spectacle of this shy man with his burning faith in the capital importance of a piece of research trying, in vain, to persuade those who alone could have made its practical application possible, to see as he did.' But, in reality, it proves to be more rewarding to discover exactly what Fleming *did* do with penicillin between 1928 and 1940.

The third mystery involves wider issues. Just how did Fleming, who had discovered the *bacteriological* effect of penicillin, become the world hero when Florey and his team in Oxford discovered and proved its almost miraculous *therapeutic* power twelve years later? In most of the Fleming biographies the Oxford work is acknowledged but not emphasized. In some it is barely mentioned, and in one, credit for the clinical work done in Oxford is actually given to Fleming and St Mary's Hospital – a gross mis-statement of fact. Earlier newspaper reports are probably to blame for this misconception – one that has rooted itself widely. John Sheehan, in *The Enchanted Ring*, published in 1982, describes how the version of the penicillin story popular in America has fused Fleming's discovery with the Oxford work, so that Fleming has been canonized while Florey and his team 'have fallen into the shadows of history'. To Fleming's biographers it seems to be a just and natural consequence of his achievements that he should make triumphal world tours, during which he received 25 honorary degrees, 15 civic freedoms and over 140 orders, decorations, major prizes and other honours. But these events are quite at variance with the shyness and modesty emphasized as characteristic of Fleming, and they also seem to be unjustified by the facts of scientific history. The explanation may lie in what seems to have been an efficient and somewhat mysterious exercise in public relations.

There is one writer on Fleming who is notably exempt from the criticisms implied above. In his book, *The Birth of Penicillin*, published in 1970, Ronald Hare was the first to analyse the scientific facts of Fleming's discovery of penicillin and his activities thereafter. One result was the revelation of the astonishing sequence of chance events that made the discovery possible, and Hare's own ingenious theory of how they came about. Next, his book casts doubts on Fleming's supposed struggle to develop penicillin as a therapeutic agent, and describes, in fact, a surprising inactivity. Then, in 1979, Hare reported his discovery of unpublished experiments that give a convincing explanation for Fleming's lack of enthusiasm. It was this work that helped to persuade me that another biography of Fleming was needed.

My own interest in Fleming stems from the time of the epoch-making penicillin work in Oxford. Before that, I had given him little thought. As a junior hospital pathologist in the 1930s I had met him briefly at medical functions, and remember two of his lectures during which I was impressed by his clever practical demonstrations. I attended two of Almroth Wright's soirées, where I marvelled at Fleming's 'germ paintings'; and one of Wright's famous tea parties – a terrifying experience for a young outsider from St Bartholomew's Hospital. But Wright's influence had extended even there – I well remember the tedium of doing 'opsonic indices' and preparing vaccines, and my lack of faith in the real value of either. At that time Fleming seemed but a dim figure on a stage dominated by Wright, and until I went to Oxford in 1941, I had barely heard of penicillin.

In Oxford, we soon became aware of Fleming's rise to world fame and of the fact that it seemed, at least in the newspapers, to be based on work that we had seen done by Florey and his colleagues. I must confess that it was with a lingering sense of injustice that I wrote a biography of Howard Florey some years ago. This was not lessened when none of the commercial publishers whom I approached showed any interest either in the subject or the author except one, who suggested kindly that I should write a biography of Fleming instead. 'At least,' he said, 'everyone has heard of *him*.' So, the book on Florey having eventually been published, I have now taken his advice.

The present book is, so to speak, the other side of the equation. And I should say at once that any resentment that I might have felt for Fleming at the outset quite evaporated as I studied his life and work in detail. He was, I am sure, an honest, likeable and truly modest man, and a highly talented and original scientist who believed that he had sound reasons for what he did and did not do about penicillin. But when the antibiotic revolution swept the world it was Fleming who was carried on the wave of an enormous public gratitude. In the circumstances, it would have been almost impossible for him to have abdicated this position. And if he had, the credit for a new era in medicine might well have slipped away – not to Oxford, but out of Britain and across the Atlantic.

Work on this book began in Ayrshire, in the district in which Fleming was born. The Dick Institute in Kilmarnock has a fine reference library with many books on local history, files of local newspapers and – most valuable of all – an admirable unpublished book by Robert Fleming, Alexander's brother, giving a vivid account of their Ayrshire boyhood and early years in London. This is almost the only such account, and it has been the basis for the opening chapters of most biographies of Fleming, including my own. Some days spent in and around Darvel and a visit to Lochfield Farm high on the bleak hillside above it gave substance to Robert Fleming's narrative, and the feeling of a strongly individual and essentially Ayrshire–Scottish community. One does not joke about Covenanters in Darvel! They are still remembered with fierce pride.

From the upland wilds, the trail led to the confined silence of the Manuscript Department in the British Museum. Here are deposited the Fleming Papers, collected by Lady (Amalia) Fleming. They can be divided into two categories – writings by Fleming, and writings about him. It was the former that were of most value, and of these his laboratory notebooks were paramount. Anyone familiar with laboratory research and with some knowledge of the then-contemporary field can follow a line of investigation running through the jumble of figures and routine entries typical of such notebooks. Fleming's were most rewarding, and to find the first entries describing lysozyme and penicillin was a thrilling experience.

Fleming's other writings were of less interest. There are almost no personal letters, and most of the diaries that have survived contain only scattered notes of appointments. There are scripts of speeches and lectures, but these are formal affairs that reveal little of the speaker. For a picture of Fleming, the man, one has to rely on the many letters written about him soon after his death. These were in response to an appeal by Lady Fleming for personal reminiscences from his colleagues, friends and students for use by her chosen biographer. It is inevitable that such letters should be mostly laudatory, but they contain revealing and amusing anecdotes. A selection of these was used by André Maurois and I cannot avoid duplicating some of them. I have included one or two less complimentary items not used by him and others with a bearing on the arguments developed here.

The Florey archives at the Royal Society contain some correspondence with Fleming and also four volumes of press cuttings on penicillin for the years 1942–1945. Reading these almost creates a disbelief in one's own knowledge of the facts, but at least an understanding of how Fleming became a world hero. It seems that Fleming had his own book of cuttings selected for the wildness of their inaccuracies about himself, and this is not among his papers. But what he called the 'Fleming myth' is well represented in the Florey collection. Visits to St Mary's Hospital and the Wright–Fleming Institute were essential to gain a picture of Fleming's place of work over fifty years, and another to The Dhoon, his country house in Suffolk, explained its fascination for him.

Meanwhile I had been corresponding with people who had known Fleming, and interviewing as many as was practical. Sadly, five of those who were helping me have died during the course of this work. They are: my old friend Sir George Pickering, FRS, Professor of Medicine at St Mary's from 1939 to 1956; Dr V. D. Allison, who had worked with Fleming on lysozyme and who remained his friend thereafter; Professor F. Bustinza, a fervent admirer of Fleming, who kindly sent me his books about him and many papers and photographs; Dr Thomas Hunt, who had known Fleming as a colleague and as his family physician; and Vivian Pitchforth, RA, Fleming's most frequent companion at the Chelsea Arts Club. I record here my gratitude for their letters and the considerable help I received.

When the writing of the book was almost complete, Professor Hare sent me a copy of his essay on Fleming's scientific work, which he has submitted for publication in *Medical History*. This was indeed generous because he knew that my book was likely to appear before his essay, and he believed that I would find what he had written helpful. This it certainly was. Having read his essay, some puzzling entries in Fleming's notebooks and odd remarks by his colleagues suddenly assumed significance. I had myself been misled by the 'Fleming myth' into believing that he had been depressed by a failure to develop penicillin during the years that followed his discovery. Having read Hare's essay, I realized what Fleming had contentedly been doing with penicillin during these years, and I discovered for myself further evidence of his real major interest. In consequence, I rewrote the chapter concerned with this period, changing its title from 'The Twelve-Year Gap' to 'Twelve Busy Years'. Hare's essay has completed his own convincing and original study of Fleming's work, and I am most grateful for this preview of it.

I have tried to convey, to the best of my ability, an objective and impartial account of the events of Fleming's life and the details of his scientific work. For the benefit of non-medical readers I have avoided technical jargon as much as possible, but I think that most people now know a good deal more about scientific medicine than doctors perhaps realize. Fleming's own notebooks and published papers form the basis for the account of his scientific career. For the personal side, I have had to rely on material provided by his family, friends and colleagues, some of which has appeared in previous biographies. In particular I have followed Maurois's account of the closing scenes of his life, since these must have been described to him at first hand by Lady Fleming. Only in the last chapter of this book do I make my own assessment of Fleming as a scientist and a man. This is a subjective one, but I hope it is unbiased. Readers will have had the facts before them, and they can form their own opinions.

It is a pleasure to thank those who have been so generous with their time and trouble on my behalf. First and most constant in her efforts is my wife, Dr Hilary Macfarlane, who has worked with me throughout the research and the preparation of the manuscript. The staff of the Dick Institute at Kilmarnock, and the Rector of the Academy there, were helpful and informative. I owe special thanks to Mr William Gray of Symington, formerly Secretary of the Darvel Fleming Memorial Committee. He knew that my views on Fleming differed from his own, yet he guided us to Lochfield Farm and around Darvel, and did a good deal of local research on my behalf and maintained a long correspondence. Both he and his wife were kindness itself, insisting that we should stay with them.

In London, the staff of the British Library were as helpful as their rigid rules allowed, and the librarians at the Royal Society were, as always, willingly co-operative. Among members of the staff at St Mary's Hospital I have received much help and many letters from Professor A. A. Glynn, then Director of the Wright–Fleming Institute, Mr K. Lockyer, Secretary of the Medical School, and our friend Dr J. F. Ackroyd. In Suffolk, Dr Robert Fleming, Sir Alexander's son, spared time from his busy practice to talk about his parents, to take us to see The Dhoon and later to write a long account in answer to further questions. Mr Angus Fleming, son of Sir Alexander's brother Robert, gave us an informative interview, supplemented later by several detailed letters. Dr Donald Fleming, son of Sir Alexander's half-brother Tom, wrote a most interesting letter, and sent copies of family papers and a complete family tree. We did not meet Lady (Amalia) Fleming, who lives in Athens, but she has written letters, sent photographs and given permission to quote from Sir Alexander's writings.

We had two meetings and, of course, much correspondence, with Professor Ronald Hare, to whose work I owe much of the new material in this book. We recall with pleasure a visit to Dr and Mrs V. D. Allison at Emsworth. Their memories of Fleming and his family were fresh and vivid, and they had a fine collection of Fleming 'memorabilia' including one of his famous *P. notatum* medallions. Dr Allison also wrote to me at length about Fleming, and gave me copies of his own papers and lectures. Another visit was to Mrs Barbara Hunt, who also had personal memories of the Fleming family.

I wish to record my thanks to the many other people who took much trouble to write in answer to my requests for information about Fleming, his work, and the historical background to it. They are: Sir Edward Abraham, Dr A. R. Butler, Mr J. V. Chapman, Dr J. A. Charles, Mrs Vera Colebrook, Professor J. G. Collee, Mr D. B. Colquhoun, Dr J. A. Cross, Mr Ian Curteis, Dr D. P. Cuthbertson, Mr F. Donnelly, Mr S. F. Everitt, Professor G. J. Fraenkel, Dr Norman Heatley, Dr W. E. van Heyningen, Dr Gladys Hobby, Professor Dorothy Hodgkin, Dr N. Howard-Jones, Mr R. M. Howitt, Mr J. Hunter, Dr Charles Jack, Dr B. Juel-Jenson, Professor R. R. H. Lovell, Mr L. J. Ludovici, Sir William Maycock, Dr L. M. Miall, Sir Ashley Miles, Sir David Phillips, Professor R. R. Porter, Dr Beatrice Pullinger, Dr A. H. T. Robb-Smith, Mr N. H. Robinson, Mr Giles Romanes, Professor D. Rowley, Miss Audrey Russell, Professor J. C. Sloper, Professor A. L. Stalker, Dr J. M. Stengle, Professor Gordon T. Stewart, Dr C. R. la Touche, Dr T. I. Williams and Mr David Wilson.

Mr T. H. H. Hancock, Secretary of the Chelsea Arts Club, and Mr J. Bulpin, of the London Scottish Regiment, have been most helpful in obtaining information about Fleming's membership of, and activities in, these organizations. Dr P. N. Cardew, of the Photographic Department, St Mary's Hospital Medical School, showed us a fine collection of photographs of Almroth Wright, Fleming and their colleagues, and has provided selected copies to illustrate this book. Mr J. Hunter, of the Dick Institute, has researched local history on my behalf, and also provided photographs.

Mr R. S. Crespi, of the National Research Development Corporation, has given advice on British patent law current in the 1930s, and Lloyd's Maritime Records have confirmed details of Fleming's ship travel.

I wish to thank Mrs R. Ryan, who very kindly translated for me the Spanish text of Professor Bustinza's book on Fleming. I am grateful to Mrs B. Clapton and Miss G. Carroll for doing most of the typing, and to the Gairloch Construction Company for much photocopying.

Finally, I gratefully acknowledge grants of £500 each, made on the recommendation of Professor G. V. R. Born, by Messrs Pfizer and Messrs Merck and Co. Inc., towards the expenses of collecting material.

R.G.M.

Acknowledgements

Permission for quotations from copyright material is gratefully acknowledged from the following writers and their publishers, agents or literary executors, the material concerned being identified by the relevant chapter/note numbers unless otherwise stated: Messrs Curtis Brown Ltd, London, on behalf of the Estate of André Maurois, (Preface, 8.9, 14.12, 18.6, 18.18, 19.12, 19.17); Mr R. M. Howitt, (7.9); Mrs Vera Colebrook, Mr Giles Romanes and Messrs William Heinemann Medical Books Ltd, London, (7.11); Mr Giles Romanes, (p. 77 and p. 198); Mr Angus Fleming, (8.3); Lord Moran, (8.17); Dr V. D. Allison and the Editor of the *Ulster Medical Journal*, (10.14); the Editors, the *Proceedings of the Royal Society*, (11.1); the Editor, the *British Journal of Experimental Pathology*, (12.1); the Editor, the *Journal of Pathology*, (14.1); the Editor, the *Proceedings of the Royal Society of Medicine*, (14.2); the Secretary, the Royal Institute of Public Health and Hygiene, (14.3); the Editor, the *British Dental Journal*, (14.5); Mr Ian Curteis, (14.13 and 17.3); Messrs Methuen Ltd, London (14.15); Lady (Margaret) Florey, (16.6, 18.15 and 18.26); Lady (Ann) Chain, (16.12 and 21.27); Lady (Amalia) Fleming, (17.6, 18.14 and 19.30); the Editor, the *British Medical Journal*, (17.12b); Mrs Lucia Fulton, (18.9); Dr G. M. Little, (18.27); Dr Hugh Clegg, (19.14); the Editor, the *Daily Mail*, (p. 210); Mr L. J. Ludovici, (19.23); Professor A. L. Stalker, (19.26); Professor R. Lovell, (19.27b); Messrs Robert Hale Ltd, London (19.28); Professor D. Rowley, (19.34); Dr W. E. van Heyningen, (19.35 and 22.6); Professor R. Hare, (19.36); the Chairman, *St Mary's Hospital Gazette*, (19.36 and 20.36); Professor F. Bustinza, (20.4–10); Messrs Wayland Publishers Ltd, Hove (20.13, 21.1 and 22.10); Messrs Butterworth Ltd, London (21.18); Mr A. J. P. Taylor, (21.25); the Medical Research Council and the Controller, HM Stationery Office, (21.26); Mr G. S. Pitchforth, (21.28); Mrs Robert Cruickshank, (22.7).

The author wishes to acknowledge the permission granted by the Officers of the Royal Society for the publication of historical information in the Society's records.

Permission has also been kindly granted for the reproduction of illustrations as follows: Department of Audio Visual Communication, St Mary's Hospital (Dr P. N. Cardew): Plate 2a. Lady Fleming and the British Library: Plate 1a and b. Professor Ronald Hare: Plate 2b and c.

Contents

Contents

Illustrations

Inside front cover, Plate 1

(a) The first entry on penicillin in Fleming's notebook
(b) The next experiment on penicillin recorded by Fleming

Inside back cover, Plate 2

(a) Fleming's photograph of his original penicillin plate
(b) Ronald Hare's photograph of an experimental 'penicillin plate'
(c) Ronald Hare's photograph of his next experimental plate

But *Facts* are cheels that winna ding,
An' downa be disputed.

ROBERT BURNS *A Dream*

I

The Ayrshire Background

Alexander Fleming was born on 6 August 1881 in a remote farmhouse near Darvel in Ayrshire. The great hills and valleys of this south-western area of Scotland in which he spent the first fourteen years of his life, and the people whose families had lived there for centuries, created an environment so strongly individual that it could not have failed to mould his character.

Ayrshire is a county of contrasts. In the west is the fertile coastal plain with its woods and quiet rivers and the wide, level farmlands that have made its agriculture famous. But a few miles inland the hills begin, and there is a complete change of scene. These hills are the outposts of the Southern Uplands which roll eastwards, not just across most of Ayrshire, but on across Scotland to the North Sea. Rising to rounded summits over 2,500 feet in height, the Uplands are bleak and almost barren, supporting no more than isolated sheep farms where life has changed very little since Fleming was a boy.

The Irvine valley is one that penetrates into the western edge of this hill country. It forms a pass into Clydesdale, and provides a route for the Ayr–Edinburgh road and, in pre-Beeching days, for a railway. Darvel, Newmilns and Galston – known as the Valley Burghs – are three little lace-making towns strung out along a five-mile reach of the Upper Irvine river. The stream is powerful and once turned the wheels of many textile mills. It rises a few miles above Darvel and flows westward between high hills which, at Galston, subside abruptly into the coastal plain.

This lower entrance to the valley was guarded by Loudoun Castle, the fortress home of the Campbells of Loudoun since the twelfth century. Like their kinsmen the Campbells of Argyll, the Loudoun family were authoritarian landowners deeply and deviously involved in the violence and political intrigue that beset Scotland until the mid-eighteenth century. An earldom of Loudoun was created in 1633, which passed through the female line to the Hastings family in 1804. Loudoun Castle, commanding one of the few passes from the coast, was besieged many times and burned and rebuilt twice. It was finally destroyed by fire in 1941 and is now in ruins.

It was John Campbell, Fourth Earl of Loudoun, who largely created the pleasant, well-wooded landscape and prosperous farms of the Irvine valley.[1] He began in 1733, when peasant farmers lived in isolated hovels and gained a bare subsistence from a few acres of soil and a few animals on the common grazing. John Campbell planted a million trees and miles of hedgerows which still give shelter along the floor of the valley and its lower hillsides. He built substantial farmhouses with enough enclosed land for a reasonable living, and many miles of roads to serve them. He introduced a system of land drainage and crop rotation. All this was considered progressive or oppressive, depending on the point of view. The agriculture of the district, and the standard of life for perhaps fifty of its farmers was greatly improved. But most of the peasant farmers lost what little they had. They could choose to become hired hands on the now-larger farms; to find work in the towns; to emigrate or starve. Far up the bleak hillsides one can still find memorials to their former way of life – the ruins of the tiny cottages they had once occupied.

At Darvel the hills have drawn so close to the river that the little town consists of not much more than its Main Street, extending for about half a mile along the floor of the valley, a few short cross-streets and the textile mills. Squarely in line with Main Street like some colossal monument, the extraordinary volcanic mass of Loudoun Hill 2 miles upstream virtually blocks the head of the valley. The hills flanking Darvel rise, at first gently, then steeply, for a thousand feet or more. Their lower slopes, sheltered by John Campbell's beech trees and hedges, support prosperous farms. Above these the hedges give way to 'dry-stane dyking', and higher still there is the open rough grazing and then the peat bogs and heather of the moorland wilderness. Even these uplands provide a living for a few hill farmers. Remote and isolated, reached only by long, steep tracks, each small homestead with its huddle of sturdy outbuildings is a miniature fortress defying the elements.

From these heights the urban ribbon is out of sight and the limitless view is of rolling hills. On a fine day the vast expanse of blue sky, the green valleys and the purple summits dappled by racing cloud shadows have an undeniable beauty. The air is fresh and clean, and there is an exhilarating sense of space and freedom. For those with happy childhood memories of this upland world, the flute-notes of the curlew, the high, clear whistle of the golden plover and the scent of peat smoke must evoke nostalgia.

This was the natural environment in which Alexander Fleming spent his boyhood. Strong though its influence must have been, it was the people around him who ensured that he became one of themselves. The popular image of the typical Lowland Scot is familiar enough – he is supposed to be dour, pawky, canny with his money, serious, literal-minded and humourless. He speaks a strange dialect, the Scots or Doric vernacular, largely incomprehensible south of the Border – or north of the Highland Line. This picture is, of course, a caricature. The charge of meanness is unfounded. The Scots, while aware of the value of money are, in general, hospitable and generous. The second misconception is the supposed lack of humour – the Scot likes to poke fun slyly and with a straight face. As regards the Scots tongue, it is the language immortalized by Burns, the poet of the Ayrshire countryside. It has as many roots – including the eleventh-century English imported by Queen Margaret – as there are different racial elements in the people who speak it. As we shall see, Alexander Fleming acquired the true Scottish characteristics and, like most expatriate Scots, he retained them tenaciously throughout his life.

Ethnically the people of Ayrshire are of very mixed descent. A main strand is Celtic; for several centuries before and after the Roman occupation – which must surely have added its own genetic traces – Ayrshire was part of the Celtic kingdom of Strathclyde, and many present-day place names have Gaelic derivations. In the sixth century there began a long period of domination by the Saxon kingdom of Northumbria which ended with the unification of the Scottish kingdom in the eleventh century. There followed the interminable wars with the English, involving frequent invasions and occupations that must have contributed Anglo-Saxon and Norman elements. This confusion was compounded by the Vikings who, as incessant raiders and even coastal settlers, are probably responsible for the Scandinavian strain still clearly to be seen in the physique of some Ayrshire people.

The last major addition to this ethnic mixture came with the Reformation and the consequent religious persecutions in France and the Low Countries. Protestant refugees, Flemish and Huguenot, fled to Britain and many to Ayrshire, which was by that time solidly Presbyterian. Those who settled in and around the Irvine valley brought with them their crafts of weaving and lace-making. The name Fleming became a common one in this area – there is a village called Flemington to the east of Darvel, a Fleming Street in Darvel itself, and three families of Flemings were recorded as living in Main Street in 1845. The name was probably given, rather indiscriminately, by the natives to newly-arrived Flemish neighbours. These proved to be hard workers who largely founded the textile industry of the Valley Burghs. They soon integrated with the community and, by intermarriage, contributed another strand to be woven into the already complex racial pattern.

Ayrshire remembers with justifiable pride its history and its heroes and Darvel has its share of both. Maps of Scotland mark the sites of three historic battles at or near to Loudoun Hill. Wallace's Cairn commemorates the ambush of the English forces there by which he began the Scottish War of Independence in 1296. The second was the Battle of Loudoun Hill in 1307, in which Robert Bruce defeated the English army and regained sovereignty for Scotland. The third was the Battle of Drumclog in 1679, in which the Covenanters of the Irvine valley routed Government forces commanded by the supposedly invincible John Graham of Claverhouse. Among more peaceful Ayrshire heroes, Robert Burns the poet probably ranks second only to Shakespeare in world opinion, and Sir Alexander Fleming, by his discovery of penicillin in 1928, brought about the greatest of all advances in clinical medicine.

But pride is not the only element in the Ayrshire people's view of their history. As in any long-established community, folk-memory selects and preserves the more dramatic episodes – real or legendary – complete with their emotional implications. And when the past was in sober reality as wild and turbulent as it had been in Ayrshire, centuries-old grievances maintain an almost permanent significance. For example, no account of Fleming's Ayrshire background, however brief, could be complete without some account of the Covenanters. His own ancestors were in their ranks, and some of his biographers have imagined the Covenanting spirit as a component of his own character. Most Scots will need no description of these formidable zealots – they are widely venerated to this day. But others may appreciate a few words on their origin and activities.

The Covenant of 1557, drawn up by John Knox and his followers, bound its adherents to enforce Presbyterian Calvinism in Scotland and abolish Roman Catholicism. Its authority was unchallenged until the Union of the Crowns in 1603 placed James VI not only on the throne of England but at the head of its Anglican church. When he was tempted to assert a similar religious authority in Scotland he created a violent opposition which, during the reign of Charles I, flared into armed rebellion. The Covenant was revived in 1638, largely by the Campbells of Loudoun and Argyll, and its more active adherents – the Covenanters – became the military wing of the Presbyterian church. It was to their army that Charles surrendered at Newark in 1646 during the English Civil War, but the enforcement of the Covenant in England, which had been pledged in return for the alliance with the parliamentary forces, was not honoured. This was seen as a betrayal that has never been forgotten nor quite forgiven in Scotland.

The Covenanters had little comfort from Cromwell – he treated them with the even-handed severity he used on all trouble-makers. And the restoration of the Stuart monarchy brought them, particularly in the south-west, more than twenty years of guerrilla warfare. Charles II's reorganization of the Presbyterian church along Anglican lines was bitterly opposed by armed Covenanters. In the eyes of the Government they were fanatical rebels; in the eyes of the local population they were heroes in the Old Testament mould, smiting the enemies of the Lord, and ready to die for their faith. As a result, Ayrshire was put under an army of occupation. There were ambushes, night raids, massacres, martyrdoms, murders, torture, betrayal and great cruelty on both sides.

It was during this period that the famous battle of Drumclog took place, in which the Covenanters – many from Darvel – slaughtered Graham's dragoons as they floundered in a bog and were ordered by their leader to kill those they had taken prisoner. The story of this battle (which is remembered by some present-day inhabitants of Darvel with a clarity of detail suggesting that they were actual participants) is the central episode in Scott's *Old Mortality*. The period that followed was grimly known as the 'Killing Time'. It brought, indeed, even more ferocious repression and reprisal that only ended with the deposition of the last of the Stuart kings, and the accession of the strongly protestant William of Orange.

Ayrshire and the south-west had little part in the subsequent Jacobite rebellions. The people there hated the Stuarts and had no love for their Highland supporters who seemed, during their marches through the area, to be as wild and foreign as a horde of Tartars. When, after 1745, the Highland clan system and its Gaelic culture were systematically destroyed, few Lowlanders knew or cared about the almost genocidal changes in the north-western half of Scotland. Indeed, almost none of them had ever ventured there.

During the eighteenth century Ayrshire settled into peaceful and profitable righteousness. Years of turmoil had taught its people to guard their tongues and to distrust strangers. They were careful, too, about property and money, having so often lost both in the past. They retained a strong religious voice, keeping their ministers to the narrow path of strict Calvinism. Nevertheless, released from the unifying force of persecution, the church began to disintegrate. Theological differences caused a bewildering series of secessions, splittings, reunions, regroupings and reforms so that by the end of the nineteenth century the people of Darvel, for example, had to choose between at least seven Presbyterian denominations.[2] The differences were on theological detail, but the similarities were fundamental. All condemned present earthly pleasures and promised a future of eternal damnation for the vast majority of their members.

Meanwhile Darvel had grown in size and importance. Alexander Fleming's fame has stimulated a flurry of historical speculations on the origin of its name. One authority has pointed out that Derval and Loudun are adjacent places in Normandy and suggests that the Campbell family originated there.[3] The word Darvel has also been supposed to mean 'hidden valley' in Old English, 'river valley' in Old Scots, and 'dark vale' – a name quite unjustifiably attributed to Mary, Queen of Scots on her way to imprisonment in England.

Darvel, in reality, seems not to be a very old-established place, since a reference to Darnvaill in the Loudoun records of 1509 is said to be the first written evidence of its existence.[4] Its expansion from a few scattered cottages began about 1750, when a continuous row of dwellings was built along the north side of the highway. Thirty years later work on the south side began and the long Main Street took shape. The census of 1790 showed a population of 400, and by 1848 there were three schools, four churches and 1,400 inhabitants. The growth was the result of the lace industry. Hand-loom weaving had been established by the refugees from France and Flanders who found the Irvine valley favourable to their work. Thanks to the skill of these settlers the district became famous for the artistry of its silk and cotton lace fabrics.

Fortunes fluctuated during the nineteenth century. The Hungry Forties brought poverty, near-starvation, and epidemics of Asiatic cholera. To make matters worse, the introduction of the power loom in the industrial cities threatened the existence of the hand-loom weavers. They began to drift away to other work, houses stood empty and grass grew in Main Street. It was Alexander Morton who saved the little town. Himself a weaver, he adopted the new technology by installing the first power loom in Darvel in 1875, and persuading a number of his fellow weavers to follow suit. Lace curtains were then in great demand and the combination of the old arts with power weaving soon restored the Darvel fortunes. Mill after mill was built, and by the end of the century they were supporting a population of 3,000 in prosperity.

What was the social life of Darvel when Alexander Fleming was a boy? Not very different, probably, from that of any small, semi-rural, semi-industrial Scottish community in the 1880s and '90s. It was very much church-dominated, but contemporary local newspapers give glimpses of secular diversions and excitements. There were edifying lectures arranged by the Darvel Institution Committee, masonic meetings, canary shows and – very occasionally – the daring inclusion of a concert (vocal and in-strumental). The young engaged in athletic sports and there was evidently local support for curling, quoiting and football teams. It was a close-knit community in which almost everyone was related by blood or marriage. They tell the story, against themselves, of the commercial traveller – a foreigner from twenty miles away – who became benighted in Darvel. The Turf Hotel was full, and he sought a night's lodging in house after house and in vain. At the sixth he exclaimed in despair to the woman who was turning him away, 'Guidness, are there nae Christians in this toun ava?' Shutting the door in his face she answered, 'Nay, we're maistly a' Mortons and Clelands.'[5]

One's picture of small-town Scottish life as it was in those days partly depends on what books one reads. The so-called Kailyard School of Barrie and others portrays a serious piety and reserve shot through by shafts of whimsical humour and romance, and the gleams of pure gold in every heart. To read *The House with the Green Shutters* by George Douglas, himself the son of a small Ayrshire farmer, is to be given a grim picture of latter-day malignants and hypocritical street-corner moralists united only by their schemes to pull down those more successful than themselves. There is some truth, perhaps, in both extremes.

The present-day visitor to Darvel will find that Main Street is recognizably the street shown in the photographs of a century ago. Loudoun Hill still looms at the end of it. Many of its single-storey houses have survived; the Turf Hotel remains the dominant building, the churches still stand. There are, of course, recent changes. The town has acquired a new school, with playing fields and a handsome park on land left by a change in the course of the river. The most relevant additions are those which honour Darvel's first Freeman and its most famous hero. At either end of the town, where new housing estates have extended its length, there are road signs identifying Darvel as the birthplace of Sir Alexander Fleming. And about half-way along Main Street an impressively designed memorial garden is the setting for his life-size bust in bronze.

Fleming was not, in fact, born in Darvel but at Lochfield Farm on the Glen Water, 4 miles to the north and 800 feet up on the bare and windswept hillside. Here is another memorial to him – a simple, rough-hewn slab of Cumberland granite with the inscription 'Sir Alexander Fleming, discoverer of penicillin was born here at Lochfield on 6th August 1881'. This little monument must be one of the few additions to Lochfield Farm since he was a boy there. To reach it one must climb steep and narrow roads to the farm gate and then another half a mile of rough track over braes and gulleys to the farm itself. This is a compact block of whitewashed stone buildings alone on the hillside and visible for miles. The house, facing south, is part of this block and with byres and barns on either side forms three sides of a square enclosing the yard. Photographs taken a century ago show a barn and a large tree which have since disappeared. Behind the house there is a ridge that gives some shelter from the north, and beyond this the rough pasture rises to the boggy, heather-covered moors. To the south there is a wide view of the Irvine valley, dominated by the sphinx-like Loudoun Hill, but the little towns along the river are too deeply set to be visible.

The Flemings of Lochfield

Not all the Flemings of the Darvel area were weavers. Some who settled in the part of Strathavon known as Flemington became farmers. One of these, Hugh Fleming, was born in 1773 at Low Ploughland, a substantial farm just to the east of the Loudoun Hill watershed. In due course, Hugh married Mary Craig from the neighbouring farm of High Ploughland, and had nine children, including Hugh II, born in 1816. The Craigs were descended from active Covenanters, and it was one of these who had carried the standard at the Battle of Drumclog, now in the Museum of Antiquities in Edinburgh.[1] Hugh II worked at Low Ploughland until his father died in 1855 and left the farm to John, the eldest son. Hugh then moved out and rented, from the Earl of Loudoun, the 800-acre farm of Lochfield, a holding largely devoted to sheep, but with 40 or 50 acres of arable land and keep for a small herd of cattle. Installed at Lochfield, he married Jane Young and their first child, Jane, was born in 1862. Hugh III followed in 1864, Thomas in 1868 and Mary in 1874. The farm and the children thrived, but their mother's health did not. She developed pulmonary tuberculosis and died in the year of Mary's birth.

Left with a lonely homestead and four children to look after, Hugh Fleming remarried in 1876. His new wife was Grace Morton (unrelated to the mill-owner), one of the twelve children of a Darvel farmer, and they soon embarked on a second family of four children. Grace II was born in 1877, John in 1879, Alexander (Alec) in 1881, and Robert in 1883. Their mother was an admirable person who so succeeded in uniting the whole family that her stepchildren loved her, and no difference between them and her own children was ever noticeable. In this she had a willing ally in Jane who, twenty years older than the two smallest boys, took them under her wing. But poor Jane's life was a short one. Before Robert was old enough to remember her, she had married Dr Lyon of Darvel and within a year had died of small-pox. During her illness, Grace Fleming nursed her devotedly, thus showing the courage and affection that had endeared her to her stepchildren.

A year or so before his death in 1888, Hugh Fleming suffered a stroke and became an invalid. Alec and Robert, then about six and four years of age respectively, remembered their father only as a kindly, grey-haired man confined to his chair by the fireside. His eldest son, Hugh III, had been taking on more and more of the running of the farm and, at twenty-three, was quite capable of its complete management. It was naturally assumed that, in due course, he would inherit the tenancy, but Lochfield could provide a living for only one farmer, and others of the family would have to make their lives elsewhere. Naturally, their father worried most about his three youngest sons, and he urged Hugh and Tom to do the best they could to give them a start in life.

Tom was at that time a medical student at Glasgow University. He was a clever boy who had gone from Darvel School to Kilmarnock Academy, and thence to study medicine. The cost of this must have been a drain on the Lochfield income, but the Scottish respect for the learned professions justified every sacrifice that enabled a promising boy to become a lawyer, doctor, teacher or – supreme achievement – a minister of the kirk. In relation to today, Tom's expenses would not be heavy. Medical students in those days put up with hardships that would be thought intolerable now, and most earned what they could in their spare time in casual jobs.

On 27 October 1888, the local Irvine valley newspapers reported the death of 'Hugh Fleming, farmer, of Lochfield, aged 72.' Beyond this bare announcement there were no obituary tributes. He had been a hard-working, conscientious and successful farmer who had raised a large family despite the poverty of his land. He would have had little time, and possibly little inclination, for the community activities that eventually earn obituaries. His son Hugh, as expected, was confirmed by the Earl of Loudoun as the new tenant of Lochfield.

Life at Lochfield, as in most farms, followed the pattern of the seasons. Superimposed on the daily routine – the feeding of humans and animals, the fetching of water from the spring, fuel for the fire, the milking of the cows, the work in the dairy (Mrs Fleming was famous for her cheeses) and the care of three or four hundred sheep – there were seasonal bursts of activity, anxiety and, with good fortune, great satisfaction. Lochfield was busiest and most anxious at lambing time, when bad weather or some other disaster could bring near-ruin. Hugh bore the brunt, with many sleepless nights in the open. When shearing-time came, the flock had to be rounded up and clipped by hand. Since this was impossible for one man, farmers with their dogs and older children formed communal shearing gangs that moved from farm to farm with a good deal of cheerful noise, to do the work and consume the food and drink provided by the hostess of the day.

May and June were the months for cutting peat, the fuel used for all cooking and heating. The peat was cut from banks on the moor about a mile above the farm. After stripping the turf and heather, slabs of the soft peat were cut with the long-handled peat-knife, and laid out in rows to dry until it was firm enough to be picked up. Then it was piled on to long, low peat barrows and taken down the rough hillside to be stored under cover. About fifteen tons of half-dry peat would be moved in this way each year. It was in many ways an ideal domestic fuel. It cost nothing – except labour. It was clean, and could be made to burn slowly or brightly with little smoke and a sweet, unforgettable aroma.

Then would come the haymaking, when every able-bodied adult and child on the farm would snatch an opportunely fine spell of weather to mow the grass, spread and turn it, and finally build it into haycocks on tripods. Harvest time was the occasion for imported labour. Itinerant harvesters from the cities and Ireland came to earn a pound or two, free board, a bed on the straw in the barn and something of a summer holiday. The men would cut the corn with scythes, while the women gathered it into sheaves. By the 1890s, horse-mowers were coming into use on farms like Lochfield, and reducing the need for temporary labour. But when Alec and Robert were children, two Irish harvesters came for about six weeks every summer and the little boys remembered listening entranced to strange stories told in almost unintelligible accents. Later, they were to discover that their own broad Scots Doric would sound almost as outlandish in London.

There were other regular visitors to the farm. Travelling grocers ('cadgers') came in horse-traps, lightly loaded because the hills were steep. They were welcomed by the children because, if the cadger made a sale, they got some small treat. Then there were the packmen, with a load of fancy goods on their backs, who hoped for a free meal and some business with the women of the family. Travelling the country widely, they were the main purveyors of news and gossip, and the children drank in every word of even the most improbable stories.

By modern standards, it was not only the notorious city slums that were overcrowded in those days. One of the visiting salesmen lived in a tiny, two-roomed cottage above Darvel with his wife and no less than twelve children, all of whom apparently thrived. By comparison, Lochfield farmhouse was fairly spacious. Even so, the four adults and four young children who lived there in the 1880s had to be fitted into the three bedrooms and the box bed behind a sliding panel in the kitchen. And there was room for visitors – usually relations of whom the Fleming family had enormous numbers. Clearly the bedrooms and even the beds must on occasions have had two or three occupants. One frequent visitor, Guy Fleming, was no relation, despite his name. He would appear at irregular intervals, work on the farm of his own volition for two or three weeks, and then vanish. The children saw nothing strange in this, and it was only years later that they learned that Guy had what is now known as a 'drink problem' and used Lochfield Farm as a drying-out place.

Life in the house itself was typical of that in any remote farmhouse of the period. There were none of the amenities thought essential today. Paraffin lamps lit the kitchen, candles the bedrooms. Open fires and the kitchen-range provided the heat. There was no piped water, no bathroom, no indoor sanitation. People washed in the kitchen sink in water drawn in buckets from the spring above the house. On grand occasions enough would be heated on the stove for a bath in a tin tub in front of the kitchen fire. The kitchen was the nerve-centre and the living-room for the whole family. There was plenty of good, fresh food, and appetites to match. There was warmth, companionship, the smell of home baking and the scent of peat smoke. This was the place to be when the rain-laden winds roared in from the Atlantic, or the east winds brought the frost and snow.

If life was tougher for an Ayrshire upland sheep farmer than for his counterpart in, say, Thomas Hardy's Wessex, it was still idyllic for the children. Apart from an occasional stint as sheep-minders, the younger ones had no set chores about the farm. When not at school they were free to play in the barns and outhouses, and to roam the hills, glens and moors to their hearts' content. The farmland gave them plenty of scope, covering an area about two miles long from east to west, and a mile wide. There was a fence along the eastern boundary which was also the Lanarkshire border. The northern limit was marked only by the edge of a large bog known as Juck's Haggs (Duck's Bog) which separated the Lochfield land from that of Overmuir Farm. Three streams ran through the Lochfield glens. The Glen Water on the western boundary was a sizeable tributary of the Irvine, and at Lochfield tumbled between steep banks of sandy clay, and outcrops of rock that formed waterfalls and deep pools. The smaller Loch Burn ran westward, close below the house, to join the Glen Water, and the Calder Burn, which formed the southern boundary of the farm, ran eastwards by a chance alignment of the Loudoun watershed, to enter Avondale. Dividing these glens were Lamb Hill, Rough Hill and Whiteknowe, all nearly 900 feet in height, while Carse Hill and Ellrig, some 300 feet higher, were a mile or so to the north. Scattered about this wild countryside were the ruins of the tiny farmsteads that were abandoned when John Campbell's reforms created larger farms in the eighteenth century.

The Fleming children knew every inch of their 800 acres and much of the country around them. They seem to have been quite free of the usual parental admonitions not to get wet, dirty or tear their clothes. No one, apparently, worried about the more serious risks of getting lost (mists come down quickly on those hills) or drowning or falling off cliffs. So they learned to look after themselves and became tough and confident. Some of their games were pretty hazardous. The peat barrows made splendid toboggans on the steep slopes, but it was the barrows and not bones that got broken. They bathed in the deep pools and clambered about the waterfalls, though none of them could swim. One game might have been the last for Alec, a competition to see who could roll fastest downhill. Alec, as always determined to win, chose a dangerously steep slope ending in a sheer drop into a rock-filled gulley. The other children watched, horrified, as he rolled and bounced quite out of control and then miraculously stopped just short of the probably fatal precipice. But all Alec said, when he had collected himself, was: 'Ah cam doun tha quick'.

Alec and Robert were almost inseparable. Robert, the younger by two years, records that Alec never took the big-brother line or pretended to be cleverer when games later gave way to more serious and profitable pastimes. These involved acquiring skills that many a poacher would have envied and, by effortless observation, a knowledge of the wildlife around them that naturalists gain with difficulty. Alec's favourite sport was trout fishing. The boys used home-made rods and tackle and their methods did not conform to angling club rules. They fly-fished when conditions were right, but a worm-baited hook was more productive. The surest method was 'guddling' (tickling) which needs patient, barely perceptible hand movements and a lightning-quick grab on the half-hypnotized trout.

Robert tells a fishing story that illustrates several facets of the Fleming character. Despite the later tendency to describe Alec and the Flemings as 'staunch Covenanters', Robert makes no mention of religious or church affairs and writes that they had no knowledge of Covenanting ancestors until the spotlight of Alec's fame was turned on his family history. But when they were children there were probably family prayers, and Bible readings on Sundays, and certainly all games and sports on the Sabbath were forbidden. One Sunday, however, Robert and Alec went fishing and caught several fine trout – the Devil's luck, no doubt. Since they could not take these home legitimately, they put them, still alive, in a little pool from which they could not escape, and returned innocently from their walk. Early next morning before going to school, they recaught their fish and produced them triumphantly for breakfast. Their mother professed astonishment at their phenomenal skill, but the probability was that she and the rest of the family (who could scarcely contain themselves) knew quite well how it had been achieved. Straight-faced charades of this sort were a family speciality, and Alec Fleming was apt to play them all his life.

Another sport was rabbiting. Rabbits abounded in those pre-myxomatosis days and were good both for food and fur. The boys of course, were too young for guns and they rightly thought snares and traps cruel. So their caught their rabbits with their bare hands. There were always three or four collies at Lochfield, two being trained working dogs, plus a young one in training, and an old pensioner. It was the pensioner who went with the boys on their rambles. He might have lost his speed and stamina, but he had kept his nose, and would soon know if a rabbit was hiding under some overhanging bank. The boys would then simultaneously slide their arms from either end into the superficial burrow, and the one that grabbed the rabbit's hind legs kept it. Another method needed almost incredible quickness and agility. The boys had observed that rabbits, hiding from their approach under grassy tussocks, would stay motionless if they thought themselves unseen. Having, in fact, seen the rabbit, the boys would walk past it looking the other way, and then whip round and dive on the unfortunate animal. Robert remarks that only a *small* boy can achieve this timing – larger ones fall too slowly!

Birds were a constant interest. Alec and Robert knew every kind by name, and the movements of the migrants. Swallows nested in the barn, plovers (peewits) near the grazing lands, and golden plovers on the moors. There were curlews (whaups) with their haunting flute-notes, larks and meadow-pipits singing on the wing, moss-cheepers, land rails, and mavis (thrushes) singing near the house. Further afield, sand-martins made their nests in the braes, and sandpipers, ring ouzels, herons and snipe in the marshes, wild duck and gulls of many kinds nested on Juck's Haggs and hawks abounded. The boys observed all these, and made a fair amount of pocket money by collecting plover's eggs, then a great delicacy in fashionable restaurants. They were paid 4d each for the eggs by a Darvel grocer (the consumer paid 5/- each) but were careful always to leave some in each nest for the mother bird to hatch.

Game birds were carefully preserved by the Earl of Loudoun's keepers, for the annual slaughter by visiting sportsmen. Butts would be built on the Lochfield moors, and from the Glorious Twelfth onwards the hillsides would echo to the barrage of gunfire. The Fleming boys had no part in or liking for this ritual – their sympathies were with the birds. The Earl was said to get a larger income from letting his shooting than from his farms. It seems that he was beginning to need it, since the once-wealthy family had run into financial trouble some years before.

Such was the summer background at Lochfield, when the sunshine was strong and warm in the clear air and any shower could be seen approaching for many miles across the vast landscape. Winter was a different world. The hills were often lost in low cloud, and anyone on them might be lost too without a good knowledge of the landmarks and a natural sense of direction. And there was the wind. On an unsheltered Lochfield hillside it would be impossible to stand upright in winds that sometimes reach 100 miles an hour. That is why buildings are massive, roofs heavy and everything moveable well secured. After the winds, the snow. It happened that, during the ten years from 1885, the winters were unusually cold and the snowfalls heavy. Robert recalled that a changed note in the howl of the wind would herald a blizzard. The hills naturally took the worst of it, with drifts ten to twenty feet deep. The first concern was for the sheep. Instinctively they would make for some hollow where the snow would bury them completely. Huddled together in this natural igloo they could survive for days, but they had to be found and dug out as soon as possible. The difficulty of finding them can be imagined, but there was often a tell-tale sign on the surface of the snow. Their warm breath

would melt a blow-hole and then, condensing around it, form a conspicuous yellow stain – just the colour, as Alec was to remark years later, of
penicillin. When the sheep had been dug out, it was the turn of the
farmhouse, when drifts had blocked doors and windows; and the long
road down to Darvel would sometimes remain impassable for days.

In the long winter evenings the children played the games that most
Victorian children played, but were great inventors of new ones. Family
games remained a Fleming speciality to be handed down to the next
generation, and Alec in particular never lost his enjoyment of them. His
brother Robert does not mention any interest in literature nor the sort of
books they read. It is doubtful if there were many at Lochfield, though a
few 'improving' books were obligatory in any God-fearing family.

Social life, in the modern sense, hardly existed. People hesitate to 'drop
in for a chat' if this entails an eight-mile walk. The Flemings of Lochfield
did not take part in the social excitements of Darvel, nor in the games of
bowls, quoits, football and curling which the residents there supported.
But they saw a good deal of the Loudon children from Overmuir Farm,
two miles to the north across the bog. The families used to combine for
Hallowe'en and Christmas parties at one house or the other, showing that
extreme Presbyterianism did not weigh too heavily on them. The Free
church condemns to this day such pagan frivolities, and when the Flemings
did go to church, it was to the Church of Scotland at Newmilns, where
there was a warmer side to a predominantly cold religion.

When Alec was five, he went to school. By good fortune, a tiny school,
Loudoun Moor, had just been opened about a mile from Lochfield, on the
Glen Water. The school house, built like a Highland croft cottage, had a
single classroom where nine or ten children, almost all Flemings or
Loudons, were taught by a young woman in her early twenties. There
they learned the three R's and some history and geography, but it must
have been well taught, because children from this little moorland school
were always ahead of their contemporaries in Darvel School when the time
came for them to move there. The young schoolteacher in Robert's time
was Elizabeth Haddow, who had relaxed but effective methods. In winter
she and her class did their lessons round the fire (each child brought one or
two pieces of peat for this every day) and in summer by the open window
or even down by the river. This would not have pleased the schools
inspector, a foreigner from Ayr. One day, when his trap came into view in
the distance on an unexpected visit, Lizzie Haddow and her flock had to
creep round to the back of the school and climb in through the window.
They were all demurely in their places – slightly breathless – by the time the
inspector strode into the classroom.

The children walked to school in all weathers. The Flemings got there by
a short cut across the moor and a rickety plank over the Glen Water which

had no handrail and a tendency to be swept away when the river was in spate. Then they had to take the longer way by the road and the stone bridge at Laigh Bradley, where there was a cottage with an apple tree. This tree was the only one within miles to bear good fruit and its ancient owner guarded it from the schoolchildren like an enraged Ladon – but usually weakened and gave each one a precious apple. Much has been made of the fact that Alec sometimes walked barefoot to school with an inference of the direst poverty and hardship. This impression is quite false. The Fleming children were well-clothed, fed, and shod, but though Wellington boots might have done for the Duke they were not then generally available. If the children had to cross wet or muddy ground they took off their boots and stockings and carried them. Bare wet feet can be dried, wet boots and stockings stay wet all day.

Both Alec and Robert enjoyed their years at the little moorland school and maintained that they had learned faster there than anywhere else. The young teachers evidently enjoyed their spell of duty there, and were sad to move on after a year or so. One of them, Marion Stirling, who taught Alec, wrote to him from Durban when he became famous, rejoicing in his marvellous discoveries and success.[2] She remembered him 'as a dear little boy with dreamy blue eyes'. Later, many people were to notice that his eyes were remarkable – large, very blue, observant and yet often fixed in a blank, disconcerting stare on some effusive stranger or voluble colleague.

At the age of ten, Alec left the moorland school for the larger one at Darvel. The headmaster, Peter Gorrie, was a cousin of Mrs Fleming. Darvel was by then a prosperous little town. Alexander Morton's mills had revived its fortunes, and a proper water supply and drainage system had restored its health. Morton's business was to expand into England and Ireland and employ 2,000 people. He had interests, too, in horticulture and horse-breeding, and it was through fields full of his horses that the short cut to school lay. It was a walk of four miles there and four miles back. In winter it had to be made in darkness morning and evening, and on bad days Alec must have arrived soaked to the skin. His mother used to give him two large baked potatoes fresh from the oven to keep his hands warm in his pockets, and to eat later. But he seemed none the worse for these hard conditions; there is no mention of illness. Indeed, Alec attributed his physical stamina to his tough upbringing, and maintained that he learned to observe every change in the things to be seen on his twice-daily walks, so that to him they were never dull. But when the weather was really atrocious or the road deep in snow, he would spend a night or so in Darvel with 'Auntie Grace' – in reality a great-aunt.

It was in the school-yard at Darvel that Alec had the accident that changed his profile and led to the persistent myth that he had been a noted boxer. Charging round a corner he had collided, literally head-on, with a smaller boy charging in the opposite direction. Alec's nose took the brunt, and it was only when the swelling had gone down that the fact that it had been badly broken became apparent. The bridge of his nose was flattened, spoiling what had been good looks. Plastic surgery was then unknown.

Alec did well at Darvel school, and was ahead of most of his contemporaries. Soon his future must be decided. His father had died when he was seven, leaving nothing much more than the tenancy of the farm to Hugh, and the wish that he and his brother Tom would look after their young half-brothers John, Alec and Robert. Since there were no prospects for them at Lochfield, it was Tom who helped to give them a start in life. His own medical career had not begun smoothly. He had gone into general practice in Wigton, Cumberland, but his health broke down and he had to sell his practice. After a voyage to South Africa to recuperate, he set up in practice in the Marylebone Road, London, with his sister Mary as his housekeeper. At first he had few patients, but a retired ophthalmic surgeon was pleased to teach Tom the theory and practice of his subject. So Tom became an oculist and soon worked up a thriving practice, mainly in detecting faults in refraction and correcting them by suitable spectacle lenses.

In 1893, Tom was able to suggest that John, then aged fifteen should join him in London and become apprenticed to the optical firm that supplied him with lenses. John agreed, and went to live with Tom and Mary. His apprenticeship cost a premium of £50 and, like most trade apprentices in those days, he did a great many menial tasks and received low pay.

Meanwhile Alec had transferred to Kilmarnock Academy at the age of twelve. Once more he was ahead of his contemporaries by at least a year, and clearly had a quick intelligence, an excellent memory and the urge to learn. But he did not exert himself unduly, being fortunate enough to absorb what his new school had to offer with little apparent effort. He could extract the essential facts from a book or a lesson, tuck them away in his memory and recall them at will, even years later. But he was also observant and critical, drew his own conclusions from what he learned, and wasted little time in talking.

Kilmarnock was then a busy town of about 30,000 inhabitants, noted for textiles, leather and dairy produce and its railway works, iron foundries and coal mines. The first Scottish Lord Mayor of London (Sir James Shaw) was a Kilmarnock native, as was Alexander Smith the poet. But the main literary distinction was that the first edition of Burns was published in 1786 in Kilmarnock, and the Burns Museum and Library there are famous.

The Academy, founded in 1633, to which Alec went as a pupil in 1893, was then on the London Road near the river. It was not until 1898, three years after he left, that the Academy moved to its present imposing site near the Dick Institute.[3] When he entered the school, there were about 700 pupils, none of them boarders. The curriculum was surprisingly comprehensive: English, Latin, Greek, German and French; history, geography, geology, and astronomy; arithmetic, algebra, plane and solid geometry, trigonometry, and mechanics; chemistry, physics and biology. On the more practical side there was agriculture, domestic economy, book-keeping and shorthand ('phonography'). There were organized games and sports and a school orchestra. Pupils paid ten shillings per quarter for each subject, with an average total of £10 per annum – a sizeable sum in those days. There were bursaries to be won, but there is no record that Alec ever held one, or won any prizes during his short time at the Academy.[4] He was only there for eighteen months. During the week he stayed with an aunt in the town, and went home for weekends. The railway extended at that time only as far as Newmilns, and unless Alec could catch the horsebrake there, or get a lift to Darvel, he had a six-mile walk home to Lochfield late on Friday nights, and another in the early hours of Monday morning. Alec was probably not sorry when, in the summer of 1895, Hugh decided that he should accept an offer from Tom to live with him and John and Mary in London, and was even more pleased when Robert joined them all six months later.

As it turned out, the boys who left Lochfield – Tom, John, Alec and Robert – did very well indeed in their chosen professions. Hugh, the farmer, devoted himself to Lochfield until his death in 1943 at the age of seventy-nine. In 1921 he had been able to buy the freehold for £3,750 when the declining Loudoun fortunes forced the sale of forty-five farms.[5] Despite his brothers' phenomenal success he remained the acknowledged head of the family and insisted that he had had the best life of them all.

3

The Flemings in London

'The noblest prospect which a Scotchman ever sees is the high road that leads him to England', said Dr Samuel Johnson.[1] When he made this famous remark in the Mitre Tavern, Fleet Street, in 1763, he was speaking from an experience of Scots but not of Scotland, to which he went for the first time ten years later. Boswell writes that 'if he was particularly prejudiced against the Scots, it was because they were more in his way; because he thought their success in England rather exceeded the due proportion of their real merit; and because he could not but see in them that nationality which I believe no liberal-minded Scotsman will deny'.[2] By 'noblest' therefore, Johnson meant 'most profitable' and he resented the fact that when the Scots succeeded in England they remained obstinately Scottish.

From the beginning of the nineteenth century an increasing number of well-to-do Lowland Scots were taking that profitable road, while tens of thousands of their destitute Highland compatriots were being shipped like cattle to the bleak wilderness of Nova Scotia. The Lowland exodus did not mean that Scotland had lagged behind England in the industrial, scientific or academic fields. The Scottish Universities were almost as old, just as learned and more practical than the two English universities. Their medical schools were so far ahead of anything that England could offer that many English doctors trained there. Lister's epoch-making research was done mainly in Edinburgh and Glasgow, and Simpson's work on anaesthesia was part of another medical revolution. In science, engineering, architecture, and literature the list of Scottish nineteenth-century pioneers could be far extended. Why then, did ambitious, well-educated young Scots flock to England? One answer is that at home they would have to compete with other ambitious, well-educated young Scots, and in England most of their competitors would be merely the English.

The Fleming migration to London was an example of this trend, made possible by Tom's foothold there. As a general practitioner who had simply put up his plate and waited for patients his first year had been a lean one. The residents of the area were either wealthy people who could afford fashionable doctors, or the very poor who were treated free in the local hospitals. But when Tom began to specialize his fortunes changed. Local doctors and even Harley Street consultants referred patients to him, and when Alec and Robert came to join him at 144 Marylebone Road there was a brass plate by the door, engraved 'Dr T. Fleming, Oculist', and a busy consulting room.

It would be tempting to contrast the confinement, noise and dirt of London with the wide, clean Ayrshire landscape and to dwell on the things the boys had left behind them – the fishing in the Glen Water, the song of the larks, the note of the curlew and the frisking of the lambs in the soft, warm winds of spring. But in reality the entrancing new phenomenon of London excluded regret and demanded the fullest investigation and exploration. Uncle Willie Morton had brought Robert, then aged twelve, down to London at Christmas, 1895, and had taken the whole family to the theatre to see *Charley's Aunt*. The two youngest had to stand at the back of the gallery, and the play was quite beyond them, but it was an unforgettable first visit to a theatre.

Thereafter the boys settled down to explore and enjoy London as they had explored and enjoyed their Ayrshire glens. Clearly, London was a strange and wonderful place. Their house was built close above the Metropolitan underground railway from Paddington to Moorgate. Every few minutes the house would shake as a steam train rumbled beneath it, and smoke billowed from the gratings along the centre of the Marylebone Road. For all they knew, the whole of London shook and fumed like this. Road traffic was horse-drawn, ranging from the heavy drays with their huge shire horses, two-horse omnibuses and trams, and seedy growlers, to the spanking hansom cabs and elegant carriages. Noise must have been one of the strongest impressions: there were barrow-boys, costermongers, and porters pushing their handcarts with warning cries to the crowds of pedestrians; the shouts of drivers; the clatter of iron-shod hoofs and iron-tyred wheels on the stone setts; the bells of buses, trams and cabs; and the muffled snorting of the underground. Then there was the dirt: horse-dung littered the streets and became churned into a sludge that joined the garbage in the gutter and choked the drains. Ladies lifted their skirts to keep them clear of the filth at unswept crossings. A million chimneys poured greasy smoke into the air from the coal fires that heated every home and powered every factory. Sometimes the air could hold no more, and laid down its burden in fogs as thick as pea soup. For the boys, they added to the glamour.

Alec was delighted to regain Robert as his companion. With several months of London life to his credit, he was the natural leader in their expeditions. But, once more, Robert stresses that he was never domineering. He made his own judgements from what he saw and left Robert to do the same. In fact, the boys scarcely spoke, merely drawing attention to some weird or wonderful sight by a nudge or a nod. They were, of course, tireless walkers, and most of central London was within their range. But when they had a few pennies they would treat themselves to their favourite form of transport, one of the General omnibuses. The boys always scrambled for a seat next to the driver. From their farm experience they knew good horse-handling when they saw it, and delighted in the skill with which their driver wove in and out of the traffic like a charioteer, hurling incomprehensible shafts of cockney insult at every competitor for the right of way. They went to the Tower, St Paul's, Westminster, the Kensington museums, picture galleries, the British Museum and, almost on their doorstep, Madame Tussaud's, the Zoo, and the Regent's Park lake, where they could hire a boat for sixpence. There was no limit to the wonders around them.

But sightseeing was for the evenings and weekends. John was working with his optical firm, and Robert had joined Alec at school. Tom's choice for their further education turned out to be a good one. They both went to the Regent Street Polytechnic, which provided day and evening classes at almost nominal fees for anyone wanting to learn. It was the creation of Quentin Hogg, an Old Etonian educational philanthropist. In 1882 he acquired the disused building of the Polytechnic Institution, where mid-Victorian audiences once came to be astonished by the marvels of science, such as crackling discharges of electricity, the magic lantern, and the celebrated Pepper's Ghost – all done by mirrors. Hogg replaced these entertainments with more solid education but retained the name Polytechnic. When Alec and Robert enrolled there, they did so in the commercial school, since Tom, after his slow start in medicine, felt that a business career was safer than a professional one. Both boys were, educationally, at least two years ahead of their contemporaries at the Polytechnic, and Alec had moved up four classes in his first two weeks. The teaching they received was obviously effective, to judge by subsequent events, but it did not include Latin, which Alec was later to regret.

At school, and even at home when Tom was entertaining, the boys had to contend with a feeling that they were foreigners. They had arrived in London with – at best – broad Ayrshire accents and – at worst – lapses into the unintelligible Scots Doric. But, although shy at first, and the targets at school for the usual English jokes about the Scots, they soon found that the English, in fact, have an instinctive respect for the Scots and are quick to claim any Scottish ancestry that they themselves may have. A Scottish accent was not a serious social disadvantage, whereas in those days any English local or regional accent would put one beyond the pale of London middle-class society. The boys did their best to acquire standard English, but they never lost their soft Ayrshire burr, and resorted to the vernacular in moments of stress. However, they soon lost the sense of inferiority felt by all country boys transplanted to a great city. The Fleming boys soon had the best of both worlds. While retaining their love and knowledge of the country and the habit of observation and curiosity that goes with it, they quickly adapted to city ways and thus had the advantage of the London native.

When he was sixteen, Alec left school having passed all his courses with ease, and took a job in a shipping office in Leadenhall Street. He was not an office boy in an obscure firm, as described by several writers; he was a junior clerk in the America Line, one of the crack companies of the North Atlantic trade. Their ships were the *St Paul, St Louis, City of Paris* and *City of New York*, twin-screw liners of 10–12,000 tons and speeds of 21 knots, built between 1889 and 1893. They were then, and for several years to come, among the largest and fastest of the Atlantic liners. Alec was paid ten shillings per week, which he calculated was twopence-halfpenny per hour. His job was to copy letters and documents, enter accounts in the ledgers, and prepare the cargo manifests and the booking of the steerage passengers, all, of course, by hand. It was a boring job, relieved only by the need to carry messages and papers to other firms.

Alec made no special friends either in his office or in the City, and his four years there were, from the point of view of his career, wasted. The daily journey from Marylebone to Leadenhall Street was by the sulphurous and suffocating Metropolitan Railway or, if time allowed, by bus. The City clerks were particular about their dress – straw hats in summer, bowlers in winter, tight tweed jackets and trousers, high starched collars and a touch of latitude in a choice of neck-ties. Here, Alec showed his independence – he wore a bow-tie then and no other sort for the rest of his life. Robert used occasionally to join him for lunch in one of the City eating houses. Their favourite was Wilkinson's, noted for its 'beef-à-la-mode'.

Meanwhile the Flemings had moved from Marylebone Road to 29 York Street, off Baker Street, where Tom set up a new consulting room. Mary was housekeeper for them all, and mothered the younger ones. It was a happy, self-contained family. Tom saw to it that there was always something to occupy and amuse them at home. He was an adept at inventing competitions that were both exciting and instructive, such as historical, geographical or mathematical quizzes in which each entrant put a penny in the kitty and the winner took all. Alec did a shade better than the others, Tom a shade worse, but the odds were fairly even.

Not all Tom's ideas were good ones. One evening he came home with a pair of boxing gloves and said that the boys should learn to box. With one glove each, they had to fight single-handed, the larger of the pair having the left-hand glove. Tempers became so strained during these bouts that Mary put the gloves in the dustbin and the family took to ping-pong, whist, bridge, nap and poker.

In 1898 Mary left to get married. Her husband was James Douglas, a London veterinary surgeon, and they later emigrated to New Zealand. Mary's place in the Fleming home was taken by Grace, the eldest of the second family, who left Lochfield to join them in London. Soon after,

Robert, then sixteen, went to work in the optical firm that employed John.

On 9 October 1899, President Kruger of the Transvaal delivered an unacceptable ultimatum to the British Government and thus precipitated the Boer War. That a 'handful of Boer farmers' could actually declare war on the most powerful empire on earth was greeted in London with almost hilarious incredulity. But this mood soon changed to one of shock when the Boers, invading British territory, drove almost all the available defenders into Kimberley, Mafeking and Ladysmith, and then surrounded and besieged them. When the last days of the nineteenth century had ebbed away, the twentieth began with the British armies in South Africa facing extermination or surrender. The whole of Cape Colony was virtually at the mercy of the Boer forces, and there was an evident inclination in its Dutch population to welcome them with open arms.

Once the gravity of the situation had been grasped by the British government, it acted firmly. An army corps under Lord Roberts and Lord Kitchener was sent out from England to meet the threatened invasion, and to relieve the besieged garrisons if possible. This move seriously depleted the regular army in Britain, and Roberts launched a recruiting drive to strengthen the volunteer regiments that later formed the Territorial Army. These regiments had county or regional associations, and one of them, the Highland Armed Association of London, had been formed as a defence against an invasion by Napoleon. During the Crimean War, it reappeared as the London Scottish Rifle Volunteers, and has retained this identity ever since. Its uniform resembled that of the regular Highland regiments, but the kilts were of hodden grey, so that clan rivalries in the choice of a tartan were avoided.[3]

At the beginning of 1900, with Mafeking, Kimberley and Ladysmith still besieged, there was an enthusiastic response in London to the call for volunteers. John and Alec Fleming enlisted immediately as privates in the London Scottish, and Robert joined too, on reaching the age of eighteen in October 1901. The regimental headquarters at Buckingham Gate provided amenities that were social as well as military. Training was a part-time occupation for the evenings and weekends, with route marches and summer camps. All the Fleming boys enjoyed the club-like companionship and facilities of the regiment. Among their fellow privates there were City clerks, artisans, doctors and lawyers. Off duty, the officers mixed freely with the other ranks, seeming to prefer their mess to their own – they were, first and foremost, all Scots in a foreign city. The training was little hardship to the country-bred Flemings, and their only complaint on the long route marches was that, being in H Company, they were so far behind the band that they could not hear it. One notable march was from Aberdeen to Blairgowrie, a distance of about sixty miles, undertaken in pouring rain in August 1901.

The London Scottish sent three detachments to South Africa, but none of the Fleming brothers was posted overseas. The year 1900, which had begun so badly for Britain, saw a series of military successes. Ladysmith, with its 22,000 besieged soldiers and civilians almost at their last gasp, was relieved on 28 February. The delirious celebrations in London following the news of the relief of Mafeking on 17 May were an index of the deep anxiety that had prevailed. Though there were still two years of guerrilla fighting ahead, the Boer resistance weakened steadily, and there was no need to draft many more Territorial volunteers to the war zone.

Alec and Robert therefore remained in London, but were active in regimental affairs. They became, for example, fine rifle shots, and were in the teams that competed at Bisley and won the Daily Telegraph Cup. Robert was the better marksman of the two, and went on to shoot for Scotland,[4] a distinction mistakenly given to Alec by later writers. Another activity was swimming. None of the boys could swim when they came to London, but they joined the regimental swimming club and learned to such good effect that within a few months they were in the water polo team. But Robert stresses that the matches they played were scratch affairs. Alec and Robert were never more than moderate players, and later reports of Alec's prowess were much exaggerated. But one water polo match in which Alec played was, he often claimed, to influence his career and, if so, then the future history of medicine. This was a game played against St Mary's Hospital Medical School.

In Barrie's *What Every Woman Knows* one of the characters says 'A young Scotsman of your ability let loose upon the world with £300 – what could he not do? . . . especially if he went among the English!'[5] It was not quite £300, but £250 each that set all four of the able young Scots of York Street on roads to great success and, in Alec's case to undreamed-of fame. Their little fortunes came through the will of Uncle John Fleming, their father's eldest brother, a bachelor who had farmed Low Ploughland near Darvel since 1855. The eight surviving Lochfield Flemings inherited between them their father's eighth share of his brother's estate which, since each got £250, must have been about £16,000 – a considerable one for a hill farmer. Each of the London brothers made good use of his legacy. Tom opened a consulting room at 42 Harley Street, from which his practice grew rapidly. The younger boys had to wait until they were twenty-one before receiving their shares. When they did, John and Robert used their money to set up their own optical business, which developed into a large company with branches throughout Britain and in the United States. And the prospect of Alec's legacy determined a complete change of course for him in 1901, over a year before it was paid.

Though Alec had done his work at the shipping office well, it did not interest or satisfy him, and he could see no chance of quick promotion. Tom knew this, and now that his own practice was flourishing, he had come to feel that medicine would, after all, provide a good career for one of his young brothers. John and Robert were enjoying their work; Alec was not. So Tom suggested that he should stop being a clerk and become a medical student. Alec agreed, not because of any burning enthusiasm for medicine – which surely would already have become evident in a doctor's household – but because it offered an escape from the Leadenhall Street trap.

The first obstacle in this new path was the fact that Alec, by then nearly twenty years old and two or three years older than most first-year medical students, had none of the qualifications he needed for acceptance by a London school. These schools were affiliated to London University, and students who wished to enrol for their preclinical courses had to have passed the London matriculation or some other acceptable examination. Alec had done none of these things. Tom discussed the problem, and was advised that Alec should work for the diploma of the London College of Preceptors which would be accepted as equivalent to matriculation. It was then that Alec regretted the absence of Latin from his Polytechnic courses, for this was an obligatory subject. Undaunted, he found a teacher to coach him in the evenings, and in July 1901 he sat for the examination. He passed in Scripture, History, English Language, English History, Geography, Arithmetic, Algebra, Geometry, Book-keeping, French, Latin, Heat, Light and Sound, Physiology, Geology and Shorthand. He not only passed, he was first in the list in the English subjects, and equal first in General Proficiency, but he was not awarded the prize, which went to the fifteen-year old candidate with whom he had tied.[6]

That a young man who had left school at thirteen and a half, attended Polytechnic classes to the age of sixteen, and had then been a clerk for four years, should be able to take top place in an exacting open examination with apparently little effort is astonishing. But it did not surprise his family. They were quite used, according to Robert, to Alec being at or near the top of every class at school at the Polytechnic, and he had a happy flair for excelling himself at examinations. This ability, which was to be a feature of his academic career, was not the result of hard slogging. He seldom buried himself in his books in the evenings – he preferred the family competitive games. 'Competition', wrote one of his contemporaries, 'was the breath of life to him.'[7] Perhaps it was the competitive element in examinations that brought out Alec's best efforts – which were very good indeed.

With Alec about to start on his medical career it is time, perhaps, to take a closer look at him as a person. He was a fair-haired young man, pleasant-faced despite the deformity of his nose, which certainly looked as if it had been acquired in the boxing ring. His most noticeable feature was the eyes. No longer the 'big, dreamy blue eyes' of 'the dear little boy' at the moorland school, they were now large, observant and penetrating. He would sometimes use them in what Leonard Colebrook described as a 'basilisk stare' that was often taken for rudeness, but which some women found fascinating.[8] His habit of staring in this way at some long-winded or pompous speaker and then turning away without a word was disconcerting. A distinguished epidemiologist, who was certainly neither long-winded nor pompous, has described such an experience, which occurred when he had become famous: 'I had what I thought was a good idea, and wanted to discuss it with Fleming,' she said, 'so I went to see the great man, who waved me to a chair. I sat down and began talk. He stared at me without moving a muscle. I began to falter, then forgot what I had intended to say, mumbled something and bolted. He never said a word.'[9]

Alec was below average height, even for those days when people were, in general, shorter than today's average. On joining the London Scottish his height was recorded as 5 feet 5¾ inches.[10] Though he appeared to be unselfconscious about his stature, he remarked occasionally on the social and even academic advantages of being tall. For example, when a colleague told him that his son was working hard for an examination, Fleming said, '*He* doesn't need to bother about exams – he's tall. Tall people can do anything, go anywhere.'[11] But he had none of the aggressive self-assertion that some small men develop and was very popular – indeed something of a mascot – in the regiment. On long military train journeys, his large companions would hoist him onto the luggage rack, where he was more comfortable than on the crowded seats below. Physically, he was tough and strong, able to hold his own against bigger men in any rough and tumble, and to march further than they could without fatigue.

In manner, though Alec was notably a man of very few words, he was friendly and fond of company. He made few close friends, probably because his brothers were his best companions. People enjoyed his company largely, perhaps, because he was (or seemed to be) a good listener, and because he would enter enthusiastically into any amusing game or interesting project. He seemed quite without conceit and, strangely enough, without worldly ambition. He made no effort to get promotion in the City and, despite remaining in the London Scottish for fourteen years, never rose above the rank of private. He described this attitude when he spoke at a regimental dinner in 1949. 'To be humble is a great advantage. It is a wonderful thing in a company to remain a private and to watch others doing the climbing. They do it in such different ways, but all of them are interesting.'[12] He was, however, proud that three Fleming brothers had helped H Company to carry off the best shooting prizes.

With the College of Preceptors Diploma to his credit, Alec could choose from the twelve London medical schools the one that would suit him best. To his practical mind the great traditions and historical associations of the old-established ones counted for less than a convenient proximity to York Street. St Mary's Hospital, to the west, the Middlesex to the south-east, and University College to the east were all within easy walking distance of his home. What, according to Alec himself, determined the choice of St Mary's was the fact that he had played a water-polo match against their team.[13]

Whatever the reasons for his choice, it was at St Mary's Hospital Medical School that Alec enrolled, at the beginning of the academic year in October 1901. He was to spend the whole of his working life there – a total of fifty-one years, apart from the years in France during the First World War. St Mary's did much to make Fleming the medical scientist he became, and perhaps it was only under the rather peculiar conditions that existed there that penicillin could have been discovered. Penicillin made Fleming one of the most famous men in the world, and St Mary's one of its most famous hospitals. Voluntary institutions like the London teaching hospitals had their own character, their own life and ethos, set their individual stamps on their staffs and students, and inspired fierce loyalties. St Mary's had a very positive character. In its struggle to become established, to survive and then to excel, it became a forceful, energetic organism within the world of London medicine. Since it made Fleming, and since Fleming gave so much honour to St Mary's, it is impossible to do justice to the man without portraying the origins and development of the remarkable institution in which he worked.

4

St Mary's Hospital

When Alec Fleming became a student at St Mary's in 1901, it was the youngest of the twelve London teaching hospitals. It had been founded in 1845, largely because Dr Samuel Lane was tired of his repeated attempts to get a staff appointment at St George's Hospital.[1] Most of the other teaching hospitals had a much longer history. St Bartholomew's and St Thomas's date from the twelfth century, and Guy's, St George's, the Westminster, the London and the Middlesex hospitals from the eighteenth. In 1836, London University was founded, with its own teaching hospitals of University College and King's College. Then came Charing Cross Hospital, the Royal Free and finally St Mary's.

Before 1836, English medical education was fragmented. Oxford and Cambridge students did their clinical work in a London hospital, in Scotland, or on the Continent, returning to their University to take their medical degrees. Some medical students did all their training in Scottish or continental schools, which were then superior to the English ones. To add to this diversity there were private medical schools where the preclinical subjects such as anatomy, chemistry, biology and physiology were taught, and clinical work could be done as a house-pupil of some eminent doctor. After training in one or more of these ways the student obtained an official medical qualification, such as an appropriate university degree, or a diploma from the Royal Colleges of Surgeons and Physicians, or the Society of Apothecaries. Then the appearance of London University changed the whole situation. The previously autonomous hospital medical schools became affiliated to the new university, which awarded its own medical degrees, improved the standard of clinical teaching, and created preclinical schools. In consequence, London became one of the best centres for medical education in the world.

Samuel Lane, who became a fervent medical educator during these changes, was a tenacious man. He was born in 1802, the son of a London tailor, and began his medical studies at the famous Great Windmill Street school of anatomy, which had been founded by John Hunter. He then became a clinical student at St George's Hospital in 1821, and a house surgeon there in 1827. At the end of this appointment he hoped for a more permanent one on the honorary staff, but this did not materialize. So he settled down to wait for the next vacancy, and in the meantime started a private anatomy school of his own in a large house close to the hospital. This prospered, because St George's had no such school itself and because Lane had managed to capture pupils from the Great Windmill Street establishment, which had to close in consequence. Lane's school soon developed into a complete preclinical one, with several lecturers teaching the required subjects, and Lane himself in charge of anatomy. It was, in due course, recognized by the new London University. But Lane's primary ambition, to become a member of the St George's honorary staff, was repeatedly thwarted. Vacancy after vacancy occurred, and he was always passed over.

Then a financial blow fell. St George's created its own preclinical school in direct competition with Lane's, refused his offer of amalgamation, and told him that he had no chance of a staff-appointment then or later. Lane, faced with ruin, was forced to give up his siege of St George's Hospital, but a magnificent, flamboyant solution to his problems had occurred to him. If St George's would have neither him nor his school, why should he not found a whole teaching hospital of his own?

It was just at this time, and just across Hyde Park, that the need for a hospital was rousing the residents of Paddington to action. Their committee must have been surprised but undoubtedly pleased when the energetic and experienced Dr Lane appeared among them, and soon established himself as their leader. It was he who obtained the support of the Bishop of London for a plan to build a 350-bed hospital on land belonging to his diocese, and who organized a public appeal for the £15,000 that would pay for it. The need was clear enough. By that time Paddington had a population of 150,000, with an area of slums and appallingly bad sanitation behind the frontage of opulent new mansions along the Bayswater Road and Westbourne Terrace.

Forty years before, in 1800, Paddington had been a pretty village with its church of St Mary's, its green, and the Westbourne river running down from Hampstead through fields and woods. Then came the Grand Junction Canal, with an extensive basin and wharf just south of St Mary's Church, and an influx of navvies and canal workers who were housed in shoddily-built terraced cottages and tenements that sprang up around the village. Next came Brunel's Great Western Railway, with its huge terminus, extensive goods and shunting yards and another influx of workers. So this part of Paddington became an industrial slum. Smoke and dust poured into the air and on the canal banks enormous piles of London garbage rotted while supposedly awaiting removal by barge. What had been a pretty village became known as 'stinking Paddington'.[2]

Not surprisingly these conditions favoured epidemics of typhoid and cholera. The water supply was suspect and what drains there were led into the Westbourne river, which thus became an open sewer. By 1842, there was so much ill-health in the Paddington area that the provision of a hospital seemed to be the first priority, and it was then that the action committee of local people was formed and found a leader in Dr Samuel Lane. The appeal for funds raised the necessary £15,000 by 1844. The Bishop of London persuaded the Canal Company to sub-let about 1 acre of land adjoining South Wharf Road as a site for the new hospital, which at his request would be known as St Mary's. The site, with a frontage on Norfolk Place, was not ideal, being restricted in area and only a few yards from the brimming canal basin, but it was approved and plans were drawn. The foundation stone was laid by the Prince Consort on 28 June 1845.

The architect, who gave his services free, was Thomas Hopper, then aged seventy, and celebrated for designing country mansions. He carried this style into the plans for the hospital, which has a magnificent entrance hall and monumental staircase lit by a dome, and such lofty main wards that there was little room or light for what, in a mansion, would be the servants' quarters but in a hospital the essential ancillary departments. Troubles beset the building process. The contractor died shortly after it began, and his successor went bankrupt. The hospital was finally completed by a member of the committee, himself a builder, who 'hoped that he might be paid when funds were available'.

In April 1850, the first phase of the hospital was finished, providing 150 beds. A Board of Governors had been set up, and their first task was to appoint the Honorary Staff. Here they faced difficulties. They wanted the best men, but these were already on the staffs of the other teaching hospitals. They also had to contend with the suspicion, already being loudly voiced in medical circles, that self-interest had stimulated the efforts of certain members of the action committee – Dr Samuel Lane being clearly the target. To allay these suspicions the Board devised a complicated voting system to select the staff members, and this somehow produced almost exactly the suspected results. Samuel Lane became the senior surgeon and, of the other fifteen members of the new staff, one was his nephew, J. R. Lane, and four were from his original private medical school.

At this point one might ask why it was that eminent doctors should be so anxious to gain hospital appointments that entailed hard and often unpleasant work and no pay. The answer lies in the structure of the medical profession before the creation of the National Health Service in 1948. The hospitals were then maintained by voluntary contributions, and they could not afford to pay their medical staffs. But since it was only the doctors with lucrative private practices who could afford to work part-time for nothing, it followed that the senior honorary posts were usually held by the most eminent and fashionable doctors of their day, and the junior posts by ambitious young men on lower rungs of the same ladder. There was, in fact, great prestige attached to honorary consultant posts.

Rich Victorians, who had a bad conscience about the swarming slums so close to their streets and squares of magnificent houses, gave generously to the hospitals, and rewarded the doctors who worked in them by their patronage as private patients.

There were other advantages for the hospital consultants. Dealing as they did with large numbers of patients who, being poor or destitute, were grateful for any form of treatment, they gained experience and could become specialists. And, having specialized, they could then earn larger fees from private patients. Teaching students was a stimulus to the consultant, ensuring that he kept abreast of his subject. And the students would one day become doctors who would remember a good teacher and refer private patients to him. Beyond these professional advantages, there was often a humane reason for hospital work, a desire to alleviate the sufferings from disease and poverty that existed in nineteenth century cities to a degree seen now only in the 'third world'.

The successful London doctor, therefore, had a teaching hospital appointment, a house and consulting rooms in the Harley Street area, a place in Society and a voice in the affairs of his profession. The most sought-after accolades were a royal appointment and a knighthood. Of the sixteen doctors who were first appointed to St Mary's when it opened its doors, several achieved high success. Three were appointed to the Royal Household and were knighted; four were Fellows of the Royal Society, an honour given for important contributions to science. Two of the three surgeons became famous for special operations. One of these could remove a stone from the bladder within sixty seconds of making the first incision. The other devised an operation for removing ovarian cysts, which was fatal in the first four cases but successful in the fifth patient – the surgeon's own sister – and in most cases thereafter.

Having appointed its clinical staff, St Mary's turned to the creation of a medical school. This had to be housed in a separate building, estimated to cost £2,500, which was raised by a public appeal in 1852. The new building was completed in 1854. It faced South Wharf Road, and adjoined the main hospital block fronting what is now Norfolk Place. It was planned to accommodate 300 students, with an anatomy theatre, dissecting room, laboratory, museum, library and rooms for the Dean and lecturers. Contemporary pictures show a façade resembling the stable block of one of Hopper's country mansions. The first Dean, one of the hospital surgeons, was Mr Spencer Smith. Lane and his nephew taught anatomy and Dr Handfield Jones, a physician, dealt with the new subject of physiology, only just beginning to be separated from anatomy. The lecturer in botany was John Burdon-Sanderson, who later became one of the foremost medical scientists of his day, and whose work was to have an important bearing on the career of Alec Fleming.

Burdon-Sanderson[3] was born in 1829, and after studying medicine in

Edinburgh, worked in Paris with Claude Bernard, the great physiologist, before becoming interested in botany. It was this interest that led to his appointment in the St Mary's medical school, but he was primarily a physician and became Medical Superintendent at the hospital. In 1856, under the new Public Health Act, he was appointed the first Medical Officer of Health at Paddington, a post that he held for ten years. Though at the beginning of his appointment there was no recognition of the fact that infectious diseases are caused by living organisms, it was realized that filthy living conditions and contaminated drinking water promoted epidemics such as the Asiatic cholera that London had suffered in 1849 and 1853. The new Medical Officers of Health were given wide powers, and Burdon-Sanderson began his crusade by cleaning up the Paddington canal and its banks, and converting the Westbourne stream from an open sewer into a closed one. He also dealt with the Serpentine, into which the Westbourne had emptied its sewage for so long that the lake was half-filled by stinking black sludge, and on which it was considered dangerous even to row a boat. The lake was drained, the sludge removed, and a filtration system installed that kept it filled with clean water.

As a botanist and epidemiologist, Burdon-Sanderson noticed the presence of microscopic living organisms in diseased human tissues, and he began to culture and study them, becoming one of the earliest bacteriologists. But he did not accept Pasteur's revolutionary idea that these organisms were the cause of disease, until he convinced himself that they were not the result of it. Then he became a convert to the 'germ theory' of disease and one of Lister's active supporters in promoting it. It is of particular interest to note that, in 1871, Burdon-Sanderson became probably the first medical scientist to record that moulds of the *Penicillium* group can inhibit the growth of bacteria in culture.[4] Lister made a similar observation, and, at King's College Hospital in 1882, successfully treated a chronically infected wound with a *Penicillium* culture.[5] In the same year Burdon-Sanderson became the first Professor of Physiology in Oxford, an appointment that caused serious upheavals in that ancient and conservative university. The impact of these developments in Oxford on the career of Alec Fleming will become apparent in later chapters.

From its inception, St Mary's Hospital had to struggle to make its way. The perennial problem was lack of money and, unlike the older hospitals, St Mary's had no endowments accumulated over the centuries. The medical school, designed for 300 students, opened with only 20, and for the first six years the fees they paid did not cover the costs. By 1866 the number had risen to 120, and there was the beginning of a community spirit. Rugby football and swimming clubs were formed, and a Medical Society where papers were read and discussed. In 1869 the School and Hospital Committees were thrown into confusion by the startling application by three women to be enrolled as students. Though the formal response was a stern refusal, several St Mary's men were actually sympathetic, and helped the applicants, Sophia Jex-Blake, Mary Peakey and Isabel Thorne, to found their own school, the London School of Medicine for Women, in 1874. St Mary's can claim, therefore, that some members of its staff were more receptive than those of other schools to the revolutionary idea that women might become doctors.[6]

Meanwhile the hospital itself needed money for improvements and expansion. The existing accommodation was wasteful of space, and yet badly ventilated. Another trouble was the drainage. The builders had had little experience of the new-fangled water-closets specified, and installed them in such a way that the lavatories on lower floors overflowed with the contributions from those above. The hospital had to be closed in 1875, while new 'sanitary towers' were built at each corner. It had to be closed again in 1886 while leaks were found and repaired, and similar drainage troubles closed a wing as recently as 1953. The first extension of the hospital had taken place in 1867, when the Albert Edward Wing added five new wards. And in 1882, a bequest of £25,000 allowed the building of the Mary Sandford Wing, and a new out-patient department at the junction of Norfolk Place and South Wharf Road.

In 1883, St Mary's was taken in hand by its new and energetic Dean, Dr George Field, a man with a belief in the value of publicity that he passed on to his successors. Within a few months of taking office he sent out 6,000 invitations to a conversazione at the hospital, a fund-raising exercise to which nearly 3,000 people came. The hospital was transformed for the occasion. The reception area, decorated (free) by Messrs Gillow and Mr William Morris, displayed pictures and works of art lent by various owners. The band of the Grenadier Guards, hand-bell ringers, the Gala Choir, and Mr Plater's Glee Singers provided musical entertainment in different parts of the building, while in the medical school (decorated by Messrs Marshall and Snelgrove) there was an exhibition of the latest medical inventions and the latest Victorian triumph – electric light. Refreshments were well up to this high standard, the main novelty being bird's nest soup. The whole elaborate venture was a great success, and St Mary's emerged from dingy obscurity into the profitable limelight of Society patronage.

In 1887, George Field decided that the hospital should acquire land adjoining it that fronted Praed Street. This belonged to the Ecclesiastical Commission, but was sub-let to the canal company, and was occupied by a row of houses and little shops. After two years of bargaining the canal company agreed to sell the leasehold for £8,500, and the Church Commissioners generously made over the freehold to the hospital. But the houses and shops were still there and the hospital had to buy out the occupants, an expensive process funded by repeated appeals to the public. By 1892 possession was complete and work began on the new block that would stretch along Praed Street, and be named the Clarence Wing. But it was not until six years later that the basement, housing a new outpatient department, was completed. The building managed to rise one more floor, and then work was stopped for lack of funds. The truncated façade, something of an eyesore, became known as the 'amputation stump'. But the ever-resourceful hospital authorities put its flat roof to profitable use in 1902, by erecting a large stand to accommodate some of the thousands of people lining the route of the march-past to cheer the victorious troops returning from South Africa.

During the half-century between the founding of St Mary's, and Alec Fleming's arrival there as a medical student in 1901, medicine had made more progress than in the preceding 2,000 years. One revolutionary advance had been the use of anaesthesia in surgery and midwifery, so that by 1860 no major operation was performed without it. Before then the unfortunate patient undergoing an operation had to endure the pain as best he could. He was strapped to the operating table, and the surgeon did what had to be done as quickly as possible. The speed and dexterity of the surgeons in those days was truly astonishing – stones could be removed from the bladder in about two minutes, and a limb amputated in five. But, with the patient put to sleep by chloroform or ether, the surgeon could take his time and carry out more complicated operations that would have been previously impossible.

But the mortality from any form of surgery remained distressingly high. The main cause of death was 'hospital gangrene' or 'mortification' of the wound, and about 25 per cent of surgical patients died of it. Its cause was quite unknown, but there were learned, dogmatic and quite mistaken theories. It is astonishing that the idea of contagion seems not to have occurred to those faced with obvious evidence of it. And it was the obstetricians, not the surgeons, who first, but most reluctantly accepted it. As long ago as 1795, Alexander Gordon of Aberdeen stressed the epidemic nature of puerperal fever and suggested that wound mortification might have a similar origin.[7] But his book on the subject had almost no effect, except on Oliver Wendell Holmes, whose pamphlet on 'The Contagiousness of Puerperal Fever' earned him the abuse of American obstetricians. And a similar rejection awaited Semmelweis in Vienna a few years later, though he had proved the point. All new ideas tend to provoke an automatic rejection by an entrenched and conservative profession, and in this instance the suggestion that doctors were actually harming their patients by transmitting some hypothetical and invisible 'infection' was not merely absurd – it was insulting.

It took the force of character and prestige of two of the greatest of all medical scientists to persuade an incredulous and hostile profession to recognize the existence of harmful bacteria and the infections they could cause. It was Pasteur who showed that specific animal diseases were caused by specific germs and that germs caused putrefaction of animal tissue. And this idea, relayed to Lister in Edinburgh in 1865,[8] fired him with the further idea that 'hospital gangrene' was a form of putrefaction caused by bacteria. Thus the whole future of surgery began to change.

Lister began at once to search for chemicals that would kill bacteria without harming the patient – becoming an adept bacteriologist in the process. This was the beginning of the quest for the 'ideal antiseptic', an ideal that eluded not only Lister but a host of other workers for the next seventy years until Alexander Fleming found it. Lister had to make do with the best he could find – dilute carbolic acid, just strong enough to kill germs and weak enough not to kill the living tissues of the patient. Believing that most harmful germs came from the air, Lister introduced his famous spray that filled the operating rooms with a fine mist of carbolic, and which must have been almost as unpleasant for its human occupants as for the germs it was aimed at. The dramatic decrease in post-operative infections that followed was probably due less to the carbolic than to the awareness of the existence of dangerous germs, and the need for strict cleanliness. The improvement was particularly striking in the results of surgery during the Franco-Prussian War of 1870, and Lister was acclaimed on the Continent before being fully appreciated in Britain. But the results of his work, taken together with that of Pasteur and Robert Koch, established the 'germ theory' of disease and the recognition that infectious diseases of all sorts are due to an invasion of the body by virulent micro-organisms.

Another name must be added to the list of pioneers in the battle against infectious disease. Deaths from typhus, cholera, typhoid and dysentery during the Crimean War of 1855 far outnumbered those caused by the enemy. It was the astonishing Florence Nightingale who headed a crusade against the appallingly insanitary conditions in the British military hospitals, and against the prejudice and incompetence of the authorities that condoned them. This crusade did not end with the war, Miss Nightingale continued it as a tyrannical invalid for the next twenty years, bullying the military authorities into providing an efficient army medical and nursing service.[9] Her achievements had their effect, of course, on civilian hospital practice, and provided the administrative foundation for the Listerian revolution in surgery. With the £50,000 raised by public subscription, Florence Nightingale founded the school for nurses that bears her name. Thus, for the first time, hospital nurses were properly trained and given a background of medical knowledge that made them the colleagues and not merely the servants of the doctors.

5

Alexander Fleming – Medical Student

Alec Fleming was one of the eighty new students entering St Mary's in October 1901. Queen Victoria had died in January of that year, and the coronation of Edward VII had been delayed by a dramatic illness cured by equally dramatic surgery. Medicine had started its ever-accelerating progress, and the British Empire, struggling to conclude the Boer War, had started on the long decline that few of its citizens then recognized.

Alec was twenty when he began medicine, at least two years older than most new entrants, who had come straight from school. For these the change in academic habits was not great; there was simply a continuation of classes, lectures and community life, though with more freedom. For the provincial boys there was the heady experience of living in the wicked metropolis and in the rather bohemian lodgings that catered for students. In an attempt to exert some quasi-parental control – and also to augment its income – St Mary's had established a Residential College in Westbourne Grove a few years before. This had proved a financial disaster, and in 1900 it had closed, leaving the Medical School with debts that burdened it for years to come.

Both the school and the hospital were, in fact, in dire financial trouble, the result of the airy optimism of the Dean, George Field, who retired in 1900. His 'build now, pay later' policy had doubled the size of the hospital during the seventeen years of his office, and doubled the number of students in the school. The speaker at the Staff Dinner who proposed the health of the retiring Dean referred to 'the great debt of gratitude' that both hospital and school owed to Dr Field. The gratitude was real enough. So unfortunately was the debt. A great deal of the new building had not been paid for, and there were no profits from the school to pay the teachers. It needed the firm hand of the new Dean, Dr Caley, and the new Secretary, to save St Mary's from extinction as a teaching hospital. The man appointed Secretary on Dr Field's retirement spent a few days going through the books and then promptly resigned. His successor, Dr Matthews, was made of stronger stuff. He remained to juggle the books until they balanced.

One of the causes of the financial troubles was the increasing cost of medical education. New subjects were appearing almost every year, needing new laboratories, equipment and staff. Bacteriology, once a branch of botany, was by 1900 an important medical science and a part of the students' training. Physiology was taking its first steps into vast, unexplored fields, and what had been 'chemical physiology' was becoming a subject in its own right, soon to be called 'biochemistry'. To meet these new demands the school borrowed £4,000 to modernize the old buildings dating from 1854. The hospital had the same sorts of problems. Improved medical treatment cost more and, unlike the students, the patients paid no fees. It was not surprising that the Clarence Wing, begun so proudly in 1892, had only just appeared above ground when Alec arrived, and was not completed until 1904. St Mary's always had been, and always would be, short of money and would have to fight for life in the competitive world of charitable institutions.

For Alec, becoming a medical student was more of a change in mental habits and less in ways of life than for his fellow freshmen. He had left school at sixteen, and would have to adjust to high-pressure learning. On the other hand, the initial distractions of London were behind him; he was familiar not only with its streets but with all the tricks of survival, and he was living at home within a few minutes' walk of the hospital. Added to this, he had the advantage of his Ayrshire upbringing. It had given him physical stamina; the boyhood ability to take a day's work and an eight-mile walk without fatigue remained with him for most of his life. It had given him too his interest in living things and developed the naturalist's powers of critical observation.

Alec seems to have been a model student from the first. He settled down to acquire fascinating new knowledge and entered into the community activities of the students, as he was still doing in the London Scottish Regiment. By strenuous lobbying, the students had persuaded the hospital to provide them with a common-room and restaurant in the basement of the Mary Sandford Wing, and this was the centre of their social life until 1931. There were several sporting clubs, the rugby football club being the most important since it brought prestige to St Mary's when successful in the pitched battles for the Hospitals Cup fought out every year by the twelve London medical schools. Alec did not play rugby, but being an excellent shot, he was a star member of the rifle club. He also played water polo. He was active in the Dramatic Society, where, because of his small size, he was often cast in female roles. It is on record that the two feminine leads in a production of Pinero's *Rocket* were played by Alexander Fleming and C. M. Wilson – better known later as Lord Moran.[1] Alec was also a member of the Medical and the Debating Societies; despite his almost impenetrable silence he enjoyed companionship and revelled in competition.

London medical students in those days had a reputation for high spirits bordering on rowdyism. Their clinical work, particularly in the slum homes of their maternity patients, gave them an experience of the seamy side of life – and death – and of a squalor, dirt and poverty that must have shocked the sensitive. But it seldom depressed them. Unlike many students of today, they were not political animals.

There was then no time-limit on a medical student's studies. He could hurry or dawdle through his courses and examinations at his own pace. Some, with private means, treated their medical school as a convenient club, delaying qualification by several years. A very few prolonged their training from a wish to specialize or to do research, taking time off to work as demonstrators or to study abroad.* But there was little official encouragement for research. It was regarded as a hobby for those with a strange urge to discover things, and who could afford to spend time on expensive, unpaid and usually fruitless work. Very few hospital consultants did any serious research, nor did they expect their students to challenge accepted ideas.

By 1900, medical studies were separated into the preclinical and the clinical courses. For the first two years students learned something of the rapidly growing scientific basis of medicine. This began with biology, chemistry and physics, with some of which Alec was already familiar. The study of the minute structure of the different tissues and organs (histology) was also begun, involving the cutting and staining of sections and their examination under the microscope. The students paid about £25 for tuition each year, and had other expenses. They had to buy books, dissecting instruments and other equipment, and usually their own microscopes. Alec learned his biology from W. G. Ridewood, a distinguished zoologist who was Director of the Natural History Department of the British Museum.

The Lecturer in chemistry was also a distinguished man. He was Sir William Willcox, a great figure in the medico-legal world, often appearing as an authority on poisons in murder cases. He was the first of a series of St Mary's men to excel in medical jurisprudence, being followed by A. P. Luff, Bernard Spilsbury and Roche Lynch. In Alec Fleming's time as a student, biochemistry had not yet emerged as a specific subject, and the known chemical processes involved in respiration, digestion, muscle contraction and so on, were within the province of chemical physiology. Physics for medical students was limited to heat, light, sound, mechanics, and a very little electricity. The electrical nature of nerve impulses was only just becoming apparent. X-rays were still a scientific curiosity, having been discovered by Röntgen in 1895. It should be recorded, however, that a St Mary's man, Dr A. P. Laurie, a lecturer in chemistry, had been astonishingly prompt in applying the new discovery. In 1896 he managed to photograph a stone in a patient's bladder, using a twenty-minute exposure to a

---

* Two of the most eminent medical scientists of their day were Sir Charles Sherrington who took ten years to qualify, and Sir Bernard Spilsbury who took nine years.

primitive X-ray source.[2] But it was not until 1913 that the hospital had an X-ray department.

During his first year at St Mary's, Alec sat for the hospital entrance scholarship and won it. It was worth £145, enough to pay all his medical tuition fees. And at the end of that first year he also won the chemistry prize and the biology prize. As already mentioned, Alec's phenomenal success in examinations was not the result of obvious hard book work – all who knew him at that time are agreed on that point. At home in the evenings, he always had time for the family games. When he did read a textbook, Robert Fleming describes him as flipping over the pages, apparently taking in the gist at a glance, and groaning when he caught out the author in some mistake or contradiction.[3]

C. A. Pannett, who was so often the runner-up to Alec in the annual contests for prizes and scholarships, complained that he had to work much harder to gain second place than Alec did to get the first. Pannett ascribed this success to an almost uncannily accurate prediction of the examiners' questions.[4] But he bore Alec no ill-will, and remained one of his closest friends throughout his life, becoming himself a distinguished surgeon. Various writers, baffled by Alec's effortless academic successes, credited him with a photographic memory, stored with pages of print that he could recall at will. But his brother Robert believed that Alec had something much more valuable; a selective, penetrating mind in which essential facts were arranged in a logical and easily memorized framework. And he had a canny (not uncanny) insight into the workings of his examiners' minds, coupled with the ability to convey what they wanted with the brevity and clarity that no examiner, wearied by rambling, wordy ignorance, can resist.

In his second year Alec moved on to human anatomy, physiology and organic chemistry. The lecturer in physiology was A. D. Waller, a Fellow of the Royal Society, a professional medical scientist and research worker, and the discoverer of the pattern of electrical impulses generated by the beating heart. (Waller had not developed this discovery and the man who did, Willem Einthoven, was awarded a Nobel Prize for producing the electrocardiogram.) Alec attended the systematic lectures and practical classes by which physiology was taught. Whole tracts of what is now elementary physiology were then unknown. Vitamins had not been discovered; hormones and the functions of the endocrine glands were only just beginning to be recognized, and diseases such as pernicious anaemia and diabetes were usually fatal because they were due to a break-down of physiological systems that were then not even known to exist.

By contrast, anatomy was a circumscribed and stable subject. It had been the essential study for the medical profession for about 2,000 years and every bone, muscle, tendon, ligament, nerve, blood-vessel and organ visible to the naked eye had been named in all its parts – in Latin. The

Greeks had been admirable anatomists and great logicians. They and their followers had believed that, given the facts of anatomy, the functions and disorders of the body could be deduced by pure reason. The classical ideas on bodily function and disease were, as far as observed facts went, perfectly reasonable. But they were also absurdly wrong. Observation and deduction are not enough, and until William Harvey added the essential stage of experiment, there was no conception of the true function of the heart and lungs or the circulation of the blood. Harvey's work was indeed the practical beginning of the scientific method – observation, hypothesis, experiment – fostered by the founders of the Royal Society in 1660, which made possible accelerating advances in every branch of science.

Despite the rise of physiology, early-twentieth-century medical students were still expected to master as much anatomy as their mediaeval predecessors. They had virtually to learn by heart the contents of massive text-books and had to dissect for themselves every part of the human body. The dissecting-room, with its rows of partly dismembered corpses laid out on the tables, was a shock to the more squeamish of the new students. But familiarity bred a sort of detachment, and indeed the bodies, like Egyptian mummies, had been so carefully preserved by injection that it was difficult to imagine that they had ever been alive. The student paid a fee for the body assigned to him – it would be a regular companion for about a year – and the school had to meet the cost of acquiring and preparing it.

Some of Fleming's biographers have described the colourful and brilliant Clayton Greene as being his anatomy teacher, and have supposed that his flamboyant methods were an early inspiration to the future scientist. But W. M. Clayton Greene did not teach Alec, because he was not appointed to the school until 1905. Alec's anatomy teacher was J. E. Lane, Samuel Lane's great-nephew, and there could have been few duller lecturers. In a flat monotone he would recite from memory a sufficient number of pages of Gray's *Anatomy* to occupy the statutory hour. Alec became equally knowledgeable, because he won the Anatomy Prize in 1902, and he also won the Physiology Prize, which needed a logical rather than a repetitive approach. But anatomy obviously attracted Alec, because he became a prosector (student demonstrator) in 1903 and won the Senior Anatomy Prize in 1904. He had, at that time, the idea of becoming a surgeon, and his remarkably deft fingers would have been a great asset. He also won the Histology Prize, having become a skilful microscopist and section-manipulator, and these distinctions brought him an added bonus, the Junior General Proficiency Prize. He was indeed a most admirable student.

Meanwhile, the close-knit Fleming community at 29 York Street had come to an end. Hugh, the farmer of Lochfield, had at last decided to marry. The bride, to the family's delight, was 'the girl next door', Kate Loudon of Overmuir Farm with whom they had played and gone to school as children. Hugh's marriage meant that his step-mother, Grace, no longer had to keep house for him, and she transferred her attention to her own children in London, buying a house in Ealing to which they all – except Tom – moved. Tom disposed of 29 York Street, and moved to an apartment near his consulting room at 42 Harley Street. But he was a frequent visitor to the new family home in Ealing.

At St Mary's, Alec had added pharmacology and organic chemistry to his studies and, as was by now expected of him, won the prizes for both subjects in 1904.[5] This was the end of his preclinical years, and he sat for what was then known as the Intermediate MB examination of London University. Unlike Oxford and Cambridge, London did not award a degree at this stage, and their medical students remained undergraduates until their clinical studies were completed. Alec passed his Intermediate MB examination in July, 1904, with distinctions in physiology and pharmacology.

With the examination behind them, Alec and his classmates were let loose in the hospital as clinical students. They were attached, like apprentices, to one or other of the senior clinicians, each of whom had his entourage of a junior consultant, registrar, house-officer, and several students known collectively as a 'firm', and responsible for appropriate wards and outpatients. Until the 1930s, students were expected to do a good deal of minor medicine and surgery now done by doctors and nurses and, by contrast, many of the chores now done by porters and orderlies. Students were, in fact, useful, and they paid fees for the privilege. They learned by practical experience and trial and error. The errors, mostly minor, were the patients' misfortune, but they seldom complained. Most were pathetically grateful for any treatment, and fiercely loyal to 'their' hospital. In the outpatient department, students lanced boils, drained abscesses, stitched up cuts, dressed wounds, extracted teeth, passed catheters, and learned to treat fractures and dislocations. They also learned to sort out those who were really ill from those who only wanted free board and lodging.

In the wards, under the stern eye of the ward sister, patients were less at the mercy of the students. Much of their training took place during the consultant's rounds, when the art of diagnosis from the history of the patients' illness, and from the classical methods of 'inspection, palpation, auscultation and percussion' was demonstrated by the chief. Ten or twelve students in turn then examined the shivering patient, endeavouring to feel or hear what they were supposed to. There were no X-rays and virtually no laboratory reports to help in the diagnosis, or to guide treatment. Nevertheless, a good clinician could weigh up the signs and symptoms and make a fairly accurate diagnosis within the limited range of diseases then recognized. But medical treatment was dismally ineffective. In fact, the clinical textbooks that Alec Fleming had to read, and the practice of medicine in which he was instructed, are so different from the experience of today that they need some description. Only doctors and nurses old enough to remember the pre-antibiotic days can have any true appreciation of the medical revolution that has taken place.

In those days a large proportion of the patients that filled the hospitals were children and young adults suffering from bacterial infections of one sort or another. The clinical textbooks gave much of their space to descriptions of these, and to the largely ineffective methods of treatment. The diseases were usually classified according to the parts of the body affected: for example as meningitis, sinusitis, tonsillitis, pneumonia, enteritis, peritonitis, and so on. But the relatively new science of bacteriology had at least identified the enemy – the essential first step in the long battle to defeat it. And since Alexander Fleming's life work was to lie in the field of bacteriology, and its main purpose was to discover ways to overcome the dreadful ravages of infection, it is logical at this stage to glance, very briefly, at the subject that he was beginning to study.

There are thousands of different sorts of bacteria – microscopic, single-celled organisms. Most are harmless to man; some are useful, as, for example, soil bacteria and those causing fermentation. A few are extremely harmful, being deadly invaders of living tissues, or producers of toxins so poisonous that minute quantities are lethal. These are the pathogenic bacteria, and the main study of medical bacteriologists. Their detailed classification is extremely complex – and made more so by several changes in official terminology during the past fifty years.

A very few main characteristics will serve to identify the major groups. The first is shape. Elongated or rod-shaped bacteria are bacilli, round ones are cocci. The cocci which grow in clumps, like a bunch of grapes, are staphylococci; those which form chains are streptococci. Long spiral or wavy bacteria are spirochaetes. Spirochaetes and some sorts of bacilli are actively mobile, cocci are not. Then there is the matter of reproduction. All bacteria multiply by simply dividing so that one organism becomes two – a process that can occur every twenty minutes under favourable conditions. Some bacteria produce spores, minute and very resistant 'seeds' that can survive – perhaps for years – if conditions for growth are unfavourable. Different growth requirements define different bacteria. Some grow best at blood heat ($37°C$), some at lower temperatures. Some need oxygen – the aerobes; others will only grow in the absence of oxygen – the anaerobes. Finally, a simple staining reaction, devised by Gram, separates all bacteria into two groups. Those that lose the stain on washing with alcohol are classified as Gram-negative, those that retain it are Gram-positive.

The common killers in Britain among these bacteria were the streptococci, staphylococci, pneumococci, meningococci, tubercle bacilli, diphtheria bacilli and the typhoid and paratyphoid bacilli. The *Streptococcus pyogenes* was the dreaded invader of wounds, causing a spreading infection that could be fatal in a few days. Even an infected pin-prick might be lethal. This was the organism, too, responsible for most cases of puerperal fever, scarlet fever, erysipelas and some cases of pneumonia, ear infections and meningitis. The *Staphylococcus aureus* was the common cause of boils, carbuncles and other skin infections, not usually dangerous, but occasionally leading to widespread and very dangerous dissemination. The staphylococcus was also the common cause of osteomyelitis in children, a long drawn-out, crippling and often fatal infection of the bones.

The pneumococcus was the cause of lobar pneumonia, then a very common and dangerous illness. In a hospital like St Mary's whole wards would be full of patients suffering or recovering from it. The illness itself was bad enough, but the common complication of empyema (pus in the pleural cavity) was worse. The only effective treatment for an empyema was the surgical removal of several inches of one or more ribs, and the insertion of a tube through which the pus drained – perhaps for weeks. There was no specific treatment for pneumonia (nor, indeed for almost any infection) but doctors had their own pet theories. The usual treatment for pneumonia was the application of a hot poultice to the affected side of the chest, but Dr D. B. Lees, a physician at St Mary's, believed that cold discouraged the growth of the pneumococcus, and treated his pneumonia cases with ice-bags.[6] One patient with pneumonia of the left lung was being treated in this way when Dr Lees went off on holiday. The man then developed pneumonia of the right lung, and the physician deputising for Dr Lees believed in hot poultices. So the unfortunate patient had ice packs to the left, and hot poultices to the right side of his chest. He recovered.

The tubercle bacillus was the cause of a vast amount of ill health. Tuberculosis of the lungs in Britain killed 53,000 people, mainly young adults, in 1900, and made permanent invalids of several times this number. Tuberculosis also affected bones and joints, the kidneys and lymph glands and caused an invariably fatal form of meningitis in children. Diphtheria, often an epidemic disease of children, was due to the invasion of the nose and throat by the Klebs–Löffler bacillus. This produced toxins which caused a swelling and exudate that might rapidly asphyxiate the patient and also damage the nerves and heart. Diphtheria, in 1903, was one of the very few infections for which a specific remedy had been produced. This was antitoxin, made from the blood of horses immunized by repeated injections of small doses of the toxin. If antitoxin was injected early enough in a case of diphtheria, the toxins were neutralised and their harmful effects avoided. It was the first glimmering of light in an otherwise dismal picture, the first signs that bacteria could be fought with specific and sophisticated weapons.

Virulent sporing bacteria can be dangerous because the resistant spores can lie dormant perhaps for years, particularly in soil or road dirt containing horse manure. One of these organisms is the tetanus bacillus, a common inhabitant of the intestine of the horse. It is an anaerobe producing in infected tissues a toxin that causes generalized muscular spasms so severe that they are usually fatal. As in the case of diphtheria, an antitoxin had been produced, but this was only effective as a prophylactic, given as soon as possible after wounding and before the toxin could be produced. Another sporing anaerobe, *Clostridium welchii*, was one of the organisms causing gas gangrene, mercifully rare in peace-time, but a terrible invader of battle-wounds. The infection, usually starting in a dirty wound, spreads with terrifying speed along muscle tissue, which becomes blackened and distended with gas in a few hours. A lethal toxin is also produced but antitoxin is ineffective and the only treatment then was immediate amputation – if it was possible. A third sporing killer is the anthrax bacillus, an aerobe. Anthrax is primarily a disease of sheep and cattle, but the spores can infect man through some minute cut or abrasion, or even by dust breathed in the lungs. Once it has gained access to the body, the anthrax bacillus multiplies rapidly in the blood of the victim and, in those days, caused almost invariable death. It was fortunately a rare disease, but became of interest to military authorities in 1940, when its use in germ warfare was the subject of extensive experiments. Gruinard island off the west coast of Scotland, used in testing, is still heavily contaminated with anthrax spores and probably will remain so, perhaps for centuries.

Abdominal infections were caused by many different bacteria. The most prevalent were the intestinal (enteric) fevers due to the typhoid and paratyphoid bacilli. They had a high mortality, were endemic in places with poor sanitation, and became epidemic at times, particularly among the troops during campaigns such as the South African War. At the time that Alec Fleming was a medical student, Sir Almroth Wright, who had become bacteriologist and pathologist at St Mary's in 1902, had produced a prophylactic vaccine against typhoid, about which there will be more in later chapters. Cholera was another acute and epidemic intestinal infection, usually conveyed by contaminated drinking water. By 1900 it was rare in Britain, but there had been several major epidemics during the previous fifty years.

Abdominal organs such as the kidneys, bladder and gall-bladder could be the site of acute infections by the pyogenic (pus-forming) streptococci and staphylococci. One common and very dangerous infection was only just becoming recognized. This was appendicitis. It had not been realized that the appendix was the primary site of an infection that had been called 'perityphlitis' which often led to peritonitis and death. Until Lister's pioneer work with antiseptics made abdominal surgery reasonably safe, no surgeon would have dared to operate on patients who must have been suffering from appendicitis.

It took a royal occasion and one of the most courageous medical decisions ever made, to bring appendicitis and its surgical treatment to general recognition. The coronation of Edward VII was fixed for 26 June 1901. By 24 June all the elaborate preparations were complete and most of the Heads of State of the world (crowned or otherwise) had assembled in London. And on that day the king became suddenly ill with abdominal pain and fever. Next day, Sir Frederick Treves diagnosed 'perityphlitis' with impending peritonitis, and said that only immediate operation could save the king's life. The king refused, saying, 'I must and will go to my Coronation.' 'Then, your majesty,' Treves is reported to have answered, 'you will go as a corpse.'[7] The king was persuaded. The ceremonies were cancelled and the assembled kings and dignitaries departed. Treves operated, removed a grossly infected appendix, and the king was out of danger within two weeks. One of the men to take credit for the success of this surgical drama was Lord Lister, who was rightly one of the first recipients of the newly created Order of Merit in the delayed Coronation honours.

To conclude this very incomplete account of the miseries caused by bacterial infection, one should mention two diseases that, in those days, were unmentionable in polite society. These were syphilis and gonorrhoea. The fact that venereal diseases were unmentionable did not reduce their enormous prevalence, nor were they confined to the lower orders of society. Infected prostitutes were the main vector for dissemination, but virtuous women were infected by their less virtuous husbands.

Syphilis is caused by a spirochaete. It is an extraordinary infection, going through three distinct phases over a period of many years. The first phase is no more than a local sore. A few weeks or months later widespread skin ulcers develop, with other unpleasant manifestations. Later – perhaps by years – a far more serious phase of degeneration of the blood vessels, bones, nerves, brain and personality takes place. Another distressing feature is that syphilis can be passed to the unborn child, so that it comes into the world already deformed and infected. Syphilis, historically known as 'the pox', was for centuries the scourge of millions, monarchs and paupers alike, and the quackeries of the 'pox doctors' were in great demand.

Gonorrhoea, due to the gonococcus, is less serious. Often causing no more than inflammation and a discharge, it was commonly referred to by patients, as 'a dose' – to the confusion of ignorant medical students – and a cause of ribaldry rather than concern. But it had serious complications. It could cause blindness in new-born babies, by infecting the eyes. It could also cause sterility, and a form of arthritis.

It should now be said that almost all these diseases that featured so prominently in Alec Fleming's hospital training have, through medical advances in which he himself played a major part, virtually disappeared. Many doctors practising today will never have seen a case of puerperal fever, septicaemia, lobar pneumonia, tuberculous meningitis, or tertiary syphilis. Memories are short. It is only by re-creating the terrors and miseries of the past that we can appreciate what has been won by those who fought so long and so hard against bacterial disease.

When Fleming was a student the very existence of this enemy had only been realized during the previous thirty years, and the battle against it had scarcely begun. Indeed, the absence of any effective treatment was so deeply rooted in the medical mind that doctors were scarcely aware of any deficiency. But there was one man among Alec's teachers who preached a veritable crusade against the bacteria he saw as the greatest enemy of the human race. This, of course, was Almroth Wright, recently appointed Professor of Pathology. He was an astonishing man, dazzlingly erudite, full of ideas and enthusiasm, fascinating to an entourage of able young men, many of whom became his life-long disciples. Fleming was among the students who sat enthralled at his lectures, while whole new worlds of medical science – almost science fiction – opened out before them. Fleming, with his Scottish caution was at first sceptical – he demanded facts. But he succumbed in the end, and Wright was to become the most powerful influence in his working life.

Though Alec, as a student, was already impressed by Wright, he had no clear idea of becoming a bacteriologist, being inclined towards surgery. Surgeons were the élite of the profession, the men of action, the heroes of life-and-death dramas. Manual dexterity backed by a sound knowledge of anatomy was the basis of their success, and Fleming had both these advantages – in fact, as noted, he was marvellously deft with his hands. So, in January 1905, he took and passed the Primary Examination for the Fellowship of the Royal College of Surgeons. In the meantime he had collected the Pathology Prize, the Medicine Prize, the Medical Jurisprudence Prize and the Second General Proficiency Prize.

He then went on to do his training in obstetrics, which involved practical instruction in delivering babies and the prompt actions needed when things went wrong. During the first part of the course this was carried out in the labour ward of the hospital, with expert supervision and the best equipment available. There could have been no greater shock for nervous, inexperienced students when they were finally expected to deliver babies in the mothers' own homes. These were usually in the worst of the Paddington slums. A whole family might live in a single, ill-lit, ill-ventilated, verminous and filthy room, with but one bed, and with only one lavatory and water-tap for perhaps a dozen such families. Babies usually arrived at night, and the anxious student, summoned by some child, or the possibly drunken father, would find his way to a scene worthy of Hogarth. Children, friends and relatives were likely to be crowded into the stifling space, presided over by the local, unqualified 'Sarah Gamp' – the tribal midwife – who knew very well that the beardless boy with the black bag was an utter novice. Most births went smoothly, provided the student interfered as little as possible. Occasionally things went wrong, when he had to act effectively if he could, or summon help if he could not. But the arrival of a new little life, despite these deplorable surroundings, was an event of great satisfaction and, even in these poor and overcrowded homes, usually one of joy.

With the passage of his clinical years, Alec continued to collect his prizes – the Third General Proficiency Prize in 1906 and the Psychological Medicine Prize (a daring subject in those days). Then he began to take his final examinations. Although he had passed his Intermediate MB, BS in London University, he elected to sit for the so-called 'Conjoint Board' examinations of the Royal Colleges of Surgeons and Physicians. Many candidates chose this qualification because it could be taken in stages and was therefore supposed to be an easier path than that of the London MB, BS. But Fleming took all four parts in July, 1906, and passed with ease. He was then a qualified doctor, with the letters MRCS, LRCP, after his name.

This was not the end of his studies; in fact, it might be said to be the beginning of his definitive career. There were many choices open to him. He could apply for a house appointment at St Mary's or some other hospital, or he could have gone straight into general practice. In fact, he elected to stay on in the medical school to work for his London MB, BS. His choice was directed by the same sort of chance that had sent him to St Mary's. It happened that one of Almroth Wright's most ardent disciples, John Freeman, was also an enthusiastic member of the St Mary's rifle club, as was Fleming. The team had won the Hospitals Cup in 1905 and had hopes of winning the Armitage Cup at Bisley. Fleming's departure might spoil the team's chances, and Freeman was anxious to keep him.[8] But Fleming needed a job that would give him both a salary and time to work for his examination, and, as it happened, Almroth Wright had a vacancy for a junior assistant. Freeman suggested to Wright that Fleming was the very man, and to Fleming that this was the very job for him. So, in the summer of 1906, Fleming, with no great enthusiasm, joined the staff of Wright's department, as a temporary measure, and remained there for the next forty-nine years.

6

Almroth Edward Wright

In 1906, when young Alec Fleming joined his department, Wright was forty-five years old and at the height of his powers. In that year he was knighted, though this was a move in the game being played by Lord Haldane, Minister for War, against the Army medical authorities who were refusing to adopt Wright's inoculation policy.[1] In the same year he became a Fellow of the Royal Society, which must have pleased him more because it showed an appreciation of his work as a scientist. Wright had a justifiably high opinion of his own merits, and he liked the people whom he respected to share it. He was, in fact, one of the most outstanding figures of his day, who influenced profoundly a number of very able men. The most notable of these was Alexander Fleming, and no account of his career can be separated from that of Wright's.

Almroth Edward Wright was born on 10 August 1861 at the Rectory at Middleton Tyas, Yorkshire. He was the second of the five sons of the Reverend Charles Wright, the curate to the Rector, Dr Blackwood. Charles Wright came of a staunchly Protestant County Dublin family, with estates at Floraville, Donnybrook. Charles entered Trinity College, Dublin, and became an Old Testament scholar, learned not only in the Latin and Greek texts, but in Hebrew, Arabic and Irish. He was ordained and received his first curacy from his friend, Dr Blackwood, at Middleton Tyas.

It happened that, when Blackwood and his wife, Lady Alicia, were visiting Geneva, they met two young Swedish girls. They were the daughters of Professor Almroth, a noted chemist, who had recently died, and the girls were on a personal pilgrimage to the birthplace of Calvinism. The Crimean War had begun, and Lady Alicia Blackwood set off for Scutari to become one of Florence Nightingale's assistants, sweeping the Swedish girls along with her as amateur nurses. On their safe return to Middleton Tyas, the girls were informally adopted by the Blackwoods, and the Rectory became their home. It was also the home of the young curate, Charles Wright, and it was not long before he and Ebba Almroth married.

During the next six years Ebba had five children, all boys. In 1863, when Almroth Edward was two years old, Charles Wright became Chaplain to the English Church in Dresden, and five years later moved to Boulogne, where he founded the British Seamen's Institute in the Boulevard Daunou, by the River Liane. Meanwhile he was gaining an international reputation for Old Testament scholarship. Both parents undertook the education of their children, and an excellent one it turned out to be. Almroth, for example, attended no school until he was over fifteen. During most of this time, the family income did not exceed £400 a year, and Almroth later declared that he was brought up in an atmosphere of intellectual riches and material poverty 'entirely favourable to the growth of the life of the mind'.

Certainly the children thrived on this sort of life. The eldest became Lord Chief Justice of Trinidad; Almroth, one of the great medical scientists of his day; a third was the first Librarian of the London Library and translator of Tolstoy; and a fourth was the Major-General of Engineers who overcame the formidable supply problems of Allenby's campaign in the Middle East in the First World War. With a firm base in the classics and mathematics, they had a wide range of languages. Both parents spoke several fluently, and the children had lived in Germany and France. It was a strict and austere household. Frivolity was frowned upon. On Sundays all the blinds in the house would remain drawn, and the hours not spent in church would be devoted to Bible study and meditation.

In 1874 Charles Wright became Vicar of St Mary's, Belfast, and when he was fifteen, Almroth went to the Academy, where he studied for two years. He then entered Trinity College, Dublin, reading English, French, German, Spanish and Italian literature, gaining first-class honours and the Gold Medal in his BA degree in 1882. Astonishingly, he had also read medicine at the same time, qualifying in 1883. He then had to decide between the different careers that were opening up before him. During his medical studies he had been much influenced by Dr J. M. Purser, who introduced him to the use of the scientific method in medicine, which Wright adopted with an evangelical enthusiasm. Though this method of observation, hypothesis and experiment had been preached for centuries, the clinical practice of medicine had remained largely empirical. Physicians learned to recognize and classify diseases, and to give some indication of the probable outcome. But they had neither the knowledge nor the means to influence this outcome significantly. Wright, only too well aware of these deficiencies, had no wish to become a clinician. But the idea of *scientific* medicine attracted him, and he obtained a scholarship of £100 that would enable him to work for a year with the pioneers of medical research in Germany.

Thus, at the age of twenty-three, Almroth Wright went to Leipzig to study with Cohnheim, the great pathologist. He learned to observe the white cells of the blood, and their ability to pass through the walls of vessels inflamed by bacterial infection so that they accumulated in the tissues to form pus. He thus already had an interest in the white cells when Metchnikoff described them some years later as 'phagocytes' (meaning 'swallower cells') and emphasized the importance of 'phagocytosis' in the natural defence of the body against bacterial invasion.

Wright's studies with Cohnheim were sadly brief, because Cohnheim died in August 1884. But he stayed in Leipzig to work with Ludwig, the physiologist, and Weigert, the histologist. From Ludwig he learned physiological recording techniques, and from Weigert his methods for staining tissues and bacteria. He learned, too, that the essential requirement for any scientific advance is a reliable method for observing and measuring the phenomenon being studied, a lesson that remained with him all his life.

It was an exciting time in medical research on the Continent. Every improved method of investigation – even the microscope – opened up vistas of new knowledge and dazzling new ideas. But when Wright's year there was over, and he returned to London in 1885, he found that the conservatism of British clinical medicine had been largely unmoved by the advances in pathology and physiology. There was no opening for him in scientific medicine. No hospital had a bacteriological laboratory, and there were no suitable posts available in any of the universities. So Wright entered for, and won, a scholarship of £200 to read law. This he did with his usual application, and developed an interest in logic that was to remain a life-long one. But when the £200 was gone, he had decided that he did not want to be a lawyer, and was still without a career, despite qualifications in three professions.

With what had become a characteristic versatility, Wright entered for the Civil Service Higher Examination, and obtained such excellent marks that he was immediately offered a clerkship in the Admiralty. He then began to lead something of a double life. By day or, rather, by part of the day, he was a passable Civil Servant, properly dressed and doing all that was expected of him with contemptuous ease. It was difficult for his superiors to reconcile the shortness of his hours at his desk with the excellence of his work – they could not decide whether to promote him for his ability or to sack him for laziness. The laziness was an illusion. Wright was spending every available hour, in the early mornings before Civil Servants went to work, and in the evenings until late at night, doing medical research at the Brown Institute in the Wandsworth Road.

The Brown Animal Sanatory Institute[2] deserves a more prominent place in medical history. The first experimental pathology laboratory in Britain, it was established by the bequest of an eccentric Irishman named Thomas Brown, as a centre for investigating and curing 'maladies of Quadrupeds and Birds useful to man'. In the event, it became an institute of animal pathology that certainly proved useful to human medicine. John Burdon-Sanderson had become the first Professor Superintendent in 1871, and he was followed during the next twenty years by some of the most distinguished of medical scientists, including C. S. Roy, Victor Horsely, and C. S. Sherrington.

Almroth Wright chose to do unpaid research at the Brown Institute because L. C. Wooldridge, whom he had met in Leipzig, was working there. Wooldridge was a young physiologist with ideas so original that they did not appeal to the professors, and Wright, who was already developing the rebel streak that was later to scandalize the medical profession, was much impressed by them. They had done some strange experiments together in Leipzig, and it was this association that continued at the Brown Institute while Wright was an Admiralty clerk. The subject that interested them was blood coagulation, a natural phenomenon that has challenged physiologists for centuries.

The blood in normal blood vessels is a freely circulating fluid, but if it escapes from these vessels it solidifies within a few minutes. This mysterious transformation is part of the normal defence against bleeding to death from a wound, and in conditions such as haemophilia, in which clotting is defective, persistent bleeding from even trivial injuries could be fatal. When Wright became interested in the subject there was no effective treatment for haemophilia, and he tried to find one for several years. Wooldridge believed that the plasma, the fluid in which the living cells of the blood are suspended, is itself alive – a sort of protoplasm. Clotting, he thought, was analogous to the coagulation of protoplasm that occurs in dying or injured cells. Wright helped to devise experiments to test Wooldridge's ideas, and produced a method for measuring the clotting time by drawing blood into a fine capillary tube, and at set intervals of time blowing a small portion of this on to filter paper until a solid thread appeared. The method, described by Wright in one of his early papers, was used in medical practice for many years.[3]

The Superintendent of the Brown Institute at that time was C. S. Roy, who had also worked with Cohnheim. He was impressed by Wright's ability, and when he became Professor of Pathology at Cambridge, he offered Wright a post in his new department. Wright accepted and left Whitehall for Cambridge in 1886. There he worked with Henry Head on the relationship of the emotions to the visceral sensations associated with them. The question 'Do sensations cause the emotions or do emotions cause the sensations?' still teases psycho-physiologists. Wright had his own firmly held ideas, which he was to expound for many years. In particular, he regarded 'belief' as a mainly physical event, and he would certainly have approved of the meaning implied by the modern phrase 'gut reaction' – though he would equally certainly have coined a grand classical name for it.[4]

Cambridge soon palled on Wright, because, as he explained to a friend, he found that Cambridge scientists did not take him at his own valuation. False modesty was not one of Wright's faults. He was, in many ways, an intellectual giant, very conscious of the lesser stature of his colleagues and apt to demonstrate the differences at every opportunity. This did not make him popular. When, in 1888, he won a Grocers' Scholarship, he left Cambridge to study for another year on the Continent. There he chose to work in Marburg with von Recklinghausen on pathological anatomy, and with Kulz on diabetes – then an unexplained disease – and in Strasbourg with Hoppe Seyler, the great physiological chemist.

At the end of his year, he married a Cambridge graduate, Jane Wilson, the daughter of a County Kildare JP. And he also accepted a Demonstratorship in the University of Sydney. This could be either in anatomy or physiology, and on the voyage the toss of a coin decided the issue in favour of physiology. Wright enjoyed his time in Sydney, but his wife was homesick for England. After two years he gave up his post, partly on her account, but also because he saw no chance of promotion. For him, no subordinate role was tolerable for long – he had to dominate.

When he returned to Britain in 1891, he had no job. He could find nothing that suited him, and spent two years working in the Laboratory of the Colleges of Physicians and Surgeons in London. From there he published 11 papers, the first in the series of 150 written during his career. Five were on blood coagulation, in one of which he described how decalcifying salts such as oxalate or citrate prevent clotting.[5] He seems to have been the first to suggest that these salts could be used to keep blood fluid, and sodium citrate was, in fact, used in this way for transfusion purposes during the First World War, and has been ever since. Other papers reported his work on diabetes, acidosis, the optical principles of microscopy, colour blindness, and visual phenomena such as the apparent colour of shadows. It was a series showing an astonishing breadth of interests, and great originality.

In 1892, with no settled appointment, and a wife and child to maintain, Wright urgently needed a salary. Then he was offered the post of Professor of Pathology in the Army Medical School at Netley Hospital, by Southampton Water. He accepted gladly, describing it later as 'the best stroke of luck that ever a man had'. And, as it turned out, it was also one of the most important and rewarding appointments that the Army Medical Service had ever made. But at first it seemed a surprising one. Wright was a civilian with no experience of army medicine, and little of pathology. And, at thirty-one, he was much younger than some regular officers who had been passed over for the post, and who resented this fact.

A professor of pathology is expected to teach his subject and to do research. In the Army School the emphasis was on the pathology of wounds, the infections to which they were liable, and also the infectious diseases which often caused more casualties among troops in the field than did enemy action. During the previous twenty years the success of Lister's antiseptic surgery had finally convinced the army surgeons, who had then developed an almost immovable faith in chemical antiseptics for the treatment of infected wounds. It was to take all Wright's efforts during the next twenty years to convince them that this faith was misplaced. But for infectious diseases such as typhoid, typhus, cholera and dysentery there were no remedies, other than the prevention achieved by improved sanitation. Wright, as a pathologist, was concerned with the more specific sort of prevention that Pasteur's work was beginning to reveal.

In 1796, Edward Jenner had shown that people inoculated with cow pox (*variola vaccinea*) became immune to smallpox. The wide adoption of this manoeuvre, which he called 'vaccination', has eliminated smallpox, but until Pasteur's work some eighty years later both the nature of the infection and of the process of immunization were quite unknown, and in no other disease was similar immunization attempted. In 1880, Pasteur discovered that cultures of chicken cholera bacilli that had lost their power to infect, could immunize against infection by virulent bacilli. He recognized the similarity of this phenomenon to Jenner's earlier work, and that a general principle might be involved, namely that inoculation of pathogenic organisms, made harmless in some way, could produce an immunity to natural infection by the same organism. He went on to apply this principle to anthrax and rabies by inoculating with living but attenuated cultures. Pasteur called his immunizing agents 'vaccines', in honour of Jenner, and it became clear that their use might have a wide application in preventing infectious diseases of all sorts, provided that the organisms responsible could be suitably reduced in virulence so as to allow safe inoculation.

By 1892, when Wright went to Netley, the principle of vaccination had made little headway beyond Pasteur's work, and though Wright was to be a pioneer in the coming advance, he was not at first concerned with it. He was not a trained bacteriologist, though he had to become one in order to teach his students. He had plenty of time for research, and most of this he spent on blood coagulation experiments. Having shown the importance of calcium in the clotting mechanism, he came to the conclusion that calcium deficiency was the cause of the bleeding in haemophilia, and for many years remained convinced that suitable calcium treatment would cure the disease. His conclusions were logical but, as it happens, wrong. Haemophilia is due to the hereditary lack of one of the twelve protein factors now known to be involved in the normal clotting mechanism.[6]

After about a year at Netley, Wright did become involved in bacteriological problems. A colleague, David Bruce, had recently discovered the organism that causes Malta fever – one of a group now called the *Brucella*. Malta fever is a prolonged, relapsing illness, difficult to diagnose because the organism is difficult to find. Many patients with suspected Malta fever were sent to Netley, and Wright set out to devise some test that would identify the infection. Widal, in France, had shown that the blood serum*

---

*Serum is the clear fluid that exudes from a solid blood clot. It is useful to immunologists because it is free from cells and does not clot.

of patients recovering from typhoid fever caused typhoid bacilli to clump together into visible masses. This 'agglutination' was due to the development in the patients' blood of a specific 'antibody', a protein that stuck the typhoid bacilli together. The presence of this antibody not only explains the natural recovery from typhoid, and the immunity that follows it, but it also provides a very useful diagnostic test. If, after about ten days of fever, a patients' serum develops the ability to clump typhoid bacilli, then that patient very probably has typhoid. Wright saw that this agglutination test could be applied to Malta fever, using suspensions of *Brucella*. The results were brilliantly successful, and marked the beginning of his career in immunology.

From improved diagnostic tests, Wright passed to possible improvements in the treatment or at least prevention of infective diseases. Early in 1893, Waldeman Haffkine, a Russian bacteriologist working at the Pasteur Institute in Paris, came to visit him at Netley. Haffkine was on his way to India to carry out experimental inoculations against cholera, the first extension in man of Pasteur's work. Haffkine proposed to use a live but attenuated cholera vaccine, but he had also found that a vaccine killed by heat had some immunizing power. Wright began experiments with heat-killed Malta fever vaccines, and decided that they were protective in monkeys. He was sufficiently sure of his results to vaccinate himself with a killed culture, and then tested his immunity by injecting a virulent one. His confidence was misplaced, because he developed Malta fever, and was miserably ill for several weeks. But his faith in the principle of vaccination remained unshaken.

While he was ill, he had plenty of time to think, and he thought about the nature of immunity. It was clearly related to the appearance in the blood, after vaccination or infection, of antibodies that could clump, kill, or dissolve the bacteria involved, or combine with their toxins to render them harmless. Various names describing their function had been given to these antibodies, such as 'agglutinins', 'lysins' or 'antitoxins'. They were specific in the sense that they would react only with the particular organism or toxin that had stimulated their production. It was supposed that these organisms and toxins contained chemical 'antigens' that determined the appearance of exactly corresponding antibodies. Even dead organisms could promote an active immunity to live ones, and such an active immunity might last for many years. Moreover, serum from an immunized person or animal could be injected into a patient and confer a 'passive immunity', though this would last for only one or two weeks. This passive immunity was the basis of the successful treatment of diphtheria, and the prevention of tetanus, by injecting the serum of horses already immunized by vaccination.

As Wright pondered on these things, he decided to experiment with typhoid. Though improved sanitation had greatly reduced its prevalence, typhoid was still killing about 5,000 people a year in Britain, and 35,000 in the USA.[7] And in wartime, the danger of typhoid among the troops was greatly increased. During the Franco–Prussian War, 60 per cent of the casualties in the German forces were due to typhoid. The disease itself is due to an invasion of the bloodstream by typhoid bacilli in the bowel. If the blood already contained typhoid antibodies, then the invasion might be defeated at the outset. But it would be dangerous to vaccinate with a live culture, even if attenuated, because just one virulent organism could cause an attack of typhoid fever, which had a mortality of about 20 per cent.

As soon as he recovered, Wright began to tackle the problem. First, he standardized his vaccines, so that he knew the number of bacteria in each dose. Then he measured the response in the recipient of the vaccine by the appearance in the blood of antibodies lethal to typhoid bacilli. He was thus able to compare the immunizing power of vaccines killed by various means, such as by heat, or by different antiseptics and chemicals. It was an arduous process, involving hundreds of experiments. To begin with, most of these were done in animals, but later Wright himself and a courageous band of volunteers were the test subjects. The final conclusion was that a heat-killed vaccine produced a satisfactory response. After inoculation, there was a period of two to three days during which the slight normal power of the blood to kill typhoid bacilli was actually reduced – the so-called 'negative phase'. Then there was a rapid rise in typhoid antibody, reaching a peak in about fourteen days, and persisting for months or even years.

Wright was then ready – and anxious – to try his vaccine on a large scale. But neither the Army nor civilian authorities were willing to sanction a novel and potentially dangerous experiment. He had no rank to impress those with military authority nor, with his lack of clinical experience and his unorthodox ideas, did he impress influential clinicians. But he published a paper on his typhoid vaccine in 1897, and soon after he was asked by the superintendent of a lunatic asylum in Kent to use it to control an outbreak of typhoid there. Twelve members of the staff had already contracted typhoid, and 84 of the remaining 202 staff volunteered to be inoculated. No cases of typhoid occurred among these, but there were 4 cases among the uninoculated 118. Apart from a slight fever for about twenty-four hours after inoculation, and a sore arm for a few days, Wright's vaccine produced no ill-effects. Despite the small numbers involved, this preliminary trial was promising.

In 1898, some of the British troops posted to India were inoculated against typhoid by medical officers trained by Wright, and when he went there as a member of the Plague Commission a year later, he persuaded the Indian Army authorities to inoculate 4,000 volunteers. Within a few months it became clear that these men were protected against the typhoid endemic among the other troops. Back in Britain, Wright obtained a grudging permission from the War Office to inoculate those who volunteered for it among the troops bound for the South African War. He prepared large amounts of vaccine at Netley and expected an enthusiastic response. In this he was disappointed. Medical officers were either ignorant of, or unimpressed by the arguments in favour of the inoculation, and they had no conception of the appalling death-toll from typhoid that lay ahead for their men when they got to South Africa. All they knew for certain was that Wright's vaccine often produced a reaction severe enough to keep a man off-duty for two or three days. Some were so opposed to it that they dumped the suplies of vaccine over the sides of their troopships as they steamed down Southampton Water, and some of the boxes were washed ashore almost at Wright's feet at Netley. The result of this apathy – even hostility – was that only 14,000 out of 330,000 troops were inoculated.

With only 4 per cent in the inoculated group, statistical analysis of the results had a poor base. And the results themselves were highly unreliable. Under active service conditions records were muddled or lost, and the practice of one hospital sergeant illustrates the sort of hazard that makes fools of statisticians: in every case of typhoid he recorded that the patient had been inoculated because, he said, 'it stands to reason that if he got typhoid, he must have been inoculated with it'.[8]

There were, in round numbers, 58,000 cases diagnosed as typhoid, with 9,000 deaths, among the British forces in South Africa. Wright was convinced that his figures showed a significant protection by his vaccine. But the War Office and the medical profession were not convinced. Professor Karl Pearson, a famous statistician, launched a heavy attack on Wright's methods of analysis which, with Wright's equally forceful counterblast, led to a battle of words that filled the correspondence columns of the medical press for months. Wright was a born fighter, and the struggle to get official recognition of the value of vaccination against typhoid took much of his time and energy up to the outbreak of the First World War in 1914.

This battle, however, was largely fought after Wright left Netley in 1902, to become Professor of Pathology at St Mary's Hospital. Though he had made many friends, particularly among the younger officers, and attracted the band of devoted disciples known as 'Wright's men', he had not been happy in the stuffy army atmosphere. Some of the rules and regulations seemed to him to be fatuous, and he made no secret of his feelings. On one occasion, when his military laboratory assistant was required to take part in a parade, Wright stalked onto the square and plucked the man out of the ranks under the nose of an apoplectic Commanding Officer. On another, when giving evidence to a military tribunal, the President asked him if he had anything more to say. Wright replied 'No, sir. I have given you the facts. I can't give you the brains.'

When the opportunity to go to St Mary's Hospital arose, Wright was happy to take it, and his army superiors must have been happy that he should do so.

7

The Inoculation Department

When Almroth Wright took up his appointment at St Mary's Hospital in November, 1902, he filled two vacancies. In that year, H. G. Plimmer, FRS, resigned his post as Pathologist to join the staff of the newly-founded Lister Institute, taking with him A. Paine, the hospital bacteriologist. St Mary's therefore expected to appoint two men, but when the committee came to interview Almroth Wright they were so dazzled by his command not only of pathology but bacteriology that they agreed to give him full charge of both departments. In spite of this increased scope, Wright was at first much worse off than he had been at Netley. Instead of the spacious laboratories and undemanding duties, he now had cramped rooms, almost no funds for research, and responsibility for all the routine hospital pathology and bacteriology as well as the undergraduate teaching. And his salary of £300 per annum was considerably less than that of the post at Netley.

The reason why Wright chose to take this apparently retrograde professional step was his vision of a revolution in medicine that he himself could bring about if he could apply his ideas in a general hospital. Just as Samuel Lane had chosen St Mary's as the setting for his medical school, so Wright saw it as the setting for clinical research. He was convinced that appropriate vaccination could not only prevent but cure many of the bacterial diseases for which there was then no effective treatment, and for the rest of his life he worked to this end. It did not matter to him that at first he was uncomfortable, burdened with routine work, and poorly paid. He was quite confident that he could soon improve the material conditions by exercising the force of his personality on colleagues a good deal more flexible than those with whom he had been in conflict in the army.

Wright was, indeed, an extremely impressive person. Intellectually, he was a heavy-weight, and he had a physique to match. He was a huge, ungainly bear of a man, tall and with a frame so massive that William Bulloch described him as 'within a near shave of being an acromegalic'.[1] But, despite the size and apparent clumsiness of his hands, he was surprisingly deft with the minute pieces of glassware with which he loved to work. If his body was bear-like, his head was leonine. With his sandy hair and moustache, and his steel-rimmed spectacles, he reminded Leonard Colebrook of John Tenniels' lion 'blinking lazily at Alice' over the cake in *Through the Looking-Glass*. He was as often known as 'the old lion' as 'the old man' in later life.

Wright's department in 1902 was housed in two rooms in what had been the old out-patient department. They were ill-equipped, ill-lit, and shaken every few minutes by the trains in the Underground Railway, which made microscopy difficult. Wright at once demanded, and got, more equipment and space. He made an immediate impact on the students. His lectures attracted growing audiences; staff members began to join them, and then progressive young doctors from other hospitals. He held them spellbound by his command of language, with apt classical and literary allusions, and scathing criticisms of current medical thinking. He created persuasive visions of a new era in which logic and science, by replacing the stagnation of centuries, would defeat disease. 'The physician of the future', he used to declaim, 'will be an immunizator.'[2]

On the more practical level, Wright had to fulfil his statutory duties. But he did not intend to spend his time doing routine post-mortem examinations and histology. There were two young demonstrators in his department, John Wells and Newport Kilner, to whom he deputed this work, and also a medical student working as a voluntary assistant because he was fascinated by pathology. His name was Bernard Spilsbury, then aged twenty-five, who had come to St Mary's from Oxford in 1899 to do his clinical work, but who spent so much of his time in the post-mortem room that he had delayed his qualification.[3] He was invaluable to Wright, and when he finally qualified in 1905, he joined his staff as a lecturer. He was appointed Morbid Anatomist to the hospital in 1907, later becoming world-famous as a forensic pathologist. Wright had other devoted assistants: Stewart Douglas, who had worked with him at Netley, joined him at St Mary's on being invalided out of the army, and during the next few years John Freeman, Leonard Colebrook, Parry Morgan, John Matthews, Carmalt Jones, Leonard Noon, and then Alexander Fleming, made up a staff of talented and enthusiastic young men.

Fleming was not, at first, one of Wright's charmed devotees. Freeman had contrived his appointment largely to keep him in the rifle team, and Fleming had accepted it because it would pay a small salary while giving him time to work for his London MB, BS and to decide whether or not he wanted to be a surgeon. His Scottish caution was not entirely dispelled by Wright's eloquence. While he was making up his mind about the post in the pathology department, Freeman took him to hear one of Wright's special lectures. All Wright's staff attended his lectures, and they never knew what he was going to say. At the conclusion of this one, and when the applause was over, Freeman said to Fleming, 'Wasn't that marvellous!' To which Fleming replied, 'I'd rather have facts than a lot of hot air' – or words to that effect. But he took the job.

Though Wright's knighthood and his election to the Royal Society in

1906 greatly strengthened his position in the 'establishment' he himself was a violent critic of this establishment. 'I make it a principle never to write anything that won't give offence to somebody,' he once remarked to Leonard Colebrook, and much that he wrote did greatly offend the fashionable London doctors. They used to call him the 'Paddington Plato', the 'Praed Street Philosopher', 'Sir Almost Wright' or 'Sir Always Wrong'. What infuriated the medical pundits most was Wright's habit of appealing over their heads to the lay public by writing articles or letters in the newspapers, which was considered highly unethical.

One notorious example was a long article published in 1905 in the *Liverpool Daily Post*.[4] Headed 'The World's Greatest Problem', it began: 'Of all the evils that befall man in his civilized state, the evil of disease is incomparably the greatest . . . If the belief is nurtured that the medical art of today can effectively intervene in the course of disease, this ought to be dismissed as illusion.' He described the medical profession as ignorant, impotent, complacent, and guilty of deceiving their patients. In a passage that must have enraged Harley Street, he wrote of 'the careless rich who nurture the comfortable faith' that if they fell ill their wealth could buy a cure from the best (i.e. the most expensive) doctors. They should be disabused of this illusion. The most famous of doctors was no more able to cope effectively with illness than the humblest general practitioner. Wright's solution to his 'greatest problem' was for the rich to spend their money on medical research rather than on their fashionable doctors.

If Wright had enemies in Harley Street he had powerful friends among the intelligentsia of London, and these were active on his behalf. They included Arthur Balfour, who had been Prime Minister from 1902 to 1905; Lord Moulton, an Appeal Judge; Lord Haldane, Minister for War; and Bernard Shaw, who was fascinated by Wright's command of language and his radical views on every conceivable subject – except women. With such men, and many others, behind him, Wright could afford to offend those whom he considered to be enemies of progress. He numbered some statisticians among these, particularly those who criticized the validity of his conclusions. Wright distrusted statistics, believing that, however elegant the mathematical method, it could not turn unreliable observations into reliable ones. 'What comes out of the mill depends on what you put into it.' He believed in what he called 'the experiential method' – based on the almost intuitive conclusions that a worker draws from his own experience in the laboratory or the wards, by an application of 'diacritical judgement'.[5] Wright has expounded at length on 'diacritical judgement' but the exact nature of the process remains unclear.

So Alec Fleming had joined a department humming with a life and activity derived almost entirely from Wright's own enthusiasm. The staff consisted of eight or nine young graduates and as many visiting doctors – often foreign – as space would allow. Everyone worked hard, and frequently into the small hours. Wright worked with them at the bench, and every new observation or discovery was discussed freely. Lunch consisted of sandwiches eaten in the laboratory, or a meal in a nearby public house. Tea-time was a break for general discussion. Wright took the chair, and pulled his intellectual rank. No one spoke until he had opened the discussion which could be on any subject from philosophy and morals to gardening or women. Wright dominated such assemblies, even when the most distinguished visitors were present. He had travelled widely, and had met almost everyone of consequence, not only in medicine and science, but in many other fields. He was a classical scholar who spoke seven languages and could read eleven, and had a prodigious memory. He claimed that he could recite over 200,000 lines of verse, and he had a disconcerting habit of using apt quotations in conversation and suddenly challenging his listeners to identify the source. It is not surprising that most of them held him in such awe that they dared not contradict even his most outrageous statements.

After this somewhat daunting 'tea-party' it was back to the bench until dinner-time. Some went home for a meal, some to local restaurants. Wright would take any distinguished visitors out to dine. Then they would all come back to the laboratory until the day's work was done. There followed the 'midnight tea-party', and a renewed but more relaxed discussion, usually on the results and discoveries of the day, and on plans for the morrow. It was sometimes 2 or 3 a.m. before the last had gone home, but they were all at their benches punctually at 9 a.m. next morning.

Fleming's part in all this scientific and mental activity was at first a very low-key one. Conversation had never been his strong point, and he hardly opened his mouth. One of his colleagues claimed, years later, that trying to converse with Fleming was like playing tennis with a man who, when he received a service, put the ball in his pocket. Wright particularly disliked such a reaction. 'There are three degrees of discourtesy in conversation,' he used to say, 'to contradict; to change the subject; and to receive it in silence.' Fleming's silence baffled him. He claimed that Fleming could only speak Eskimo, and that he would have to learn the language to communicate with him. (Wright did, in fact, learn Eskimo, but not for that reason.) He also claimed that Fleming, being a Scot, believed in magic, knew all the poetry of Burns, and being a Covenanter, knew the Bible by heart. Wright used to tease him by quoting Burns and telling him to complete the verse – a challenge usually ignored. Once Wright quoted a verse he had written himself. 'Who wrote that?' he shot at Fleming. 'Burns, I suppose,' said Fleming – to Wright's delight. But people began to notice that when Fleming did say something it was usually very much to the point. And his habit of staring at a speaker and then turning away without a word left the talker with the uneasy feeling that he had somehow made a fool of himself.

Despite his habitual silence, Fleming became a popular member of the staff. He was good-tempered and easy-going, and took part in all the activities within the laboratory and outside it with obvious enjoyment. He became 'little Flem' to everyone, and it was not long before he began to display his practical ingenuity and an astonishing manual dexterity that allowed him to devise, make and use some bit of equipment to meet the latest of Wright's ideas. Wright would expound on some problem, and elaborate airy schemes for solving it. Fleming would listen in silence, retire to his bench and produce a practical, working solution within a few hours, usually in the form of a neat new method or a minutely constructed gadget. Sometimes, when Wright was being more than usually fanciful, Fleming would wait until he had finished and then say, laconically, 'It won't work sir.' Wright, quite unused to objections from his own staff, was apt to go through the whole exposition again, as if he supposed that Fleming was deaf. When he had finished, Fleming would say, simply, 'It won't work.' As he was invariably right, his judgement as well as his skill came to be respected.

The work that so excited Wright and every member of the department was their research on the immunity conferred by vaccination. Wright suffered from what he called 'pain in the mind', an almost physical torment, described by him as 'the emotional tension intolerant of intellectual impasses',[6] not only in science but in moral and social issues. A scientific drive was thus combined with Wright's desire to ease the world's suffering, and the immediate object was an effective treatment for bacterial disease. He was convinced that the solution lay in the natural defences of the body against bacteria, and their artificial stimulation so that they were enhanced to the point of invulnerability. But his method was always 'to look below the surface of things, to proceed from the known to the unknown', and at that time very little *was* known about the mechanism of immunity, natural or enhanced. It was recognized that, after an infection or vaccination by some sorts of bacteria or their toxins an immunity developed to the particular type of organism involved, and that this was often associated with the appearance in the blood of specific antibodies, such as agglutinins, lysins, or antitoxins. But what exactly these antibodies were, how they were produced and how they worked was not known. It is only now, over seventy years later, that the origin of the antibodies, their molecular structure, and their biophysical reactions with specific target molecules on the bacterial surface, are being elucidated.

In the early years of this century, Wright and his young men 'with fire in their bellies' as he liked to say, could only try to stimulate the natural immune mechanism and measure the response. In any science, the main advances come through new methods, and it was here that Wright and Fleming made their best contributions. On the bacteriological side, they had to identify organisms, grow them in pure culture, kill them by various means, suspend the dead bacteria in a suitable fluid to make a vaccine, and standardize the dose by counting the number of organisms per unit volume. All these stages needed special methods, and many of these were innovations. It should be mentioned here, perhaps, that the organisms were identified and separated by first 'plating out' the mixture of bacteria present, for example, on a throat swab, by smearing the swab across the surface of a solid culture medium, such as agar or gelatine, contained in a flat, circular plate, known as a 'Petri dish'. Then the glass cover would be replaced, and the plate incubated. Within twenty-four hours or so, the plate would become covered with visible colonies of bacteria, each one of which had grown from a single organism. Different organisms often produce recognizably different colonies, and a colony of the desired organism could then be picked up on a sterile platinum wire loop, and transferred to a suitable liquid medium, where it would grow as a pure culture of that particular organism. It was from these pure cultures that the vaccines were made.

Wright and his staff injected these experimental vaccines into animals or, more often, into themselves, or into patients who might be expected to benefit. But the essential investigation was to measure the response in the blood, and it was here that new methods were needed. A practical difficulty was that of getting enough blood to work with. In those days, before well-fitting syringes and sharp needles were available, the taking of blood from a vein was difficult and usually one had to make do with the drop or two of blood obtainable from a skin prick. Wright solved the problem by scaling down all his tests so that they would work with one or two drops of blood. He did this by using fine capillary glass tubes – which he drew out himself from larger bore tubing – to replace the more usual test tubes. The simplest example of this technique is the so-called Pasteur pipette. It is made by softening in a flame the middle section of a length of glass tubing, and then pulling the two unheated ends apart so that the soft central part is drawn out into the long, fine tube. This is then cut in the middle, to form two 'pipettes', each with a stem of the original tubing – about 8 mm in diameter and a long, fine nozzle about 1 mm in diameter. The pipette can be fitted with a rubber teat, so that fluid (or air) can be drawn into it. This was Wright's basic piece of equipment, and he elaborated it in various ingenious ways, and devised an endless series of 'micro-methods' by which tests could be carried out in these tiny glass capillaries. For example, by making a mark on the capillary, he could draw up a volume of blood, then a bubble of air, followed by successive, but separated, volumes of the test reagents (such as suspensions of bacteria) and allow them to mix in the wide portion of the pipette. After a given time, a sample of the mixture was blown down into the capillary, where it could be studied under the microscope. Some of the elaborations of this method involved multiple bulbs, and convolutions, but the underlying principle remained simple and elegant. It was laboratory engineering on a minute scale, which has become the basis of many modern automated methods. Wright described it in his famous book *The technique of the teat and capillary glass tube* which became a classic.[7]

The use of these methods soon suggested that people could recover from many sorts of infection without antibodies developing in their blood. Wright therefore began to think of the possible importance of the white cells as antibacterial agents. Many earlier microscopists had observed these cells collecting at the site of inflammation. But there was no clear idea that this behaviour was defensive until Metchnikoff, a Russian marine biologist, saw that these cells swallowed bacteria, and suggested in 1882 that this was an important function. The white cells of the blood (leucocytes) are of three main types: the granulocytes, the monocytes and the lymphocytes. It was the granulocytes that were the active swallowers of bacteria. Metchnikoff coined the name 'phagocyte' to describe them, and 'phagocytosis' became the technical term for the actual process of swallowing.

Wright began to study phagocytosis in normal blood and in the blood of patients recovering from infections, or who had been given his vaccines. He soon found that normal phagocytes would ingest bacteria, moving towards them like amoebae, and then engulfing them. It was tempting to suppose that this behaviour was a defence against infection, and that it might explain the natural immunity characteristic of different species of animals. Some animals are quite immune to infections that are lethal in other animals, or in human beings. Conversely, man is immune to a number of animal infections. Phagocytosis was, when Wright took up its study, beginning to be recognized as a part of this mechanism of immunity.

Wright and his staff, including Fleming the apprentice bacteriologist, spent most of their time studying phagocytosis. As with any scientific research, the first requirement is a method for measuring what is being studied. A drop of blood (containing phagocytes) was mixed with test microbes on a glass slide, and covered to prevent drying. After a set time, the cover-slip was removed, the blood spread out into a thin film, dried and stained. The film was then put under the microscope, where the phagocytes were easily seen, and also any microbes inside them. The average number of microbes ingested by each phagocyte was calculated by counting both the microbes and the cells. The result compared with the normal figure, was the 'phagocytic index' for that particular blood sample, against that particular microbe.

Wright found that the phagocytic index did not vary greatly in normal people, but during infections might be significantly lower than normal and then, in the recovery stage, higher than normal. After vaccination, the index against the organism in the vaccine dropped below normal for two to three days, and then rose rapidly above normal, maintaining this level perhaps for months. Wright therefore concluded that both a natural infection or artificial vaccination somehow stimulated phagocytosis. He knew that vaccination led to the production of antibodies in the blood, and he then had the idea that there might be a special sort of antibody that stimulated phagocytosis. This idea led to many experiments, and the observation that normal phagocytes were particularly attracted to microbes that had been coated by something in the blood of people who had previously been infected or vaccinated with that sort of microbe. This of course, supported the theory that a special antibody was involved, one that made the offending microbe more appetizing to phagocytes in general. Wright, who loved coining names from his classical storehouse, called this still hypothetical antibody 'opsonin', meaning, in Greek 'I prepare food'. Opsonin was apparently present at a rather low level in normal blood, but could be greatly increased by vaccination. The study was put on a more quantitative basis by using 'standard' microbes and 'normal' phagocytes. The test then consisted of mixing the microbes with the serum of the patient, so that they might be coated with the opsonin in that serum, and then offering them to the normal phagocytes. The average number of microbes swallowed was calculated, and the whole process was repeated, using normal serum in place of the patient's serum. The ratio of the two averages (patient's figure divided by the normal figure) was the 'opsonic index' for that patient's blood. The point has been laboured, perhaps tediously, only because the determination of opsonic indices became the key measurement of the effect of Wright's vaccination programme, and a major occupation for him and his staff for many years.

This was the work that Wright and his devoted team were doing when Fleming joined them. And the necessity to work into the small hours was due to the fact that the opsonic index of a sample taken, say, at 2 p.m., could not be measured until 2 a.m. No one complained. They were all fired with Wright's own enthusiasm. This was a period in which it seemed to them that a new era of effective medical treatment was dawning. Most doctors had by then accepted the fact that appropriate vaccination could prevent certain diseases. Smallpox was the best example, though at first even this had won only a grudging acceptance. Pasteur's demonstration of the protection against anthrax in animals, and of rabies in man, had been convincing, and Wright's own work on typhoid was beginning to establish itself. The principle was being extended to cholera, plague and Malta fever, though on an experimental basis.

But Wright went much further than the prophylactic use of vaccines. From his work on opsonins he came to believe that their stimulation by vaccination could cure an existing bacterial disease. This, most doctors could not understand or accept. They maintained that a patient suffering from boils, or pneumonia or tuberculosis was already invaded by staphylococci, or pneumococci or tubercle bacilli, and that to inject more of the same organism seemed useless or even harmful. Wright's view was that in such 'localized' infections the immune mechanism of the body had not been fully stimulated. Then suitable vaccination would increase the production of opsonins, and a new army of defensive leucocytes, which together would overcome the invaders.

It was difficult to reconcile such diametrically opposed points of view, and other workers failed to get good results by his method of curative vaccination. But Wright attributed these failures to ignorance of the finer points of his technique. Vaccination, he argued, would only be effective if the natural swings in the opsonic index of the patient were carefully studied and the vaccine given at the beginning of an upswing. It was only specially equipped and well-informed pathologists, he asserted, who could get good results from the method. The obvious implication was that its best practitioners were Wright and his staff and the best equipment for it was to be found only at St Mary's. Wright pointed this out at every opportunity in lectures, speeches, and in the medical and lay press. The result was that large numbers of private and hospital patients came to him for vaccine therapy.

By 1907, Wright was attracting so many pupils and visitors to his laboratory, and so many patients to the wards of St Mary's hospital, that the need for an expansion of accommodation became acute. The Chairman of the Board of Governors, H. A. Harben, recognized this, and offered Wright the use of three wards in the Clarence Wing, and their ancillary rooms. These wards had never been occupied because the hospital had not raised enough money to equip and staff them. Wright and his staff were by then financially self-supporting. The private patients they treated paid fees into a hospital account on which he could draw, and several of his rich friends had been so impressed by his 'new gospel' that they made generous contributions towards the cost of his research and the salaries of his assistants.

On receiving Harben's offer, Wright approached Arthur Balfour, Lord Moulton, Rupert Guinness (later Lord Iveagh) and Max Bonn, all of whom were deeply interested in his work. With their help enough money was raised to equip the empty space in the Clarence Wing to provide laboratories, and two special wards for patients under treatment by Wright's methods. The new unit was named 'The Inoculation Department'. It was an autonomous organization, independent of both the hospital and the medical school, and with its own committee under the chairmanship of Arthur Balfour.[8] Not surprisingly, Sir Almroth Wright was a member of this committee – with, in fact, the most powerful voice in its operation.

The Inoculation Department had its own finances. It paid a rent to the hospital for its accommodation, and the cost of medical services and salaries, as well as all laboratory expenses. Its income came from the fees paid by private patients and from the sale of vaccines prepared in the department to the medical profession. These were distributed by the pharmaceutical firm of Parke, Davis and Company, and contemporary catalogues show what a wide range of diseases were supposed to be amenable to vaccine therapy.[9] There were special vaccines for acne, pyorrhoea, boils, pneumonia, bronchial colds, influenza, gonorrhoea, sore throats, intestinal troubles, tuberculosis and even cancer – though it was admitted that the organism *Micrococcus neoformans*, said to be found in almost all malignant tumours, was probably not the cause of them. The advertisement proclaimed that all these vaccines had been 'prepared in the Vaccine Laboratory of the Department of Therapeutical Inoculation, St Mary's Hospital, London W1 under the supervision of the Director, Sir Almroth E. Wright, MD FRS etc.' Not surprisingly the vaccines had a very wide sale to doctors who had probably been unable to cure such diseases by more conventional means, and the Inoculation Department received a large and steady income from this source for many years. It also received an initial endowment of £17,000 subscribed by members of the committee and other well-wishers. It was, from the first, a private clinical research institute inspired by one man, and responsible for the treatment of patients. As such it was unique in Britain at that time.

Wright and his staff moved into their new and far more spacious laboratories in 1908. Though, from a technical point of view, they were much better off, the increased space meant an isolation of interests and a loss of the 'happy family' atmosphere of the old, crowded laboratory. Shared discomforts endured for the sake of a common purpose tend to promote easy personal relationships rather than friction. John Freeman lamented this change, and Wright agreed: 'Yes,' he said, 'I'm afraid the best sauces are all cooked in little saucepans.' The move also provided wards for Wright's patients – the first research wards in Britain. A proportion of these patients were suffering from various forms of tuberculosis. Wright had great faith in his vaccine – 'tuberculin' – and his staff too were convinced of its good effects. Unfortunately other methods of treatment were also used at the same time, so that it was not easy to identify the real cause of any improvements. The same sort of criticism applied to many other sorts of infection treated by the vaccines. Chronic skin infections, persistent ulcers, recurrent boils, bronchitis, sinusitis, gastritis, colitis, arthritis, rheumatism, all were candidates for vaccines. Many results seemed dramatically successful. But in all such conditions spontaneous cures or remissions are not uncommon – many patients get better with no treatment at all.

Within a year or so Wright had a staff of about fifteen paid or voluntary assistants. The hospital routine bacteriology was supervised by John Freeman who, for a time, lived in Wright's household. The making of vaccines for sale was the responsibility of S. R. Douglas, Wright's Assistant Director. Hospital pathology was in the hands of Bernard Spilsbury. But all these people had time for research, either as members of Wright's team or along their own lines of interest. John Freeman, for example, became one of the pioneers in the field of allergic disorders such as asthma and hay fever. They were also free to engage in private practice, with their own consulting rooms in the Harley Street area.

Wright used to maintain that his laboratory was 'a republic – as all the world ought to be'. In fact, it was a benevolent dictatorship. Though Wright seldom gave direct orders, his intellectual ascendancy was such that his 'suggestions' had the force of commands, and in the 'democratic arguments' he enjoyed conducting there was no serious challenge to his supremacy. As a scientist, he had an ambivalence often amounting to self-contradiction. Though he preached the exercise of the scientific method, he actually believed that the powers of human reason were more important than experiment.[10] Having constructed some reasonable theory, he would 'prove' it by a minimum of experiment and then only to convince possible unbelievers. A favourite saying of his was 'One experiment suffices, if properly performed, to establish the truth of a principle'. In biological science, this is an outrageous generalization. He also used to say 'Random experimentation in the laboratory is *the* sin against the Holy Ghost',[11] meaning that every experiment had to be part of a preconceived pattern of investigation. It was a good thing for the future of medicine that Alexander Fleming did not always follow this precept.

8

The Pre-War Years

Fleming's post in the Inoculation Department was neither a permanent nor a full-time one. Though an active member of Wright's team, he was also working for his London MB, BS degrees. In 1907 a paper appeared in *The Lancet* on 'Therapeutic Immunisation' – an exposition of Wright's belief in the value of vaccination in the treatment of existing infections.[1] The authors were Wright, Douglas, Freeman, Wells and Fleming, and it was the first of the many papers to bear Fleming's name. A year later he published another, also in *The Lancet*, with Leonard Noon, on the accuracy of Wright's method for measuring opsonic indices, which was a practical defence against those critics who thought the procedure unreliable. And one on the same subject appeared in *The Practitioner* by Fleming alone. Fleming was thus already making his name as a bacteriologist but, even after two years, he had not quite made up his mind where his future path lay.

In May 1908, Fleming sat for his MB, BS examinations, and passed with honours and the London University Gold Medal. And in the same year he won a second gold medal, this being the Cheadle Medal for Clinical Medicine awarded by St Mary's Hospital. Fleming's entry was an essay entitled 'The Diagnosis of Acute Bacterial Infection'. It was an admirably methodical and lucid exposition of the clinical value of applied bacteriology, and it was published in the *St Mary's Hospital Gazette* in 1909.[2] It reflects, of course, Fleming's experience in Wright's department, but also his own powers of critical analysis and judgement. But he had not lost his hankering for a career in surgery. He had already passed the primary examination for the Fellowship of the Royal College of Surgeons, and in 1908 decided that he would work for the final part. This would need practical experience in operative surgery, and so in that year he became Casualty House Surgeon, a post that he could hold while still working in Wright's laboratory. In this way he gained experience by carrying out minor operations himself and assisting at major ones. He took the examination in June 1909, and passed with ease.

The possession of the FRCS would have entitled Fleming to set up in practice as a surgeon, and to be considered for a staff appointment at one of the London hospitals. In the event, he decided to remain with Almroth

Wright. It would have been difficult to exchange the excitement and enthusiasm of the laboratory pioneers for the long, slow climb up the ladder of conventional surgery. But Fleming was one of the very few laboratory workers to be a fully qualified surgeon, and a later cartoon of him by H. M. Bateman is captioned 'The only FRCS never to have done an operation'. Curiously enough, having achieved this rather irrelevant academic status, he never bothered to take his London MD, the higher degree that would have been appropriate, and which he could have obtained with ease and probably with honours. It is, perhaps, an illustration of his easy-going attitude to his career and of a lack of personal ambition, that he did not exert himself to acquire a doctorate.

Meanwhile the Fleming family arrangements had changed yet again. The house in Ealing, which had served as a home for John, Alec and Robert when their mother moved down from Lochfield Farm in 1903, was exchanged by her after a few years for a roomy flat at 125, Clarence Gate Gardens, at the Regent's Park end of Baker Street. This, of course, was more convenient for Alec, who was once more within fifteen minutes' walk of St Mary's. John and Robert, who also lived there, had started up their own optical business as partners and it was already flourishing. The three brothers remained close friends and companions, often joined in the evenings by Tom for the usual family games. They were still members of the London Scottish Regiment, and John and Alec were active in the shooting team that won several important events.

Robert records that Alec's professional interest was obviously shifting. He talked less about surgery and more about Wright's ideas. Then he began to put these into practice on his own family. If any one of them had a sore throat, a cold, or some other minor ailment, Alec would take swabs and blood samples to the laboratory, and come back with a vaccine which he would inject into the victim. 'I must have had my arm punctured and injected with hundreds of different kinds of dead microbes in those days', Robert wrote; 'Alec must have jabbed killed microbes into himself many more times. Here again Alec was a master of technique. He could insert the needle of a syringe into you so that you hardly felt it.'[3] Alec, in fact, was becoming a dedicated follower of Almroth Wright.

One of Alec Fleming's earliest personal interests in the field of therapeutic vaccination concerned the treatment of acne. This is a chronic infection of the skin of the face, neck, chest and back occurring particularly in adolescents. It produces unsightly pustules and small boils, with sometimes permanent scarring, and is extremely disfiguring and distressing. Fleming studied the bacteriology of this condition, finding the frequent presence of a specific bacterium, the acne bacillus or *Corynebacterium acnes*. He made a vaccine from cultures of this organism, which appeared to give good therapeutic results, and published a paper on the subject in *The Lancet* in 1909.

In 1909, Fleming became involved in the laboratory diagnosis of syphilis. Clinical diagnosis could be difficult and it was important to recognize it, because of the danger of personal and congenital transmission. The invention of an extremely ingenious and reliable laboratory test by the German pathologist A. von Wassermann in 1906 was therefore a great practical advance. Since this test was of immediate concern to Fleming, and because it illustrates the sort of immunological principles with which he was constantly working, it is worth describing it in bare outline. It had already been shown, by Wright and others, that the presence of antibodies in a patient's blood was a useful diagnostic sign that he had been exposed to the sort of microbes against which the antibodies reacted. In typhoid, for example, there was a simple test for the presence of antibody – the visible clumping of known typhoid bacilli. But the spirochaete of syphilis is a very delicate organism that could not then be grown in pure culture, and thus could not be used to demonstrate directly the presence of syphilitic antibodies in a patient's blood. There is, however, an indirect, or two-stage, way for detecting them.

When an antibody in serum reacts with its target antigen, another component of normal serum known as 'complement' is used up, or 'fixed'. So the presence or absence of complement after the addition of an antigen to serum indicates whether or not there had been an antibody to react with it. The presence of complement can be demonstrated by a second stage of the test. For this, a lytic antibody (haemolysin) against sheep red blood cells is made by vaccinating a horse with these cells. This haemolysin will, when mixed with the sheep red cells, visibly dissolve them – but only in the presence of complement. If complement is absent, then the red cells remain visibly intact. The reaction is thus an indicator of the presence or absence of complement.

Wassermann used this principle in a two-stage test for syphilis. In the first stage, he incubated the patient's serum with syphilitic antigen. For this antigen, he chose liver tissue from still-born syphilitic babies, which was known to be swarming with spirochaetes. If, in this first stage of the test, the patient's serum contained antibodies against the spirochaetes (indicating that he had syphilis), then these would react with the antigen, and complement would be fixed. In the second stage, sheep red cells mixed with haemolysin were added. If complement had been fixed in the first stage, the red cells would remain intact, and the test was positive for syphilis. If the red cells were lysed (dissolved – see footnote p. 100), releasing their haemoglobin, then complement had not been fixed in the first stage, and the test was negative for syphilis.

The Wassermann reaction soon became established throughout the world and clinical laboratories were expected to be able to carry it out. The Inoculation Department, of course, was much involved with it, and its ingenuity must have appealed to Wright as a triumphant example of applied logic. It was, in practice, far more complicated than the bare bones described above, and many things had to be controlled. One practical difficulty was tackled by Fleming. As described by Wassermann, the test needed more blood than could be easily collected from a skin prick, so Fleming devised a micro-method using only one or two drops of blood. He published three papers on this improved method during 1909 and 1910,[4] and he became much in demand as a diagnostician of syphilis, not only by the London hospitals, but by Harley Street consultant physicians.

Unfortunately for those who, like Wright, believed in the power of pure reason, the theoretical basis for the Wassermann reaction had meanwhile been destroyed. In the process of carrying out control tests workers had discovered the astonishing fact that normal liver worked just as well as syphilitic liver. The presence or absence of spirochaetes made no differ- ence, and it was pure luck for Wassermann that syphilitic antibodies happen to react specifically with a substance present in various normal body tissues, including liver. This discovery made the test much easier to carry out – syphilitic livers are not easy to come by – and its accuracy was unimpaired. But faith in applied logic must have been shaken when the great success of an elaborately reasoned test was found to be quite fortuitous and also inexplicable. Biological research cannot be done with confidence from the armchair.

Fleming's growing practice received a greater impetus when, in 1910, there was a revolutionary advance in the treatment of syphilis. Hitherto, as in most incurable diseases, there had been a host of fashionable but ineffective remedies. Then Paul Ehrlich, in Frankfurt, began a systematic attempt to synthesize new chemical compounds that would be more poisonous for microbes than for men. He was looking for what he called a 'magic bullet', something that would hit only its selected target. What he found, after reputedly testing 605 new compounds, was an arsenical derivative that was highly toxic for the spirochaetes of syphilis and much less so for humans. This was dioxy-diamino-arsenobenzene which he called '606' and later 'Salvarsan'.

The new compound could be given by injection so that it reached every part of the body, and destroyed the spirochaetes wherever they might be. This systemic use of an antibacterial agent was a departure from the prevalent local use of antiseptics, which can work only where they are applied. Salvarsan was not strictly the first 'chemotherapeutic' agent to be given systemically so that it worked throughout the body. Quinine, which kills the malarial parasite, had been used in this way, quite empirically, for many years. But Salvarsan was the first such product of chemical synthesis. Its great limitation was that it only worked against the spirochaete – it had no effect on other virulent organisms. And the use of '606' in syphilis remained the only successful application of the synthetic chemotherapeutic principle for the next twenty-five years.

It happened that Almroth Wright was a personal friend of Ehrlich, and he was one of the first to receive a supply of the new wonder drug for clinical trial in Britain. Wright was sceptical, on principle, of any chemical method for treating an infection, and he handed his supply of Salvarsan to Fleming and Colebrook to try out on syphilitic patients. Fleming, already well-known for his improved diagnostic test, was now in enormous demand from clinicians anxious to try the new drug. It had to be injected directly into a vein, and Fleming was adept at such injections. With his neat, deft fingers, and a virtual monopoly of the drug itself, he attracted patients from all over London and, whether he sought it or not, soon found himself with a flourishing private practice. It was said, by one of his colleagues, that he asked the Post Office to change his telephone number to 'Paddington 606'[5] – a change that did not happen and a story that may not have been true. But he was depicted in a cartoon by Ronald Gray dressed in the uniform of the London Scottish with an enormous syringe instead of a rifle, and the caption 'Private 606'.[6]

Within a year of the introduction of Salvarsan its success in clearing up the lesions of syphilis was accepted with astonishment by the doctors and with heartfelt gratitude by thousands of patients. Fleming and Colebrook published a paper in The Lancet in 1911, setting out their excellent results, and emphasizing that the unpleasant side-effects described by other users could be avoided by careful technique.[7] So Fleming's reputation in the field of antibacterial therapy grew, not only as one of the very few doctors who could cure syphilis safely, but also as an authority on the preparation and use of vaccines. To deal with the many private patients who were referred to him, he rented a consulting room at 30 Devonshire Place, John Freeman's house.

Despite these growing activities, Alec's life at that time was beginning to expand beyond professional circles. An Australian colleague at St Mary's, Dr Page, took him to meet some friends who lived in Warwick Gardens. They were the Pegrams, who were well-known in the art world. Fred Pegram was a celebrated etcher and illustrator; one brother-in-law was Townsend, the art editor of Punch, and another was Ronald Gray, the painter. Alec Fleming was a great success with the Pegrams and their friends, and became a frequent visitor. He had no pretensions about art, but was a good listener, and they found such modesty in a successful medical scientist most appealing. He entered into the spirit of their entertainment and played long and complicated games with Marjorie Pegram, the small daughter of the family, with unfeigned enjoyment. She found his invention in miniaturized golf, using every room in the house, 'terribly exciting'.

This predilection for any sort of game remained a permanent trait in Alec's character. Even his younger brother Robert, who also had it, recognized that in Alec it was more pronounced and wrote 'he had something of the boy in him always'. As members of the West Middlesex Golf Club, the brothers were often subjected to Alec's improvised rules – such as a round to be played with only a putter. In the Freeman house, where he had a consulting room, Alec would spend any spare time, between appointments, pitching coins on to a particular square on the carpet in competition with Mrs Freeman. Two students at St Mary's, anxious to see how Fleming made a piece of equipment, went nervously to his laboratory. He willingly showed them the tricks of glass-blowing, and then rapidly made for them a beautiful glass cat and a series of scampering mice. His favourite laboratory game was to grow pictures, designs and miniature rock gardens on agar plates sown with bacteria that would develop various bright colours. He had collected a whole range of these chromogenic bacteria, with which he painted pictures that would appear, as if by magic, twenty-four hours later. Even his serious work in the laboratory was, to him, exciting and amusing. 'You treat research like a game,' Wright complained to him. Certainly Fleming did not suffer from Wright's 'pain in the mind'. While Wright tilled his intellectual soil with infinite labour, Fleming observed, so to speak, the wild flowers in their natural state and enjoyed them.

The Pegrams and their circle positively adopted Alec. It may seem odd that these talented, sophisticated and cosmopolitan people should have been so attracted to the silent Scot who knew so little of the social world and nothing about art and artists. But, as with Wright and his clever friends, Fleming was a good foil. His silence seemed to imply an intelligent and admiring interest that was endearing to compulsive talkers. Occasionally he would interject a remark that was often unexpected and disconcerting, and he was no respecter of persons. One day at lunch with the Pegrams, the great George Moore was expounding the beauties of biblical language, with illustrations from the prophet whose name he pronounced 'Ezkiel'. 'Ezekiel,' said Fleming clearly, without looking up from his plate. Moore paused, astonished, in mid-sentence, and then returned to 'Ezkiel'. 'Ezekiel,' said Fleming again, impervious to the consternation among the lunch party. That George Moore should be interrupted was bad enough, but to be *corrected* . . . !

The Pegrams were much impressed by the stories they heard from their friends of Fleming's success in treating ailments that had defeated other doctors. They often asked him about these 'wonder cures' and were delighted by his humorous modesty when he replied, 'It was nothing to do with me – he would have got better anyway', or 'I'm damned if I know what was wrong with him'. Such remarks were typical of Fleming throughout his life, and were always attributed to a laconic self-depreciation. It was seldom believed that he could be speaking the simple truth. But his successes were real enough, and when Fred Pegram's brother-in-law, the painter Ronald Gray, developed tuberculosis of the knee, Alec was asked to treat him. Gray was then staying with the Hammersleys, a family of merchant bankers with an elegant house and a wide circle of cultured friends. Gray was put to bed there, and Fleming started a course of vaccine injections. During his frequent visits to the patient, Alec met other visitors, including Mrs Richard Davis, wife of a Bond Street antique dealer. She became a great admirer of Alec, and invited him to the parties she gave for her colourful friends.[8] There he met the Wertheimers, rich and famous art collectors, and became a regular visitor to their palatial house, described by André Maurois as 'full of beautiful furniture and rare porcelain, with a perfectly trained staff and a table which abounded in delicious food and wine'.[9] Alec had indeed come a long way from the little stone house on its bare hillside above Darvel.

Ronald Gray recovered from his tuberculous infection, and Alec's vaccine was naturally credited with the cure. But tuberculosis was an unpredictable disease, often with spontaneous remissions. And it could also respond to the sort of treatment, such as rest in bed and the splinting of infected joints, that was used in conjunction with vaccine therapy. No clear figures were published from Wright's department showing the success-rate of vaccine therapy compared to other forms of treatment, either in tuberculosis or in other sorts of infective disease. Wright relied on his 'experiential method' and 'diacritical judgement' and remained convinced for many years that vaccines were curing his patients.

On his recovery, Ronald Gray began to take Alec as his guest to that Mecca of artists, the Chelsea Arts Club in Old Church Street. Alec enjoyed this. The free-and-easy bohemianism delighted him; and the good food, convivial conversation in the bar, spiced with scandalous stories of the private lives of the famous, were very much to his taste. And once more, the apparently shy little Scottish doctor proved to be a great social success. He was always ready for any sort of game, from croquet or bowls to snooker or bridge. He was a frequent and welcome guest, and after he had treated several members for various ailments it was proposed that he should be elected 'Honorary Bacteriologist', on the condition that members would get free treatment from him.

The Chelsea Arts Club had been founded in 1890.[10] When Chelsea had been engulfed by the expansion of London, it retained the bohemian character it had gained during the eighteenth century and became known as the 'London Latin Quarter'. But it lacked a social focus for its bohemians, until a group of artists, including Stirling Lee, Frank Brangwyn, George Clausen, J. M. Whistler, Wilson Steer, Ronald Gray and several others, decided to form a club. A Scottish painter lent premises at 181 King's Road, where the first committee installed a billiard table, furniture and fittings, kitchen, dining-room and bar. The club opened with ninety members in March 1891, and was limited to 'men professionally engaged in all forms of Visual Arts'. An early rule decreed that 'no bicycles, dogs or women will be permitted on the club premises'.

The success of the club was immediate, despite recurring trouble with the steward who felt it necessary personally and frequently to sample the 'wet stock' – a difficulty resolved when he succumbed to an attack of delirium tremens in the basement. His successor proved to be an inspired cook, whose savouries became famous throughout the art world, and invitations to the club's 'Monday Dinners' were eagerly sought. By 1901 larger premises were needed, and the club moved to 143 Old Church Street, a site that gave room for a bowling green, and croquet lawn. Among the members when Fleming joined them as 'Honorary Bacteriologist' were William Orpen, Augustus John, A. J. Munnings, Phil May, Max Beerbohm, John Sargent, John Lavery, Walter Sickert, and Fred Pegram who had been Chairman from 1904 to 1906.

Fleming was as popular at the Chelsea Arts Club as he was in the London Scottish Regiment and St Mary's Hospital. He seems to have impressed the exuberant artists with an undefinable personal quality that inspired affection and respect. They were undoubtedly in awe of him as a doctor, yet he was easy-going and good-tempered, never taking offence at personal chaff and banter. They noticed that he often evened up the score by some sly leg-pulling done with a perfectly straight face that much amused those able to detect it. He was an avid player of any sort of game that was suggested, and he often excelled by unorthodox methods. As a croquet player he was famous for confounding the opposition by quite unexpected tactics. He brought the same skill to billiards and snooker – probably his favourite game. His play often attracted onlookers, some of whom were apt to give advice. Fleming would listen in silence and then play quite a different stroke with complete success. Nothing gave him more pleasure than the most outrageous of flukes. He brought the same style to all card games (often inventing new ones) and even to chess. He was hardly ever seen without a cigarette dangling from his lips.

Fleming's membership of the club was, according to the rules, anomalous. There was no statutory basis for the election of an Honorary Bacteriologist, and at that time he hardly had the distinction required for the honorary membership reserved for such people as the current President of the Royal Academy and a very few world-renowned figures in literature and music. He was then about thirty years old with, as yet, no great eminence in medicine and none at all in any of the arts. Ronald Gray, to make an honest member of him, devised a scheme that would allow him to qualify as 'professionally engaged in the visual arts'. All Alec had to do was to paint a picture that would be accepted for exhibition by an art gallery and actually sold. Alec, always ready for such things, agreed, though the only pictures he had ever painted had been done with bacteria. The story of the picture that he produced has been told in different versions by different writers. Ludovici, in a biography based on interviews with Fleming himself, writes that it was 'a view of the Children's Ward at St Mary's'.[11] Maurois, writing some years after Fleming's death is quite specific: 'Gray forced a brush into his hand and *ordered* him to paint a farm scene. Much against his will, Fleming produced a cow . . .'[12] Whatever its ostensible subject – which may not have been very apparent to the viewer – Gray took it, with a deliberately atrocious daub of his own, to a gallery exhibiting 'modern' art. Both pictures were accepted quite seriously, and Fleming was delighted to hear critics praising his work as an example of 'sophisticated naivety'. But no one seemed anxious to buy it, and Gray had to persuade a friend to do so. He had achieved two objectives. Fleming was technically an artist, and the critics of 'modern art' had been fooled.

Fleming could meet great men of literature and learning not only in his new club, but in the unlikely setting of the Inoculation Department. Almroth Wright had a reputation as an original thinker, talker, writer and polemicist, that went far beyond the bounds of medicine and science, and he attracted equally radical thinkers sometimes of opposite views. One of these was Bernard Shaw, who used to visit Wright at St Mary's for a good argument. On one of these visits, probably in 1905, Wright showed him the work on phagocytes. Shaw was fascinated – though he refused to believe that there were hundreds of millions of cells in every drop of blood. This was, he said, no more credible than the 'yarn that the sun was 93 million miles from the earth'. While he was talking, John Freeman came in to ask Wright if he could take on the treatment of another patient. After a discussion, they decided that they could not – they already had as much work as they could handle. Turning to Shaw, Wright said, 'The time is coming when we shall have to decide whether this man or that is most worth saving.' 'Ha!' said Shaw, 'there I smell drama!'[13]

A week or so later, Wright heard that Shaw was writing a play in which he would be portrayed as one of the main characters. Wright protested to Shaw, arguing that he was already unpopular with the medical pundits, and to be staged as a hero would increase their dislike. Shaw replied that he need have no fears. In the play, the hero made no medical mistakes and was loathed in consequence, whereas the king's physician made nothing but mistakes and was loved by all. So *The Doctor's Dilemma* was produced in 1906 at the Court Theatre, a brilliant satire on the medical profession. Granville Barker played Sir Colenso Ridgeon, a somewhat exaggerated picture of Wright. The dilemma that confronted Ridgeon was whether to treat an honest, decent 'sixpenny doctor' or a scoundrelly blackguard of an artist with real genius – he could not treat both. After much verbal agonizing, Ridgeon treats the doctor and refers the artist to the eminent, stupid physician, Sir Ralph Bonnington, who kills his patient by failing to recognize the importance of determining the opsonic index when stimulating the phagocytes by vaccination.* The fact that the artist left a charming widow who had become an admirer of Sir Colenso Ridgeon adds another dimension to the ethics of the dilemma.

When Wright went to see the play he walked out during the performance at the point when the fashionable physician kills his patient by injecting vaccine at the wrong time. He was indignant that Shaw had contrived a situation for which there was no scientific justification. 'Shaw is not interested in truth – only in circus tricks,' he said afterwards. But they continued to meet and argue. Except for a mutual dislike of hidebound medicine, they disagreed on almost every topic. The main bone of contention was 'The Woman Question'. For some reason that psychologists with a knowledge of his background might be able to explain, Wright had – or professed to have – a profound contempt for the brains and morals of women. No women were employed in his department, even as secretaries – he himself had a male secretary. And he had a stock of anti-feminine aphorisms which he would fire off at the least provocation. The following are a few examples:

'Woman has only one moral claim upon man, and that is to be treated always with the courtesy due to intellectual inferiors'.

'Women belong to the logical underworld'.

'Man is the prototype of the human species, woman the aberration'.

'Women object to definitions. They don't consider it an advantage to know what they are talking about'.

These and many more can be found in Wright's book, *Alethetropic Logic*.[14]

Shaw defended the female of the species against these opinions. Wright considered that any man who supported women's rights must be emasculated – a naturalized woman. His prejudice here is truly astonishing. For example, he rejected the inductive logic of John Stuart Mill for no better reason than that Mill had petitioned parliament on behalf of women's rights. Wright argued that Mill was therefore not fully masculine and thus could not be logical. Yet Wright's own 'Alethetropic Logic', on which he worked for most of his life to convey 'a logic which searches for the truth' is very like Mill's attempt to put the inevitably imaginative process of 'induction' on a solid logical basis. About Shaw, Wright made the same judgement. Imputing a lack of masculinity to Shaw, which he associated with his vegetarian habits, Wright said to him, 'God help the women of England, Shaw, if you ever have a mutton chop!'[15]

Wright was naturally a bitter opponent of the Suffragette Movement that, in 1910, reached a crescendo of violent demonstrations. He wrote a

* Bernard Shaw, who wrote in this play: 'There is . . . only one genuinely scientific treatment for all diseases and that is to stimulate the phagocytes', was not the only champion of this view. The hero of Wells's *Tono-Bungay* describes the fabulous patent medicine as 'Worster Sauce for the Phagocyte. It gives an appetite . . .'

three-column letter to *The Times*[16] headed 'Militant Hysteria' which Shaw denounced as 'the wildest letter ever written'. The two (basically friendly) antagonists agreed to a public debate, to be held in the St Mary's Medical School. Lord Moran (as he later became) describes it:

'Shaw arrived in a blue reefer coat and a red tie. When he sat down I felt sorry for Wright. I felt that he had been pulverised, but at the end of his reply I blushed to think that Shaw, who was after all a guest, had been so mercilessly shown up . . . Every single sentence was a direct hit; there was not a single word that did not contribute to the confusion of the enemy.'[17]

Wright kept his professed contempt for women until his last illness, when he asked for a female nurse 'as being more comforting'. His anti-feminine attitude, defended on logical grounds, was actually emotional and often illogical. One of his own epigrams is revealing: 'Ill-groomed and ugly women annoy men; carefully groomed and good-looking women trouble them.' Perhaps he disliked or was afraid of being 'troubled'. Strangely, while he deplored the supposed lack of deductive logic in the feminine mind and its habit of forming intuitive judgements, he tended towards the same thought processes himself. The 'diacritical judgement' on which he set such store in his 'experiential method' seems to be a prime example of Wright's self-contradiction. Diacritical judgement appears (to the author) to depend largely on what most people would call intuition.

From time to time Wright, with a ponderous and patronizing show of affability would stage what he called '*damennachte*' in his department – soirées to which his staff and colleagues could bring their ladies. Simple demonstrations of the wonderful work being done by men – tailored for weak intellects – would be set up to impress these ladies, with such amusing aspects of science as Fleming's 'germ paintings'. Wright would take favoured visitors round, explaining the laboratory work with elaborate simplicity but dazzling them with a torrent of literary quotations in half-a-dozen languages. However low Wright's opinion of women might be, he took great pains to impress them. His mother came to one of these soirées. She proved to be a very tall, gaunt and formidable old lady. Wright treated her with great courtesy, but used to tell her that she was 'an old pagan', apparently a reference to her ultra-Protestant beliefs. She had once told a friend that 'Almroth was always my failure – I could never make him do what I wanted'. On the other hand, one of his brothers maintained that for her, Almroth could do no wrong. 'If he had committed murder, she would have said: "And a fine, manly thing too."'[18]

Perhaps the seeds of Wright's attitude to women are to be found in his early home life. From both parents he received a barrage of religious dogma. He responded by rejecting the basis of orthodox Christianity as illogical and unscientific. In his childhood his mother had been the dominant figure. Old photographs suggest that she could probably have picked up her husband with one hand, and she had a strength of character to match her physique. The fact that Almroth was able to rebel says something for the force of his own personality. In defying his mother, had he defied the whole female sex?

9

The Casino at Boulogne

At the beginning of 1914, the shadow of war had not yet touched the ordinary people of Britain. They were aware, perhaps, of the 'Balkan question', but Balkan wars seemed to be a local pastime without danger to world peace. They were not aware of the danger of alliances that committed the great powers to preserve the integrity of small and volatile states – alliances that formed an interlocking mechanism like the deadly clockwork of a time bomb. Nor did most people worry about the increasing instability of power in Europe – the growth of German arrogance, the signs of disintegration within the Austro-Hungarian Empire, the French dreams of revenge for the war of 1870. Such things might have worried those whose job it was to think about them but most people simply went about their business and planned their usual summer holidays.

Alec Fleming's business as a bacteriologist at St Mary's and as a private consultant continued to expand. Vaccine therapy may have had an uncertain scientific base but the sale of St Mary's Hospital vaccines became increasingly lucrative. Wright had supporters among the medical profession, as we have noted, and there must have been many waverers who were prepared to try a course of vaccines when other methods of treatment had failed. Among pathologists, Wright's ingenious techniques (many of which had been perfected by Fleming) had won general approval. But even here there were critics. When Jules Bordet invited Leonard Noon and John Freeman to demonstrate some of these methods at the Pasteur Institute in Paris, the opinion was expressed that they were more suitable for conjurers or for amusing children than for serious laboratory work.[1]

In April, 1914, Alec Fleming resigned from the London Scottish Regiment. He had belonged to it for fourteen years, taken part in most of the regimental activities, and distinguished himself as a marksman and a swimmer with medals and trophies to his credit. But he had never risen above the rank of private – another example of a lack of personal ambition to which he himself was to refer many years later. He was sad to give up the long association but it was difficult for him to attend regimental functions, and he had a new social outlet at the Chelsea Arts Club. He went there whenever he had an hour or two to spare, usually in the early evening and before returning to the laboratory, or to his consulting room. On several occasions he went to the Chelsea Arts Ball, the annual riotous assembly in fancy-dress at the Albert Hall. Once he went as a golliwog, and the next year as a small girl. His taller friends took it in turns to see that he came to no physical harm in the crush. They need not have worried. Fleming, for his size, was a good deal tougher than they were.

Alec, John and Robert Fleming were still living with their mother in Clarence Gate Gardens in 1914. None of the brothers had married, but Robert, the youngest, had become engaged. His fiancée was a girl of nineteen, named Ida Tomkinson, who became a great favourite with the family. But her first meeting with Alec illustrates the abrupt and disconcerting manner he often had with strangers. Ida, on her way to a dance, was wearing her best evening dress. Alec inspected her in silence, and then said, 'I suppose you think you look nice.' The poor girl, speechless with embarrassment, never forgot – or entirely forgave – Alec's reception of her. Robert, writing of this incident, explains that Alec had no intention of being rude. His 'I suppose you think you look nice' really meant 'I think you look nice' – according to Robert.[2]. But Alec often made such unexpected, and sometimes hurtful, remarks without Robert to explain them.

During these last few pre-war years, the pattern of summer holidays had changed for the Fleming boys. Previously they had gone to Lochfield whenever they had time to spare. Hugh and his wife welcomed their visits, and for a few days they could re-live their childhood pleasures. No one minded the makeshift accommodation – Robert enjoyed sleeping in the box-bed in the kitchen. But as they grew older and busier these visits to the north became less frequent. Alec began to join his new artist friends on their painting holidays, particularly the Pegrams who had a cottage in the beautiful Suffolk countryside near Mildenhall. The tranquillity of the gentle rivers, great trees and lush meadows had an irresistible appeal for Alec. It was an escape from the noise and dirt of London and yet a complete contrast to the bleak hills and moors of his boyhood. He joined the sketching parties on their rambles in search of a subject and, while they worked, he fished or swam. A few years later he was to find his own country home near the Pegrams' cottage, and almost all his spare time would be spent there.

On 28 June 1914, the heir to the Austrian throne, Archduke Francis Ferdinand, was assassinated at Sarajevo. A Serbian conspiracy was at once suspected and Austria, with the approval of Germany, sent a virtually unacceptable ultimatum to the Serbian government. The reply was considered unsatisfactory, and Austria declared war on Serbia on 28 July. But the Serbs had an alliance with Russia, and the Tsar ordered the mobilization of his armies on the Austrian border. This move brought an Austro-German treaty into effect, and Germany too ordered mobilization, ostensibly to meet a threat from Russia. But France was pledged to support Russia in any conflict with Germany, and was, indeed, in no doubt of

Germany's intentions towards herself. France mobilized, and Germany declared war on 3 August, immediately invading Belgium to attack France from the north. The final stage in this catastrophic chain reaction was the guarantee, by Britain (among the other European powers) of the neutrality of Belgium. So Britain honoured what the Kaiser had dismissed as a 'scrap of paper' and declared war on Germany on 4 August. Thus, within a few days, Austria, Germany, France, Russia, and the British Empire were committed to a war that would last for four years, kill over eight million of their young men, maim millions more and devastate a great part of Europe. And before it was ended, many other nations from America in the west to Japan in the east would become involved.

Almroth Wright's reaction to the war was immediate and practical. He placed his whole department at the disposal of the government for the production of vaccines. When there was some official hesitation in the acceptance of this offer, Wright used his now familiar weapon of a direct appeal to the public. On 28 September he published a signed article in *The Times*: 'On the Inoculation of Troops against Typhoid Fever and Septic Infection'. In this he produced overwhelming evidence for the value of prophylactic vaccination against typhoid, with figures derived from America, India, Germany, France and Japan, where his vaccine had been used in hundreds of thousands of troops. Wright seemed justified in his contention that anti-typhoid vaccination should be compulsory in the British Army. But he was on much less certain ground when he advocated vaccination against septic infection.

Wright's tactics, though unpopular with the medical authorities, enlisted a good deal of public support, and though the results of anti-typhoid vaccination had been available for years, the British Army made it compulsory only after Wright had publicized them. Then Sir Alfred Keogh, Director-General of the Army Medical Service, agreed that Wright's department at St Mary's should be mobilized to produce typhoid vaccine on an unprecedented scale, and some ten million doses were prepared there during the course of the war.[3] Thus the men of the British army and navy were protected almost from the beginning of the war. The appalling sanitary conditions of the trenches during the next four years were exactly those that would favour the spread of typhoid, but the death-rate from this disease was less than ten per cent of what it had been during the Boer War, when only a small proportion of the troops had been vaccinated. It has been calculated that, without Wright's vaccine, over 120,000 deaths from typhoid might have been expected in the British European army, instead of the 1,200 that actually occurred.[4]

But, on the other issue, vaccination against septic infection, Keogh was unconvinced. More research was needed, and the final decision was that Wright himself should provide and direct a research unit to study the bacteriology of wound infection and the best methods for overcoming it.

This unit would be based on a military hospital in France, where patients were sent as soon as possible after wounding. These wounds were often of the sort very liable to infection, with dirt and fragments of clothing driven deeply into the tissues by shrapnel. No one knew what went on in such wounds, what bacteria might flourish there, what the natural defences of the body might be. The practice of military surgery was in part based on the tradition of centuries, and in part on the Listerian principle of attacking dangerous germs by chemical antiseptics. The wound was opened up, foreign bodies, dead tissue and dirt were removed as far as possible, and the whole area was then irrigated with antiseptic solutions or packed with antiseptic dressings. Only after days or even weeks of such treatment, when the inevitable sepsis was declining, was it considered safe to close the wound by sutures and allow healing to take place.

Since Fleming, in particular, was to spend the war years and many years thereafter in studying antiseptics, their value (if any) and their adverse effects, it would be appropriate to give a brief account of them. The word 'antiseptic' seems to have been first used in its modern sense by Sir John Pringle, the eighteenth-century physician. During his service with the Duke of Cumberland in the campaign against the Jacobites in 1745, Pringle acquired a grimly practical experience of military surgery and medicine. He used the word 'septic' in its Greek sense of 'rotten', to describe what was then called 'mortification' and in a paper to the Royal Society in 1750 suggested various 'antiseptic' measures that might reduce its terrible prevalence in wounds.[5] The idea that sepsis was due to living micro-organisms was only conceived following the work of Pasteur, Koch and Lister 120 years later. Lister worked for years to find his 'perfect antiseptic', one that would destroy germs without harming living human tissues. He never found it, and the best that he could do was to use chemicals, such as carbolic acid, in a dilution that was lethal for germs and apparently non-lethal for tissues. But, though it was easy to discover the effect of a chemical antiseptic on microbes in culture, it was far more difficult to find out what it was doing to them in the depths of a wound, and also to the tissue cells that were fighting their own battle for survival.

There is no doubt that Lister's antiseptic campaign brought about a new era in surgery. Surgeons and their assistants became aware of dangerous germs and the necessity for the strictest cleanliness and the sterilization of all instruments and dressings. From about 1900 onwards, surgeons wore sterile operating gowns, rather than frock coats, and even caps and masks. Sterile rubber gloves were slow to be adopted. Halsted, the famous surgeon, introduced them not for his own hands, but to protect the delicate hands of his instrument nurse (whom he subsequently married) from the effect of carbolic acid.[6] Some surgeons then began to wear them, but in the standard textbook of surgery that Alec Fleming read in 1906, their use was dismissed as a passing fad. Slowly, surgical technique progressed from the antiseptic to the aseptic – to the prior exclusion of germs from the operation site, rather than their destruction by chemicals during the operation itself. Under these aseptic conditions major surgery could be undertaken without much risk of subsequent infection – an enormous advance. But the surgical treatment of already infected wounds was a very different matter.

It was specifically to study this problem that Wright and his staff of bacteriologists were posted in October 1914 to Boulogne – in uniform. Wright was given the acting rank of Lieutenant-Colonel, S. R. Douglas of Captain, and Alec Fleming, after fourteen years in the ranks of the London Scottish, became a Lieutenant. Leonard Colebrook, Parry Morgan and John Freeman were also on the strength of the unit. Their living quarters were in a house which Wright acquired in the Boulevard Daunou, by the River Liane, close to the Seamen's Institute founded by his father forty-five years before. There Wright, surrounded by his faithful disciples, lived throughout the war, and was looked after by the parlourmaid, Lucienne, and her old mother, the cook. And there, at various times, he had his usual influx of distinguished visitors – Princess Marie Louise, Sir Berkeley Moynihan, Sir William Osler, W. H. Welch, the American pathologist; Harvey Cushing, the neuro-surgeon; Georges Dreyer, the Professor of Pathology in Oxford; and a number of war correspondents including Dawson of *The Times* and, most frequently, Bernard Shaw. This was the social background for Wright's team – a brief and quite spartan respite from the mounting horrors of their work as doctors.

Wright's unit was attached to a British Army General Hospital housed in the Casino. This might imply luxurious accommodation, with large, ornate rooms, soft lighting and plush furniture. In fact, the wedding cake exterior of the Casino (which was destroyed during the Second World War) came to house conditions of stench, filth and despair worthy of Scutari. Sir Alfred Keogh, DGMS, said in October, after inspecting such hospitals, 'We have, in this war, gone straight back to all the septic infections of the Middle Ages.'[7] The once-elegant rooms of the Casino were crammed with row after row of camp beds, on which lay the wounded from Mons, Ypres and the Marne, at first still in muddy, blood-stained uniforms. The army services were overwhelmed by the sheer numbers of casualties. Men who had lain wounded on the battlefields for hours or even days had, after a brief field-dressing, to be transported to Boulogne where they endured long delays before their turn came in the operating rooms. Almost all the wounds were dirty and already infected. The field dressings had become what Wright called 'a putrefactive poul-tice'. Gas gangrene was the most dreaded of these infections. Beginning in the dead tissues of a wound it spread with terrifying rapidity along even healthy muscles which within a few hours became distended with gas and putrefaction. Prompt amputation of a gangrenous limb might save a man;

delay was inevitably fatal. Another lethal infection was tetanus, usually striking without warning, and even after quite minor wounding. But the vast majority of wounds were infected by the so-called pyogenic bacteria, the common streptococci and staphylococci. Sometimes the victim died from an invasion of the bloodstream, that is, from septicaemia. More often the wound suppurated, discharging pus perhaps for weeks, until the natural defences of the body slowly gained the upper hand, and new tissue grew to fill in the cavities and heal the wound.

The first accommodation assigned to Wright for his laboratories was atrocious. It consisted of two or three badly-lit and unventilated store-rooms in the basement of the Casino. A leaking pipe ran along the wall carrying sewage from the make-shift wards on the floor above. Wright ordered that this should be flushed through with lysol every morning, but this did little to reduce the stench that increased during the day. Soon, Wright could stand these conditions no longer, and demanded new quarters. He got them – in the rooms of the fencing club on the top floor. These had more light and space but they had their own drawbacks. There was no water, gas or drainage. Here, Fleming's technical ingenuity proved invaluable. He contrived incubators heated by paraffin stoves, bunsen burners running on alcohol, glass-blowing burners using fire-bellows, and a system of petrol cans and pumps to supply water.[8] He said, years later, that it was one of the best laboratories he had worked in. Certainly it suited Wright who had always been happiest with simple, home-made apparatus – his beloved capillary tubes and rubber teats, a few glass slides, a dab of vaseline or plasticine and a blob of sealing wax. Surrounded by his devoted young men, and faced by the dreadful reality of thousands of deaths from wound infection, Wright settled down to the hardest and most harrowing work of his career.

The first task was to identify the commonest infecting organisms and their source, and this was done by Fleming. He took swabs from all wounds before, during and after surgery and – all too often – in the post-mortem room. He examined the bullets, shell fragments, shreds of clothing, dead tissue and bits of bone removed by the surgeons. He then cut samples of the men's clothing uncontaminated by wound exudate, and cultured them. The results of this latter study showed that 90 per cent of these samples grew *Clostridium welchii* – the organism causing gas gangrene, 30 per cent grew tetanus bacilli, 40 per cent streptococci, and 15 per cent staphylococci. The men's own clothes were therefore a major source of infection. The high incidence of gas gangrene and tetanus organisms could be explained by the horse manure on the well-tilled fields of Flanders, since both organisms flourish in the intestine of the horse. But both are anaerobic organisms, which do not grow in the presence of oxygen. How then, did they become invaders, in a wound exposed to the air, of tissues supplied with oxygen by the blood? Fleming showed that these anaerobic organisms would grow in porous material if aerobic organisms such as streptococci were growing in the surrounding fluid and consuming the oxygen. The aerobes and the anaerobes were, in fact, symbiotic. In the type of wound that so often led to gas gangrene or tetanus the superficial tissues were heavily infected with aerobic organisms and in the depths and crevices there was dead tissue and the oxygen-free conditions needed by the lethal anaerobes.

Fleming wrote two papers on his findings for *The Lancet* in 1915.[9] In this first comprehensive study of the bacteriology of wound infection he described the bacteria responsible, their frequency, origin and conditions of growth. He had also observed the blood cells in the wound exudates, and studied their behaviour by observing them under the microscope. He found that in fresh wounds, or untreated ones, the exudate abounded with active phagocytes, busily swallowing bacteria. But where antiseptics had been applied phagocytes were few in number, and these mostly dead or dying. It seemed likely that they had been killed by the antiseptic. Not so the bacteria that should have been killed – these were still flourishing.

These results did not greatly surprise Wright, who had for years believed that the phagocytes were more easily killed by chemical antiseptics than were the invaders themselves. But the conclusion that antiseptics were not only useless but harmful in the treatment of infected wounds was totally unacceptable to army surgeons. It had taken years to move the ponderous mass of medical opinion in the direction of Lister's revolution and now it had a momentum that resisted any further deviation. Sepsis was due to germs; germs were killed by antiseptics; it followed that antiseptics would overcome septic infection. When it became obvious to the surgeons that the antiseptics they were using were *not* curing sepsis, and that patients were dying in thousands, their first reaction was to demand more powerful antiseptics, and the help of the bacteriologists in finding them.

Wright and Fleming set out to discover why it was that chemicals that could kill bacteria in a few minutes in the test tube failed to do so in a wound. One answer lay in the nature of the wound itself. Most wounds – particularly those caused by shrapnel – were a labyrinth into which dirt and foreign bodies had been driven. It was in these recesses that bacteria flourished, producing their toxins, and spreading death to the surrounding tissues. And antiseptics, applied from the surface, never reached these ramifications. Fleming demonstrated this with an 'artificial wound', made from a test-tube from the heat-softened walls of which he had drawn out a number of hollow spikes. He filled this spiked tube with infected liquid, and then emptied it. Next he filled it with antiseptic solution and incubated it for twenty-four hours. Finally, he emptied the antiseptic from the tube, and replaced it with liquid culture medium. On further incubation the original organisms grew vigorously. They had been lurking in the hollow spikes, untouched by the antiseptic.[10]

In the real wound, the antiseptics not only could not reach the crevices, they were rapidly removed by the discharge of fluid and pus. And they were also removed by adsorption on to dressings, and dead tissue. Fleming used to demonstrate this by filling a test tube with a highly coloured antiseptic such as gentian violet, and then pushing a plug of cotton wool like a piston down to the bottom, with a glass rod, so that the fluid was forced up through the wool. The fluid that appeared on top of it was quite colourless – all the antiseptic had been absorbed by the plug.

The third and most important factor in the failure of antiseptics to control infection was their harmful effect on the white blood cells. The pus that discharged from an untreated infected area was composed of countless millions of these cells, most of which were phagocytes containing ingested bacteria. Fleming showed again and again that when antiseptics had been applied, these phagocytes were killed while the bacteria survived. He also showed that most antiseptics reduced the natural antibacterial power of blood serum by destroying certain enzymes. By a most ingenious trick he illustrated this in the case of gas gangrene organisms. To a row of tubes containing blood serum he added increasing concentrations of carbolic acid, then inoculated them all with the bacteria, and covered the surface of the liquid with a layer of melted vaseline which soon solidified. On incubation, any gas formed by the growth of the bacteria forced the vaseline plug up the tube, the height reached indicating the amount of growth. This demonstration showed dramatically that the presence of carbolic acid up to a concentration of 0.5 per cent actually favoured the growth of the gas-gangrene organism in serum.[11]

Armed with such laboratory evidence – and far more than can be described here – Wright began his campaign to change wound treatment. He wished to prohibit the use of all antiseptics harmful to phagocytes or the tissues. He advocated that after the earliest possible surgical removal of all dead tissue, dirt, foreign bodies, etc., the wound should be irrigated with strong, sterile salt solution that would promote the flow of lymph containing phagocytes. ('The leucocyte is the best antiseptic,' Wright used to say.) Then the wound would be closed as far as possible and protected by sterile dressings. This regime was successful, if applied early enough and before infection had set in, as many of the younger medical officers who had worked with Wright were able to show. But in large, jagged or heavily infected wounds it was quite impractical, a circumstance that led to the persistence of the 'antiseptic school' and provided ammunition for Wright's opponents.

The most powerful of these opponents was Sir Arthur Sloggett, who had become DGMS in France. He objected to a memorandum being sent by Wright to the War Office, maintaining that Wright had exceeded his authority, and recommended that he should be recalled. But Wright, with his usual heavy-weight panache had also sent copies of his memorandum to Lloyd-George, the Prime Minister; Lord Derby, Minister for War, and Arthur Balfour. Opinions on Wright's proposed medical and administrative recommendations for better treatment for the wounded were so mixed that his memorandum was shelved – a common bureaucratic device – and no one got what they wanted. Wright was not recalled; neither did he get official support for his reforms.

In the civilian medical hierarchy, Wright's main opponent was Sir William Watson Cheyne, President of the Royal College of Surgeons. Cheyne had the greatest veneration for Lister, with whom he had worked, and any criticism of antiseptic treatment was, for him, sacrilege. When Wright published his report in 1915,[12] Cheyne replied with an article urging a return to the strong carbolic used by Lister.[13] Wright responded with all his polemic gusto, in an article for the *British Journal of Surgery*, which had published Cheyne's paper and invited Wright to reply. But Wright's reply was too strong for the editors, who refused to publish it because it held up Cheyne to ridicule. *The Lancet*, however, had no such scruples, and printed it in September 1916.[14] There followed a heated exchange of letters in *The Lancet*, described later by an eminent physiologist as 'an unedifying rough and tumble'. Though Wright was scientifically correct, his methods of expressing his views were so abrasive that he did his cause little good with those in authority.

So, except for those who had worked with Wright, army medical officers continued to use antiseptics. Many new ones were tried, each with a short-lived enthusiasm that underlines their real lack of effect. Carbolic gave way to sodium hypochlorite, 'eusol', iodine, iodoform, and various dyes such as gentian violet, flavine, acridine, and so on. Fleming tested each of these in the laboratory and the wards with impartial care. He came to the conclusion that none was effective, with the possible exception of Carrel–Dakin solution. This contained hypochlorite, which was so unstable that it lost its antiseptic power in the wound within minutes and turned into a simple salt solution. But this salt was just what Wright had advocated. Fleming published twelve papers on his work at Boulogne, which established him as the bacteriologist with the greatest practical experience of wound infection, and one who had made many original observations and devised many ingenious techniques. Wright's campaign, largely based on Fleming's work, made little headway during the First World War. But it gradually changed the medical attitude to the treatment of wounds in the years that followed and in the Second World War, the standard surgical procedure was almost exactly that which he had advocated twenty-five years before. Like many unpopular innovators, he got little credit when proved right.

There was one immensely important medical advance that the pressures of war had stimulated. This was the development of blood transfusion technique. One of the last of Fleming's wartime papers describes 'Blood

Transfusion by the Citrate Method'.[15] The discovery of the blood groups by Karl Landsteiner in 1901, and the introduction of a reliable method for 'grouping' blood donors and recipients by Ottenburg in 1908, had made compatible transfusions possible. Wright had contributed indirectly to transfusion technique when he suggested, in 1894, that blood could be kept fluid (uncoagulated) by adding salts that bound calcium. Sodium citrate is such a salt, and it had become the most widely used anticoagulant for blood transfusion work.

Their experience of the terrible and tragic fate of so many of the wounded in the Casino at Boulogne left an indelible impression on Wright and his staff. In later years they could hardly bear to recall their desperate and often unavailing work in the wards. But away from the hospital, Wright had established the same sort of intellectual camaraderie that he had created at St Mary's. If he was not too tired after the day's work, there would be hours of stimulating talk. During the long, cold winter evenings there would be a blazing fire in the living-room of the house in the Boulevard Daunau, to which Wright would attend himself. When it would not draw well, he would stimulate the draught by the common practice of holding a sheet of newspaper across the fireplace. When, as often happens, the paper began to scorch, Wright used a method – the product of purely logical invention – for preventing it from bursting into flames. He would at once make a hole through the paper at the point of scorching so that cold air was drawn through it. This effective trick greatly impressed Harvey Cushing, who often referred to 'Wright's punctures' when talking or writing about his experiences in Boulogne. Wright also describes it in his book, *Alethetropic Logic*, together with two other practical examples of applied reasoning, an improved method for swatting flies, and another for cutting the finger nails of the right hand.[16] But philosophy might have been responsible for burning down the house in Boulogne. Wright and Bernard Shaw were arguing the finer points of morality with such absorption that they failed to notice that the chimney was ablaze and the room full of smoke. Freeman and Lucienne rushed into the street to see if the roof too was alight, but fortunately it was protected by a covering of snow. The two philosophers continued their discussion quite unperturbed.

Looking back to this period during which the battle against infection was never more desperate, and when the conflict of medical opinion was never more bitter, it seems strange that no one moved in the direction so plainly indicated by Salvarsan. Wright and Fleming were intent on showing that locally applied antiseptics could not reach deeply infected tissues, and anyway did more harm than good. Wright was further intent on his conviction that the only way to overcome bacterial infection was by so stimulating natural immunity that the invaders were defeated from within the patient's own body. His conservative opponents were intent on producing ever stronger local antiseptics, and on proving that Wright was wrong. But between them lay the unseen road that stretched from Salvarsan to chemotherapy and the antibiotics. Salvarsan was the magic bullet with a single bacterial target, an agent that could be injected into the body to be carried to every tissue in the body. Ehrlich conceived of similar systemic antibacterial agents that would be active against a wide range of pathogenic organisms. But, as a general concept, it failed to arouse enthusiasm and it did not, for nearly thirty years, stimulate large-scale research. If the need for such a substance was appreciated at all, it was never stressed in the voluminous discussions on the treatment of infected wounds during the First World War.

From Boulogne to Lysozyme

The war years brought major changes to Alec Fleming's professional and personal life. His experiences in Boulogne had shown him, as nothing else could have done, the ravages of bacterial infection – the universal enemy of all mankind. Wright had once told him that he treated his work as if it were a game. No one could treat the work in France as a game – it was a battle against death that was lost all too often.

But Fleming's love of real games was not entirely crushed. For example, he used to play golf at Wimereux on Sundays, walking the two miles to the links along the sandy coast when he could not get an illicit lift in a staff car. As usual he preferred his own rules to those of the Royal and Ancient, sometimes making putts lying flat on the green and using the club like a billiard cue, or putting between his feet with his back to the hole. These antics shocked a self-important Staff Colonel, who told Fleming to behave himself. One day, among the sand dunes bordering the fairway, Fleming saw the Colonel drive a long ball from the tee. It rolled to a halt not far from him, out of sight of the Colonel. Fleming picked it up and – with a truly impish inspiration – dropped it into the hole.[1] After a long search it was discovered there and the delighted Colonel celebrated his hole-in-one in the traditional manner, Fleming being among those treated to a drink. Myth has it that Fleming was able to repeat this joke more than once, and the Colonel's reputation for veracity – as well as his pocket – suffered in consequence.

In 1918, Fleming was appointed bacteriologist to a special hospital at Wimereux, dealing with wounds involving bone fracture. This type of injury was particularly liable to gas gangrene, and Fleming's observation that anaerobes flourish in the presence of an aerobic infection led to a surgical regime that reduced its incidence significantly. Fleming also developed his practical methods for blood transfusion, publishing a paper in *The Lancet* in 1919 with Dr A. B. Porteous,[2] who was also his partner – or opponent – in his games of eccentric golf. Between them they laid out a putting course in the grounds of the hospital, and used to play at night, by the light of the candles marking the holes.

Meanwhile, Fleming had done something so unexpected that none of his colleagues at Boulogne would believe it until he produced photographic evidence. He had got married. When the Fleming family had been living at Clarence Gate Gardens, they became friendly with two Irish girls – twin sisters – who ran a private nursing-home in Baker Street. They were Sarah (Sally) and Elizabeth, the daughters of Bernard McElroy, a County Mayo farmer. Both girls were trained nurses. Sally was extrovert and energetic, and made a great success of the nursing-home, which she had started herself. Elizabeth had joined her, after the death of her Australian husband. She was shy, quiet and retiring.

The romance between Sally and Alec must have been based on the attraction of opposites, though they were the same age. She was a little taller, bubbling with Irish volubility and sentiment, and she was a Roman Catholic. Perhaps Alec aroused the protective and maternal instincts that had made her a nurse beloved by her patients. She may well have perceived behind his almost impenetrable silence the vulnerable sensitivity of a small boy. She certainly admired his professional distinction and had faith in a great future success. For his part, Alec became devoted to the gay, charming Irish girl who could speak and laugh for both of them, and who was also competent and practical. Whether Alec actually asked her to marry him seems doubtful, and from later remarks by Sally, it is likely that it was she who did the proposing.[3]

Sally and Alec were married on 23 December 1915, during one of his leaves. They set up house in a flat in Bickenhall Mansions, but soon Alec had to return to Boulogne, and Sally continued to run her nursing-home. As with so many wartime marriages, a settled home life had to wait until after the Armistice. Meanwhile, old Mrs Fleming became ill, and Sally's sister, Elizabeth, came to the Clarence Gate Gardens flat to look after her. She was an ideal nurse, and John Fleming, still living with his mother, found her gentle nature very attractive. Soon afterwards they too married, so that there was a double bond between the Flemings and the McElroys. Old Mrs Fleming who had done so much to make a home for her sons until they were safely settled, was now free to return to Scotland to live with her married daughter, Grace, while John and Elizabeth kept on the Clarence Gate Gardens flat.

There were two momentous events in 1918, one universally acknowledged, the other often forgotten. The first was the Armistice of 11 November. After four years of almost static slaughter on the Western Front, the stalemate was broken by a series of Allied offensives in September, and an advance began across the miles of devastation that over four million men had died to gain or defend. When the German armies had been pushed back to the line from which they had started in 1914, their morale collapsed. The navy mutinied, the Kaiser abdicated, and at 5 a.m. on 11 November, the Armistice was signed in Foch's railway carriage in the Forest of Compiègne. By 11 a.m. the First World War was over. Eight and a half million combatants had been killed, twenty-one million had been wounded, and perhaps a million or more were missing, presumed dead.

But if one war was ending, another was just beginning. In May 1918, a pandemic of influenza began in Europe, apparently in Spain. It quickly spread through the warring nations, including the United States. The attack rate was high, but the mortality relatively low. But towards the end of this first wave of the pandemic, there was an ominous increase in the death rate. Young and apparently healthy adults began to succumb to a fulminating congestion of the lungs. Army medical officers were suddenly confronted by soldiers with all the signs of asphyxia, as if they had been gassed. Many died, and at post-mortem, the lungs were found to be full of fluid. Then the epidemic subsided in August and in the excitement of the summer victories it attracted little attention.

In October the second wave of the pandemic struck, and spread with devastating effects to every part of the globe. It was far more virulent than the first wave, and the fatal pneumonic infection now occurred with terrifying frequency. Healthy young people could report sick with a mild fever on one day and be dead on the next. There was nothing that the doctors could do. In the worst cases the patients simply drowned in their own pulmonary exudate, and by the end of 1918, over twenty million people had died,[4] a death-roll dwarfing that of the war itself.

In the Casino at Boulogne, as in every military and civil hospital, cases of influenza far outnumbered the wounded. Even though only those desperately ill were admitted, and though these were dead or better within a few days, all available space was crammed with make-shift beds. The first priority was to try to relieve the asphyxia which, in some cases responded to the oxygen and suction treatment used for cases of gassing. The second priority was to discover the reason why a relatively mild disease had suddenly become a killer on the scale of the Black Death. Alec Fleming, of course, as one of the most competent of British bacteriologists, was at the forefront of these investigations. Every day he took swabs and samples from all living sufferers, and from the scores of those newly dead. At that time, the cause of influenza was supposed to be a bacillus that had been discovered by Pfeiffer in 1893, and successively known as Pfeiffer's bacillus, the 'Influenza bacillus' and, later, '*Haemophilus influenzae*'.

Fleming paid a great deal of attention to this bacillus in his search for the cause of the fulminating infection of the lungs. But he found that different strains of the bacillus occurred in different cases and that it was not always present in the worst-affected lungs.[5] In those cases the exudate was swarming with the streptococci, staphylococci and other pyogenic organisms with which he had been dealing during his four years work on wound infection. It seemed clear that the influenzal infection, mild in itself, could so damage the membranes of the air passages that they become, in effect, an open wound vulnerable to just the infections that had afflicted the battle casualties. Once more he was brought up against the same problem. Even when the invader was identified, there was no available means for killing it without also killing the tissues it was invading.

Fleming was right in supposing that the high mortality in the pandemic was due to secondary infection by pyogenic organisms, but he was not the discoverer of the real cause of influenza itself. In 1919, Japanese bacteriologists showed that cultures of Pfeiffer's bacillus did not cause influenza and not long afterwards the real culprit was identified as a virus.

In January 1919, Alec Fleming returned to the Inoculation Department at St Mary's. It was an index of his growing reputation that the Royal College of Surgeons invited him to give the Hunterian Lecture in that year. In this he presented a masterly summary of his work on wound infection, and of the experiments showing that undamaged and active leucocytes were more effective in controlling infection than were chemical antiseptics. This seems to have been Fleming's first important lecture, and he arranged his material logically, clearly and briefly. But he was not a good lecturer. What he said was impressive, but the way in which he said it was not. His manner was self-deprecating, and his voice carried no conviction – in fact sometimes it did not carry at all. These shortcomings as a lecturer were to determine the course of later events.

Alec had returned to an unfamiliar domestic life as a married man. At first he and Sally continued to live in the flat near John and Elizabeth at Clarence Gate Gardens. The two couples formed contrasting pairs. Sally, like John, was gay and loquacious. Alec and Elizabeth were calm, reserved and usually silent. Religion, which might have been a source of friction, seems to have been nothing of the sort. The Presbyterian Fleming brothers and their Catholic wives seemed to have been completely tolerant of each other's beliefs. The girls went to Mass on Sundays. Their husbands certainly did not go with them, or to any church at all regularly.[6] The Covenanting spirit attributed to Alec by some of his biographers is probably mythical. He was always ready for an argument with his family on almost any topic, but he and Sally, who had a strong mind of her own, made no serious efforts to change or even challenge each other's religious views.

Alec soon picked up the social threads broken by the war. His artist friends received Sally with enthusiasm, and after visits to the Pegrams' Suffolk cottage, she began to share Alec's love for the gentle countryside there. She decided to sell her nursing-home and devote herself to domesticity and her husband. Not long afterwards, in 1921, the Flemings were staying with the Pegrams. Alec and Sally had become interested in antiques, and were always on the look-out for auction sales where bargains – perhaps unsuspected treasures – could be picked up. One day they saw the notice of a sale to be held at a nearby house, at Barton Mills. They went to the sale, hoping to acquire a fireguard for their London home. History does not reveal whether or not they got their fireguard, because at the end of the sale they bought the house itself. They had already fallen in love with it, and when the bidding faltered at £400, Alec on an impulse entered the fray and bought it for £500.[7]

The Dhoon – a strange and unexplained name – is a charming house of the early Georgian period, with a symmetrical façade and a red-tiled roof. It is built of lath and plaster on a timber frame, as are many such East Anglian houses. It had six bedrooms and three living-rooms, and a garden of about three acres including a paddock and many fine old trees. At the bottom of the paddock was the river Lark, an idyllically pretty stream of limpid green water winding mysteriously through almost impenetrable willow woods. It was probably this river that hooked Alec. It was big enough for boating and fishing, and there was even a little island, reached by a footbridge, that was part of the garden.

From the moment of its acquisition The Dhoon became Sally's main interest and Alec's main relaxation. They bought a car, and drove there from London almost every weekend (petrol then cost about one shilling per gallon). They both became devoted gardeners, and the three neglected acres were a challenge indeed. Within a few years there was a croquet lawn and a tennis court; hedges were planted to enclose a formal garden and the kitchen garden, and the paddock became an orchard. Much of this work they did themselves, but labour in those days was plentiful and cheap, and a full-time gardener achieved more than the weekend owners could possibly have done. Sally planned the flowerbeds and borders, Alec was a somewhat eccentric experimentalist. But he had a marvellous way with cuttings. Envious visitors complained that he would almost absent-mindedly cut a shoot from some tree or shrub and shove in into the ground where it immediately took root and flourished. Certainly a great number of the beautiful trees that now adorn the grounds of The Dhoon began life in this way nearly sixty years ago.

Alec had other interests there. The fishing in the river was good – pike, perch and gudgeon abounded. Though he had begun his sporting life as a fisher of the nobler trout, he enjoyed any sort of angling. So he built a boat house and bought a punt. There was also swimming. The river was eight or nine feet deep by the island, making an ideal bathing pool. And, of course, there was tennis and croquet. Alec brought the same skill and guile to croquet as he did to billiards and snooker, often disconcerting opponents by unexpected tactics and outrageous flukes. Midnight croquet, with candle-lit hoops, became a feature of life at The Dhoon. The country around Barton Mills was interesting because the village stood at the junction of three different types of landscape. To the north was the then barren heath of Breckland, on the estate of Lord Iveagh, a great benefactor to St Mary's and a personal friend of Alec's. Lord Iveagh's environmental experiment was the reclaiming of Breckland. To the east of Barton Mills was typical fen-land, and to the west and south, the rolling hills of Cambridgeshire.

Meanwhile the Flemings had moved house in London. The flat had been convenient while Sally was working, but had not much else to commend it. Alec liked to go to the Chelsea Arts Club from his laboratory for a game of billiards or snooker before going home for dinner. Since the Club was to the west of St Mary's, and the flat to the east, his evening journeys were annoying. Then came an opportunity to move to Chelsea itself. The parents of Ronald Gray, his artist friend, had an engineering business with premises in Danvers Street, near Old Church Street. These included a house, No. 20, which became vacant. Gray suggested that the Flemings should rent it, and they agreed with enthusiasm. The house was divided into two flats, and the lower one gave them all the space they needed. Danvers Street was quiet and secluded, close to the Embankment and within a few minutes' walk of the Club. The Flemings were then ideally housed. They had a charming country house, and an attractive town house in one of the best parts of London, close to their friends and not too close to St Mary's. Living a discreet distance from his hospital protects a doctor from many an unnecessary call during off-duty hours.

Though Wright had returned with most of his original staff to the Inoculation Department, the former energy and enthusiasm had flagged. Everyone was tired and shaken by their experience in the army. Wright had lost some of his supreme confidence and authoritarianism, and his staff could even question the validity of some of his techniques without risking expulsion.[8] The tea-time discussions still took place, but the sparkle had vanished. When Wright and Bernard Shaw took part in a debate of the sort that dazzled the audience before the war, the result was merely the depressing spectacle of two old men trying in vain to recapture a lost brilliance.

Things had not gone well for Wright, professionally or personally. His faith in vaccine therapy had been shaken by lack of success. His theories were logical, yet this was evidently not enough. Wright's quite typical reaction was to blame conventional logic, and to seek a new system of reasoning. It was an exercise that absorbed a great deal of his time and energy for the rest of his life, and the results of his labours are described in the posthumously published book *Alethetropic Logic* (see p. 77). But his interest in philosophy meant a decline in his interest in the Inoculation Department, and he left most of its administration to Fleming and most of its research to younger men.

Wright's domestic life had also suffered. His wife had left him, not for any scandalous reason, but simply because she found his overbearing attitude to women, including herself, no longer tolerable. Wright scorned what he called 'voluptuary pleasures', such as the enjoyment of food, drink or the arts. He ate very little, and particularly abhorred expensive food or drink – to the consternation of the society hostesses who hoped that in him they had bagged a notable lion for their dinner parties. He never smoked, and never drank anything more alcoholic than two ounces of light beer. He had been passionately fond of music as a young man, but turned his back on it. 'Art is a whore I played with in my youth', he said in later life.[9] Once, his wife persuaded him to take her to a symphony concert at the Queen's Hall. He became so lost in the music that, when it was over, he stalked out hatless and coatless into Portland Place and pouring rain, with Lady Wright trailing behind him and begging him in vain to take a taxi because her dress was being ruined.

Wright's only voluptuary pleasure was his garden at Southernwood, his country house at Farnham Royal in Surrey. The Colebrooks were his closest friends, geographically and personally. They too had a house at Farnham Royal, and while Dorothy Colebrook kept an eye on the domestic arrangements at Southernwood, Leonard was Wright's devoted amanuensis in the laboratory, helping to prepare his lectures, transporting him to appointments and even arranging for a barber to come to the laboratory to cut his hair every month.[10] Wright was not a rich man. He had inherited virtually nothing from his parents, but he had earned up to £6,000 per year in private practice before the war. He had therefore been able to save 'a few thousand', which was the extent of his private fortune. But when he returned to St Mary's he determined to devote himself entirely to the work of the laboratory and to his search for a new system of logic, and he made a considerable financial sacrifice. He gave up private practice, and his only source of income was a personal grant from the Medical Research Committee, soon to become the Medical Research Council. This grant continued until he was sixty-five, in 1926. Thereafter the Inoculation Department paid his salary until he retired in 1946 at the age of eighty-five.

Wright's example was followed by Alec Fleming. He, too, gave up private practice and did not reopen his consulting room. His financial position is not clear. His salary from the Inoculation Department was under £1,000 per year but, when S. R. Douglas, who had been in charge of the production of vaccines, left for an appointment at the National Institute for Medical Research, Wright promoted Fleming to take his place. The manufacture of vaccines for sale was a profitable function that made the Inoculation Department financially independent, but, unlike its research, its commercial activity was not publicly paraded by Wright. Fleming's remuneration (if any) for its exacting and responsible direction was never mentioned. However, it seemed that the Flemings were living very comfortably. They entertained a good deal both in London and at The Dhoon, and Alec would often take several guests at a time to lunch or dine at the Chelsea Arts Club.[11]

It is at this period (1921) that Fleming's laboratory notebooks, deposited at the British Museum after his death by Lady (Amalia) Fleming, begin to be of interest. The earlier ones, covering the countless experiments on opsonins and vaccines from 1908 to 1914, and the seemingly endless work on antiseptics and wound infection at Boulogne, consist mainly of lists of patients' names and columns of figures, so abbreviated as to be almost unintelligible. But the notebook labelled No. XVII (16 March 1921–2 February 1922)[12] contains the record of Fleming's first great discovery, one much stranger than his later discovery of penicillin and probably an essential preliminary to it. The notebook begins with terse – almost shorthand – jottings of experiments on phagocytosis, the preparation of vaccines and antitoxins. They illustrate the tentative probings by which bacteriology advances. Any one of them might reveal something interesting, or even a winner that could carry the work into a new country.

When the winner arrived, in November 1921, it was such a dark horse that only the most observant of eyes would have recognized it. The first words to indicate it appear on the page dated Nov 21, under the heading 'Bacteriophage'. Bacteriophage is a viral parasite of certain bacteria which usually kills them. It had been discovered by Twort in 1915, who observed a 'glassy degeneration' of the affected colonies, followed by their dissolution. In 1921, d'Herelle had suggested that bacteriophage might function in natural immunity, and claimed to have treated intestinal infections with it. With this fresh in his mind, Fleming's 'Bacteriophage' heading in his notebook might mean that he intended to work on it himself, or that he believed that he had already found an example of it among his cultures.

Below this heading is a sketch of three 'streak' cultures across a blood-agar plate. These had been made by drawing a bacteria-charged platinum loop across the surface, so that the organisms would be spread along the line and grow into separate colonies. The streaks were labelled respectively 'Staphyloid coccus from A.F.'s nose'. 'Staph albus (Hazlett)' and 'pneumos.' 'A.F.' is evidently Fleming himself, 'Hazlett' is unidentified further, and 'pneumos' probably indicates a known culture of pneumococci. The note below the sketch explains that Fleming had taken some of his own nasal mucus, diluted it with saline, centrifuged it, and then placed a drop of the clear fluid (which contained no visible organisms) on each of the three streak cultures before incubating them for eighteen hours. The sketch shows the appearance after incubation. The 'A.F. coccus' streak had grown nothing in the vicinity of the drop of mucus, but the other two streaks had grown thickly from end to end.

On the same day Fleming set up a similar experiment, using a wider selection of bacteria, 'coli, pneumos, staph, strep', and again 'A.F. coccus'. The first four were unaffected by the mucus, but the A.F. coccus failed, once more, to grow in its vicinity. On 23 November he did a very dramatic experiment. He had grown his A.F. coccus in broth until it formed a turbid suspension. He then added a drop of the diluted mucus and within five minutes the turbid fluid had become clear. He tried to repeat this with suspensions of other organisms, but none was cleared except a culture of *Staphylococcus albus* (usually non-pathogenic) and of cholera bacilli, which both showed 'slight clearing'.

Taken as they stand, these entries by Fleming give no hint of his line of thought or its origin. Clearly they record experiments arising from some previous observation. Research workers do not always stop to write down everything they do when they have come upon something exciting and, like a dog casting round to pick up the scent, they are rapidly probing the possibilities by quite tentative experiments. It is only later, when the research line has become clear and the work needs to be published that they try to present it as a logical sequence from a definite beginning.[13] Since Fleming did not do this in any of his papers on lysozyme, its beginning is an unsolved mystery. It is no part of the purpose of this book to add to the myths already surrounding Fleming's work, but the lysozyme story cannot be made intelligible unless it is given a beginning. Fortunately this can be done with reasonable confidence by combining two sources of informa-tion. One is derived from what Fleming did write; the other is the account given – admittedly many years later – by Dr V. D. Allison who, as a young Belfast graduate, was actually working with Fleming when he discovered what was later called lysozyme.

In a lecture to the Ulster Medical Society in 1974, Allison, by then a distinguished bacteriologist, described how he began to study bacteriology in the Inoculation Department, in 1921:[14]

'Early on, Fleming began to tease me about my excessive tidiness in the laboratory. At the end of each day's work I cleaned my bench, put it in order for the next day and discarded tubes and culture plates for which I had no further use. He, for his part, kept his cultures . . . for two or three weeks until his bench was overcrowded with 40 or 50 cultures. He would then discard them, first of all looking at them individually to see whether anything interesting or unusual had developed. I took his teasing in the spirit in which it was given. However, the sequel was to prove how right he was, for if he had been as tidy as he thought I was, he would never have made his two great discoveries – lysozyme and penicillin.

Discarding his cultures one evening, he examined one for some time, showed it to me and said "This is interesting." The plate was one on which he had cultured mucus from his nose some two weeks earlier, when suffering from a cold. The plate was covered with golden-yellow colonies of bacteria, obviously harmless contami-nants deriving from the air or dust of the laboratory, or blown in through the window from the air in Praed Street. The remarkable feature of this plate was that in the vicinity of the blob of nasal mucus there were no bacteria; further away another zone in which the bacteria had grown but had become translucent, glassy and lifeless in appearance; beyond this again were the fully grown, typical opaque colonies. Obviously something had diffused from the nasal mucus to prevent the germs from growing near the mucus, and beyond this zone to kill and dissolve bacteria already grown.

Fleming's next step was to test the effect of fresh nasal mucus on the germ, but this time he prepared an opaque, yellow suspension of the germ in saline and added some nasal mucus to it. To our surprise the opaque suspension became in the space of less than two minutes as clear as water . . . it was an astonishing and thrilling moment [and] the beginning of an investigation which occupied us for the next few years.'

Allison's account is simple, clear and convincing. It conveys the unique thrill felt by every research worker who makes an entirely new discovery and realizes that it may lead him into unexplored fields and to unknown wonders. It explains why Fleming did the first experiments described in his notebook, but in one respect it conflicts with what he wrote. Allison is confident that the strange, yellow coccus was a chance contaminant from the air or dust, while Fleming, in recording it as a 'staphyloid coccus from A.F.'s nose', seemed to have believed that he himself had been harbouring it. As will be seen later, Allison's is the more reasonable supposition. Myth-makers have been busy on this point, and some of their creations will be discussed in Chapter 21.

From 23 November, the experiments recorded in Fleming's notebook followed a logical sequence. He first had to discover if this strange lytic* activity (which might have been due to bacteriophage) was peculiar to his own nasal mucus. So he tested samples from many other people – including his friend Ronald Gray – and found the same activity in all of them. It also seemed to be a normal property, and not the consequence of the common cold infection. And, for technical reasons that he explained later, he concluded that bacteriophage was not involved. Next, he tested the other fluids related to nasal mucus. The tears, for example, drain into the nose (as Allison said 'We swallow our grief') and tears proved to be highly active. There was activity too, in saliva and sputum. Widening the field, he tried blood serum and plasma, peritoneal and pleural fluid, and pus – all showed lytic activity.

Fleming must have been surprised and excited to find his bacteriolytic agent as a normal component of such different body fluids. For the first time in his career, instead of treading the well-worn paths established by Wright, he was exploring something that he himself had discovered. He had visions of a previously unknown and possibly important part of the defences of the body against bacteria, a natural antiseptic complementing the phagocytes, opsonins and antibodies that had so tediously occupied the energies of all who had worked with Wright during the past twenty years. It is not surprising that Fleming followed his new line with an enthusiasm greater than he had shown for any previous work and that he should always maintain that this was the best research of his career.

Fleming, as it happens, had made, not one, but two, interlocked discoveries. The first was the 'A.F. Coccus' as he then called it. This was a large, gram-positive coccus, easily cultivated on ordinary media, with

---

* Lysis in this sense means the dissolution of cells or bacteria.

what was to prove to be a unique sensitivity to the lytic agent. It must have been a rarity, for Fleming had never seen it before, and neither he nor Allison ever found it again in its natural state.[15] Its origin in Fleming's laboratory remains a mystery, but reason favours Allison's view that it was an airborne visitor, rather than Fleming's supposition that it came from his own nose, since he had shown himself that his nasal mucus destroyed it in a few minutes. Whatever its origin, this A.F. coccus, carefully maintained in culture, was to remain the best indicator of the lytic activity that Fleming and Allison investigated during the next five years. And it must be emphasized that it was the chance arrival of this very rare organism on a culture of nasal mucus that presented Fleming with his second discovery – that normal body fluids possess bacteriolytic activity.

During the next few weeks Fleming filled the pages of his notebook with experiments designed to discover the natural distribution of the lytic agent, which bacteria were affected by it, and what it might be. Having found it in human body fluids he went on to examine every sort of tissue obtainable in the operating theatre and post-mortem room. The lytic agent seemed to be everywhere; in skin, mucus membranes, most internal organs and tissues, particularly in cartilage, even in hair and nails. Nor was it limited to the human species – it occurred too in the first animals examined, rabbits, guinea pigs and dogs, though there was a wide variation in its power and distribution in different animals.

In the search for natural sources of lytic activity the A.F. coccus was used as the indicator in two ways. In the simplest, the test fluid or tissue extract was added to a suspension of the coccus to see if clearing occurred. Or, if the activity was weaker, the sample was added to a tube of liquid culture medium sown with A.F. coccus which, after incubation, indicated any inhibition. A more sensitive method was the 'well-plate' used by Fleming in his work on antiseptics. For this, he cut with a cork borer a number of round holes in the solid gelatine or agar of a culture plate. He placed in these holes discs of paper soaked in the test fluid, or slices of tissue, or a mixture of test substance and melted agar. He then covered the surface of the plate with a thin layer of melted agar, which filled all the holes smoothly, and when this had set, sowed the whole area thickly with A.F. coccus. After incubation, the coccus would have grown except in the areas in which lytic agent had diffused from the 'wells'. In this way slight degrees of activity could be revealed and many different samples could be tested on one plate.

For the investigation on the different bacteria susceptible to lysis there were again two methods available from the work on antiseptics. One was to add dilutions of the standard preparation of lytic agent to culture tubes sown with the different bacteria, and record inhibition of growth after incubation. The other was the 'gutter plate'. Fleming made this by cutting a long strip or gutter across the surface of a culture plate. He filled this gutter with melted agar mixed with lytic agent and, when this had set, streaked cultures of the different organisms to be tested across the gutter at right angles to it. After incubation susceptible organisms would have failed to grow near the gutter, insensitive ones would have grown right across it.

The results of these bacteriological tests must have reduced Fleming's hopes that he had discovered an important natural antiseptic. For, of all the organisms tested, A.F. coccus remained by far the most sensitive, while the virulent staphylococci, streptococci, pneumococci and the coli-typhoid group were all scarcely affected by the lytic agent. A number of non-pathogenic airborne organisms were susceptible, also some varieties of staphylococci and streptococci that were only occasionally pathogenic. It seemed, therefore, as if the lytic agent attacked only harmless germs, and that its discovery was more of academic interest than a contribution to practical immunology.

On the third aspect of the research, the nature of the lytic agent, Fleming and Allison, not being chemists, could make little progress. But they found that the active agent was destroyed by heating to 70°C, and that it could be precipitated by alcohol, acetone, picric acid and other chemicals that precipitate proteins. From these findings and the fact that the lytic agent actually dissolved or digested bacteria, Fleming concluded that it was probably a ferment, or, as we would say now, an enzyme. (An enzyme, usually a protein, is an organic catalyst that promotes chemical changes without itself being changed. Enzymes are produced by living things and are responsible for most of the chemical reactions essential to life.) Fleming's conclusion that his lytic agent was an enzyme was sixteen years later proved to be correct, but not by him.

In December 1921, Fleming presented his findings, as far as they had gone, to a meeting of the Medical Research Club. This had been founded in 1881, largely by Almroth Wright, to bring members together to hear papers about work in progress, discuss them, and suggest further research. Fleming, as already mentioned, was a poor lecturer. His usual flat monotone, unrelieved by highlights of emphasis or humour, was often inaudible. Worse still, he gave the impression that he had little enthusiasm for his own subject, and would 'throw away' really important points with a self-deprecating shrug.[16] On this occasion he had a difficult subject to present, needing lucid exposition and explanation to convey the interest and possible importance of quite novel observations. It seems that he conveyed none of these things. All that his listeners could gather was that some rare and harmless germ of which they had never heard was soluble in tears or saliva. The almost inevitable question in their minds must have been 'So what?'

But, when Fleming had finished, and the Chairman asked for comments, not even this question was asked. No questions were asked, and there was no discussion. After minutes of embarrassing silence, while Fleming stood waiting on the platform, the next paper was called for, and he had to return to his seat. What would later be regarded as an historic event in medical history seemed to have sunk without a ripple.

From Lysozyme to Penicillin

The apathy shown by the Medical Research Club towards Fleming's newly discovered bacteriolytic agent did not dampen his own enthusiasm. In fact, the tempo of his work with Allison quickened. More human and animal fluids and tissues were tested, and almost all contained lytic activity. Then Fleming turned to the vegetable kingdom. The activity was discovered there too – particularly in the turnip, though later Fleming was to find it in a wide variety of plants, flowers and vegetables. At the same time the work on the germs susceptible to lysis was also widened, and the nature of the lytic process studied. Fleming watched through his microscope as bacteria in the presence of tears became swollen and transparent and then simply disappeared.[1]

This work, of course, demanded a steady supply of the active agent. For the first few weeks human tears provided this and Fleming, Allison, members of the laboratory staff – even unwary visitors – all had to shed copious tears in the cause of science, aided by a drop or two of lemon juice in the eyes.[2] When such 'volunteers' dried up, laboratory boys were bribed with a few pence per cry. *Punch* got wind of these strange rites at St Mary's and published a cartoon by J. H. Dowd,[3] showing a brawny drill-sergeant birching a small boy whose streaming eyes dripped into a bottle labelled 'tear antiseptic', while other small boys queued to get their whack and their pennies.

Fortunately a much better and more convenient source of the lytic agent was soon found. On 12 January (1922), Fleming's notes record that egg-white possessed great activity,[4] and from then onwards it became the main provider of experimental material. By the end of January, Fleming decided that he had enough data for a formal scientific paper. He produced a manuscript and submitted it to Wright for approval. Wright clearly did approve, and showed this in three practical ways. Firstly, he considered the work sufficiently interesting and important to 'communicate' it himself to the Royal Society – of which he was a Fellow – so that it would appear in the Proceedings and thus rank as a work of scientific distinction. Fellows of the Royal Society could promote the work of their protégés or colleagues, who were not themselves Fellows, in this way. Sometimes the 'communication' was read at a meeting before publication, but this was not obligatory.

Wright also took the trouble to invent new words to identify Fleming's 'lytic substance' and the lysable microbe – scarcely a trouble perhaps, since he loved coining classical neologisms and his *Alethetropic Logic* is so full of them as to be almost unreadable. So, when Wright submitted Fleming's paper to the Royal Society on 13 February it contained two names that Fleming had not used in his notebook. The lytic agent was called 'lysozyme' and the organism originally known to Fleming as 'A.F. coccus' had become '*Micrococcus lysodeikticus*'. Cultural factors had placed it in the *Micrococcus* group, but 'lysodeikticus' – an awkward word meaning in Greek 'indicates lysis' – was a typical Wright invention.

It may be of interest here to record the evolution of the terminology used in Fleming's own notes at this time.[5] 'A.F. coccus' was his term until 16 February, when it became '*Micrococcus lyticus*' until 3 March, and '*M. lysodeikticus*' thereafter. The lytic agent originally labelled 'bacteriophage' became 'lytic substance' until February, then 'microzyme' until April, and finally 'lysozyme'. Thus, Fleming did not adopt for several weeks the names written into his paper by Wright. However, 'lysozyme' and '*M. lysodeikticus*' became the permanent names and have remained in use to this day.

Wright's third expression of his interest in Fleming and his work was that in 1922 he proposed him for election to the Fellowship of the Royal Society.[6] Though he cited the new work on lysozyme in support of Fleming's candidature, there was much previous research to his credit, particularly the work on the bacteriology of wound infection, the continuing work on antiseptics, and the invention of a number of neat and clever technical methods. To become a Fellow of the Royal Society was regarded as one of the highest honours that a scientist could achieve, and even to be proposed for election was a considerable compliment.

The Royal Society was – and still is – the most respected, influential and exclusive scientific society in the world. It was founded by its first royal patron, Charles II, in 1660 as the Royal Society of London for the Promotion of Natural Knowledge. Its Fellows were exponents of the 'new philosophy' and the experimental method, and their quest for scientific truth often brought them into conflict with religious dogma. The advance of science during the next two centuries was greatly assisted by the radical influence of the Royal Society. But, by the nineteenth century, and in the changing climate of critical thought, the Royal Society had become a respected part of the Victorian establishment. As professional scientists increased in number, so the Fellowship of the Society grew, but it continued to be filled by only a small proportion of those who had achieved scientific distinction. From 1857 to 1966 the Society occupied beautiful apartments in Burlington House, adjoining those of the Royal Academy. In 1922, when Fleming was first proposed as a candidate, there were 480 Fellows. These were drawn from every branch of science:

anatomy, astronomy, botany, chemistry, engineering, geology, mathematics, medical science, physics, physiology, and zoology. It was rare for a practising medical doctor to become a Fellow, because medicine had for centuries been more of an art than a science. There were, of course, exceptions. Lister, for example, had been President of the Royal Society.

In the 1920s the number of new Fellows elected each year was limited to 15, and these were more or less equally distributed between the ten or eleven scientific disciplines. In any one year, therefore, only 1 medical scientist might be elected. The first step towards election was to be proposed by a Fellow, seconded by another and supported by at least 4 others familiar with the candidate's work and prepared to sign a certificate setting out its merits. At that period, this certificate entitled the candidate to be considered for election every year for five years. If he were not elected during this time, the certificate lapsed but, after an interval of three years, it could be renewed for a further five years, a process that could be repeated indefinitely.

Each year the relative merits of the work of all the candidates were considered by separate committees appropriate to their different fields of research. The task of these committees was one of painful elimination. The list of candidates that each had to consider might contain 40 or 50 names which, after several meetings, had to be reduced to 2 or 3 in order of preference. Thus 10 committees might between them submit 20 or 30 names to the next arbiter, the Council, which would reduce the number to 15. Finally, these 15 names would be put before the whole Fellowship for approval. So, in 1923, Fleming's name appeared for the first time on the long list of candidates, and it was to remain there, apart from the statutory intervals, for the next twenty years.

Fleming's first paper on lysozyme appeared in the Proceedings of the Royal Society, in 1922.[7] Its title was 'On a Remarkable Bacteriolytic Element found in Tissues and Secretions'. In the introduction, Fleming gave only scanty information on the genesis of his discovery:

'The lysozyme was first noticed during some investigations made on a patient suffering from acute coryza. The nasal secretion from this patient was cultivated daily on blood agar plates, and for the first three days of the infection there was no growth, with the exception of an occasional staphylococcus colony. The culture made from the nasal mucus on the fourth day showed in 24 hours a large number of small colonies which, on examination, proved to be large gram-positive cocci . . . The microbe has not been exactly identified but for the purposes of this communication it may be alluded to as the *Micrococcus lysodeikticus*.'

Fleming described how drops of diluted nasal mucus placed on cultures of this organism inhibited their growth, and visibly cleared thick suspensions of it. He continued:

'These two preliminary experiments clearly demonstrate the very powerful inhibitory and lytic action which the nasal mucus has upon the *M. lysodeikticus*. It will be shown later that this power is shared by most of the tissues and secretions of the human body, by the tissues of other animals, by vegetable tissues, and, to a very marked degree, by egg-white.'

But nowhere did Fleming explain why he should have added dilute nasal mucus to cultures of this organism in the first place, particularly since, later in the paper, he referred to it as 'the nasal coccus' which might have suggested that it would thrive in nasal mucus. This enigmatic beginning to his paper, which must have puzzled anyone who thought about it, is so abrupt that Hare has suggested that some part of it must have been omitted in error.[8] The missing sentences might have described Fleming's observation that the organisms near the mucus on the original plate were obviously undergoing lysis, and thus explain why he had done the experiment with which the paper opens. But, as it stands, the experiment seems to be dangerously close to the random category condemned by Wright as '*the* sin against the Holy Ghost'.[9] If an explanatory passage had indeed been accidentally omitted, then Wright would have been responsible, since Fellows communicating papers to the Proceedings were, at that time, supposed to edit them.

The rest of Fleming's paper set out the available data on the natural distribution of lysozyme, its simple chemical and physical properties, and the list of susceptible organisms. At the end, Fleming allowed himself to speculate – a rare indulgence for him – on the possible biological importance of lysozyme. Hitherto, he pointed out, it had been supposed that a function of tears, saliva, sputum and mucus secretions was to rid the body surfaces of bacteria by washing them away. But now he had demonstrated an active antibacterial property. He had shown that 75 per cent of the 104 strains of airborne bacteria and a number of other strains of non-pathogenic staphylococci and streptococci were destroyed by lysozyme. He suggested that these organisms could not be pathogenic, precisely because they were susceptible to lysozyme. By inference, he might have suggested that organisms that were resistant to lysozyme were pathogenic precisely because of this resistance. In his first paper he did not go so far, and only gave a hint of his developing belief that lysozyme was in the front line of the natural defences of all living things against their eternal predators – the bacteria. Such defences are literally a vital function. As soon as an animal dies and its active defence ceases, the bacteria invade the body and destroy it.

The argument that lysozyme must have a biological function because it is so widely distributed in living things is, of course, teleological – a scientifically discredited principle – and Fleming was always searching for facts that would support this hypothesis. During the next five years he continued his work on lysozyme with Allison, who had obtained a Beit Fellowship that allowed him to prolong his research in Fleming's laboratory and to use its results in an MD thesis. Between 1922 and 1932 Fleming published eight papers on lysozyme, and five of these were with Allison as co-author. Allison's part in this work has tended to be undervalued by writers on Fleming. For example, in Fleming's bibliography in the *Biographical Memoir* published by the Royal Society in 1956, Allison's name is omitted from the authorship of three of the papers in which he had collaborated.[10]

By the summer of 1922, Fleming and Allison had added some significant facts which they published together in the *British Journal of Experimental Pathology*, and in the *Proceedings* of the Royal Society. One was that lysozyme was not related to bacteriophage. Then a fishing week-end at The Dhoon led to the discovery that pike's eggs were particularly rich in lysozyme. Thereafter, Fleming's pursuit of science could be combined with that of his favourite sport as one sort of fish after another was added to the list of lysozyme sources. The woods and hedges yielded the eggs of many birds, and the garden its flowers, plants and vegetables. Fleming sent Allison to the Ministry of Agriculture laboratories at Weybridge to collect tears from horses, cows, hens, ducks, and geese (pigs proved to be unco-operative) and then to the London Zoo for samples from fifty different species of animals.[11] Most contained lysozyme, though in varying amounts. But this work merely confirmed its wide natural distribution. Facts about its biological function were needed to confirm Fleming's belief in its importance.

Facts did emerge, though piecemeal and rather reluctantly. For example, Fleming and Allison discovered that they could produce complete resistance to lysozyme in organisms normally susceptible to it – even in *M. lysodeikticus*. They did this by repeatedly culturing the bacteria in the presence of partially-lethal concentrations of lysozyme, selecting the survivors and sub-culturing.[12] The demonstration that such a resistance could be acquired supported the idea that, in the remote past, harmless bacteria could have acquired it and thus become present-day pathogens. A more positive step in the same direction was provided by Frederick Ridley, the young ophthalmologist who joined Fleming in 1926 to study lysozyme in relation to eye infections. Ridley showed that when a staphylococcus that had lost its virulence was made resistant to lysozyme it regained its ability to cause conjunctivitis.[13]

Another fact to emerge was that the resistance of the important pathogenic bacteria to lysozyme was by no means complete. At the beginning of their work Fleming and Allison had used tears diluted 1 in 100 – in order to conserve a scarce commodity – and it was with this material that they had studied bacterial sensitivity. But when egg-white lysozyme became available they were able to show with a much more powerful preparation that lysozyme could inhibit pathogenic staphylococci, streptococci, meningococci, and typhoid and anthrax bacilli.[14] Ridley carried this observation further when he showed that *undiluted* tears could kill some virulent organisms. Lysozyme might indeed be important in protecting at least the eyes against infection.

A third line opened up from the observation that leucocytes contain lysozyme. Fleming, of course, was particularly interested in the phagocytes and the effect on them of antiseptics. In 1923 he began to use the simple and effective 'slide-cell' that had been devised by Wright and his colleagues and described by them in a paper to *The Lancet* so lengthy that it had to appear in three instalments.[15] Fleming's own description is brief:

'The slide cells . . . are made from two microscope slides separated by five strips of vaselined paper arranged at intervals transversely to the long axis of the slides. By means of these strips of paper the space between the two slides is divided into four very thin compartments or cells open at each end.'[16]

Each cell could contain about a drop of fluid, and this could be any desired mixture of blood, serum, leucocytes, bacteria and antiseptic. Having been filled, the ends of the cells were sealed with wax, and the preparation incubated and observed microscopically at various times to see what was happening.

Fleming's first experiments with these slide cells continued his long-running battle to show that chemical antiseptics were worse than useless. He set up mixtures of serum, phagocytes, staphylococci and dilutions of twenty different antiseptics used by surgeons. After incubation he found that in the slide cells containing *no* antiseptic, the phagocytes had killed 98 per cent of the cocci. But with weak concentrations of antiseptic it was the phagocytes that had been killed, while all the bacteria flourished. The phagocytes in fact were much more vulnerable to antiseptics than were the bacteria. This was a neat and elegant confirmation of his earlier work at Boulogne. But now he went further, and considered the prospect for the use of such chemicals, given by injection. He concluded: 'These experiments show that there is little hope that any of the antiseptics in common use could be successfully introduced into the blood stream to destroy the circulating bacteria in cases of septicaemia'.[17] This conclusion seems reasonable enough at first sight, but it is the sort of unjustified generalization from a bench experiment to the living body to which Wright's teaching so often led. There are countless known and unknown differences between an artificial mixture in a glass container and the conditions in the living body. There was only one certain way to discover what an antiseptic could do to bacteria in the circulating blood and that was to inject it and see what happened.

From chemical antiseptics Fleming soon returned to his natural antiseptic, lysozyme. He showed in slide cells that even his strongest preparations had no adverse effects on living phagocytes, they remained as active and viable as in normal serum. Then he considered that since the phagocytes themselves contained lysozyme it might be concerned with their ability to digest the bacteria they had swallowed. This digestion was the essential second phase of effective phagocytosis. If the swallowed organism remained alive it would kill the phagocyte. To examine this point, Fleming and Allison studied in slide cells the phagocytosis of lysozyme-sensitive organisms as compared to those made lysozyme-resistant by selective culture. The results, which they published in 1927, were clear-cut.[18] The sensitive strains were swallowed and digested, the resistant strains were swallowed, but remained intact and alive in the phagocytes. Ridley added his own contribution to this research when he found that leucocytes normally contained enough lysozyme to digest most pathogenic organisms.[19] It seemed likely, therefore, that leucocyte lysozyme might be important to phagocytic function.

It was inevitable that, during these years of work on lysozyme, Fleming's thoughts should turn to some clinical application for it. He had studied every new chemical antiseptic as it appeared and had dismissed it as virtually useless. Now, for the first time, he had himself discovered an antiseptic that was apparently harmless to living cells and tissues. Fleming and Allison, having discovered that egg-white lysozyme was not destroyed in the stomach, tried the effect of large doses given by mouth on patients with intestinal infections. They did find a reduction in the number of intestinal streptococci in one case, but the benefit to the patient was not obvious. Then they injected egg-white lysozyme intravenously in rabbits to see if the blood level could be raised. Immediately after the injection it was, but within six hours it had returned to normal.[20] So lysozyme seemed to be rapidly eliminated until the natural balance was restored. Repeated injections might have maintained it, but here there was another difficulty, the development of allergic reactions.

Fleming was well aware of this danger, because allergy had become a major part of the work of the Inoculation Department. John Freeman had a clinic for sufferers from asthma, hay fever, urticaria, and other allergic disorders. His treatment was based on identifying the particular 'allergen' to which the patient had become sensitive, which might be a pollen, mould, some food-substance, or dust. Then he made a 'vaccine' from the offending substance and, by starting with minute but increasing doses, 'desensitized' the patient. It was a treatment that often worked, and he had a large practice. One of his assistants was a mycologist, Dr La Touche, who cultured moulds, collected from the houses of Freeman's asthmatic patients, in the room immediately below Fleming's. Fleming was well aware, too, that even normal people can be sensitized by an injection of a foreign protein, such as egg-white, so that repeated injections of his lysozyme preparations could cause severe or even fatal reactions. But a paper published with Allison in 1924 contains the suggestion that an intravenous injection of egg-white might overcome a generalized infection by lysozyme-sensitive microbes.[21]

When Ridley joined him in 1926, Fleming hoped that he would be able to purify lysozyme and rid it of the egg-white proteins. Ridley knew more biochemistry than anyone else then in the Inoculation Department, having taken a course in it while working for a BSc degree. But the purification of lysozyme was a problem beyond his limited experience and laboratory facilities. It was, indeed, only solved eleven years later in the Oxford laboratory of Sir Robert Robinson, one of the greatest organic chemists of his day.

Though Fleming was, during this postwar decade, doing the most original and best sustained research of his career, and describing it in a series of scientific papers and lectures, he failed to convey his conviction of its importance, or even to arouse the interest of most of his colleagues. For the clinicians, lysozyme seemed to have no practical significance. Its impact on the bacteriologists can be judged from the fact that their contemporary standard textbook dismissed it in two lines.[22]* The biologists, who should have been intrigued by something that might have been a factor in the evolution of pathogenic bacteria, were not impressed by Fleming's presentation of such a possibility.

This uncertainty about Fleming's scientific contributions was reflected in the decisions of the Royal Society Selection Committees. Every year, from 1923 to 1927, the committee dealing with medical science, which included real experts in Fleming's field, had examined the merits of his work, and had placed it below the best of that of their many other candidates for election. Much of Fleming's work had been more or less routine bacteriology, distinguished by ingenious new techniques but, with one exception, not by outstandingly original discoveries. The one exception was lysozyme, and at that time no one knew what to make of it. It might be an important scientific contribution – or it might not. Until this doubt could be resolved, Fleming's work on lysozyme did not justify his election to the Royal Society.

During the immediate postwar period there had been marked changes in the fortunes of St Mary's Hospital Medical School. There had been a disastrous decline in the number of students in the years before the war, with an intake of only nineteen in 1914, and this had continued despite the fact that St Mary's had admitted women students to its clinical courses from March 1916. In 1920, Dr Charles McMoran Wilson was appointed Dean, in succession to Sir John Broadbent. Charles Wilson, though three years younger than Alec Fleming, had been his contemporary throughout their student years at St Mary's and they had both been keen participants in the School's activities. On the outbreak of war, Wilson became Regimental Medical Officer to the 1st Battalion, Royal Fusiliers, and three years

---

* It may be of interest to record that the Proceedings of a Conference on Lysozyme, held in 1972 to commemorate the 50th anniversary of its discovery, fill a book containing 641 pages, and references to 2,586 papers on the subject.[23]

in the trenches made an indelible impression on his mind. His famous book, *The Anatomy of Courage*, is a revealing record not only of its subject but of its author.[24] He is better known as Lord Moran, the title conferred on him in 1943.

When he became Dean, Wilson found his School in dire straits. The buildings were not just inadequate, they were almost derelict. The student intake was low, despite the feminine component, and the official view of the University was that St Mary's had no future as a clinical school. Wilson refused to accept this dismal judgement. One of his first innovations was to establish medical and surgical professorial units, under a new London University scheme, which not only raised the academic prestige of the School, but brought in substantial funds from the University Grants Committee. This move was not entirely popular with the St Mary's consultants who feared the intrusion of university appointees. But the first Professor of Surgery was one of their own colleagues, C. A. Pannett, Fleming's student friend and rival for so many prizes and honours.

Wilson's next step was to change the system by which entrance scholarships were awarded on the results of examination. He was convinced that character is of greater importance in a doctor than the ability to score high examination marks, and he replaced the written papers by an interview – usually with himself. He was looking for a combination of strength of character and excellence at games – which he believed often went together – and awarded the scholarships to those who passed both tests. In consequence, St Mary's began to gain tough, energetic young sportsmen – particularly rugby footballers. It also gained, through the generosity of Wilson's friend, Lord Beaverbrook, a splendid new sports ground at Teddington. Soon it began to excel in the inter-hospital and university sporting events, amid a tendency among the losers to complain about 'professionalism' and 'football scholars'. But the overall effect was what Wilson wanted. Sporting successes were a good advertisement for his School; students were eager to enrol and, by 1924, the admission of women – which had never been popular among the majority of the staff – was stopped. St Mary's, which had had such a precarious existence ever since its foundation, and had seemed on the verge of extinction in 1920, became within a few years a thriving – even aggressive – organization.

Alec's position in the Inoculation Department had become secure in 1921, when Wright gave him the title of Assistant Director. This did not please John Freeman, Alec's senior by several years, who had expected that, in the relatively near future, he would succeed Wright. Wright had certainly led him to suppose this, referring to him as 'my son in science'. On this occasion it seems that Wright placated him with promises, and was not above making the same promises, in the greatest secrecy, to Fleming. In fact, Wright could not do without either of them – they were the twin backbones of his department. Freeman ran the routine bacteriology, and

Fleming the production of vaccines and the general laboratory administration. Wright, lost in rarefied thought for most of his time, was quite incapable of mundane practicality. He kept his two capable and middle-aged lieutenants in his department by encouraging each one to believe that, when the 'Old Man' retired in a year or so, he would become Director. In the event, as mentioned earlier, Wright did not retire until 1946, in his eighty-fifth year, when Fleming was already sixty-five, and Freeman past retiring age.

Readers of the small print of Fleming's papers should have noticed an apparently momentous change in his status, and in that of the Inoculation Department, that took place in 1922. In July of that year a paper by Fleming cites him as 'Director of the Department of Systematic Bacteriology' in 'The Pathological Institute, St Mary's Hospital'.[25] It would seem, therefore, that Fleming had become director of a new department, that the Hospital had gained a new Institute of Pathology, and that the Inoculation Department had ceased to exist. These inferences were only true on paper – in reality nothing had changed. No one had gained or lost any space, money or executive authority. The changes in titles – made more confusing by the conflicting accounts of St Mary's historians – were the surface indications of deeper moves by Charles Wilson to bring Wright and his autonomous Inoculation Department into the jurisdiction of the Medical School.

The existence of a virtually private research institute within the Hospital was a challenge to his authority that the new Dean found difficult to accept. Yet Wright's position was almost unassailable. He was Bacteriologist to the Hospital, and Professor of Experimental Pathology in London University. His Department, which cost the Hospital and School nothing, gave valuable services to both. The Hospital received a free laboratory service, advice and treatment for its patients, the upkeep of the 'Research Ward', and rent for the space occupied by the Department. The School received free lectures and teaching from Wright's staff and, of course, the prestige of his fame. It was, therefore, expedient to leave things as they were, and yet politically untidy to do so. Wilson wanted his School whole and complete, without embedded foreign bodies – even such a pearl as Wright's world-famous laboratory.

There seems to be no available record of the ways and means by which the Inoculation Department was apparently absorbed. If Wright seemed to give way, then it was the sort of judo move that uses the opponent's momentum to his own disadvantage. What Wright agreed to was the creation of an 'Institute of Pathology and Research' with himself as its Principal. It consisted of six departments – Anatomy, Systematic Bacteriology, Clinical Bacteriology, Chemical Pathology, General Pathology and Experimental Physiology – each with a director who would have a voice in the controlling council. Such was the new Institute – on paper. In fact all the 'new' departments already existed and their respective heads merely changed titles. Two of them had made up the old Inoculation Department under Fleming and Freeman respectively and their separation was supposed to dissolve it. The other four had not been connected with the Inoculation Department, and perhaps Wilson hoped that Wright and his two henchmen would be outvoted in any conflict of interests.

It was a strange situation in which it was not clear who would swallow whom. Wright might have tried to assimilate the other four departments, but the men already in charge of them would have proved indigestible. In the event, it was the Inoculation Department that proved indigestible – fatally so, in fact, to the Institute of Pathology. By 1929 the Inoculation Department had reappeared, unchanged by its nominal extinction, while the Institute of Pathology and Research had, in Zachary Cope's words – 'quietly lapsed'.[26]

Meanwhile Alec Fleming's domestic life was thriving. On 17 March 1924, his wife gave birth to a son, Robert. He was a much-loved arrival after nine years of childless marriage. Sally began to spend more time with her baby at The Dhoon during the summer, often joined by nephews and nieces, the children of Robert and Tom Fleming. About this time she decided that her friends and relations should call her Sareen. 'Sareen' had, she said, a proper Irish sound, but the real reason was that to the children she had become 'Aunt Sally', which she disliked. Being a firm-minded woman, she effected the change almost overnight, and 'Sareen' she became and remained for the rest of her life.[27]

Alec enjoyed his holidays and week-ends at The Dhoon, often surrounded by children. The garden, steadily developing as he planned and planted, the paddock bordering the river, the little island and the river itself, all these were a constant delight. There were endless opportunities for the games he loved to invent, for swimming, fishing and for the observation of a wild life as varied and unrestrained as that of his native hillsides. The Flemings maintained their close family ties. Robert and his wife Ida lived at Radlett, with their children, Angus, John and May. They often stayed at The Dhoon and remembered the extraordinary games of golf in the garden over courses constantly revised by Alec and with an abundance of hazards such as flower-beds, cold frames and, of course, the river.

John Fleming, Robert's partner in their successful optical business, had moved with his wife Elizabeth (Sareen's twin sister) to live in St John's Wood. They remained childless. In 1922, Tom Fleming died. After his marriage in 1909, he and his wife Florence had lived in Ealing, with their children, Rosamund, and Donald. There were often family parties in one or other of the Fleming households in the London area, and every Christmas as many as possible spent the day together. From time to time there were visits to Lochfield, where Hugh was still farming and nothing seemed to change. Old Mrs Fleming lived with her married daughter, Grace, in Ayrshire, until she died in 1928.

In 1925, the Inoculation Department gained a new recruit, Ronald Hare, a St Mary's graduate who had won a £200 scholarship to do bacteriology and research. Hare was to be the author of *The Birth of Penicillin*, an admirable book, in which he gives graphic descriptions of Wright and his department at that time, a most illuminating account of Fleming's discovery of penicillin and of Fleming himself. Hare describes him as a small man with a large head, blue eyes, a bent nose, and a broad Ayrshire accent. He seemed to lead a blameless and contented existence, divided between his laboratory, his club, his flat in Chelsea, his country house, and his interest in antiques and auction sales.[28] He had a good collection of pictures by Wilson Steer, Philip Connard, Ronald Gray and other artist friends, and good taste in acquiring others. One day he remarked to Allison that some etchings by Whistler were being sold at Sotheby's and suggested that they should go and bid for them. At £30, they proved too expensive but Fleming encouraged Allison to buy three sketches by a little-known artist named Pablo Picasso. He got them for £3.[29]

When, in 1926, Wright had to retire from his University Chair of Experimental Pathology at the age of sixty-five (but from no other appointment) Charles Wilson took the opportunity to procure a Chair of Bacteriology for the Medical School, and to ensure that Fleming should occupy it. But it was not until September 1928, that the appointment took effect, and even then Fleming was reluctant to use his new title – apparently to spare the feelings of John Freeman who once more must have felt supplanted by him.

To Hare, Fleming seemed relaxed and never in a hurry. He arrived at nine every morning and left at five in the afternoon. The old days, when Wright's staff would work all night on some exciting project, were gone, with so many other pre-war things. Fleming habitually went from the laboratory to the Chelsea Arts Club, where he had tea, played chess, snooker, or cards, had a drink and then went home for dinner at 8 p.m. His closest companion, who writes of the happy hours he spent with him at the Club, was Vivian Pitchforth, the artist.[30] Pitchforth was stone deaf in consequence of his war service in the artillery. Since Fleming seldom spoke and Pitchforth could hear no conversation, the two men enjoyed their games with no verbal distractions and became firm friends.

In the laboratory, Fleming, though equally taciturn, liked company. He attended all the scientific meetings, never refused an invitation to lecture, and often entertained visiting scientists at the Chelsea Arts Club. Hare remembers him as always ready for a gossip in the Department. The door of his room was habitually open and visitors were welcome. If no one dropped in to see him, he would wander into the main laboratory for a chat. This usually involved Fleming planting himself in front of the fire, with his hands in his pockets and a cigarette dangling from his lips, while he looked more or less into space. On rare occasions, Hare writes, he would utter a few words on the marriage of a colleague, the state of the stock market or some current scientific scandal. But, one morning in the autumn of 1928, he had something to show to anyone who was interested. This was a culture plate – one that he had rescued from being discarded. It showed a blob of mould, the growth of which had clearly disagreed with the staphylococci that covered the rest of the plate. Thus was the discovery of penicillin announced to its first audience.

The Discovery of Penicillin
1. The Bare Bones

No one to whom Fleming showed his mouldy culture plate on that September morning in 1928 realized that they were looking at something that would eventually revolutionize the practice of medicine. What they saw, when Fleming pointed it out to them, was that it was covered with the recognizable colonies of staphylococci, except in the vicinity of a growth of mould near the edge of the plate. In this area the colonies were ghost-like and transparent, and quite close to the mould there were none at all. Fleming had often demonstrated plates showing just this sort of effect produced by lysozyme, and part of the lack of interest in this particular one was due to the fact that he had become something of a bore on this subject. The general impression was that here was another example of lysozyme, which was being produced by a mould. Fleming himself at first thought that this was the case. But he recognized something exciting which evidently escaped his colleagues. This mould was, unlike the familiar lysozyme, capable of attacking a common pathogenic organism.

It is clear that, if Fleming felt excited by his discovery, he failed to communicate this feeling to the people who looked at his culture plate. So no one paid much attention to what they said, or to what Fleming said, and there was nothing to fix the incident firmly in their minds. It was only some fifteen years later, when the truly historic importance of the episode became apparent, that the first eye-witnesses tried to recall precisely what had happened. It is not surprising, therefore, that their accounts of an event that had left little impression at the time should be coloured by their later knowledge of its significance. When the available facts surrounding the origin of Fleming's plate are examined in detail it will be seen that it can only be explained by a series of chance events of almost incredible improbability. Truth, in this case, is so much stranger than even the most blatantly fictitious stories of the discovery of penicillin, that these will, for the present, be ignored.

The most certain foundation on which to reconstruct the details of Fleming's discovery, and his early work on it, must be provided by what he actually wrote at the time in his laboratory notebooks and in his paper published in 1929. Unfortunately these writings, like those on lysozyme, provide only a very incomplete picture. The gaps can be partially filled in from relevant contemporary events and from a knowledge of the way in which bacteriologists in general, and Fleming in particular, worked in those days. Archaeologists and palaeontologists are prone to reconstruct the probable form of a buried building or an extinct animal from no more than a few stones or bones. Such reconstructions are inevitably hypothetical, and therefore controversial. But, as Wright so often said, one can only progress by advancing from the known into the unknown.

The first clue to the work that Fleming was doing when he happened to observe the antibacterial effect of this particular mould is given in the paper in which he first described it:

'While working with staphylococcus variants, culture plates were set aside on the laboratory bench and examined from time to time. In the examination these plates were necessarily exposed to the air and they became contaminated with various micro-organisms. It was noticed that around a large colony of a contaminating mould the staphylococcus colonies became transparent and were obviously under-going lysis. (See Fig. 1).' (See Plate 2a.)

Figure 1 was a photograph of the now-famous plate, and it shows very clearly the accuracy of Fleming's description.[1] But as a description of an epoch-making event, it is tantalizingly incomplete. What, for example, were the 'staphylococcus variants'? What was the culture medium? Does 'set aside on the laboratory bench' mean (as it seems to mean) that the plates were not incubated? Does 'from time to time' mean intervals of hours, days, or weeks? And where did the contaminating mould come from? None of these questions can be answered from Fleming's published writings, nor from his notebooks, nor by his later lectures and reminiscences.

There is, however, another clue in the work that Fleming was doing in 1928. He was a recognized authority on the staphylococcus group of micro-organisms, and he had been invited to contribute a section on the subject to a new book, *A System of Bacteriology*, that was being published in nine volumes by the Medical Research Council.[2] His contribution (which appeared in Volume Two in 1929) involved him in a good deal of reading and some practical work beginning in 1927. In the course of this, Fleming had come across a paper describing variations in the colour of staphylococcal colonies, that seemed to be related to their virulence. The *Staphylococcus aureus* is the common virulent strain, and this produces golden yellow colonies on solid culture media. But it was suggested that interesting colour changes took place if the cultures were made and incubated for twenty-four hours in the ordinary way, and then kept at room temperature for several days. These colour changes indicated the presence of staphylococcal variants, and their virulence was of interest.

Fleming decided on a personal study of these variants, and enlisted the help of D. M. Pryce, a research scholar. They cultured staphylococci from boils, carbuncles, abscesses, and nose, throat and skin infections. The cultures were made by smearing an infected swab or platinum loop across the surface of a solid medium such as blood-agar, contained in Petri dishes. After sowing these plates, they were then incubated, and within a few hours the surface would become dotted with staphylococcal colonies, each one of which had grown from a single organism. The mature colonies would be round, smooth, opaque little domes, about 1–2 mm in diameter. If incubation was prolonged, growth continued, and the colonies would merge. If incubation was stopped at an early stage, and the plate kept at room temperature, little further growth took place, and the colonies remained the same size. But some changed colour, which was the point of the investigation. So Fleming and Pryce took their plates out of the incubator, piled them on the bench, and looked at them every few days to see what was happening.

In February 1928, Pryce transferred from Fleming's laboratory to study morbid anatomy, and Fleming carried on the work by himself. At the end of July he and his family went off to spend their summer holiday at The Dhoon. Meanwhile Dr S. R. Craddock had replaced Pryce as Research Scholar in Fleming's laboratory, and it was arranged that he should work in Fleming's room while the latter was away. Hare, who has produced his own reconstruction of the events surrounding the discovery of penicillin, obtained much information from Stuart Craddock himself and from his notes.[3] Craddock told him that, before going on holiday, Fleming put a number of culture plates into a pile at the end of the bench, where they would be out of the sunlight, and also out of Craddock's way.

Pryce, Fleming's former assistant in his work on staphylococci, spent part of his holiday with Hare, and returned to St Mary's at the beginning of September. When Fleming also restarted work, Pryce 'dropped in' to see how the investigation was going. There is no certain date for this momentous call, but from Pryce's impression and other evidence, Hare believes that it took place on the morning of 3 September. Pryce found Fleming sorting out the stacks of plates that had been left on the bench during his absence. He had examined many of these and discarded them by piling them in a shallow tray of lysol where – if they had been immersed in the antiseptic – the cultures would have been killed and the plates made safe for the technicians who would clean them. Fleming grumbled to Pryce about the amount of work he was having to do since Pryce had left him, and then began to show him what was on the plates. As it happened, a number of the plates that Fleming had dumped into the tray of lysol were high and dry above the liquid. And it was from these discarded plates that Fleming picked a few at random to show to Pryce. Then, as he was making this cursory second inspection, he suddenly noticed something about the appearance of a plate he was about to hand to Pryce. 'That's funny,' he said, and looked more closely. He then pointed out the now famous zone of disappearing staphylococcal colonies around a large blob of mould. Pryce went off to his proper employment, and thought very little more about what had happened, until some twelve or thirteen years later.

But Fleming who was, like most acute observers, an avid collector of strange phenomena, was elated by his find. He took up a minute sample of the strange mould on a platinum loop and sub-cultured it into a tube of liquid medium. In his published paper he wrote that this was Sabouraud's medium, a peptone-agar mixture used for moulds and fungi, but from his notebooks it seems that he found ordinary meat broth quite satisfactory. During the rest of the day he showed the plate to anyone who happened to visit him, including E. W. Todd, who had just returned from New York; Hurst Brown, a Canadian Rhodes Scholar; and C. J. La Touche, the mycologist from the laboratory immediately below Fleming's who was cultivating moulds obtained from the homes of Freeman's asthmatic patients. None of these visitors saw much significance in Fleming's demonstration. Fleming also took the plate along to show to the various people in the 'main laboratory' (including Ronald Hare) when he went there for his usual gossip. He often produced oddities of this sort, and the mouldy plate, looking very like one of his lysozyme tricks, did not strike anyone as particularly exciting. Finally, Fleming showed his plate to Almroth Wright, when he came into the laboratory during the afternoon. If Wright's reaction was more enthusiastic than that of his colleagues, it has found no place in the records.

Fleming was evidently not discouraged by this failure to share his interest. We know that he photographed the plate and made it permanent by exposing it to formalin vapour (as he did for preserving his 'germ paintings'), which killed and fixed both the bacteria and the mould. So the original plate, kept safely by Fleming during the years when it seemed to be of no interest, was subsequently resurrected to become a world-famous object, now in the British Museum.[4] His care is evidence that he believed this discovery to be of unusual importance, but if it was made on 3 September, then there is a gap of nearly two months during which he did no recorded experimental work on it. The first description of an experiment on the mould, to survive in his notebook, is dated 'Oct 30. 28.'[5]

This entry is rather ambiguously headed 'Staph inhibiting mould' – the first evidence of an interest in any sort of mould in his notebooks. There follows a pencil-sketch showing the circular outline of a culture plate, the surface of which has various features. There is a long, shaded streak running vertically across the right-hand side of the culture area, with the word 'Mould' written across it. An arrowed note in the margin reads 'grown 5 days on bench before plating others'. This clearly refers to the mould, and 'others' refers to a number of horizontal streaks running from the left of the plate towards the mould. Each streak represents the growth of a different organism cultured by smearing a charged loop across the surface of the medium to the edge of the mould. Three of these streaks, labelled 'coli', 'coli' and 'Hay' respectively, show that these organisms have grown almost up to the mould. Two, labelled 'Sarcinae' and 'staph', stop 3 cm short of the mould colony. There are also faint outlines of three other streaks, all labelled 'Staph', but the drawing here seems to have been partly erased. (See Plate 1a.)

This experiment confirms the original observation that staphylococcal colonies have not formed on the surface of a culture plate in the vicinity of a growth of this particular mould. On the other hand, organisms labelled 'coli' (almost certainly *Bacillus coli*) and 'Hay' (not otherwise identified) grow quite happily right up to the edge of the mould. The inference is that something diffusing through the medium prevents the growth of, or destroys, staphylococci, but not the other organisms. It is therefore a selective bacterial inhibitor or lysin. The second point – and as will be seen later, this is an extremely important one – is that Fleming grew the mould colony on the plate at room temperature for five days *before* sowing the other organisms. He must then have incubated the plate at 37°C in order to produce the appearance shown in his sketch, because these other organisms will hardly grow at all at room temperature. It is clear, therefore, that by the time of this experiment Fleming must have discovered that the mould grew best at lower temperatures than the bacteria he was studying. And, from later evidence, it is probable that he had also discovered that he could not repeat his original observation by deliberately 'contaminating' a culture of staphylococci with mould *after* their colonies had grown. Yet this latter sequence of events has generally been supposed (except by Hare) to have led to his discovery. This is a rather complicated matter that will be clarified in Chapter 21.

The experiment described on 30 October must have been set up six or seven days earlier. The next page in the notebook, also dated the 30th, describes a second experiment. Fleming took an 'extract of staph inhibiting mould made in N salt 24 hours at 37°C' and centrifuged it to throw down the solids. To 0.5 cc of the clear supernatant of this extract he added 0.25 cc of a thick suspension of staphylococci, and incubated samples of the mixture at 45°C and 56°C for three hours. He then recorded that there was 'considerable lysis of staph in tube with mould extract' kept at 45°C. At 56°C there was no such effect. He concluded: 'therefore mould culture contains a bacteriolytic substance for staphylococci'. As will be seen later, this conclusion was not strictly valid. (See Plate 1b.)

Thereafter in the notebook there are forty-eight pages up to March 1929, setting out experiments on the mould. The work follows distinct and fairly obvious lines. First, Fleming had to secure a supply of what he called 'mould juice' which was, in effect, filtered broth in which the mould had grown. He tried various ways of growing the mould to get the best yield, and found that ordinary bacteriological nutrient broth gave good growth. He then made many experiments to find the best temperature and duration of incubation, and settled down to discover what his mould juice would do to bacteria, using the gutter-plate technique that he had developed for studying lysozyme. He filled the gutter with a mixture of heat-melted agar and mould extract, and when this had solidified, streaked cultures of the organisms at right-angles from the gutter to the edge of the plate, which he then incubated. The inhibitor in the gutter diffused rapidly through the medium, so that in a few hours it formed a zone on either side. In this zone organisms sensitive to the inhibitor refused to grow and the length of the streak showing growth indicated the degree of sensitivity of that particular organism.

Working with this method, Fleming soon had an impressive list of the organisms that were inhibited by his mould juice, including some very important pathogens. The virulent streptococcus, staphylococcus, pneumococcus, gonococcus, meningococcus and diphtheria bacillus were all powerfully inhibited. But the typhoid, para-typhoid and coliform bacilli were immune to the effect. And Fleming was interested to note that the influenza bacillus (*Haemophilus influenzae* or Pfeiffer's bacillus), on which he had done so much work, was also not inhibited. However, the pre-eminent discovery was that a group of organisms that between them caused most of the dangerous infections could be killed – apparently dissolved – by something generated by an unknown mould. Fleming, who for twelve years had been working with and thinking about chemical antiseptics and their liability to do more harm than good, must have felt that here was a natural antiseptic that might well be lethal for germs but harmless for the cells of the body. And this was one of the first aspects that he investigated.

By the end of November 1928, Fleming was doing experiments in slide-cells on the effect of mould juice on phagocytes and their ability to swallow bacteria, and found that it had no ill-effects. Yet, even when diluted one in 800, it was still lethal for the virulent bacteria. As a germicide, therefore, it was more powerful than carbolic acid, and yet it seemed quite harmless to the delicate living blood cells. It was beginning to seem, in fact, that it might be the long-sought 'perfect antiseptic'.

Further work along these lines then revealed what might be a serious limitation to clinical value. Fleming discovered that, while most chemical antiseptics killed microbes within a few minutes, the mould filtrate did not do so for several hours. He concluded, therefore, that it 'belonged to the group of slow-acting antiseptics, like flavine or novarsenobillon'.[6] And Hare has recently reported his finding of the results of slide cell experiments in the notebooks of both Fleming and Craddock that must, in his opinion, have increased Fleming's doubts of a possible therapeutic value for this new antibacterial agent. These experiments seemed to show that, in mixtures containing blood serum, the mould filtrate lost most of its germicidal power.[7] This would mean that, in wounds or septic areas where there was an exudate of serum, the mould filtrate would lose its activity before it could kill the infecting organisms.

Despite these early indications that the mould product had limitations, Fleming did not slacken his research effort. It was clearly necessary to identify the mould that had visited his laboratory, and to discover if its startling antibacterial powers were peculiar to itself, or were shared by other species and strains. There are thousands of different moulds, and Fleming, like most medical bacteriologists, knew very little about them beyond the fact that they were frequent and tiresome contaminants of bacterial cultures. So Fleming asked La Touche, the mycologist, if he could identify his strange visitor. La Touche concluded that it was one of the penicillia, of which there are scores of different sorts. He came to the conclusion that it was more like a *Penicillium rubrum* than anything else, and there is a note on this in Fleming's notebook in February 1929. Fleming accepted this provisional identification (which was later discovered to be wrong), and his mould became '*P. rubrum*' in his notebooks.

Following the classification of his mould as a *Penicillium*, Fleming coined a new word for its product. 'Mould juice' was not very elegant, and '*Penicillium rubrum* broth culture filtrate' was too cumbersome. So Fleming called its hypothetical active principle 'penicillin', and his choice seems to have been his own, not Wright's. Fleming emphasized that he applied the word to the activity of a crude mixture of substances, and not to a supposed chemical entity. It is all too easy, in scientific research, to create a false sense of reality by creating a name. Fleming did not fall into this trap, but he did believe that the 'penicillin effect' was the lysis of sensitive organisms brought about by something like lysozyme. As he also believed that lysozyme was an enzyme, he might have made his new name end in 'zyme'. Since this was an unhandy termination in this case, he chose instead the suffix 'in', which is also applied to such enzymes as 'trypsin', 'pepsin', and so on. Fleming began to use his new name in February 1929.

A parallel line of investigation was to test the antibacterial power of other moulds. It seemed unlikely, at first, that the strain that had happened to contaminate the original plate should be the only one to produce such a dramatic effect. Fleming collected moulds from everywhere he could think of; from La Touche, of course; from mouldy cheese, jam, old clothes, boots and shoes, old books, old paintings and dust and dirt generally. His search for sources of mould included the Chelsea Arts Club, which provoked a good deal of hilarity there. In all, he tested scores of different moulds classified in six different species. None of them produced any antibacterial activity except for one out of the eight strains of penicillia tested, which seemed to be identical with the original mould and which had been provided by La Touche.[8] It seemed, therefore, that Fleming's mould was something very special. Fortune had favoured him in that, and in much more than that, as will be seen in the following chapter.

Meanwhile, Fleming had set two of his young graduates the task of discovering how to produce the most active mould juice in sufficient quantities to supply his experimental needs, and also to find out something about its chemical properties. One of them was F. Ridley, the opthalmologist who was working on lysozyme, and who had some acquaintance with practical biochemistry. The other was S. R. Craddock, the Research Scholar who had replaced Pryce. Their work on producing crude penicillin and their experiments on its physical and chemical properties are mentioned briefly and occasionally in Fleming's own notes, and acknowledged in his 1929 paper. But he gave no details, either in this paper or later publications. A much fuller account of what they did is given by Ronald Hare in his book *The Birth of Penicillin*, from personal interviews with them some thirty years later, and from notes that they made at the time. The brief description of their work that follows is based on Hare's account.[9]

Although Fleming had instigated their work he gave them surprisingly little practical help. He could not – or at any rate, did not – find them bench-space in a laboratory where they would have had the basic facilities. They had to work on tables in a corridor, with a temporary gas supply through a long rubber tube from a nearby laboratory. The only water was from a tap over a sink, used for washing up, which was in the passage on the floor below, and much of their work was done here on the draining-board.

Despite these difficulties, Ridley and Craddock made good progress. They grew the mould in broth contained in large, flat-sided bottles, and found that the best growth took place at room temperature (about 18°C). The mould grew slowly, forming on the surface of the liquid a fluffy, felted mass over a period of days. Meanwhile the fluid below was acquiring a deepening yellow colour which was related to its increasing antibacterial activity. This reached a maximum in about ten days. Then the liquid was poured off from below the mould, and filtered to remove particles, first through cheese-cloth, then paper and finally forced through the pads of a Seitz-filter with the aid of compressed air supplied by the vigorous use of a bicycle pump. The filtrate was a clear, yellow liquid containing most of the original activity. It also contained all the original water, and the removal of much of this was the first step in concentration.

An easy way for concentrating watery solutions and suspensions – as every cook knows – is to evaporate the water by boiling. Unfortunately the activity of the mould filtrate was rapidly destroyed by heat, but the boiling point of water can be reduced by reducing the air pressure above it. So Ridley and Craddock put their filtrate into an air-tight distillation flask, applied a vacuum pump to the top, and sufficient heat to the bottom to cause rapid evaporation. This is the principle of 'vacuum distillation'. It depends on the efficiency of the pump and the cooling of the condenser. With high efficiency pumps, and condensers cooled in liquid nitrogen or solid carbon dioxide, water boils at 0°C and even ice evaporates rapidly, as in the process of 'freeze-drying'. But in 1928, Ridley and Craddock had to make do with very inefficient pumps, and evaporated their filtrate at 40°C. This produced what Fleming called 'a sticky mass', but it did contain almost all the original activity.

Besides the still hypothetical 'penicillin' this sticky mass contained everything that had been in the broth filtrate, except much of the water. Most of it, in fact, would be unwanted rubbish, such as the protein from the meat extract. If 'penicillin' was an enzyme – which then seemed likely – then it would be a protein too. Proteins are, in general, soluble in water but insoluble in alcohol, so the easiest first step in separating proteins from many non-proteins is to add alcohol to a watery solution of the mixture. This Ridley and Craddock did, and Hare quotes an experiment recorded in their notes for 20 March 1929.[10] They had evaporated 200 ml of filtrate down to 5 ml, and samples from this inhibited staphylococci even when diluted 1 in 3,000. They then added 90 per cent alcohol, and a heavy precipitate formed, which they separated. They tested both the precipitate and the clear supernatant fluid for penicillin activity, and to their surprise found that it was in the latter, that is, the penicillin was soluble in alcohol.

The significance of this discovery was two-fold. Firstly, it showed that penicillin was unlikely to be a protein, and thus unlikely to be an enzyme. Secondly, its solubility in alcohol opened up a convenient method for concentration (since solutions in alcohol could be readily evaporated at low temperatures), and also for partial purification. By taking advantage of these and other differential solubilities, Ridley and Craddock were able to provide Fleming with partially purified penicillin solutions that were active even when diluted 1 in 3,000 or more. But these solutions of crude penicillin were unstable. They lost most of their activity at room temperature within a few days. Then Ridley and Craddock discovered that the stability of their product was greatly influenced by the pH (an index of acidity or alkalinity) of the solutions. As the mould grew in its broth, the fluid became more alkaline (pH 8.5–9.0) and at this pH, vacuum distillation rapidly destroyed the penicillin activity. So they added acid during the process, to keep the pH at about 6.5, and found that slightly acid preparations remained active for several weeks.[11]

Fleming's own notebooks suggest that he took little part in this work by Ridley and Craddock. He titrated the material they produced by testing dilutions of it against a 'standard' culture of staphylococci. He then used it in his own experiments. These were along two distinct lines. The first was essentially bacteriological; the second was on the possible clinical value of an agent that seemed lethal to many pathogenic bacteria but harmless to living animal tissues. It was these bacteriological and clinical experiments that occupied him during the early part of the year 1929.

The Discovery of Penicillin
2. Trials and Errors

During the first three months of 1929, Fleming set out to discover which pathogenic microbes were, and which were not, inhibited by his crude penicillin. He recorded the degree of their sensitivity by simply measuring in millimetres the width of the zone of inhibition from the penicillin-containing gutter on his culture plates. Thus, *Staphylococcus pyogenes* grew up to a point 23 mm from the gutter while the *Bacillus coli* grew right up to it and scored 0 mm.[1] The list of sensitive organisms included the virulent streptococci, staphylococci, pneumococci, meningococci, gonococci and diphtheria bacilli, in that order of sensitivity, ranging from 30 mm for the streptococci to 14 for the diphtheria bacilli. The organisms that seemed quite insensitive included the bacilli of anthrax, typhoid and paratyphoid, bacillus coli and the influenza (Pfeiffer's) bacillus.

There are some obvious gaps in this list. Fleming did not test the anaerobic organisms that cause gas gangrene and tetanus, despite his great interest in them during the war. Nor did he test the tubercle bacillus, the organism that caused more deaths and ill-health in Britain than any other. This was an understandable omission, since the tubercle bacillus takes weeks to grow in culture.

On the purely bacteriological side, the point that took Fleming's fancy was the complete insensitivity of Pfeiffer's bacillus. In this he saw an immediate practical use. Pfeiffer's bacillus was of interest to those who still believed that it caused influenza and other respiratory infections, and used vaccines to combat them. But it was difficult to grow, being fastidious in its cultural tastes, rather delicate, and apt to be over-grown by just the other sorts of organisms likely to be present on throat swabs. In consequence, even if Pfeiffer's bacilli were present, they were apt to be lost. But, if Pfeiffer's bacillus is unaffected by penicillin, while most pathogenic organisms are inhibited, then a separation could be made and a pure vaccine prepared. Fleming, in fact, hit on the idea of incorporating sterile penicillin in the culture medium to isolate Pfeiffer's bacilli. In the presence of this bacteriological 'selective weed-killer' it would grow uninhibited, while most of the other germs on the swabs would be suppressed. Fleming did many experiments on this innovation, and clearly it gave very good results. Soon 'penicillin plates' became a standard medium in his laboratory for investigating throat and chest infections, and the presence or absence of Pfeiffer's bacilli was reported.

Throughout these early months of Fleming's work on his discovery the possible clinical use of penicillin as an antiseptic was very much in his mind. He explored this possibility by exactly the methods he had used to test the value of other new antiseptics. These were: the testing of ability to kill germs in culture; the testing for toxic effects on living leucocytes and, thirdly, the testing of the ability of the antiseptic to kill germs in slide cells containing blood serum. He already knew what penicillin could do to germs in culture, but, as we have seen, it took several hours to achieve its effect. He then discovered that penicillin was harmless to living leucocytes. But he also concluded from slide cell experiments done at the beginning of December 1928, that, in the presence of blood or serum, penicillin rapidly lost its activity.[2] He followed up these observations by further tests for toxicity, and by trying penicillin as a local antiseptic in cases of infection.

The means by which he extended the toxicity tests suggest that initially he had an idea that penicillin might be useful as a systemic antibacterial agent, given by injection like Salvarsan so that it reached all parts of the body. He injected his 'mould broth filtrate' into two animals, giving 20 cc intravenously to a rabbit, and 0.5 cc intraperitoneally to a mouse.[3] He reported that these injections were no more toxic than the same amount of sterile broth. The experiment appears in his 1929 paper, but not in his notebooks, and no precise date can be assigned to it. However, as Hare has recently reported, another animal experiment was recorded by Stuart Craddock. On 22 March 1929 he injected 20 cc of penicillin solution, which had a titre (strength) of 1 in 300, into the ear vein of a rabbit. He took a blood sample from the animal after a minute or so, and found that the penicillin activity in this was 1 in 16, about the level to be expected from simple dilution in the animal's blood volume. But, thirty minutes later, another blood sample showed that almost all the penicillin activity had disappeared.[4]

This experiment, combined with a previous observation by Craddock confirming that penicillin lost 75 per cent of its activity in the presence of serum in slide cell preparations,[5] and with the fact that it needed over four hours to act, must have dashed any hopes that Fleming might have had for it as a systemic antibacterial agent. He did no further animal experiments, and in consequence he did not progress to the sort of protection tests that might well have encouraged him (and others) to great efforts. As noted before, Wright had for years been preaching the supremacy of reason over mere 'random experiments'. Fleming had (or probably thought that he had) good *reason* to suppose that penicillin would be useless in the body. What would be the use of injecting something that takes over four hours to kill bacteria when it is itself destroyed in a few minutes? So he did not do the experiment.

Fleming did, however, pursue the idea of using penicillin as a local antiseptic. As a check on toxicity Craddock, with great fortitude, ate some of the mould that he had grown in milk.[6] He told Hare that it tasted like Stilton cheese, and seemed to be no more toxic. Then a patient with a gastric infection was induced to swallow a similar mould-in-milk diet three times a day. Craddock's impression was that it did him no harm and also, apparently, no good. But the first (and only) record of a clinical test of penicillin to appear in Fleming's notebooks concerns Craddock's own chronically infected nasal antrum.[7] This had troubled him for some months, and he had had an operation in which a permanent opening had been made from the nose to the antrum so that it could drain. Fleming had taken swabs from time to time and, when the infection persisted, suggested irrigating the antrum with penicillin. Craddock agreed, and on 9 January 1929, Fleming recorded the results in his notebook:

'Mould filtrate antiseptic power on Craddock's antrum. (1) Swab from antrum on blood agar, 100 staph with myriads of Pfeiffer around. Then 1 cc mould filtrate into R antrum. Enormous flow of watery fluid from R side of nose for several hours. (2) Swab 3 hours after on blood agar. 1 colony staph and a few colonies Pfeiffer. In films, as many bacteria seen after as before, but mostly phagocytosed.'

The result of this, the first clinical application of penicillin to be recorded, was thus not very conclusive. The reduction in the number of microbes may well have been due to their dilution by the violent flow of fluid, and the equal reduction in the number of Pfeiffer's bacilli (which are insensitive to penicillin) suggests that this was indeed the major factor. Craddock continued to irrigate his antrum with penicillin twice daily for several days with no clinical improvement.

Fleming then tried treating one of the surgical patients in the hospital, who was desperately ill with an infected amputation stump. He irrigated the area with a continuous flow of penicillin, but this did not control the infection, and the patient died of septicaemia.[8] In order to explain, perhaps, the disappointing results of using penicillin as a local antiseptic, Fleming and Craddock did a rather strange experiment on 2 April 1929.[9] They killed a rabbit and incubated its organs in a broth culture of staphylococci. After twenty-four hours the organs were transferred to penicillin solution and incubated for a similar period. They were then washed, sliced, and samples from the centres of the slices cultured. All grew staphylococci. The conclusion was that, while staphylococci can penetrate tissues, penicillin cannot. Thus penicillin applied to an infected surface could not reach organisms that had penetrated below it. The experiment was designed with only this local use in view, and a different result might have been obtained had the penicillin been injected into the rabbit before it was killed.

Then there was a clinical success. An assistant in Fleming's laboratory, Dr K. B. Rogers, developed a pneumococcal conjunctivitis of one of his eyes. He was a member of the rifle team that was due to compete in a shooting match, and Fleming thus had a double reason for treating the marksman's eye with penicillin. He did so, and the infection cleared up almost at once.[10] Rogers was able to take part in the match, but the result of this part of the experiment is not recorded. Fleming himself gave no details of these early clinical applications of penicillin in any of his published papers and, apart from the case of Craddock's antrum, they are not mentioned in his notebooks.

On 13 February 1929, Fleming gave a talk to the Medical Research Club on his new discovery. Its title was 'A medium for the isolation of Pfeiffer's Bacillus', and it can be inferred that he dwelt mostly on the use of his mould as a selective inhibitor in bacteriological cultures. He must have mentioned the wide range of pathogenic organisms that his mould filtrate inhibited in order to make the point that it would be useful to anyone trying to isolate Pfeiffer's bacilli from a mixed culture. The Medical Research Club had heard Fleming describe such technical tricks before, and on this occasion it must have seemed that he had simply discovered a strange mould that inhibited some bacteria but not others, and had used this selectivity very neatly to favour the growth of Pfeiffer's bacillus – an organism that no longer greatly interested the majority of bacteriologists.

When Fleming had finished his talk he waited, as was usual, to answer any question. But his experience when he launched lysozyme at a similar occasion was to be repeated. There were no questions, and no discussion. The reason, almost certainly, was that, as with lysozyme, even those who had been able to hear what Fleming had said, had understood very little of what they heard and nothing at all of its implications. They asked no questions because they could think of nothing sensible to say. No one in the audience, not even Fleming himself, had any idea that this occasion would later be recognized as an historic one. Sir Henry Dale, Director of the National Institute for Medical Research, who was the Chairman at this meeting, admitted years later that he too had sensed nothing of much importance in Fleming's presentation.[11] Dale was in 1929 one of the foremost of physiologists and greatly experienced in recognizing fruitful lines of research. Even for him there were no premonitions.

Meanwhile, Ridley and Craddock were pursuing their experiments on the production and properties of penicillin and supplying Fleming with crude material for his own tests. These activities made very little impression on the other members of the Inoculation Department staff. There was nothing of excitement or urgency in the atmosphere, merely an all-pervasive musty smell from the large quantities of growing mould, and the vapours of the ether and acetone used in the attempts to purify its product. What that product might be did not seem of much interest, and Hare remembers that the main impact of the work on the Department was the physical presence of two large men (both Ridley and Craddock were rugby football forwards) working in the narrow passage and obstructing access to the lavatory.

By April, Fleming was writing up the results of his work, and some of those of Ridley and Craddock, for a paper to be submitted for publication in the *British Journal of Experimental Pathology*. He sent this to the editors – of whom one was Howard Florey – on 10 May 1929, and it appeared a month later in No. 3, Vol. 10, of the *Journal*. Though its publication attracted very little medical or scientific attention at the time – or, indeed, for the next twelve years – it has since become a classic. It is now regarded as one of the most important medical papers ever written, the starting point for a clinical revolution that has affected the lives of almost every human being on earth. Original copies and reprints at present command prices of one or two thousand pounds on the collector's market, and since it is not likely to be readily available to the general public, a brief summary of its contents might be useful.

The title is: 'ON THE ANTIBACTERIAL ACTION OF CULTURES OF A PENICILLIUM WITH SPECIAL REFERENCE TO THEIR USE IN THE ISOLATION OF B. INFLUENZ.E' (The quaint spelling of the last word seems to be a printer's convention in the use of capital letter diphthongs.) The following text occupies thirteen pages, including four pages of tables and illustrations, one of which is a photograph of the original mouldy culture plate. In a thirteen-line introduction Fleming describes how cultures of 'staphylococcus variants . . . were set aside on the laboratory bench and examined from time to time', and how one became contaminated with a mould around which the staphylococcal colonies were 'obviously undergoing lysis'. Observing this he subcultured the mould and found a bacteriolytic activity in the broth in which it had grown, which he proceeded to investigate.

The next section deals with the character of the mould, the colour changes that it undergoes during the first few days of growth, and the production of a deepening yellow colour in the culture fluid. Fleming reports that the broth becomes alkaline during this process, that the yellow pigment is not extracted by chloroform, and that growth is most rapid at 20°C and slow at 37°C. He then states that the mould is a *Penicillium* and most closely resembles *P. rubrum*, a mould 'not uncommon in the air of laboratories'.

In the third section Fleming describes his study of the ability of other moulds to produce a similar antibacterial activity. He tested strains from six different species, including eight strains of *Penicillium*. None of these produced any inhibitory activity, except one of the *Penicillium* strains which 'had exactly the same cultural characters as the original one from the contaminated plate'. He goes on to state that he will use the word 'penicillin' instead of 'mould broth filtrate' throughout the rest of the paper.

The fourth section describes the method for testing antibacterial activity, and the sensitivity of different sorts of bacteria. The titre of the antibacterial activity is recorded as the highest dilution of the preparation that will inhibit the growth of staphylococci in broth. Sensitivity is tested by the gutter plate method, and is recorded by measuring the width of the zone of inhibition for each organism tested.

The fifth section describes the properties of the crude penicillin. Rather surprisingly 'boiling for a few minutes hardly affects its activity', and boiling for an hour reduces its activity to one quarter if the fluid is alkaline, but if it is neutral or slightly acid 'the reduction is much less'. Penicillin can be sterilized by Seitz filtration. It is soluble in water and weak saline. Fleming writes: 'My colleague Mr Ridley has found that if penicillin is evaporated at a low temperature to a sticky mass the active principle can be completely extracted by absolute alcohol. It is insoluble in ether or chloroform.' The rest of this section describes the rate of development of penicillin in mould cultures under different conditions, ordinary nutrient broth and a temperature of 20°C giving the best results. The penicillin titre reached 1 in 800 in six or seven days. Storage of the filtrate at room temperature causes a decline to a titre of 1 in 40 in fifteen days, but if it is made slightly acid (pH 6.8) 'it is much more stable'.

Section six lists the organisms that are, and are not, sensitive to penicillin (which have already been mentioned), and section seven details the rate at which penicillin kills staphylococci. This rate is slow, and even after four and a half hours some of the bacteria are still alive. Fleming concludes that 'penicillin belongs to the group of slow-acting antiseptics'.

The eighth section (consisting of ten lines) deals with the toxicity of penicillin, and its injection without ill-effects into a rabbit and a mouse, its non-irritation of infected surfaces and the human conjunctiva, and the lack of interference with leucocyte function.

The next two sections (9 and 10) occupy two and a half pages, and deal with the use of penicillin as a selective culture reagent in the isolation of B. influenzae and other penicillin-insensitive organisms. There are details of twenty-five cases of supposed influenza investigated by this technique.

There follows a discussion section, which examines briefly the main findings. It includes a reference to one previous example of an antibacterial agent produced by a living organism, the 'pyocyanase' described in 1902 by Emmerich and his colleagues. This was produced by cultures of B. pyocyaneus, and it inhibited the growth of the bacilli of anthrax, diphtheria, cholera, and typhoid, but only feebly. It is in this discussion section that Fleming writes:

'Penicillin, in regard to infections with sensitive microbes, appears to have some advantages over the well-known chemical antiseptics. A good sample will completely inhibit staphylococci, streptococcus pyogenes and pneumococcus in a dilution of 1 in 800. It is therefore a more powerful inhibitory agent than is carbolic acid and it can be applied to an infected surface undiluted as it is non-irritant and non-toxic. If applied, therefore, on a dressing, it will still be effective even when diluted 800 times, which is more than can be said of the chemical antiseptics in use. Experiments in connection with its value in the treatment of pyogenic infections are in progress. In addition to its possible use in the treatment of bacterial infections penicillin is certainly useful to the bacteriologist for its power of inhibiting unwanted microbes in bacterial cultures . . .'

Fleming concludes the paper by thanking Ridley and Craddock 'for their help in carrying out some of the experiments' and La Touche 'for his suggestion as to the identity of the penicillium'. Finally, there is a ten-point summary, and No. 8 in this runs as follows: 'It is suggested that it [penicillin] may be an efficient antiseptic for application to, or injection into, areas infected with penicillin-sensitive microbes.' It seems that when Fleming submitted the paper to Wright, who, as head of the department, had to approve its publication, Wright objected to the inclusion of this therapeutic suggestion as being pure speculation. But Fleming stood his ground, Wright gave way, and the reference to the therapeutic possibilities of penicillin was retained.

Many years later, when the story of the discovery of penicillin was written and rewritten for the general public, Fleming's epoch-making paper in the *British Journal of Experimental Pathology* was referred to with uncritical reverence. Maurois, in his 1959 biography, described it as 'a triumph of clarity, sobriety and precision'.[12] This opinion is a general one, but it is dazzled by a knowledge of the tremendous consequences of what Fleming had written, and it is not an objective assessment of the paper as a scientific contribution in its 1929 setting.

One might consider, in this connection, what is expected of scientific papers, and why scientists publish them. On the latter point, the most altruistic motive is a desire to give freely to the world the results of some research that may be of academic or practical value. A less altruistic – but quite understandable – motive is the desire to stake a personal claim to a discovery and thus receive recognition and prestige if it proves to be important. There may be material benefit in the form of professional advancement for scientists making important and original discoveries, but it should be said that medical scientists in Britain prior to about 1950 neither expected nor received any financial reward for even commercially profitable discoveries.

As to what is expected of scientific papers, they should be written in such a way that the reader, if he wished, would be able to answer the three questions posed by all supposed contributions to scientific knowledge: 'Is it true? Is it new? Is it important?' Thus, the observations and experiments must be described with sufficient detail and precision to allow other workers to repeat the work and confirm – or refute – the findings. And these findings must be related to what other workers have found in the past, so that the matter of originality can be judged. On the question of importance there may be no certain or quick answer. Some discoveries have an immediate and self-evident importance, others (like penicillin) reveal their value only after years of obscurity.

How would one of Fleming's fellow-scientists have judged his paper when he read it in 1929? In general, he would have found it a well-arranged and admirably brief account of an intriguing phenomenon of the sort that Fleming had previously described when studying lysozyme. But, unlike lysozyme, which is widely distributed in nature and is of general interest in the study of natural immunity to bacterial invasion, the penicillin phenomenon seemed to be peculiar to one sort of mould which was itself peculiar to Fleming's laboratory. And if the reader had wished to repeat Fleming's observations and experiments he would have found it difficult to discover exactly what he had done. The circumstances of the original discovery, for example, are not clearly stated and, as usually interpreted, cannot be repeated. It is, in fact, almost impossible to 'discover' penicillin in the way that Fleming seems to describe – a matter that will be discussed later, in Chapter 21.

Next, the reader wishing to learn more of the production, properties and partial purification of crude penicillin would find a tantalizing lack of experimental detail. Though Fleming describes a method for 'accurately titrating' its activity he gives no figures when referring to the effect of heat, pH, and the concentration experiments of Ridley and Craddock. Nor does he say exactly how Ridley produced his 'sticky mass' except that it was by 'evaporation at low temperature' – the temperature itself and the need for a vacuum are not specified. Fleming records the very important fact that the active material can be extracted from this mass by alcohol, but does not mention the titre achieved, so that what was gained by this process is in doubt. It would be (and actually was) very difficult for later workers to repeat the experiments in these sections of the paper. When they came to do so, some errors were revealed. The mould, for example, turned out to be a strain of *Penicillium notatum*, not *P. rubrum* as Fleming had supposed. This mistake was not, of course, his fault and was not in any case very important. But when Fleming wrote that penicillin was insoluble in ether or chloroform he was proved wrong and this was not the fault of Ridley and Craddock. Fleming had, in fact, misquoted his young collaborators, whose notebooks show that they had found penicillin to be soluble in ether and acetone, and had not tried chloroform as a solvent when Fleming wrote his paper. This lapse suggests that Fleming was not closely in touch with the biochemical work, despite the fact that Craddock gave him regular written reports.

On the bacteriological sections of the paper, the reader would have agreed that they were clear and precise – Fleming was an excellent bacteriologist. And Maurois's word 'sobriety' would have been appropriate to the paper as a whole. Fleming nowhere makes extravagant claims. He went no further than to write of penicillin that, while it might possibly be useful in the treatment of infections, it was certainly of practical use to the bacteriologist. He himself had proved the latter point, and the former – as he emphasized – was no more than a possibility. The reader would have recognized that a demonstrably non-toxic agent capable of killing microbes in culture might well be useful as an antiseptic – but this had to be shown by actual experiment, and such experiments were, Fleming wrote, in progress. The results of these would, the reader might suppose, be published later. What he did not learn from this paper was that Fleming already had evidence suggesting to him that penicillin would be destroyed in the body before it had time to kill any microbes there.

On the final question, 'Is it new?', the reader would have found no answer in Fleming's paper, and he would wish to know how his discovery fitted into its historical context. There are thousands of different sorts of moulds, and there had been hundreds of bacteriologists at work since about 1870, all of whom must have had their bacterial cultures contaminated by these ubiquitous but unwanted visitors to, or inhabitants of, their laboratories. Though most bacteriologists regard moulds with the lack of enthusiasm felt by most gardeners for weeds, surely if particular moulds could not only contaminate bacterial cultures but destroy them, someone, sometime, would have noticed it. Or was Fleming's mould unique? Fleming was silent on the question of previous observations. On the possibly very rare properties of his mould he is again tantalizingly indefinite. One of the eight strains of *Penicillium* that he tested had an activity similar to his original mould and had 'exactly the same cultural characters'. Was it, in fact, the original mould still lurking in the building, or was it from another source altogether? The answer would have determined its rarity or relative abundance.

On the historical side, Fleming was probably silent (apart from his reference to pyocyanase) because he spent more time at his bench than in the dusty stacks of a library. But the Royal Society of Medicine, of which he was a Fellow, had a splendid library where he might have found a book by Papacostas and Gaté, published in France a year before, in 1928, on the extensive subject of bacterial inhibition by moulds and by other bacteria.[13] A sixty-page section of this book is headed 'Antibiosis' – a word coined in 1889 by Vuillemin – and is devoted to previously published observations on this phenomenon with several hundred historical references. Fleming could therefore have covered the historical background to his discovery with a single reference to this book in his paper. The reader, so directed, could then have learned that scores of other bacteriologists had made very similar observations, some by almost exactly the methods used by Fleming and that there had been many attempts to use such 'antibiotic' activity for the treatment of human or animal infections. Several of these previous workers had, like him, tried to extract the active agents but they had gone further than he did and had tested their products by injecting them into animals together with virulent organisms.

Though the monograph by Papacostas and Gaté is packed with information on its subject, records of some of the earliest attempts to treat infections with mould were only dug out of the archives when the eventual triumph of penicillin focused the attention of medical historians on its origins. There was a centuries-old 'folk-medicine' tradition that various mouldy substances cured infections, but what must have been one of the earliest scientific investigations of an effect on bacteria was by Sir John Burdon-Sanderson, who had for several years worked at St Mary's Hospital, Paddington. In 1871 he reported that culture fluids exposed to the air became turbid with growing bacteria but that if moulds of the *Penicillium* group happened to appear on the surface no bacterial growth occurred.[14] Joseph Lister was stimulated by this observation to study the matter himself. Working in Edinburgh he confirmed that the growth of a mould that he identified as *Penicillium glaucum* caused the disappearance of bacteria from liquid cultures.[15] The possible clinical application of such a phenomenon was as clear for Lister then as it was for Fleming nearly sixty years later. In 1872 Lister wrote to his brother about his search for a non-toxic antiseptic and ended: 'Should a suitable case present, I shall endeavour to employ *Penicillium glaucum* and observe if the growth of the organisms be inhibited in the human tissues.'[16] Though he did use his mould cultures in this way he did not publish the results. Details of one case, however, came to light in 1940, when a former patient of Lister's described to Dr Fraser-Moodie the treatment she had received from him at King's College Hospital, in 1884, when she was a young nurse. Injured in a street accident, she sustained a wound that became infected and refused to heal. Various antiseptics failed to clear the infection and then something was used that worked so dramatically well that she asked Lister's registrar to write the name of it in her scrap-book. The entry in the book, which she showed to Fraser-Moodie, was 'Penicillium'.[17]

Following these early efforts to harness the antibacterial power of a *Penicillium*, there were scores of others along similar lines, that were duly recorded and published. Pasteur and Joubert, in 1877, experimenting with the prevention of anthrax wrote of the great therapeutic possibilities of bacterial antagonism.[18] Garré in 1887 recorded other examples of such antagonism and devised a method for demonstrating it that was very like the one described by Fleming in 1929.[19] Tiberio, in Naples, made extracts of *Penicillium* moulds in 1895, showed that they inhibited virulent bacteria, and then tested them by injecting them into experimentally infected animals.[20] But the results, though encouraging, were not very convincing. In 1897, Duchesne, a young French army doctor, described the protective action of *Penicillium glaucum* when injected into animals together with normally lethal doses of virulent bacteria. He stressed the obvious therapeutic possibilities, but he himself died of tuberculosis before he could explore them.[21]

Many accounts of similar observations and trials were published during the next thirty years, and most can be found in the monograph by Papacostas and Gaté. In general, it can be said that the various antibacterial agents extracted from moulds, soil bacteria, and other organisms were either too feeble or too toxic to be effective systemic antibiotics. At the least, several workers had done animal protection tests, injecting their products into infected animals to see if they could kill the invading bacteria in the body. By this crucial test they discovered what these products could and could not do.

On the evidence of Fleming's paper there was no reason to suppose that his mould product would be any more effective than the many others that had already been described, because he had not done the comparable animal protection tests. To anyone familiar with the field, his contribution could not be expected to stand out as being either new or important. As it later transpired, his mould was indeed a very important and special one, but in 1929 he had not produced the evidence to show that this was the case, nor did he do so during the ten years that followed.

Ridley and Craddock stopped working on penicillin after a few months. Ridley returned to his work on lysozyme and published two papers on it in 1929. He left St Mary's in 1930, joining the staff at Moorfield's Eye Hospital. Craddock continued to work with Fleming, mainly on the use of penicillin in the isolation of the acne bacillus for the preparation of vaccines, and many experiments on this application are recorded in their notebooks. Then Craddock, too, left St Mary's in 1930, having obtained with Fleming's help an appointment at the Wellcome Research laboratories at Beckenham. There were no reasons, other than declining interest, why the work on penicillin by Ridley and Craddock should have lapsed, as it did, after only four months.

Strangely, it was Fleming's insistence on the usefulness of penicillin as a laboratory reagent that in the end proved to be of crucial importance to its ultimate development as the first effective antibiotic. Despite the general lack of interest in his paper, a number of bacteriologists in Britain and abroad wrote to Fleming asking for samples of the mould that would help them to isolate the elusive *B. influenzae*. Fleming thus not only kept his own culture of this particular mould going, but saw it established in other laboratories. He sent cultures, for example, to the Lister Institute, to Georges Dreyer's School of Pathology in Oxford and to Sheffield University Medical School, and on these cultures further research would be done in later years. Without the continued preservation of Fleming's strain of mould, his paper would have been no more than the record of an unrepeatable episode – a scientific anecdote. For Fleming's strain had the ability to produce penicillin at a level that put it in a class of its own, and it was one so rare that it would have been most unlikely to be rediscovered.

Twelve Busy Years

By the summer of 1929, Fleming seemed to have abandoned penicillin as a main research interest. In the five months to March 1929, he had filled forty-eight pages in his notebook with his own experiments on penicillin, and some of those of Ridley and Craddock. Then there was a gap until September, when there were three pages of experiments on the antibacterial power of penicillin compared with some chemical antiseptics. There are no available records of any penicillin work during 1930, but in 1931 there were ten pages in all, recording experiments on preserving penicillin solutions for use in selective culture media and, on 14 June, the important discovery that penicillin inhibited the anaerobic organisms causing gas gangrene. This seems to be the first such observation, but it remained unpublished. During 1932 there were five brief references to the routine bacteriological use of penicillin, and during the next four years it was referred to, in the same context, three times.

But, although he did not mention this in his notebooks, Fleming did try the effect of penicillin as a local antiseptic in an unrecorded number of cases between 1929 and 1931. The only evidence for this comes from his own brief references in later papers and lectures. In 1932, in the *Journal of Pathology*, he wrote: 'It [penicillin] has been used in a number of indolent septic wounds and has certainly appeared to be superior to dressings containing potent chemicals.'[1] Referring, presumably to the same cases, in a lecture to the Royal Society of Medicine in 1941, he said: 'It was used as a dressing on a few septic wounds with favourable results, but as in peace time septic wounds are uncommon in hospital and as the potency of penicillin rapidly disappears on keeping, the therapeutic aspect of this substance was dropped.'[2] Finally, in his Harben Lectures in 1945, he said: 'We tried it tentatively on a few old sinuses in the hospital, and although the results were favourable, there was nothing miraculous.'[3] These, Fleming's only published references to his early clinical work with penicillin, do not convey any sense of great effort or enthusiasm either on his part or that of the clinicians to whom he offered it. One cannot avoid the conclusion that neither side had much confidence in penicillin as a therapeutic agent.

It is, perhaps, not surprising that Fleming's crude penicillin used in this way was unimpressive. He, himself, had shown that local antiseptics cannot penetrate into infected wounds and are washed away by the natural exudate. But, in special situations, penicillin can be effective locally, as Fleming had shown when he had treated Rogers' infected eye so successfully. In conjunctivitis the infection is superficial. Penicillin drops can be instilled into the eye easily, frequently and harmlessly and if the infecting organism is sensitive it can usually be eliminated in a few hours. It is strange that Fleming did not pursue this line, particularly since Ridley, who worked with him, was an ophthalmologist. They could have collected a series of cases, the amount of penicillin needed would have been small, and success very likely. It was an opportunity let slip.

So Fleming had practical evidence that penicillin was 'nothing miraculous' as a local antiseptic and he must have dismissed it – on theoretical grounds – as a systemic antiseptic given by injection. In 1931 he gave a lecture at the Royal Society of Medicine on 'The Intravenous Use of Germicides'.[4] In this he listed the various chemicals that doctors had given by injection in the hope that they would kill invading bacteria without harming the patient, a hope that he showed to be a vain one. He dismissed antiseptics such as mercurochrome, sanacrysin, flavine, gentian violet and Neosalvarsan as virtually useless when injected, but predicted that there might be some hope in the future for certain mercurial compounds. He did not, in these speculations on the future, even mention penicillin as a possible systemic antibacterial agent. However, he did make one tentative prediction that it might prove to be locally useful. In a paper to the *British Dental Journal* in 1931, on some problems in the use of antiseptics, he wrote: 'Penicillin is valuable to us at present in the isolation of certain microbes, but it is quite likely that it, or a chemical of similar nature, will be used in the treatment of septic wounds.'[5]

In 1932 he was elected President of the Section of Pathology in the Royal Society of Medicine. This was, of course, an honour, showing the high regard that London pathologists felt for him. The post entailed presiding at the Section's regular meetings, and also the delivering of a Presidential Address, which could be on any subject of the new president's choosing. Fleming chose to talk about his work on lysozyme and gave an admirable review.[6]

In 1932, also, Fleming published the second of the only two papers that he wrote on penicillin before 1942, a description in the *Journal of Pathology and Bacteriology* of the use of penicillin with potassium tellurite in the selective culture of certain bacteria.[7] He gave several demonstrations of these methods in his spectacularly pictorial style, contriving that the organisms selected by the different media should announce themselves by growing in the forms of their initial letters.

In 1930, Fleming's name had reappeared on the list of Royal Society candidates. Having failed, on five occasions, to be elected in the years 1923–27, his certificate had lapsed for three years, and Wright had now proposed him for the second time, citing the recent work on penicillin in support of his claims.[8] But, as before, Fleming was not successful in being elected, either in 1930, or in the four following years, and his candidature lapsed once more. Penicillin at that time had no general scientific interest – no new principles seemed to be involved – and it had no apparent medical application apart from its use to bacteriologists.

Meanwhile, penicillin had become of academic interest to a professional biochemist. Harold Raistrick had been appointed as the first Professor of Biochemistry at the London School of Hygiene and Tropical Medicine, in Bloomsbury, in 1929. A former pupil of Sir Frederick Gowland Hopkins at Cambridge, Raistrick had become a pioneer in the field of the chemistry of moulds and their products. Within a few years he had isolated sixteen previously unknown organic compounds produced by moulds, and as some of these had commercial value he had accepted a post at the Nobel laboratories in Ayrshire. But he was more interested in chemistry than in commerce, and was glad to return to an academic post in London University.

Fleming's paper describing the strangely acting and highly coloured product of a mould appeared just as Raistrick was planning a research into chemically active mould pigments with P. W. Clutterbuck, a biochemist, and J. H. V. Charles, a mycologist. It seems that the Professor of Bacteriology, W. W. C. Topley, drew his attention to it,[9] and Raistrick naturally added Fleming's mould to his list. Since a feature was its antibacterial activity, which would have to be measured, Topley agreed that one of his own young bacteriologists, Reginald Lovell, should help with this aspect when the need arose. The aim of the proposed research was essentially biochemical, and without regard to any possible clinical use for a purified product. Despite later statements to the contrary, it was not instigated by Fleming, who has said himself that he did not know Raistrick at that time, and did not approach him.[10] And Raistrick had been told at the outset by his clinical colleagues that penicillin was too unstable and ineffective to be of medical use.[11] This in no way reduced his biochemical interest, and he and his team began work on it early in 1930.

The first requirement was a sample of Fleming's mould, which he was glad to give them when asked. On examining it, Raistrick and Charles became doubtful of its identification as *Penicillium rubrum*. They obtained a culture of *P. crysogenum*, which they thought more closely resembled Fleming's mould, but when they found that this did not produce penicillin, they sought the advice of the American mycologist, Dr Charles Thom, sending him on 14 May a sample of Fleming's mould for his opinion. Thom decided that it was a variant of *Penicillium notatum* – a rare variant, evidently, since his own strains of *P. notatum*, which he sent to Raistrick, did not produce penicillin either.

This re-classification by the world's leading authority was an academic rather than a practical advance – the biochemical problems remained. Fleming, when he heard of it, had to change his terminology in the 1932 paper on penicillin and tellurite in selective culture techniques. The change embarrassed La Touche, who wrote a letter of apology to Fleming for having misled him. It also gave later biographers scope for imagination. Maurois writes:

'Fleming learned from Thom's book that the *penicillium notatum* had been originally recognised by a Swedish chemist, Westling, on a specimen of decayed hyssop. This reminded Fleming, the Covenanter, of Psalm 51: "Purge me with hyssop and I shall be clean" – the first known reference to penicillin.'[12]

Ian Curteis in his television 'Biography of Sir Alexander Fleming' has the following conversation between Wright and Fleming, but antedated to the time of the original discovery in 1928:

'Wright: "What is the stuff, anyway?" Fleming: "I think it's a *Penicillium* – *Penicillium notatum* or something like that. First identified by Westling on a piece of the herb, hyssop". Wright: "Purge me with hyssop and I shall be clean . . ." Fleming: "Psalms". Wright: "Fifty-three". Fleming: "Fifty-one". Wright: "Fifty-three". (pause) Fleming: "Verse seven".'[13]

Having established their mould culture, the Raistrick team worked through and largely confirmed the experiments described in Fleming's paper. Lovell modified the bacteriological titration method by using pneumococci – an organism of which he had considerable experience – rather than the staphylococci used by Fleming. But Fleming's paper gave very little information on the biochemical work done by Ridley and Craddock and it seems that Fleming, despite several telephone calls from Lovell asking for bacteriological advice, told him nothing about their findings. In consequence, the team had to discover for themselves much of what Ridley and Craddock had discovered before.

The first technical advance was the finding that the mould would grow well in a synthetic culture medium, 'Czapek-Dox', containing only simple chemicals and glucose. From this the mould products could be separated more easily than from the biochemically messy meat broth. The second 'discovery' was that the yellow pigment had no antibacterial activity, but unknown to Raistrick, this had already been observed by Ridley and Craddock.[14] Raistrick's first interest centred on this pigment. Many experiments followed over a period of several months: it was identified as chrysogenin and some information on its chemical structure was obtained. The next product to be studied was a protein – also without antibacterial power – known as 'alkali-soluble protein', which was of some biochemical interest. Only when it, too, had been characterized did the team start to investigate the third mould product – penicillin.

Using his penicillin-sensitive pneumococci, Lovell found that the filtrate from the Czapek-Dox cultures had an antibacterial titre of up to 1 in 1,280. The crude solution lost half its activity in seven days, even when kept at 0°C, and the titre was down to a quarter of the original in three months. But if the solution was made slightly acid (pH 6.8) it could be kept for months at 0°C without loss of activity – another rediscovery of Ridley and Craddock's work, which from this point Raistrick and his team continued unknowingly to duplicate. Like them, they used vacuum distillation – but with better equipment – and like them they discovered the importance of adding acid during the process. Like them they found that the active material could be extracted by alcohol, and also by ether – despite Fleming's misstatement. Solubility in ether was then found to be dependent on pH. In alkaline solutions the penicillin was not extracted by shaking with ether, whereas in slightly acid solutions it was.

Having got their penicillin into solution in ether, Raistrick's team believed that the way would then be clear to obtain it in a more concentrated and purified form. But this expectation was short-lived. They soon found that the penicillin dissolved in ether was elusive. The ether could be evaporated in a current of air at low temperature, but when the ether had gone the penicillin seemed to have gone with it. Raistrick is quoted as saying 'Such a thing was never known to a chemist before. It was unbelievable. We could do nothing in the face of it, so we dropped it and went on with our other investigations and experiments'.[15]

This dropping of the project has been labelled a 'defeat' or a 'failure' by later writers who have given the impression that Fleming's work was depending on Raistrick's success. But this is a false picture. Raistrick had not set out to purify penicillin as such; it was for him only one of three chemical products of only one of the several moulds in his programme of research. When its behaviour indicated a probably strange molecular structure it became apparent that a full-scale attack would be needed to unravel it. To mount this would mean a change of direction for several people and Raistrick judged that the academic results would be unlikely to justify the effort. As for a possible therapeutic importance, this was, at that time, not a serious consideration. There was no evidence to suggest that it should be.

Clutterbuck, Lovell and Raistrick (in alphabetical order) published a paper in the *Biochemical Journal* in 1932, entitled 'The formation from glucose by members of the *Penicillium chrysogenum* series of a pigment, an alkali-soluble protein and penicillin – the antibacterial substance of Fleming'.[16] This title indicates that penicillin was not the only, or even the main, interest of the authors, and none of them continued to work on it. While they were preparing their paper for publication they were shocked and saddened by the death in a street accident of their colleague, J. H. V. Charles. But there is no reason to suppose that his death was a factor in ending their interest in penicillin. Lovell returned to his work with Topley until the autumn of 1933, when he took up the staff appointment at the Royal Veterinary College arranged during the previous year. Though he did nothing further on penicillin, he seems to have had an inkling of its therapeutic possibilities. In an interview with David Masters in 1945 he said that an animal protection test had been in his mind in 1932. He produced a card from his index referring to a paper describing the protective action of an antipneumococcal enzyme on mice infected by virulent pneumococci bearing a note written by himself 'N.B. for penicillin filtrate'. But, like Fleming, he did not do the experiment.[17]

During the early thirties, Fleming had many things to think about besides penicillin and his continuing research on lysozyme. The Inoculation Department – indeed, the whole of St Mary's Hospital Medical School – was in a state of flux. From its apparently moribund condition in 1922, when it was threatened with closure, Charles Wilson, the Dean, had revived the School to an astonishing degree. St Mary's was constantly in the news as the winner of many sporting contests, and young men anxious to distinguish themselves on the football field were soon clamouring for admission. But, as already noted, the rising intake of students put a strain on teaching accommodation that had scarcely altered for seventy years. The old Medical School building in South Wharf Road had never been prepossessing, and age had not improved it. The brick walls were blackened by soot, and inside them the stone corridors were cold and draughty, and windows and skylights were so coated with grime that little natural light penetrated to the dissecting room, the laboratories or the archaic, wooden-benched lecture theatre. Open coal fires – seldom lit – were the only source of heat.

Wilson was determined to improve this dismal setting for his beloved school. As always at St Mary's, the main obstacle was lack of money. But it was also a St Mary's principle never to allow the inability to pay to hinder the start of an expansion. In 1928 the hospital had acquired from the Canal Company a large triangular site between Praed Street and South Wharf Road on the other side of Norfolk Place from its existing buildings. The cost was £65,000 which was raised by public appeals, flag days energetically promoted by students and nurses and gifts from various charities. Wilson saw that when this site had been cleared, it would be a magnificent one for the building of a new medical school and also for new laboratories into which the Inoculation Department could move. This would allow the space occupied by Wright and his staff in the Clarence Wing to become the clinical wards for which it had been originally designed.

Wilson approached the University Grants Committee and began to canvass his many rich friends. One of these was Lord Revelstoke, the merchant banker. Wilson dined with him and was sufficiently persuasive to obtain a gift of £25,000. Lord Beaverbrook was another, and he, in a characteristic reaction to Wilson's soliciting, decided to visit St Mary's unknown and unescorted, to see the place for himself. After looking into various wards and laboratories he went down to the Outpatient Department. Going up to the small canteen which provided tea for the patients, he asked how much he would have to pay for a bun. 'Three halfpence,' said the elderly lady behind the counter. Then, looking more closely at one of the richest men in Britain, she added: 'But if you can't afford that, you can have one for nothing.' Beaverbrook was delighted.[18] He invited Wilson to come to see him and, when he arrived, asked him how much more money was needed to build the new medical school. Wilson did a sum on the back of an envelope and replied '£63,000'. Beaverbrook signed a covenant for that amount there and then.

With these funds at his disposal and £10,000 from the University Grants Committee, Wilson organized the planning and building of lavish accommodation for his students and their teachers. There were comfortable lecture theatres, modern practical class-rooms, a generous library, a fine swimming-pool, common-rooms and a restaurant. The part of the site adjoining Praed Street was offered to the Inoculation Department. Wright, Fleming and Freeman planned the laboratory of their dreams, where there would be no need for research to be done on tables in corridors, or for patients waiting for tests or vaccines to queue up on the staircase. It was only necessary to pay for it.

In June 1931, the foundation stone of the new combined building was laid by the Duchess of York (later Queen Elizabeth and now the Queen Mother), and it was opened on 12 December 1933, by King George V. It was a handsome, five-floor building in brick with stone facings, and its first floor was connected with the Clarence Wing by a bridge across Norfolk Place. The northern part of the block housed the medical school, the southern part, adjoining Praed Street, contained the new Inoculation Department, as part of a revived Institute of Pathology.

Thus, all the old laboratories in the Clarence Wing moved across the bridge to palatial new quarters. But the 'Inoculation Wards' that provided Wright and his staff with hospital beds – a rare arrangement for a pathologist – remained under his direction. Moving lock, stock and barrel from one laboratory building to another is disruptive of research and Fleming's notebooks showed a marked reduction in his experimental work for the years 1933–35. At the official opening of the new building, with Their Majesties to be shown the work of his department, Wright had decreed that his staff should set up impressive and instructive demonstrations. Fleming, however, indulged his leanings towards light relief. He prepared a display of his by-then famous 'germ paintings' created by the patterned growth of highly pigmented bacteria. There were minute rock gardens ablaze with colour, landscapes (including a picture of The Dhoon), dancing ballerinas and – in view of the royal occasion – a red, white and blue Union Jack. Queen Mary was rather puzzled by all this. As she moved away from its inspection, she was heard to say 'Yes – but what *good* is it?' Fleming seems to have been unabashed, and used to enjoy telling the story.[19]

The cost of the new laboratories, £105,000, was raised by the Inoculation Department itself, and apparently without much difficulty. Lord Iveagh, Chairman of its Committee, personally gave £40,000, other well-wishers £22,000, and the balance of £43,000 came from the surplus funds of the Department. This very healthy surplus, coupled with the fact that the Department had paid all its own running costs, the salaries of seven doctors and fifteen technicians, rent to the hospital and the laboratory expenses of a number of visiting research workers, shows how profitable its main source of income was. This source was, of course, the production and sales of vaccines.

It is quite proper that the profits from the commercial exploitation of research should be ploughed back to support further research – as was done in such famous centres as the Lister and Pasteur Institutes, as well as at St Mary's. But there is a tendency to keep this mundane profitability out of sight and, if possible, out of minds tuned to the higher things of pure research. That there was an efficient vaccine factory within the walls of the Inoculation Department was unsuspected by many of Wright's visitors, and unemphasized even by his staff. Hare writes that it was only during the occasional visits of Parke, Davis officials 'that we realized that there was a factory just next door to the laboratory in which we were working'.[20] W. M. Hughes, in his book on Fleming, refers to 'the factory on the third floor of the building and in the basement' where vaccines were prepared, and to the fact that penicillin was made there 'every week since its discovery'.[21] Fleming, though he said very little about this side of his work, had been in charge of the production of vaccines since 1920, and Hughes points out that the whole research programme depended on their sale. It was an extremely responsible job, since any mistake could be disastrous. Fleming had an excellent production staff of technicians controlled with military discipline by an ex-RAMC sergeant who had been with him in Boulogne. Against such a background Fleming's interest in penicillin for selective culture (rather than clinical use) can be explained, and also its routine weekly production for this purpose. It allowed him to isolate with much greater ease and precision the influenza, acne and whooping cough bacilli which were in good demand for vaccines.

In 1934 Lewis Holt, a biochemist, joined the staff of the new laboratory to work with Almroth Wright on the cause of scurvy, and with Fleming on the production of staphylococcal toxoid [vaccine prepared from toxin made harmless by chemical treatment]. In the course of this work Fleming showed him the lethal effect of crude penicillin on staphylococci, and Holt was intrigued. Fleming then suggested that he should read the paper by

Raistrick and his colleagues and try himself to extend their work. He did not, however, mention the experiments of Ridley and Craddock in his own laboratory. Holt was quite willing, and seems to have been an independent and original worker. He made no attempt to follow the line taken by Raistrick's team, but went straight to the extraction of penicillin from broth filtrate by shaking it with amyl acetate at a slightly acid pH, when the penicillin passed readily into the solvent. It was at this stage, but using ether, that Raistrick's team had stopped. Holt, however, made a most original move of the sort that seems obvious in retrospect. If penicillin passes from water to solvent only when the water is acid, perhaps it would pass back from solvent to water if the water is made alkaline. And this argument proved to be correct. Holt got his penicillin back from its solution in amyl acetate by shaking it with alkaline water. In so doing he removed most of the unwanted impurities and would have been well on the way to success. But he was discouraged by the lack of stability of his product and since Fleming took no great interest in his work, and Wright thought that he was misusing his time, he abandoned it after only a few weeks. Nothing was said about his results, either by Fleming in his lectures and papers, or by Holt himself until Hare, many years later, obtained the information from him.[22]

At this time (1934) Fleming was much preoccupied with vaccines in a literary as well as in a research and production context. He was the co-author, with G. F. Petrie of the Lister Institute, of a 400-page book, *Recent Advances in Serum and Vaccine Therapy*, in which his section ran to 66,000 words with nearly 400 references.[23] This very extensive review gave a complete account of the theory and practice of the use of vaccines and must have occupied much time and energy. Fleming also published a summarized version in *The Practitioner* in the same year.[24]

Fleming's diary for January 1935, records an exciting foreign excursion.[25] His friend and admirer, Dr M. Y. Young, had worked in his laboratory while medical adviser to King Feisal of Iraq, and it was through him that Fleming received an official invitation (including expenses) to attend the ceremonial opening of a new oil pipeline, as the guest of the Iraqi government. He travelled by air, then an unusual form of public transport, and described the beautiful sight of the Swiss Alps below him on his way to Rome. There he broke his journey to attend a medical congress, and with other delegates was received by the Pope – the first of several papal receptions that he was later to experience. His diary records no details other than place names and dates, but he visited Jerusalem on his way to Baghdad. He returned via Damascus, Beirut, Haifa and Alexandria. On crossing the River Jordan he obtained a sample of its water for use in the forthcoming baptism of the newly-arrived son of his friends, the Allisons. It duly fulfilled this function at the Presbyterian Church in St John's Wood, London, in March. But Allison records that Fleming had first sterilized it by filtration.[26] His bacteriological caution had evidently overcome any Presbyterian faith in the holy purity of its origin.

In 1935 there came the first news of an impending revolution in the treatment of bacterial disease – the emergence of chemotherapy. Chemotherapy had existed as a concept since Ehrlich's development of Salvarsan, and there had been continued efforts to produce chemicals that would be as effective in the body against common bacterial infections as Salvarsan had been against syphilis. Leonard Colebrook, Fleming's friend and colleague at St Mary's, had a grant from the Medical Research Council to work on the treatment of puerperal fever and he, with Ronald Hare as assistant, was director of a research unit at Queen Charlotte's Maternity Hospital. Puerperal fever, despite all precautions, still occurred in about 1 per cent of all maternity cases, and had a mortality of 25 per cent. The infecting organism was usually a streptococcus, and Colebrook, with incurable optimism, tried each new antibacterial compound as it was produced, but with little or no success.

Unknown to most doctors, work on the possible antibacterial power of certain synthetic dyes had been proceeding quietly in the laboratories of the Bayer pharmaceutical firm (a subsidiary of the giant I.G. Farbenindustrie) near Düsseldorf. There, Gerhard Domagk had been testing new compounds as they were produced by the firm's industrial chemists. It was a laborious, hit-or-miss type of research which Almroth Wright saw with disdain when he visited Domagk. He returned to St Mary's with the story of huge laboratories in which compound after compound was tested on thousands of infected animals.[27] To Wright, who believed that human reason was the only light that could show the way forward in research, such groping in the dark was a form of sacrilege. But it was precisely this sort of groping that revealed the power of Prontosil – no arm-chair logic could have done so. The logical idea behind the work was that dyes capable of staining textiles might also stain bacteria and do them harm but, as it happens, that is not how Prontosil worked.

Domagk discovered the antibacterial effect of Prontosil because he had reverted to Ehrlich's method of testing drugs on infected animals instead of relying on easier tests on bacteria in culture. In the course of this work he made the exciting observation that certain azo dyes containing a sulphonamide group, when given by mouth or by injection had the ability to protect mice from streptococcal infection. The most effective of these dyes was sulphamido-chrysoidin, a richly red compound with the trade name of Prontosil. Domagk published a brief account of this work in 1935, referring to experiments carried out in 1932.[28] He also made the surprising statement that Prontosil, lethal for bacteria in the body, had no effect on them in culture. A friend of Colebrook's wrote to him from Paris, drawing his attention to this paper, but even when he had read it, Colebrook was not impressed. Then, on 3 October 1935, he went to a lecture in London by

Professor Höerlein, Director of the Bayer laboratories, in which he gave details of a trial of Prontosil in human cases. Wright and Fleming were sceptical, the former on theoretical grounds, the latter because he thought the evidence insufficient. But Colebrook was determined to try Prontosil in the treatment of puerperal fever.

His determination was needed, because Prontosil was strangely difficult to come by. The manufacturers seemed reluctant to supply doctors wishing to test it, and there was a suspicion that there were commercial reasons, involving patents, for withholding it, or that the claims made for it would be disproved. But Colebrook persevered. He obtained his Prontosil and, after some initial difficulties, confirmed that it did protect mice infected by virulent streptococci, and that it had no effect on the same organisms in the test-tube. Though its action was obviously mysterious, Colebrook planned to use it on his patients at Queen Charlotte's Hospital, in collaboration with Dr Meave Kenny, an obstetrician, and his own bacteriological team, including Ronald Hare.

As it happened, Hare was the first patient. In January 1936 he pricked his finger on a sliver of glass infected with streptococci – the sort of minute accident that had cost the lives of so many surgeons, doctors and nurses in the past. Hare developed a rapidly spreading infection and became desperately ill, in danger of losing his arm if not his life. Colebrook took the plunge, and treated him with Prontosil, given by mouth and by injection. Hare records that he himself could not decide whether he was dying from the infection or the drug.[29] He turned a bright pink colour all over – one of the less unpleasant side effects of the dye – and Fleming, after visiting his bedside at St Mary's Hospital, said to Hare's wife in his most laconic style 'Hae ye said your prayers?' But Hare recovered and, thanks to Prontosil and the surgical skill of C. A. Pannett, regained the full use of his hand.

During the first six months of 1936, Colebrook treated thirty-six cases of severe puerperal fever with Prontosil, and there were three deaths instead of the nine that previous experience would have led him to expect. In the next six months he treated twenty-six cases and there were no deaths. Thus in sixty-four cases so treated the death rate was 4.6 per cent, instead of the 25 per cent previously experienced. Colebrook, the pioneer of chemotherapy in Britain, was criticized by the pundits, particularly Professor Topley, for not having done a properly controlled clinical trial. By statistical rules he should have left half of his patients untreated. But Colebrook, one of the most compassionate of medical scientists, believed that had he done so he would have condemned at least eight young women to death. In such a dilemma, which has so often to be faced by those who are clinically but not mathematically sure that a treatment is life-saving, Colebrook chose to save his patients rather than his reputation as a coldly logical scientist. In the event, he was justified. Chemotherapy was soon to prove itself beyond any need for statistical confirmation.

The commercial restriction on Prontosil encouraged many workers to synthesize similar compounds for themselves. This was good for medical science but bad for the manufacturers of Prontosil because more effective and less toxic drugs were soon discovered over which they had no patent rights. This new work also began to explain how such compounds exerted their antibacterial effect. Within a few months workers at the Pasteur Institute in Paris had discovered that Prontosil was broken down in the body into its component parts of the red azo dye and the sulphonamide molecule. And it was not the dye but the sulphonamide that inhibited the microbes, once it had been released from a combination that itself had no antibacterial action. Free sulphonamide was as effective against bacteria in culture as it was in the body. A mystery had been solved.

The way was thus opened for a more rapid and by now a more logical progress. Knowing what they were aiming for, the chemists synthesized a whole range of sulphonamide compounds in which the objective was a greater antibacterial power and a lower incidence of side-effects. Some of these compounds, such as sulphanilamide, sulphathiazole and sulphapyridine (better known as M and B 693) achieved a solid success and transformed the prognosis of previously untreatable infections like pneumonia, meningitis, erysipelas, scarlet fever, and puerperal fever. There were, however, serious drawbacks to these generally life-saving drugs. Not all bacteria were sensitive to them, and those that were might become resistant. The drugs did not work well on localized infections where pus had formed, and even the best could have most unpleasant side effects, such as skin rashes and persistent vomiting. The most dangerous of these ill-effects, fortunately rather rare, was a suppression of the production of the white blood cells by the bone marrow (agranulocytosis). The patient thus became deprived of circulating phagocytes and his resistance to infection could be fatally impaired – a convincing proof of the natural importance of these cells that Wright had always stressed. Thus, while the net effect of the new chemotherapy was an enormous advance in the battle against bacterial disease, there were still areas of failure and even some disasters to be set on the debit side.

In the summer of 1936 Fleming presented a paper and demonstrations of his selective culture techniques at the Second International Congress of Microbiology in London. He then became much involved in the exciting new chemotherapy. On 23 October of that year there was the first mention of sulphonamides in his notebooks,[30] and thereafter a continuous record of experiments. He applied to the new drugs all the tests that he had developed in his study of many other antiseptics. He measured the effect of the various sulpha-compounds on the growth in culture of all the pathogenic bacteria, and he tested their effect on living leucocytes by his slide-cell method. The drugs seemed to be quite harmless to the white cells and, at the same time, effective inhibitors of a wide range of virulent organisms. Fleming (like other workers) noticed that they did not actually kill the bacteria, but merely arrested their growth and multiplication. This action, which was beginning to be explained in other laboratories, was due to the fact that the sulphonamide molecule was taken up by the bacteria in mistake for a chemically similar substance (para-aminobenzoic acid) that was essential for their proper growth and metabolism. In consequence, being unable to digest the sulphonamide, they starved, but still lived.

Fleming naturally wondered how, if the sulpha drugs did not actually kill bacteria, they could so dramatically cure an acute infection in the body. He then proposed that it was the phagocytes and antibodies in the blood that killed microbes rendered starving and helpless by the sulphonamide. This was a neat combination of Wright's beloved doctrines and the new chemotherapy. Fleming then embarked on a long series of experiments on the antibacterial action of sulphonamides when combined with specific antisera and with vaccines. If, as he supposed, the natural defences provided the final and essential stage in the killing of infecting organisms, then stimulation of these defences by suitable vaccines should improve the success-rate of chemotherapy. It might also, incidentally, maintain the market for vaccines now seriously threatened by the sulphonamides.

Fleming did a number of experiments on mice and rabbits. He found that animals treated with pneumococcal vaccine alone, or with M and B 693 alone, all died when injected with 100 lethal doses of virulent pneumococci. But when both the vaccine and the drug were given, 100 per cent of the mice and 70 per cent of the rabbits survived the pneumococcal infection. He published these results with I. H. Maclean and K. B. Rogers in 1939,[31] and in a paper presented to the Royal Society of Medicine in March of that year.[32]

In the summer of 1939, accompanied by Sareen, Alec Fleming paid his first visit to the United States to attend the Third International Congress of Microbiology in New York. He gave a paper there, and the subject was again the advantage of combining vaccine and chemotherapy. The concluding lines of the published abstract are as follows: 'It is suggested that the advent of sulphapyridine increases the importance of vaccines and serums, especially in the case of organisms not extremely sensitive to sulphapyridine.'[33]

War had broken out while the Flemings were abroad and they returned, earlier than planned, on board the *Manhattan*, in mid-September. A. W. Downie, a fellow passenger, wrote later that Fleming was 'excellent company after dinner', and that rounds of drinks and anecdotes might extend into the small hours. Back in Britain, Fleming found himself much in demand as a bacteriologist with personal experience in the treatment of war wounds. During the next two years (1940–1) he published seven papers and lectures on this subject and, in most, he advocated a combination of vaccine and chemotherapy. Even in 1941, when attention was beginning to turn to the dramatic results being obtained in Oxford with *penicillin*, Fleming paid more attention, in a lecture to the Royal Society of Medicine on the treatment of wound infection, to the principle of vaccine and chemotherapy combined.[34] But, for all his campaigning, the principle had failed to establish itself, and a new era was about to begin.

It has been stated that Fleming went to the United States in 1939 'because an American laboratory was anxious to start work on penicillin'.[35] There seems to be no foundation for this, and no evidence that Fleming's visit had any purpose other than to attend the Microbiological Congress. There had been very little interest in penicillin in America up to that time. Apart from Charles Thom's identification of Fleming's mould as *P. notatum* in 1931, the first American worker to take up its culture seems to have been Dr Roger Reid at the State College of Pennsylvania.[36] Obtaining a culture of the mould from Thom in November 1930, Reid set out to discover if its ability to produce penicillin was a rare attribute. He tested twenty-three other species of moulds, including eight sorts of *Penicillia*, and none produced significant antibacterial activity. Then, returning to Fleming's strain – clearly a very special one – he began to work through the chemical extraction processes that had just been published by Raistrick. He did not, however, make much headway, though he discovered (for himself) that penicillin does not directly lyse bacteria as Fleming's paper had led him to believe. After pursuing the elusive penicillin down a number of chemical pathways, Reid gave up the chase in about 1935.

The personal side of Alec's life during this time had, apart from one tragedy, a tranquil regularity. The tragedy was the death of his brother John in 1937. John, the senior partner of the optical firm of J. and R. Fleming (of which Alec was a director) lived in St John's Wood with his wife Elizabeth. They had no children. It seems that John and Alec had been to a football match (Alec was a staunch supporter of the St Mary's team) on a bitterly cold afternoon. Next day, John developed pneumonia.[37] Two years before he had had a similar attack, but had responded to anti-pneumococcal serum. This time the serum had no effect. Nor had Prontosil. Sulphapyridine (M and B 693), which was to prove so effective in the treatment of pneumonia, was still a year away in the future, and John died. The whole Fleming family was saddened since John had been its most outgoing and affectionate member, a frequent visitor to The Dhoon and a great spoiler of his nephews and nieces. Elizabeth was desolated and, though she came to live in the top part of Alec and Sareen's house in Danvers Street, she never recovered her former spirits.

The Fleming family life went on. The Dhoon was the summer holiday home for many of them, and Alec organized an annual 'Sports Day'. Alec and Sareen spent most of their week-ends there, driving down from London on Friday evening and returning on Monday morning. It was one of Alec's games to race the local train where the road and the railway ran close together for several miles. Since Alec too often won, he used to give himself a handicap.[38] Robert, their son, was at a preparatory boarding school and spent most of his holidays at The Dhoon, with an occasional visit to Lochfield Farm, where he enjoyed sleeping in a box-bed in the kitchen. His parents had entered him for Eton (a strange contrast to Alec's own schooling) but Robert disliked the idea, and he was sent to Stowe instead, in January 1938.[39] Alec had quite a relaxed attitude to his parental responsibilities. One day when Robert was five or six years old, he, Robert and a visitor, Dr Gerald Willcox, went fishing in the punt on the river at the bottom of the garden. When Alec hooked a pike Robert's excitement was so intense that he fell overboard, unable to swim and in 8 feet of water. Alec remained calm and more concerned for his fish than his son, so that it was Willcox who had to rescue him.[40]

During the working weeks in London Alec seldom put in more than six hours a day in his laboratory – the time when Wright's staff would work into the small hours of the morning were long past. Almost every evening Alec would go along to the Chelsea Arts Club, where he had tea and then settled down for his games of cards, chess and – of course – snooker. Vivian Pitchforth was his most frequent opponent, but Alec was very popular with all members and was never short of company. He was known there as 'Sandy', though at home he was always 'Alec', and in the laboratory simply 'Flem'. It was his habit to leave the Club at about 7.45, in order to be home for dinner at Danvers Street at 8 p.m. One evening his game of snooker had outlasted its ration of time. Alec, whose turn it was to play, looked at his watch and said, 'It's late – I'll be in trouble from the missus.' He then took his cue and almost off-handedly potted all the balls remaining on the table, leaving his opponent beaten and speechless.[41]

Enter Florey

On 17 January 1929, Fleming's professional path was crossed by that of Howard Florey, the young Australian whose work twelve years later would make Fleming a world hero. On that day there is an entry in Florey's laboratory notebook headed 'Lysozyme', with a description of rats reared on a Vitamin A-deficient diet, and the statement that various organ-extracts had been 'sent to Fleming'.[1] There must therefore have been some correspondence between the two men, but none of it seems to have survived in either the Florey archives now at the Royal Society, or among Fleming's papers at the British Museum. Fleming's notebooks make no mention of Florey.

Howard Walter Florey[2] was the youngest child and only son of Joseph Florey, a native of Oxfordshire who emigrated to Adelaide in 1885 to practise his trade as a shoemaker and to give his consumptive wife a better chance of survival. The move brought commercial success to Joseph who, within a few years, became the owner of a considerable manufacturing business with branches throughout Australia. But it did not improve the health of his wife, Charlotte, who died of her disease in April 1886. Joseph, left a widower with two young daughters – Charlotte and Anne – remarried in 1889, his second wife being Bertha Wadham, an Australian-born woman of twenty-six. Bertha produced three children during the next few years; Hilda, Valetta and finally Howard, who was born on 24 September 1898.

Unlike Alec Fleming, Howard Florey was brought up in quite affluent surroundings and in the rather stifling emotional atmosphere created by an adoring mother and four adoring sisters. His father had become a rich man, and the family home was a small mansion with 10 acres of grounds in a suburb of Adelaide adjoining the Mount Lofty range. There, the Australian bush and forests of huge trees lay just beyond the paddock fence, and Howard as a boy enjoyed nothing more than exploring these fringes of the vast wilderness. In due course he went to a local school, then a preparatory school, and finally to St Peter's Collegiate School, the equivalent of a good English public school. Unlike Alec, he did not walk to his schools, he travelled by horse-tram and later by motor-bicycle. He was an astonishingly apt pupil, nearly always being top of his form, and winning most of the prizes. He was also an excellent athlete and games-player. At St Peter's he was head boy, a member of the school's cricket, football and tennis teams, and a winning runner and hurdler.

The question of his future career was decided by Howard himself. His father had wanted him to follow him into the shoe-manufacturing business, but Howard had developed a dislike for commerce and a liking for science. At that time a career in the pure sciences was not easily obtainable in Australia, and Howard was advised to study medicine, from which point many scientific paths could lead. So, he entered the Adelaide Medical School in 1916, winning a scholarship and a State Bursary that meant that his medical education would cost his parents nothing. This was just as well because Joseph Florey's company was by then in dire financial trouble, and his personal fortune was melting away. When he died suddenly in 1918 he was practically bankrupt. The big house at Mitcham had to be sold, together with most of his possessions. Bertha had a total of about £7,000 when all was settled, with a son at medical school and two jobless daughters living at home. They moved to a small house in an unfashionable suburb of Adelaide, and to a way of life very different from their previous one.

Howard's academic progress, however, was unaffected. He was consistently top in every examination and in every subject, and he won most of the prizes. He was equally successful on the games fields, playing tennis and football for Adelaide University. It is interesting to consider the remarkable similarities and differences between Howard Florey and Alec Fleming at this stage of their respective careers – though Alec was, of course, seventeen years older than Howard. Both were supremely successful in everything that they did. Both were young men of very few words – laconic, apparently shy, and taciturn. Both were highly critical of orthodox views and teaching and were contemptuous of what Florey called 'hot-air merchants'. But here similarities end. Florey, beneath a rather tough, rough manner was deeply sensitive and conscientious, unsure of himself and yet determined to succeed. He was as tense as a coiled spring. His successes were the result of hard work and intense application. In consequence, he was not particularly popular with his fellow students, who preferred their scholars and athletes not obviously to try quite so hard. For example, tennis was Howard's best game – he was almost up to Davis Cup standards – but he would pulverize a lesser opponent to the last point and without mercy. By contrast, Alec Fleming succeeded in all that he did during his medical school days without apparent effort. He seemed to be easy-going and relaxed and to win his many prizes casually. And, despite his almost pathological lack of conversation (Wright would call it 'oligophasia') he was universally popular.

Howard passed his medical finals in 1921, though not with the expected honours. Perhaps this lapse from the highest standard was due to the fact that several things were worrying him. The first was the financial plight of his mother and sisters. He felt that, as soon as he had graduated, he should take a medical job in Adelaide, help to pay their bills and look after them generally. On the other hand he desperately wanted a career in scientific medicine and research. This would entail several more years of training (which was then not to be had in Australia), with little or no pay, and poor financial prospects even in the long run. And such a course of action was within his grasp, because he had been awarded the Rhodes Scholarship for South Australia. This Scholarship would maintain him for three years in Oxford, where he would be able to study with Sir Charles Sherrington in what had become the best department of physiology in Europe. But there was another personal reason for remaining in Adelaide. He had decided that he wanted to marry Miss Ethel Hayter Reed, a medical student in the University, and a separation of at least three years would, he felt, jeopardize his chances. He was faced, therefore, by a conflict of emotions – family ties and personal feelings on the one side and on the other, a driving ambition to do medical research. It was the latter that won the day. In December 1921, he embarked as a ship's surgeon in a cargo steamer and sailed for England.

In Oxford, where Howard arrived in January 1922, he enrolled in the School of Physiology, the department originally created by Burdon-Sanderson in 1886. Sherrington had held the chair since 1917, and had become a world leader in the field of neuro-physiology, of which Burdon-Sanderson had been a pioneer. Sherrington, in fact, was one of the great physiologists of all time. He was President of the Royal Society from 1920–25, and winner of a Nobel Prize in 1932. Within a short time of Howard's arrival, Sherrington began to pay special attention to the homesick and lonely young Australian, recognizing his obvious talents and his personal needs. Sherrington became Howard's guide and mentor then and for the rest of his life. He and Lady Sherrington opened their home to him, and became parent-substitutes on whom Howard relied for advice and support.

During this, the most formative period of Florey's scientific career, it was Sherrington who moulded his ways of thinking and learning. And Florey, being a young man of strong character despite his self-doubts, was not easily moulded. But his respect and affection for Sherrington, the first great man whom he had ever met, created a complete trust that Florey hardly extended to any other person. He could not have had a better model for his own work. Sherrington was, first and foremost, an experimentalist and a master of technique, but one with an imaginative genius always ranging ahead of his experiments in the 'might-be' world from which real facts could be crystallized by further experiments. His field was the almost inconceivably complex one of the integrated actions of the nervous system, that would now, perhaps, be called the programming of a computer enormously more varied and flexible in its functions than any man-made control system ever built.

Since Howard Florey and Alexander Fleming brought quite different but effectively complementary attitudes to their research work, and since between them – but certainly not in collaboration – they have changed the face of medicine and much of human history, it is of interest to look at the contrasting characters of the two men who most influenced them – Sir Almroth Wright and Sir Charles Sherrington. Sherrington was the older by four years. Both men had similar social backgrounds, both had travelled widely in Europe and studied with the leading medical scientists of their day. Both had held a variety of appointments before settling down to their respective specialities. (Sherrington had been the first man in Britain to prepare and use diphtheria antitoxin, the patient being his own nephew.) Wright was – even into old age – an *enfant terrible*, always at loggerheads with the medical, scientific and even political establishments, a publicist continually campaigning on behalf of his own ideas. As a scientist, he was full of original notions and the dangerous conviction that they were right. Though he too was a master of technique, and preached the scientific method of 'proceeding from the known to the unknown', all too often what he and his disciples accepted as 'the known' was in reality some dogmatically-stated hypothesis of his own. And he also practised the use of what he called 'diacritical judgement and the experiential method', a process so elastic that its results could be stretched to fit almost any preconceived idea.

By contrast, Sherrington was a quiet, dedicated academic scientist, essentially humble in his attitude to the as-yet unknown, methodically pushing forward the frontiers of knowledge by meticulously controlled experiments. His inspiration lay in his perception of an understandable pattern emerging from what he had already discovered. He was universally admired and respected and thus – perforce – became part of the scientific 'establishment' that Wright professed to despise. But Sherrington was not a campaigner, publicist, or polemicist. His Oxford department had become the best of its sort in Europe because it was based on sound, hard work of the highest quality. And Sherrington was a philosopher who thought deeply but humbly about the nature of Man and his consciousness.[3] He was knowledgeable and appreciative of the arts and literature and was, himself, a poet.[4] But, unlike Wright, he did not parade his erudition.

During the first two years of his Rhodes Scholarship, Florey learned physiology from Sherrington's department, and something of the cultural ethos of Oxford. Though very much an Australian and with a natural suspicion of English traditions, manners and customs Florey was soon captivated by Oxford. He had a deep, though then quite uneducated, feeling for architecture, history and a tradition of scholarship maintained for centuries. In the vacations he travelled widely on the Continent, living cheaply, learning French and German, inspired by the art and architecture to be found in the cities of Belgium and France, Germany, Austria, Hungary and Italy. But his travels showed him a grimmer side to the picture. The post-war poverty and starvation in Austria horrified him, and he was shocked by national antagonisms that seemed, to him, a certain recipe for another war. He remained a lonely young man almost obsessed by a feeling of isolation, as his long correspondence with Ethel Reed shows. He made few, if any, close friends of his own age, with the exception of John Fulton, an American Rhodes Scholar who, like Florey, was working with Sherrington and resident in Magdalen College. But he had a chance to meet many leading scientists at conferences in Oxford, or on their visits to Sherrington himself. He wrote to Ethel almost with awe of men like Rutherford, Haldane, J. J. Thomson, Barcroft, Dale, Banting, A. V. Hill and Thomas Lewis, and it is clear that he was dazzled by them and the world they represented.

In the summer of 1923, Florey sat for his physiology examination and obtained First-Class Honours – an achievement that would ensure him a foothold on the ladder of scientific medicine. With still another year of his Fellowship to run, Sherrington offered him a post as demonstrator in his department. There he learned the art of practical teaching, and also began to acquire the skills of animal surgery. Sherrington had suggested that, as a research project, Florey should study the function and reactions of the smallest blood-vessels (capillaries) supplying the brain. This he did, and one of his several discoveries was that, at a site of injury to the lining of these vessels, the blood platelets adhere and build up into a mass that may block the vessel, or break away into the bloodstream. This phenomenon is now the basis for much current research on the ever-present problem of thrombosis. Florey collected his observations on the cerebral circulation into a thesis which brought him a B.Sc. – a higher degree in Oxford – and which was published in the journal *Brain*. He had begun his research career very well.

In 1924, on Sherrington's recommendation, Florey accepted a research fellowship in the Department of Pathology in Cambridge. Before he took up his new post, however, he went as medical officer with the Third Oxford University Arctic Expedition to Spitsbergen and North East Land. It was an experience of comradeship, adventure, hardship and some danger, that Florey never forgot. But a more mundane and practical outcome of his experience gave Florey a research interest that ultimately led him to lysozyme and thence to penicillin. Something in the environment or the diet of the expedition gave Florey a troublesome indigestion that remained a permanent disability. It was his investigation of his own stomach function that set him on this track, as will be apparent later.

In Cambridge, Florey continued his researches on capillary function, becoming interested in the mechanism of inflammation. The questions that demanded an answer were then (as they are now): why do the white cells, normally non-adhesive in the bloodstream, suddenly become sticky and adhere to the vessel wall and to each other when they enter an inflamed vessel? How do these cells then pass through the apparently intact vessel wall to accumulate in the tissues around it? What turns them from peaceful leucocytes into war-like phagocytes bent on destroying any enemy? Florey, throughout his whole working life, tried to get complete answers to these questions, using each technical innovation as it became available, up to the time of the electron microscope. Much has been discovered about the mechanism of inflammation, and Florey himself made important observations but, like all biological problems, it widens and recedes as one approaches it.

Florey was happy at Cambridge, and his work attracted the interest and admiration of influential people. He began to follow a pattern that was to become characteristic of him. A great reader of the published literature, he brought to it a critical judgement that often revealed unsuspected fallacies or incomplete experiments. When such fallacies could be exposed, or unfinished work completed by a few simple experiments, Florey would sometimes turn aside to do these himself. In this way he demolished two or three accepted theories, and provided the valid conclusions for some unfinished lines begun by other people. One of his colleagues at this time said, 'Florey was always a great finisher.'

This same tenacity applied to his own lines of research. He followed several of these for years – some during the whole of his working life – and they continued to yield valuable information not only in his hands, but in those of his collaborators and of his pupils after his death. One of these lines began with his own digestive troubles. The indigestion acquired in the Arctic persisted in Cambridge, and Florey became worried about the possible cause. He had a medical examination in London, and learned that he was suffering from 'mucus gastritis' – an inflammation of the stomach associated with too little acid and too much mucus. Florey, relieved that he had nothing worse, became scientifically interested in his own stomach functions. He taught himself to swallow a stomach tube, so that he could study what was going on. He was particularly interested in the mucus, began to study the conditions that increased or decreased its secretion in the stomach, and to wonder about its significance and function. He soon discovered that almost nothing was known about these aspects, and yet mucus was a component of the fluid that coats all the internal membranes of the body, in the eyes, nose, mouth, throat, lungs, stomach, intestines and the urogenital tract. Something was known about its chemistry, very little about its formation and secretion, even less about its function and possible importance. It was hardly an unfinished line of research – it had not properly begun. So Florey began an investigation that, with side-lines, was to be a major interest for many years. One of these side-lines was lysozyme, another was penicillin.

In 1925, Florey was awarded a Rockefeller Travelling Fellowship that would take him to America for a year. He had already had short periods of study with some of the leading Continental physiologists and pathologists to perfect the techniques he was developing for work on capillaries and lymphatic vessels. But a year in the United States would give him more extensive experience with the leaders in this field. He arrived in New York in September 1925, to work with Robert Chambers and learn to use his almost incredibly delicate micromanipulator to dissect and study single, living cells. But Chambers was not quite ready for him. Florey, impatient as always to get to work immediately on arrival in someone else's laboratory, refused to await the great man's pleasure, and made his own arrangements to go forthwith to A. N. Richards in Philadelphia, a famous American pharmacologist who had worked with Dale in England. Florey's time in Richards' laboratory was well spent because he not only acquired the valuable technique for inserting minute glass tubes into blood and lymph vessels less than a quarter of a millimetre in diameter, but he earned the respect and friendship of Richards himself, which was to prove crucial in the development of penicillin in America sixteen years later.

After spending Christmas in Boston with his American friend John Fulton, the ex-Rhodes Scholar at Oxford, Florey went to work with Carlson, a physiologist in Chicago who was an expert on stomach function. Florey discussed his interest in mucus with him, and Carlson encouraged him to embark on a systematic study of its functions and the mechanisms controlling its secretion. But science was not Florey's only interest. While in Philadelphia he became a devotee of the Symphony Orchestra there, which greatly increased his love and appreciation of music. The frequent letters that he wrote to Ethel Reed in Adelaide contain almost as much information on the concerts he had been to, as on the work he was doing.

During his visit to America, Florey received a tempting offer of a comparatively well-paid research post in the Pathology Department of the London Hospital. It was tempting because the salary of £850 per annum would make it possible for him to marry Ethel, the wished-for outcome of a long courtship by correspondence that had been hampered by Ethel's insistence on financial security and also by the fact that their letters took about six weeks to reach their destination. After much heart-searching, Florey accepted, though he would really have preferred to return to Cambridge. He finished his American visit with a few weeks in New York spent with Chambers and his micromanipulator. Then he returned to London, and Ethel agreed to join him there and marry him. Their wedding took place at Holy Trinity Church, Paddington, in October 1926.

The post at the London Hospital did not come up to Florey's expectations. The facilities for research were poor and, what was worse, the general interest of the department was centred on clinical work, with little appreciation of any research that had no immediate practical or fee-earning value. Florey was soon at loggerheads with the director of the department, whose easy-going way of life was disturbed by the constant demands of the impatient, energetic young Australian who worked twice as hard as anyone else, but not in the way he would have liked and understood. In consequence, Florey used to slip away to do experiments in the laboratories of his friends at Oxford or at Cambridge. It was not surprising, therefore, that when he was offered a post as lecturer in the Pathology Department in Cambridge, he accepted it with enthusiasm. Ethel too, was pleased. Her health was poor, and living in London had aggravated the respiratory infections from which she suffered. But perhaps her greatest affliction, and one that spoiled the companionship that she and Howard might have enjoyed, was her progressive and incurable deafness.

The Floreys moved to Cambridge in the autumn of 1927, and for the next five years Howard worked energetically and very productively at his various researches, with a lengthening list of sound, original publications to his credit. His interests continued to be focused on the microcirculation of blood and lymph, inflammation, gastric function and mucus secretion. It was the latter that introduced him to lysozyme in 1929. Florey had been much impressed by the resistance to infection of the very thin and delicate mucous membranes, despite the fact that they are constantly exposed to virulent bacteria, and are often liable to be damaged. He began to believe that mucus might be an important protective coating for these membranes, a viscous layer on their surfaces through which bacteria could not easily penetrate. Then he read a paper in which the authors had shown that a deficiency of Vitamin A caused the secretion of mucus in the intestine to cease, and that this was followed by a bacterial invasion of the intestinal tissues. Pursuing this suggestion of an antibacterial role for mucus, Florey remembered that, in 1922, Alexander Fleming – a man whom he did not personally know – had discovered the remarkable antibacterial substance that he named lysozyme, and that lysozyme was to be mainly found in mucus-containing body fluids. Florey's motto then – and for the rest of his life – was 'Do the experiment'. Wasting no time on speculation, he kept some rats on a vitamin-deficient diet and, while acquiring the technique for estimating lysozyme himself, sent various extracts of tissues and fluids to Fleming.

The results of this particular experiment are not, unfortunately, re-corded either in Florey's notes or in Fleming's, and it must be supposed therefore, that they were not dramatic. But once he had begun to work on lysozyme, Florey continued tenaciously until, in 1938, the final answers to its mode of action were obtained in his laboratory and the job was finished.

Florey's interest in lysozyme was the same as that of its original discoverer. Like Fleming, Florey was tantalized by its wide natural distribution and a conviction that it must, somehow, be an important part of the vital defences that allow animals and plants to survive in a world full of vicious bacterial enemies. But, where Fleming had speculated, Florey settled down to do experiments that would put this idea to the test, working with Neil Goldsworthy and helped by the fourteen-year-old boy, Jim Kent, who had just become Florey's assistant and who was to remain so until Florey's death nearly forty years later. What they did was to measure the lysozyme content of the saliva, tears, and the nasal, stomach and intestinal secretions from the dog, cat, goat, guinea-pig, rat and rabbit. The results seemed to be quite bewildering. Dogs, rabbits and guinea pigs had lysozyme in all the secretions tested, but the goat had none, except in its tears. Cats had none in their tears or gastrointestinal fluids, but some in their saliva. Yet all these animals normally led healthy, uninfected lives, irrespective of the presence or absence of lysozyme in various parts of their anatomy. The inevitable conclusion was that lysozyme – as measured – was not essential to their defence against infection.

Florey and Goldsworthy published their paper on lysozyme in 1930 in the *British Journal of Experimental Pathology*,[5] the journal that, a year before, had published Fleming's paper on penicillin. There was a significant Appendix to their paper, describing the inhibition of one sort of bacterium by another which they had observed during the course of their work. They published a photograph of a culture plate showing a zone of inhibition very like Fleming's, but they referred to the fact that such inhibition was 'a very well-known phenomenon' and cited the review of the subject by Papacostas and Gaté.

Despite this unpromising start, Florey remained tenaciously attached to the lysozyme problem or, rather, to the idea of a natural system of antibacterial substances present in animal fluids and tissues, of which lysozyme might be only one example. One of the puzzles of immunity is the fact that different species of animals are naturally immune – or susceptible – to different sorts of bacteria. Cats, for example, are relatively immune to tuberculosis, and guinea-pigs are highly susceptible; pigeons resist infection by pneumococci; and so on. Florey proposed to search for specific antibacterial agents in the bodies of these animals that would explain these strange differences in immunity. One of his applications to the Medical Research Council mentions the possible existence of an antipneumococcal enzyme in the tissues of the pigeon, and his intention to look for it. But, like Fleming, he was hampered by lack of expert chemical collaboration. A. A. Miles (later Sir Ashley Miles and Director of the Lister Institute) helped Florey to measure the antibacterial activity of various tissue extracts, and Marjorie Stephenson, working in Gowland Hopkins' laboratory, collaborated on the biochemical side. But nothing much was found and nothing at all was published.

In March 1932, Florey was appointed Professor of Pathology at Sheffield. This was his first experience of a post in which he would have responsibility for hospital pathology and also, of course, for teaching and research. Fortunately, the existing staff of his new department included able clinical pathologists who ran the routine laboratory work of the four hospitals in the Sheffield Group. With the most senior of these, H. E. Harding, Florey established a fruitful research collaboration, particularly on developing a treatment for tetanus by the use of curare* and mechanical artificial respiration that is the basis of the modern practice. They also worked together on gastric and duodenal secretion. Florey was then joined by Dr Beatrice Pullinger, who proved to be enormously competent, not only in reorganizing the routine work of the laboratory but in educating importunate clinicians in the best use of laboratory investigations.

On the research side Florey was as active and energetic as ever. In addition to the work on tetanus, gastric and intestinal secretion, blood capillary and lymphatic functions, and the study of the white cells of the blood, lysozyme remained one of his major interests. He had come to the conclusion that the way forward lay in discovering the chemical nature of lysozyme – what exactly was it, and what exactly did it do to bacteria? Florey made repeated applications to the Medical Research Council to obtain funds to pay a biochemist to work with him. But no money was forthcoming. He then approached Edward Mellanby, Professor of Pharmacology at Sheffield (soon to succeed Sir Walter Morley Fletcher as Secretary of the Medical Research Council), to ask for biochemical help, and Mellanby arranged for Dr Sylvia Harrison to work part-time on the lysozyme project in Florey's laboratory. But not much progress was made – the problem needed more sophisticated methods than were available.

Meanwhile Fleming, who had retained his enthusiasm for lysozyme, made it the subject of his Presidential Address at the Section of Pathology of the Royal Society of Medicine in 1932.[6] In the course of this he quoted Florey's animal results in some detail, saying that the meaning of the observed species differences was 'quite obscure'. By this he meant that the findings seemed incompatible with his belief in lysozyme as an important factor in the natural defences of living things against infection, but it is clear from the rest of his lecture that this belief remained unshaken. Fleming by this time seemed to have lost interest in penicillin, and it is a strange coincidence that the most promising work on its clinical use had just been done in the pathology department in Sheffield.

The pathologist at the Royal Infirmary laboratory in Sheffield was C. G. Paine, who had trained at St Mary's Hospital and become interested in

* The active principle of the South American Indian arrow-poison that causes paralysis.

penicillin. He had a culture of Fleming's mould, which he grew to produce enough 'mould juice' to try out as a local antiseptic. The first effort was on three cases of chronic staphylococcal infections of the skin, but, though penicillin was applied every four hours for a week, the treatment seemed useless. Evidently the penicillin was not reaching the bacteria. Paine then used his crude penicillin to irrigate infected eyes, and here he was much more successful. Two cases of gonococcal conjunctivitis in newly-born babies cleared up completely in about two days, and a case of staphylococcal conjunctivitis responded equally well. Then Paine achieved something of a clinical triumph. A colliery manager had a penetrating injury of his right eye. This became infected by pneumococci, and the operation needed to remove the foreign body could not be carried out. Paine irrigated the eye with penicillin, the infection cleared up in two days and the operation to save the eye was safely done.[7]

This sort of work with penicillin, which could so easily have been done four years before by Fleming and his ophthalmologist assistant, Ridley, would have attracted attention to the clinical possibilities of penicillin, if only it had been followed through. But Paine seems to have had no encouragement to continue his work. Though Florey certainly knew about it, because Paine told him what he had done, he took very little interest in it. He was already involved with other research lines, and his interest in antibacterial substances was centred on their possible natural existence in the body as part of the general principle of immunity, not on the particular example of a strange mould. And Florey, at that time, was not interested in treating infections. So, when Paine's mould cultures began to lose their ability to produce penicillin, and when he himself was transferred to the Sheffield maternity hospital, he gave up his work on it. He seems to have made no effort to get help from Fleming, or further cultures of his mould. At the maternity hospital he turned his attention to the streptococci causing puerperal fever. He was interested in the work being done by Leonard Colebrook on the use of arsenical preparations, and soon in the brilliant results that he was getting with the new sulphonamides. The dawn of the chemotherapeutic era extinguished, for a time, any glimmer of interest in penicillin. And yet, by proving that dangerous infections can be best overcome by introducing suitable antibacterial agents into the circulating blood, the sulphonamides created a fresh attitude of mind. In this new climate the idea of systemic antibacterial treatment flourished, and the search was on for new and better ways of achieving it.

16

The Oxford Triumph

In 1934 Georges Dreyer, Professor of Pathology at Oxford and an old friend of both Almroth Wright and Alexander Fleming, died suddenly while on a visit to his native Denmark. Dreyer had been a noted bacteriologist and, for a time, had seemed to be on the verge of a major advance in the treatment of tuberculosis. Like Wright, he believed in vaccines and had conceived the notion that available antituberculosis vaccines did not work because the bacilli had a resistant envelope which prevented their digestion by phagocytes. He then devised a chemical method for removing this envelope and produced a vaccine called 'diaplyte' composed of supposedly digestible tubercle bacilli. Initial tests on animals gave most encouraging results. Somehow the press got hold of this information and stories of a 'wonder-cure' for one of the most dreaded of all diseases made headline news. Dreyer was besieged by journalists, and by doctors and patients clamouring for the vaccine. Then came the humiliating anticlimax. Whatever it may or may not have done in animals, diaplyte did nothing for human sufferers from tuberculosis. The false hopes raised by unauthorized publicity were cruelly shattered and Dreyer – most unfairly – was discredited.[1]

Though his research career was virtually ended by this débâcle, Dreyer retained his ambitions to improve his School of Pathology. In 1922, the trustees of the Sir William Dunn Bequest, prompted by Dreyer, offered £100,000 to Oxford University to build a new pathology department. Dreyer planned the building himself down to the smallest detail, and the result was 'in every respect a model of what a pathological department of teaching and research should be'. (It had, it should be stressed, no responsibility for hospital work.) It was completed in 1926 and formally opened in March 1927. It is a handsome building at the eastern end of South Parks Road, standing in its own grounds of about 2½ acres. The laboratories, classrooms, library, animal house and service rooms are so spacious and well-designed that, despite all the changing and expanding demands of a department in the forefront of scientific research and teaching, Dreyer's original building needed no major alterations or additions for the next forty years.

Dreyer's death made vacant what was potentially the best Chair of

Pathology in Britain. Howard Florey, though considerably younger and less experienced than most of the other applicants was, to his own surprise and delight, appointed in 1935. There are wheels within wheels behind all important university appointments, but the hidden mechanisms of Oxford move in deeper and more mysterious ways than in most other institutions. Left to themselves, these machinations would doubtless have resulted in the appointment of someone else, despite Sherrington's championship of Florey. But the issue was decided by Edward Mellanby, Secretary of the Medical Research Council, a formidable, powerful man with little respect for academic protocol, who was an external member of the Board of Electors. Mellanby arrived late for the meeting because his train from London had broken down, but he was just in time to reverse the decision taken in his absence. Oxford, he felt, needed someone of Florey's energy and enthusiasm, and Florey needed the unused facilities of Dreyer's magnificent department. So Florey got the job and, seven years later, mankind got penicillin, and Fleming his world acclaim.

Florey's first task in Oxford was to revitalize the almost deserted department that was a monument to Dreyer but also something of a mausoleum. In this he had the help of the two enormously competent people who had come with him from Sheffield, Dr Pullinger to reorganize the teaching, and Jim Kent to remoralize a technical staff suffering from the effects of under-employment. For several years before his death Dreyer's failing energies had meant that there was no focus or corporate spirit in his department. When Florey arrived there was one distinguished bacteriologist, Dr A. D. Gardner, working there as the head of an autonomous Medical Research Council Standards Laboratory, housed in the Dunn School but not part of it. And there was another, Dr R. L. Vollum, a Canadian, who tended to spend more of his time at his clinical work in the Radcliffe Infirmary than at his teaching in the Dunn School. There also remained two of Dreyer's own bacteriological collaborators, Miss Campbell Renton and Miss Orr-Ewing, who continued, rather sadly, with the work they had been doing with him before his death. And there was an Australian Rhodes scholar, B. G. Maegraith, who had just taken his D.Phil., and been appointed a demonstrator. The acting head of the department, Dr Ainley-Walker, who had been Dreyer's right-hand man for twenty-five years, retired to his college affairs on Florey's arrival, and Dr A. G. Gibson, a pathologist and physician, transferred all his energies to his hospital laboratory and his wards at the Radcliffe Infirmary.

Florey realized that his department needed a transfusion of new blood to bring it to life, and he set out to attract energetic young graduates to work there. But the all-too-familiar barrier to his plans was lack of money. Dreyer had built a magnificent department but he had not obtained a commensurate endowment for it. The University paid the cost (or, rather, part of the cost) of the teaching activities, but this barely covered such expenses as heating and maintenance, and left nothing for research. Florey therefore had to beg for funds from all the likely sources – such as the Medical Research Council and other grant-giving bodies, the Sir William Dunn Trustees, the Rockefeller Foundation and so on. It was an occupation that he hated, finding it a humiliating and time-consuming exercise that too often ended in disappointment. But he did get enough money to pay one or two graduates, and he was able to attract young research workers who had their own funds – Rhodes Scholars, holders of fellowships and postgraduate students working for a higher degree. One of the first of these was P. B. (later Sir Peter) Medawar, whose work on tissue immunity was to lay the foundations of modern transplant surgery, and win him a Nobel Prize.

Florey never allowed a change of location to interrupt his research programmes. He at once looked for biochemical help on the lysozyme work, and found it in the department of Sir Robert Robinson, the Professor of Chemistry. Robinson thought that the problem would suit one of his young men, E. A. H. Roberts, and Florey was able to obtain a grant from the Medical Research Council for Roberts to collaborate with him. For the next two years, Florey, Maegraith and Roberts worked together on lysozyme, producing enough semi-purified material to allow E. P. Abraham and Robert Robinson to crystallize the enzyme in 1937.[2] One part of the problem – the chemical nature of lysozyme – was thus well on the way to a brilliant solution. Lysozyme was among the first enzymes to be crystallized, and it was the very first in which the complete molecular structure was determined, this being achieved by D. C. Phillips and his colleagues some thirty years later.[3]

The other part of the lysozyme problem – what it does to bacteria – was solved, equally brilliantly, by a new recruit to Florey's staff. This was Ernst Boris Chain, a young Jewish refugee from Hitler's regime, the son of a German mother and a Russian father. Chain had left Germany when Hitler came to power in 1933, and he was accepted as a research student by Gowland Hopkins at Cambridge. Here he did highly original work on certain snake venoms, identifying an enzyme acting on nerve tissue to cause fatal paralysis in the victim. When two years had passed and Chain had obtained his Ph.D. degree, the question of his future arose. It was at this time that Florey was on the look-out for a young biochemist who would become a member of his staff in Oxford, and on Gowland Hopkins' recommendation he offered the job to Chain. Chain gladly accepted, though academic biochemists usually prefer to work in departments of biochemistry, and the salary – £200 p.a. – was hardly princely. During the first two years in Oxford, Chain established a biochemistry laboratory at the Dunn School, and equipped it as well as he could on a strictly limited budget – Florey had to fight for every penny spent on research.

Then, in 1937, lysozyme was purified and Chain was able to start on the project that Florey had had in mind for him from the first. This was the identification of the mode of action of lysozyme on bacteria, a project closely in line with the work on snake venoms that Chain had already been doing, because lysozyme seemed very likely to be an enzyme. An enzyme acts by attaching itself to some part of a particular molecular structure, known as its substrate, in such a way that the substrate undergoes chemical change, releasing the enzyme unchanged to repeat the process with the next molecule. In the case of lysozyme, it seemed probable that it attacked some chemical structure in the bacterial cell wall so that it fell to pieces. It was Chain's task to identify what this chemical structure (substrate) was, and what lysozyme did to it. Working with an American D.Phil. student, L. A. Epstein, Chain soon established that lysozyme was, in reality, an enzyme. They then cultured enough M. *lysodeikticus* to provide 150 g of dry material per week on which to do their chemical analyses. They fractionated the bacterial cells into their chemical components and found that one of these was a polysaccharide specifically broken down by lysozyme. From that point it was a fairly straightforward task to identify this polysaccharide as N-acetyl glucosamine and to discover the precise chemical bonds disrupted by lysozyme.[4] For Chain, the lysozyme work was complete. But, in a wider context it was the beginning of a new chapter in biochemical research, one in which the molecular structure of bacterial cell walls and the processes of synthesis and hydrolysis were revealed. Every peak scaled in biological exploration reveals new mountain ranges ahead.

Though the chemistry of lysozyme and its mode of action could be defined, its importance as a natural defence against infection remained in doubt. But Florey still hoped that other natural antibacterial substances would be found. In 1936 he had a personal experience of the danger of infection. Shortly before he and his family were due to sail for Australia to visit his mother, his five-year old daughter, Paquita, developed an acute mastoid infection with impending meningitis. An emergency operation was done, and the child was treated with the newly-introduced sulphanilamide. Though she was well enough to travel when sailing-day came, the Floreys took a supply of the drug with them in case of a recurrence. This was the first sample of sulphanilamide to be seen in Australia, and it aroused considerable medical interest in Melbourne, where Florey gave a lecture. In this he emphasized the value of the sulphonamides but also their limitations and dangers, and stressed the need to look for other and better antibacterial therapeutic agents. When, two or three years later, Chain's research suddenly took an unexpected twist, Florey's mind was probably more receptive to it as a result of this experience.

In 1938, while the lysozyme work was in progress, Florey and Chain discussed a study of other natural antibacterial agents. Florey was in favour of this, and Chain began to search the literature for suitable examples. It was, of course, a laborious task because there were hundreds of published observations of bacterial inhibition or destruction by moulds and their products and by other bacteria – Florey and Goldsworthy had, in their 1931 paper, referred to this voluminous literature. Chain collected about 200 papers on bacterial inhibition by streptomycetes, fungi, yeasts, and various bacteria, and among them was Fleming's paper on penicillin published in 1929. It particularly attracted his attention because Fleming described the (supposed) lysis of staphylococci by the mould product, and Chain in turn supposed that this must indicate the action of an enzyme like lysozyme.

After discussing the results of his literary researches with Florey, Chain chose for investigation three antibacterial substances in the summer of 1938. These were a bacteriolytic agent produced by the common and harmless *Bacillus subtilis*, discovered by Maurice Nicolle in 1907; pyocyanase, derived from *Ps. pyocyaneus*, by Emmerich and Löw in Germany in 1889; and penicillin. Chain began his work on pyocyanase at once, and with one of his graduate assistants, Miss R. Schoental, a Polish biochemist. She succeeded in extracting active substances from pyocyanase, but they proved to be highly toxic to animals.

At the same time Chain began to work on penicillin with Epstein, his collaborator in the lysozyme project. Their first need was a sample of Fleming's strain of *P. notatum*. This, of course, they could have obtained from Fleming himself and, had they done so, he might have become interested in what they were proposing to do and later resentments might have been avoided. But, as it happened, Chain had to go no further than the laboratory of Miss Campbell-Renton, just along the corridor from his own, for the mould. After deciding to work on penicillin he remembered seeing her carrying flasks containing what looked like mould cultures and discovered that she had, in fact, been keeping Fleming's strain going, for bacteriological purposes, ever since Dreyer had obtained it from him in 1929.

With only the published biochemical findings on penicillin to go on, Chain began by duplicating much of the work done by Raistrick and his team. Like them, he had no knowledge of the much more extended investigations of Ridley and Craddock and of Holt. If Chain had been in touch with Fleming at that stage it is possible that Fleming might have told him about this unpublished work carried out at St Mary's – possible, but unlikely. Fleming, after all, had given no such information to Raistrick, nor had he told Holt about Ridley and Craddock's findings, and he would probably have been equally uninformative with Chain. But Chain was not in touch with Fleming, so that the matter did not arise at all. He and Epstein had to discover things for themselves and progress was very slow. There were technical difficulties over the production of adequate volumes of mould juice, the familiar problem of the instability of penicillin, and the fact that even excellent biochemists do not necessarily make passable bacteriologists. But Chain had obtained enough biochemical information about penicillin to convince him that it was a most extraordinary substance, one that provided an irresistible challenge. He had discovered, for example, that the penicillin molecule was relatively small and that it was most unlikely to be an enzyme. This was, in one way, a disappointing conclusion since he specialized in enzymes, but in another it opened up exciting biochemical possibilities.

By November, 1938, Florey, who had kept in close touch with Chain's work, was beginning to be excited about penicillin too. Though they both insisted later that their interest at that time was purely scientific, and that the possible therapeutic value of penicillin was not considered, there can be little doubt that such a possibility was at the back of their minds then and very much in the forefront a few months later. Florey mentioned, very briefly, the work on antibacterial substances in his grant application to the Medical Research Council in January 1939.[5] Then he started to take an active part in the work himself. He was beginning to realize not only the potential importance of penicillin but the practical difficulties in the way of putting these possibilities to the test. Florey was not only a hard worker and a clever scientist, he was a great organizer. He had the ability to recognize and to use the relevant special talents of his colleagues and assistants, and he had a very special quality of his own, the ability to inspire the confidence and enthusiasm of a group of experts so that they became a very effective team under his leadership. In 1939, with almost no money to fund such a research and with the shadows of war darkening the whole of Europe, Florey decided to gamble all his resources and those of his department on penicillin, a dark horse at best, and quite possibly a non-starter.

On 6 September 1939, three days after Britain had declared war on Germany, Florey wrote to Mellanby, the Secretary of the Medical Research Council, to ask for £100 to cover the cost of the special chemicals and apparatus needed for a research on antibacterial substances. He referred particularly to the agent 'called penicillin by its discoverer Fleming, which is especially effective against staphylococci and acts also on pneumococci and streptococci'. After describing previous work and future possibilities, Florey ended his application as follows: 'In view of the possibly great practical importance of the above-mentioned bactericidal agents it is proposed to prepare these substances in a purified form suitable for intravenous injections and to study their antiseptic action in vivo.' It is perfectly clear therefore that the therapeutic application of penicillin had by then become the prime objective. For the first time too since Fleming's discovery it was proposed to use penicillin as a systemically-acting bactericide, given by injection. Finally, it is also clear that Florey was thinking of its use in human patients since, in his covering letter to Mellanby, he wrote:

'I can get clinical co-operation from Cairns for any products we produce and I have tested on animals.'[6] (Cairns was Nuffield Professor of Surgery at the Radcliffe Infirmary, Oxford, and an ex-Rhodes Scholar, like Florey, from Adelaide.)

Mellanby responded promptly, but not very generously. Though he agreed that the proposed work might be of practical importance, he felt that £25 would be sufficient to launch it, and that the application for £100 would be considered 'at the proper time'.[7] There can be few Government-sponsored schemes that have started with a smaller investment and yielded a larger return! Florey refused to be daunted by this feeble support, but set about organizing his team. Chain, of course, was to be in charge of the biochemical work, and his part was to purify, to the best of his ability, the active principle of penicillin, and in sufficient quantities for the work of the rest of the team. For the production work, Florey selected N. G. Heatley, a graduate from Gowland Hopkins' laboratory, who had been prevented by the war from working as he had intended, with Lindeström-Lang in Sweden. Heatley was not only a biochemist with a good working knowledge of bacteriology, he was a genius in improvization and laboratory engineering. He was later joined by A. G. Sanders, a pathologist almost equally gifted. The formal bacteriological work, such as the investigation and measurement of the bactericidal power of penicillin on different organisms, was in the hands of A. D. Gardner (by then Professor of Bacteriology in Florey's department), and Miss Orr-Ewing. The team, as it was at that time, was completed by Florey himself, with the assistance of Dr Margaret Jennings, and, of course, the literally invaluable Jim Kent. It was their special task to study the biological effects of penicillin, such as toxicity, in animals. But Florey was the acknowledged leader of the whole group.

There could hardly have been a worse time in which to launch a major research project. The whole life of the country was disrupted by the war. There had been a mass evacuation of people from the cities to relatively safe areas – such as Oxford. There was the black-out, rationing of food, clothing and petrol, the digging of slit-trenches and air-raid shelters. Travel was difficult and many ordinary things had become unobtainable. Everyone was preoccupied with the war effort, and only too aware that the ominous quiet on the western front was merely the lull before a storm of unprecedented fury. Not surprisingly, Florey could attract little interest and no material support from the Medical Research Council or from Oxford University for some esoteric project on a strange mould. No one then (except possibly Florey himself) had any idea that penicillin could have the slightest relevance to the winning of the war. But the major consequence of this official disinterest was the lack of money. There simply was not enough to pay the salaries of the additional workers that Florey had co-opted, or the cost of essential chemicals and materials.

Florey therefore turned to America. Ever since his Fellowship with them, Florey had been on good terms with the officials of the Rockefeller Foundation, and he decided to appeal to them for a grant that would support his penicillin research for three years. He asked, in November 1939, for £1,670 per annum for salaries and recurrent expenses and £1,000 for the initial cost of equipment,[8] and he got even more than he asked for, since the Foundation gave him the grants for five years. Chain and Florey were naturally elated. With financial worries allayed they could attack the real problem – the production, purification and testing of penicillin – from every available angle. The work began in earnest at the beginning of 1940, and the first practical advances were due to the ingenuity of Norman Heatley.

The basic requirement in any hunt for an unknown substance among a mass of other and unwanted substances is a good method for recognizing and measuring the quarry. It is only by such measurement (assay) that progress – or lack of progress – can be gauged. Fleming's dilution method did not give a precise measurement of the strength of the penicillin preparations. Heatley greatly improved the assay by inventing the 'cylinder plate'. Culture plates were made in the ordinary way, and sown evenly with 'standard' staphylococci. Heatley then stood short lengths of glass tubing, usually six or eight in number, on the surface of the agar, and pressed them in slightly, so that the lower edges were embedded. He then filled each little cylinder with the penicillin solutions under test, replaced the cover of the culture plate and incubated it. The solution in each cylinder diffused into the agar in a widening circle, and if it contained penicillin, the staphylococci failed to grow within a certain distance. The diameter of this zone of inhibition was an index of the strength of the penicillin in the solution, and it soon became possible to define a 'unit of penicillin' to which reference could be made.

Heatley's second major contribution was to the process of extraction of the active material. The first step in this was the use of solvents such as ether or (later) amyl acetate. But Chain had come up against the same difficulty that had confronted Raistrick. It was easy to extract penicillin from a slightly acid solution in water by shaking this with ether, but getting the penicillin back from its ether solution entailed enormous losses. Then, in March 1940, Heatley hit on the idea of back-extraction into water that had been made slightly alkaline, arguing that it was the pH that determined the solubility of penicillin in ether relative to water. This seemed an entirely original idea and it worked brilliantly. In fact, of course, it had already been used by Lewis Holt in Fleming's laboratory about six years before, unknown to the Oxford workers, and perhaps even unknown to Fleming himself.

Heatley then devised a fairly large-scale continuous-flow extraction process. The acidified mould-filtrate flowed down a long glass tube while a stream of ether flowed up past it, in the same tube, so that the two liquids had a large, moving area of contact. The penicillin passed from the water into the ether, which was collected at the top of the tube. The penicillin was then recovered from its ether solution by reversing the process. This time the stream of ether met a flow of slightly alkaline water, into which the penicillin passed. At each stage unwanted impurities were removed and the watery solution was stable enough to preserve its activity for several months, if kept at o°C. However, the penicillin could be even more safely preserved by the process of freeze-drying, an extension of vacuum distillation. This had been introduced during the 1930s, and had wide commercial and laboratory applications in the preservation of unstable organic materials ranging from milk to blood plasma. In this process the fluid was frozen, and then water vapour was removed from the solid ice by a combination of a high vacuum with a very low temperature condenser. Freeze-drying was useful in the Oxford work, but it was not an essential part of the process, despite statements by later writers.

At first, in 1940, the main objective of crude penicillin production was to provide enough material for the biochemists, the bacteriologists and the biologists to work with. Chain, the biochemist, had been joined by E. P. Abraham, the pupil of Sir Robert Robinson. Chain thus had a brilliant collaborator and together they began the long and difficult task of purifying penicillin. The first essential, of course, was to eliminate as much as possible of the material in the crude preparations that was not penicillin. Without going into chemical details, some idea of what had to be done can be gained from the figures for the activity of the product achieved as time went by, using the 'Oxford unit' as a measure. The starting material, the mould culture filtrate, had an activity of about 2 units per ml, which would have been roughly the same as that of Fleming's 'mould juice'. By the process of ether (or amyl acetate) extraction, back-extraction into water and freeze-drying, Chain produced a brown powder in 1940 that had an activity equivalent to about 2 units per mg. By 1941, Chain and Abraham were producing material with an activity of 30–50 units per mg,[9] and felt that this must be almost pure. But two years later when penicillin really was purified, it had an activity of 1,800 units per mg.[10] In other words, nearly 99.9 per cent of the 1940 brown powder, and 97 per cent of the 1941 product, was not penicillin at all but unwanted rubbish.

By the middle of March 1940, Chain had a stock of about 100 mg of his brown powder. He had become enthusiastic about the therapeutic possibilities of penicillin and with his excitable and impatient temperament he found that the pace of the bacteriologists and biologists was intolerably slow. He had agreed that Florey should do any animal testing, but Florey was away from Oxford and he felt that he could not wait to find out if his material was toxic. Not having an animal licence, he asked J. M. Barnes, a colleague, to inject 1 ml, containing 20 mg of his powder, intraperitoneally into each of two mice. Barnes did this, not really knowing what he was injecting, and the mice were none the worse. Chain was jubilant, as well he might be, since of all the 'rubbish' in his preparation, some might well have been poisonous. Florey was naturally pleased by the result, but not by the fact that Chain had done the experiment he was about to do himself, and which Fleming had, incidentally, done eleven years before. Indeed, at this time much of the work in Oxford was an extension and consolidation of Fleming's previous observations. Florey tested the toxicity of the penicillin preparation on various animals, on leucocytes and on living tissues, and found it virtually harmless. The bacteriologists confirmed the effect of penicillin on all the organisms reported by Fleming, with the addition of a powerful inhibitory effect on the anaerobes causing gas gangrene that Fleming had observed but not reported.

Towards the end of May, Florey was ready to do the crucial experiment – the experiment that Fleming had *not* done. Florey had given penicillin by mouth and by various routes of injection, in several species of animals, tested the blood levels obtained, and the rate of decline. He discovered that penicillin was destroyed in the stomach, so that giving it by mouth was useless. All forms of injection were effective, but the blood level dropped within two hours because penicillin is excreted in the urine. With all these facts at his disposal, Florey planned the experiment that would show if penicillin could cure an otherwise certainly fatal infection in animals. In theory, it might have been argued (as indeed it had been) that since penicillin took over four hours to kill bacteria in the test tube, and was eliminated from the animal body in about two hours, it could not work systemically and the results of an experiment were bound to be negative. But Florey's motto was 'do the experiment'. He used to say 'if you do the experiment it is not certain that you will get an answer, but if you don't do it, it *is* certain that you won't get one'. Theoretical arguments, however powerful, were no substitute, to his mind, for an actual experiment.

On the morning of Saturday, 25 May 1940, while the entire British Expeditionary Force was being driven by the victorious German army into a smaller and smaller area around Dunkirk, Jim Kent prepared eight white mice for Florey's carefully designed experiment. At 11 a.m. Florey injected each mouse with 100 million virulent streptococci, a certainly lethal dose for unprotected mice. Four of these infected mice were put back in their cages. Of the remaining four, two were labelled A and two B. At noon, the two A mice each received 10 mg of penicillin by subcutaneous injection, and the B mice 5 mg. The A mice were then returned to their cages, and had no further treatment. The B mice were given 4 further injections of 5 mg each, spaced over the next ten hours. By the time Florey gave the last injections to the B mice at 10 p.m. all the untreated mice looked very ill. Heatley stayed on until 3.30 a.m., by which time all four control mice were dead, and all the treated mice seemed perfectly well. He then cycled home in the black-out, being challenged by suspicious Home Guards.

On the morning of Sunday, the 26th, Florey, Chain and Heatley met in the laboratory to see the results. These seemed clear-cut indeed. All four of the treated mice were alive, three seemingly quite normal, one of the A mice not quite as lively as the others. The untreated mice were corpses. Florey remarked that 'it looks quite promising', a typically laconic comment on what Chain, almost dancing with excitement, proclaimed 'a miracle'. Typically, too, Florey wasted no time in self-congratulation, but settled down there and then to plan the next experiments. But everyone there knew that this might be an historic moment, the first glimpse of the path leading to a new era. They did not, perhaps, realize the enormous difficulties that still lay ahead and the labour and ingenuity needed to surmount them. Even if they had, it would not have deterred them for a moment; the four lively mice and the four dead ones made them believe that there was everything to fight for.

On the following day Florey and Dr Jennings repeated the experiment using ten mice, and the outcome was the same. The dreadful possibility that the first results were due to an unrepeatable freak was thus eliminated. They then settled down to do carefully designed experiments using larger numbers of mice, graded doses of penicillin, and different infecting organisms. These experiments defined what penicillin could and could not do, how much had to be given, how often, and for how long. They found that the best results came from frequent small injections of penicillin given over a period of two–four days. Thus, in one experiment with mice infected with streptococci, injections of 0.5 mg given every three hours for forty-five hours cured twenty-four out of twenty-five mice so treated, whereas all twenty-five controls died within a day.[11] It is of interest to note that 0.5 mg of the preparation then available contained about one unit of penicillin. This was, very probably, the amount of activity present in 0.5 ml of Fleming's original, unconcentrated 'mould juice'. By simply injecting mice with 0.5 ml doses of this 'mould juice' and without any biochemical refinements, Fleming could very probably, therefore, have proved the protective power of his material eleven years before the Oxford workers did so.[12]

The Oxford team continued their laborious production of penicillin, and the steady progression of animal experiments while the 'miracle of Dunkirk' was being enacted just across the Straits of Dover. Nearly 350,000 men were evacuated from the beaches by the improvised armada of big and little ships that somehow survived the onslaught of the German dive-bombers. The success of this operation transformed it, in British eyes, into a victory. In fact, of course, it was part of one of the most shattering defeats in military history, in which Britain had lost the equipment of an entire army. Only the air-force – minute compared to Germany's – and doubtful naval supremacy, could prevent invasion. The sombre mood of that time can be gauged from the precautions taken by the Oxford team to preserve something that they had come to believe was more important to mankind as a whole than the outcome of a German invasion of Britain. They faced the fact that if invasion came their work in Oxford would probably be destroyed and their team scattered. But, if the spores of Fleming's strain of *P. notatum* could be preserved and smuggled out of the country, perhaps one of them could re-start the work elsewhere. So Florey, Heatley, Sanders and Chain smeared the spores into the linings of their coats, where they would remain viable and undetected for years.

During these anxious weeks Florey worked with undeviating dedication. He and Kent slept in the laboratory. The alarm clock was set to ring every three hours, and every time it rang there was a batch of perhaps twenty-five animals to be injected, and many more to be inspected and recorded. By July these experiments were complete, and the antibiotic potential of penicillin proved beyond doubt. While the German forces were massing for the Battle of Britain, Florey and his team wrote a paper which was published in *The Lancet* on 24 August 1940.[13] Its title was 'Penicillin as a Chemotherapeutic Agent' and its authors were listed in alphabetical order: E. Chain, H. W. Florey, A. D. Gardner, N. G. Heatley, M. A. Jennings, J. Orr-Ewing and A. G. Sanders. It is, surely, one of the most significant contributions in the history of medicine – yet it is seldom acknowledged as such. It marked the beginning of the development of penicillin therapy. The Second World War would kill millions of people. Penicillin would save the lives or health of millions beyond counting. Ahead of the Oxford team lay the next step – from mice to men. And, as Florey with daunting realism reminded them, a man is 3,000 times as big as a mouse.

The Rising Tide

Since the treatment of a human being with penicillin would need at least 3,000 times the dose for a mouse, production at the Dunn School would somehow have to be enormously increased before a clinical trial could be mounted. Florey's first reaction to this harsh fact was to try to get help from a pharmaceutical firm, which would have large-scale equipment. With the evidence of the animal experiments to offer, Florey therefore went to the Wellcome Laboratories at Beckenham. The Director, J. W. Trevan, was a distinguished physiologist and a friend of Sir Henry Dale. He was impressed by Florey's results and he and his Chief Biochemist, Dr Pope, visited the Dunn School on 15 July 1940, to see the process of production, purification and testing of penicillin.[1] But, in the event, the Wellcome organization decided that they could not, at that time, undertake the large-scale cultivation of an evidently temperamental mould and the processing of a product that had not yet been proved to be of value in human cases. In peacetime they might have gambled, but they were now fully committed to the demands of war for vaccines, antitoxins and blood plasma.

Similar disappointments followed Florey's approaches to other manufacturers, and he found himself in a position of almost intolerable frustration. Unless he could prove the value of penicillin in human patients he could not persuade a pharmaceutical firm to make it in bulk. And unless he could obtain it in bulk, he could not treat human cases effectively. It has often been stated that the war stimulated the early work on the development of penicillin. On the contrary the demands of war were a deadening obstruction to Florey's efforts, which nearly defeated him. In the prewar years, had the same evidence been available, there can be little doubt that one of the British drug firms – always on the look-out for promising new business – would have co-operated. Fleming himself, if he had seriously wanted to develop penicillin as a therapeutic agent in the 1930s could have approached his old friends Messrs Parke Davis and Co. This firm could surely have provided both the biochemical help and production facilities for lack of which Fleming's work on penicillin is usually stated to have foundered.

When the Oxford animal experiments were published in *The Lancet* on

24 August 1940, there were two immediate reactions. The first was a letter from Mellanby, Secretary of the MRC, to Florey, briefly congratulating him on his interesting work, and then going on to castigate him for having acknowledged a grant from the Rockefeller Foundation which he had received without Mellanby's knowledge or approval. Florey was not slow to point out in his reply that it was his American benefactors who had mainly financed the penicillin project because his applications to Mellanby had produced so little.[2] In comparison to the importance of the work itself, squabbles about small sums of money and parochial pride seem ridiculously petty. But feelings were hurt on all sides – including the American one – and Florey never quite regained the good relations with Mellanby that had been such an important factor in his career. An element of friction had developed, and the herculean efforts that were still to be demanded of Florey and his team were not made the easier because of it.

The second event triggered by the publication was the appearance of Fleming himself at the Dunn School on the morning of Monday, 2 September. Until he had read *The Lancet* paper, it seems that he had no idea that any work on penicillin was going on in Oxford. His arrival there was not quite the surprise that mythology has depicted, because he had telephoned to Florey a day or so before, to make the appointment. But it seems to be true that when Florey told Chain that Fleming was coming, Chain said that he had not realized that he was still alive. Somehow this story leaked out and was later suitably embellished by the media. It appears, for example, in the BBC television biography of Fleming broadcast in 1972.[3] In this, the authors of the Oxford paper are supposed to have referred in it to 'the late Professor Fleming'. His fictionally unannounced appearance in their laboratory thus provides good television drama. The scene then shifts to the Flemings' bedroom at The Dhoon.

'*Sareen*: "And what did they say?" *Fleming*: "They thought I was dead, you see!" *Sareen*: "Dead?" *Fleming*: "The late Professor Fleming." *Sareen*: "So what did you say – when you got there?" *Fleming*: "Boo!" '

In less colourful reality Fleming, in his neat suit and inevitable bow-tie, was met by Florey. 'I've come,' he said, 'to see what you've been doing with my old penicillin.' This somewhat proprietorial attitude was, of course, quite natural from Fleming's standpoint. Penicillin *was* his, in the sense that, twelve years before, he had discovered it, named it, and had used it regularly in his laboratory ever since. He had even provided the culture with which the Oxford team was working. But his choice of words struck a discordant note that was to sound again and again in later years, and still sounds today. After all their work, anxiety, and contriving, the Oxford team had come to regard penicillin as something in which they too, had proprietorial rights. In their hands a laboratory reagent had become a refined instrument of enormous therapeutic promise.

In an ideal world no scientist would have proprietorial rights in the results of his work. His discoveries would be free gifts to humanity to be used for the benefit of all, and to be taken up and developed by anyone with the ability to carry his work further. In the real world of human nature (which afflicts scientists no less than other people) there is often an understandable resentment on the part of a worker who sees his discovery being developed by someone else, and on the part of the developer who finds that the results of his labours seem somehow to become the moral property of the original discoverer.

But, at that first meeting between Fleming and the Oxford team, there was only the barest hint of this embryo antagonism. Fleming was clearly pleased that anyone should be fostering his brainchild. Florey and Heatley took a good deal of trouble to show him every detail of the Oxford work, and finally gave him a sample of their best preparation. They noticed that he paid the closest attention to everything that he saw and heard but, apart from a few questions, said almost nothing. He left the Dunn School without a word of congratulation or encouragement, and took an afternoon train back to Paddington. The Oxford workers heard nothing more from him until 15 November.

That September of 1940 was the month of the Battle of Britain and the blitz on London. On the outbreak of war a year before, plans for the massive evacuation of women, children, old people and invalids from London and other industrial cities had been put into effect, and literally millions had been moved into temporary billets in the provincial towns and villages. But the eerie calm of the 'phoney war' had lulled the fear of apocalyptic destruction and a large proportion of the displaced city dwellers, thoroughly bored by country life, had drifted back to their homes. For the London teaching hospitals, the establishment of the Emergency Medical Service involved the removal of most of their services and administration to base hospitals well outside London, but in a 'sector' allotted to each teaching hospital, leaving its buildings in the metropolis to serve as a casualty clearing station with only a skeleton staff. The St Mary's Hospital 'sector' stretched westwards and the main base was Harefield Hospital near Uxbridge. Under the evacuation plans most of the staff of St Mary's moved to Harefield and organized their clinical and teaching duties there as best they could.

Fleming, as one of the senior pathologists at St Mary's, had been told to remove himself and his laboratory to Harefield on the outbreak of war. He made no overt objection to this plan, but in fact never complied with it. Being able to delay the move for one reason or another, he managed to remain in his own laboratory throughout the war, though Paddington Station put the hospital in a prime target area for the German bombers. As it happened, St Mary's luckily escaped damage from high-explosive bombs, but incendiaries rained down on it, and only the prompt action of the fire-watchers saved it from destruction on several occasions.

Fleming seemed quite unperturbed by the wailing sirens, the barrage of the guns and the earth-shaking crump of bombs. Even under these conditions he preferred the familiar clutter of his own laboratory, surrounded by innumerable bacteriological treasures. So, instead of the St Mary's Pathology Department being staffed by a few 'front-line' juniors, with the Sector Pathologist safely based at Harefield, the position was reversed. The Sector Pathologist was happily engaged at St Mary's with the blitz raging almost unnoticed around him, and discharging his official duties by a weekly visit to his base laboratory at Harefield. He seems to have been the only Sector Pathologist to have remained at his teaching hospital throughout the war.[4] He was also living in his own home in Chelsea, until it was bombed in March 1941. And during his spells of night duty at the hospital, he shared the fire-watchers' dormitory in the basement with the students on the rota, after joining them for a pint or two of beer at the 'Fountains Abbey'. It was, in a sense, like the old days at Boulogne and he enjoyed the companionship.

Thus it was to St Mary's that Fleming returned after his visit to Oxford on 2 September. He brought back with him samples of the best penicillin that the Dunn School could produce. He tested these by his own methods, and found that they had a titre higher than anything he had handled before. On 14 November, in a lecture on 'Antiseptics in Wartime Surgery' to the Pharmaceutical Society, Fleming ended with a few words about penicillin.[5] After ten years of being used for differential culture, he said it had recently come to the fore again as a possible therapeutic agent. Workers in Oxford had a method for extracting the active principle as a solid, though not in a pure state. He himself had obtained some of this material and had found that, weight for weight, it was a stronger antiseptic than the sulphonamides. Penicillin had not yet been tried in war surgery, nor would it be tried 'until some chemist comes along and finds out exactly what it is and manufactures it'. On 15 November he wrote to Florey saying that he was sending some cultures of his mould that produced a good yield of penicillin, but very little pigment. He went on: 'It only remains for your chemical colleagues to purify the active principle, and then synthesize it, and the sulphonamides will be completely beaten.'[6]

His attitude, therefore, was that of an interested spectator of what was going on at Oxford, and he took no further active part in it. But on 29 November 1940, he received a letter from Dr Stanley White, of Messrs Parke, Davis. Dr White had himself had a letter from the parent company in Detroit, saying that they were interested in the Oxford results with penicillin and suggesting that Fleming should ask the Oxford workers if they would supply Parke, Davis with mould cultures and penicillin preparations for use in possible commercial development.[7] Fleming replied to Stanley White that the cultures being used at Oxford were derived from his original one, and that there was very little penicillin to spare. He did not pass on the Parke, Davis enquiry to Oxford, but he did give Stanley White a culture of his mould. As a result, Parke, Davis set up a production process at their Hounslow laboratories, that was almost identical with that being used at Oxford. The details of this must have been provided by Fleming, since they had not, at that time, been published. But a number of technical difficulties arose, despite the labours of Mr S. F. Everitt, the chemist in charge of the project,[8] and in view of subsequent developments in America, it was abandoned. Fleming seems not to have been closely involved in this abortive commercial effort once it had started, and there is no record of his having visited the Hounslow laboratories to observe its progress.

By that time the blitz was causing heavy casualties in London and Fleming, with his matchless experience in the treatment of septic war wounds, was kept busy in the wards of St Mary's and his sector hospitals. There had been, of course, a new dimension added to the classical treatment established during the 1914–18 war. This was the systemic and local use of the sulphonamides. These were by no means fully effective, but were a great improvement on the antiseptics against which Wright and Fleming had campaigned for years. Fleming took an active part in promoting this new regime, publishing no less than seven lectures and articles on the subject in 1940 and four in 1941. Most of these dealt with the use of the sulphonamides, and their possible combination with vaccine therapy. After the Oxford animal experiments he usually included a few remarks on the possible therapeutic value of penicillin if it could be purified chemically and produced commercially.

There was another and more positive reaction to the 1940 *Lancet* paper on penicillin. When he read it, Dr M. H. Dawson of Columbia University and the Presbyterian Hospital, New York, was filled by hope that penicillin might save the lives of patients suffering from bacterial endocarditis, the condition in which he specialized, and which even with sulphonamide therapy, was almost invariably fatal. In this disease the valves of the heart become invaded by bacteria – usually a particular strain of streptococcus – which could not be dislodged by any available treatment. In consequence the blood was constantly infected, the valves themselves became destroyed, and the patient died within a few weeks or months. Dawson, himself suffering from a progressive and incurable muscular disease, determined to produce enough penicillin to try on his otherwise doomed patients. He obtained a culture of Fleming's mould from Dr R. D. Reid, of the Pennsylvania College of Agriculture, who had worked with it in 1933. Then, with Dr Gladys Hobby, a microbiologist, and Dr Karl Meyer, a biochemist, Dawson organized a penicillin production effort in the University classrooms very much on the Oxford model. Within a month or two they had produced enough crude penicillin to give by injection to three of Dawson's patients, beginning on 15 October 1940. Evidence suggests that the dose used must have been very small. There were no ill-effects but there was also no improvement, and the infection persisted. Dawson realized that the dosage was inadequate, but he could not increase his supplies of penicillin. Finally, like Paine, he showed that it was effective as a local antiseptic in a few cases of eye infections.

Dawson presented his findings at a meeting of the Society for Clinical Investigation in New York in May, 1941, but they seemed unspectacular and aroused little interest. Dawson died from his *myasthenia gravis* in 1945, unrecognized as the first person to have used penicillin systemically. It was only many years later that the details, obtained from Dr Gladys Hobby by Lennard Bickel, were published in his book *Rise Up to Life* in 1972.[9]

Meanwhile the work in Oxford was gaining momentum as the year 1940 drew to its close. Florey's efforts to obtain commercial help in Britain had virtually failed. The flicker of interest by the Wellcome organization, fanned, it seems, by Sir Henry Dale, led to a few small-scale experiments at Beckenham, which by the end of 1940 had not even produced a reliable assay method. Florey, still determined to carry out a clinical trial, was therefore thrown back on his own resources, of which the most effective was his own character and his power of leadership. He decided that, if existing pharmaceutical factories could not or would not help, then the Sir William Dunn School of Pathology would itself become a factory.

The decision to turn an academic university department into a factory was a courageous one for which Florey took full responsibility, and for which he should therefore get full credit. If the venture had failed, it would have been seen as an outrageous misuse of University property, staff, equipment and time, and Florey, as he well knew, would have been severely censured. An output of 500 litres of mould filtrate per week would be needed to provide within a few months enough penicillin to treat five or six patients. Up to that time the mould had been cultured in a variety of makeshift containers – flasks, flat-sided bottles, petrol cans, biscuit tins and other things that had been adapted by the ingenious Heatley. But the best results had come from the use of ordinary hospital bedpans, and so Heatley designed a special container on the bed pan model, and Florey was able to persuade a pottery manufacturer in Stoke to make 600 such vessels. Heatley collected most of the batch himself in a borrowed van two days before Christmas, 1940.

From that point the process of scaling-up production went forward in an atmosphere of excitement and optimism. Florey was able to engage a team of six 'penicillin girls' who became adept in the technique of inoculating the culture vessels under sterile conditions, using paint-sprays to distribute the spores. These girls were paid less than £2.00 per week by the Medical

Research Council, and Florey had to fight to get their wages raised to £2.50 on the argument that they could earn more in local factories. The students' classroom became the inoculation department, the preparation room the incubator where the racks of culture vessels were kept at constant temperature for fourteen days before being harvested. A range of laboratories became the extraction and purification rooms, and others the bacteriological, chemical and biological control sections.

Laboratory-scale apparatus was too small to be useful, and Heatley turned to available dairy equipment. The mould filtrate was stored and transported in milk churns: milk-coolers kept the various fluids at the required temperature during the extraction processes, and continuous-flow Alfa-Laval centrifuges, of the cream-separator type, divided the emulsions and suspensions into the desired fractions. The process involved large quantities of ether and, later, amyl acetate, which had to be stored, pumped, extracted and re-used under conditions that no factory inspector or fire officer would have sanctioned for a moment – had he known about it. The risk of fire or explosion was alarming, and the fumes of these solvents were unpleasant and even dangerous. But at that time no one at the Dunn School bothered about such things. Infinitely greater hazards were being cheerfully faced by those fighting the war in the air or at sea, and the victory to be won in that laboratory building promised to be as great as any victory ever won by force of arms.

By the beginning of January 1941, there was enough penicillin to justify plans for a clinical trial. Chain and Abraham had improved the purification. Their product now had an activity of 30–50 units per mg, and was thus about twenty times stronger than the material used for the animal experiments. Part of this improvement was due to the introduction of column chromatography, a process in which the solution containing a mixture of organic substances is passed through a column of some insoluble but adsorbent powder such as alumina. The different components of the mixture tend to be adsorbed by different layers in the column, and if these components are coloured, the layers in which they have become trapped are shown by the colour they have acquired. Most of the active penicillin, for example, was found in a well-marked yellow-brown band. This could be separated from the other and unwanted bands by extruding the column from its enclosing tube, cutting it up with a knife, and eluting (extracting) the penicillin from the brown-stained powder with a suitable solvent.

The first practical step into the clinical field was to get collaboration at the Radcliffe Infirmary, since none of the Dunn School workers were themselves clinicians. Florey went to see the Nuffield Professor of Medicine, L. J. Witts, with whom he had worked in Cambridge in 1927. Witts agreed to help, and assigned one of his Nuffield Research Students, Dr Charles Fletcher, to the project. The next move was to discover if the penicillin preparation could be safely given to a human being. Unaware of Dawson's work, the Oxford team supposed that penicillin had never before been injected in man, and there was no guarantee that its non-toxicity in the animals tested meant that it would be non-toxic in humans. (Strangely enough, it was later discovered that penicillin *is* toxic to guinea pigs, which had not been used in the preliminary experiments. If they had been, there might have been a crisis of confidence and serious delay.) There was only one way to discover if their penicillin could be injected safely into a human being, and that was to inject it.

This posed, of course, an ethical problem, because such an injection might do unexpected harm. There would have been no shortage of volunteers from the Dunn School staff, but neither Witts nor Florey felt justified in subjecting a healthy young adult to something that might do permanent damage. A more ethical course would be to use the penicillin in a patient likely to die of an infection which it might possibly cure. But in a desperately ill person it would be impossible to tell whether or not the injection had produced an adverse reaction. So it was decided to look for a patient known to be dying from cancer who would agree – having been told the facts – to receive an injection of penicillin. Fletcher found such a patient in the hospital, a Mrs Elva Akers of Oxford, who knew that she had only a month or two to live, and readily agreed to the experiment.[10] On 17 January 1941, he injected 100 mg of penicillin intravenously, with Witts and Florey standing by to see what would happen. At first nothing happened, but then Mrs Akers began to shiver, and her temperature rose – she was having a rigor.

Rigors of this sort were not an uncommon reaction to intravenous infusions of any sort of fluid, including blood transfusions, and they were due to 'pyrogens', traces of bacterial products that might contaminate even the sterile distilled water used to make infusion fluids. Florey's first response to this adverse reaction was therefore one of annoyance rather than dismay, and he went straight back to his laboratory to look for pyrogens in the penicillin solution. There is a very sensitive test for these, and when he found them, it was not a serious problem to remove them by more selective chromatography.

As soon as it was clear that Mrs Akers had suffered no other ill-effects, a systematic investigation in healthy volunteers was begun to determine the most effective methods for giving penicillin, the amounts needed to maintain a bacteriostatic level, and the ways in which it is eliminated from the body. It was soon found that, however it was given, it was rapidly excreted in the urine. As Florey remarked, keeping up an effective blood level was like trying to fill a bath with the plug out. But there was no way of putting the plug in, and the only course was to pour penicillin into the bloodstream fast enough to keep the level up. Penicillin was destroyed in the stomach, and unless it could be protected from the stomach acids, it could not be given effectively by mouth. With facts about the blood levels achieved and about the levels needed to destroy bacteria in the body, Florey felt that they were ready to treat their first case of serious sepsis. This methodical, painstaking groundwork was typical of all Florey's experimental work, and the reason for much of his phenomenal success.

Fletcher found a suitable patient on 12 February 1941. He was Albert Alexander, a 43-year-old policeman, who had been fighting a losing battle against a relentlessly spreading infection for the past two months. This had begun in a scratch on his face from a rosebush. Staphylococci and streptococci had invaded the tissues of his face to reach his eyes and scalp. He had received massive doses of sulphonamides, and numerous abscesses had been drained surgically. His left eye had to be removed on 3 February, and then his lungs and a shoulder became infected. He was clearly on the verge of death. Fletcher gave him an injection of 200 mg of penicillin on the 12th, followed at three-hourly intervals by doses of 100 mg. Within twenty-four hours there was a dramatic improvement in his condition, his temperature fell to normal and his appetite returned. By the 17th, the swelling of his face had subsided, and his right eye had become normal. Treatment with penicillin was then stopped, since it was hoped that the danger was over, and supplies were very limited. All the urine he had passed during treatment was taken to the Dunn School, and the penicillin contained in it extracted and re-injected.

For the next ten days the improvement in Alexander's condition continued, and Fletcher began treatment of a second patient on 22 February. This was a boy of fifteen who was desperately ill with streptococcal septicaemia following an operation on his hip on 24 January. Fletcher gave him 100 mg every three hours for five days. Within two days his temperature became and remained normal, and he made a complete recovery from what had seemed a certainly fatal condition. But just as the treatment of this second patient had finished, and with it all the available supplies of penicillin, Albert Alexander began to suffer a relapse. The infection had not been completely eradicated by the five days of penicillin treatment, and it returned in full force. No doubt a second course of penicillin might have saved his life, but there was now none to give him, and he died of staphylococcal septicaemia on 15 March. The doctors who had observed his case were quite convinced that the use of penicillin had produced an almost miraculous improvement, but the cold fact was that the patient was dead. The second patient, however, was an unqualified success.

The third patient was treated in May, when a new supply of penicillin had been produced. He was a man with a 4-inch carbuncle on his back, a form of staphylococcal abscess that usually needed surgical excision and took weeks to heal. The man was severely ill, with fever and enlarged glands. Penicillin was started on 3 May, and by the 10th the carbuncle had virtually disappeared, healing without even a scar. This was indeed a dramatic result, since it was clinically unprecedented.

The fourth patient was a little boy aged four and a half who had developed an infection of his eye socket after an attack of measles. The infection had then spread into the base of the skull, causing the condition of cavernous sinus thrombosis which was then invariably fatal. Sulphonamides had been given without effect. Penicillin treatment was started on 13 May, when the boy was semi-comatose, with gross swelling of the face and eyelids, and signs of meningitis. By the 16th he was dramatically better, with the swelling subsiding rapidly, and by the 22nd he was eating well, talking, and playing with toys. The penicillin was stopped, and the improvement continued. But on the 27th he suddenly had a convulsion and died. Post-mortem examination showed that though the infection had been completely eliminated, it had weakened a blood vessel in the brain, which had given way. Again, there was no doubt of the effect of the treatment on the infection, but the patient was dead.

The fifth patient was a boy aged fourteen with staphylococcal septi-caemia from an osteomyelitis of the left femur. By 6 June he was acutely ill, with signs of kidney infection. On that day Fletcher began a slow intravenous infusion of penicillin and during the next two weeks gave 17.2 g, by far the largest dose yet given. The result was a complete cure, and it was this case that began to prompt the use of the word 'miracle' by the doctors who knew only too well the almost invariably fatal outcome of such an infection. The sixth case was a baby boy aged six months who had a staphylococcal infection of the urinary tract. On 5 June, he was given penicillin by mouth, with enough alkali to neutralize the acid in the stomach and prevent it from destroying the drug. This treatment worked. Penicillin appeared in the urine, and after a week the infection was cured and the baby recovered completely. Finally, penicillin was used successfully to treat four cases of acute eye infection.

Reviewing these cases, the Oxford clinical and laboratory workers could have no doubt about the tremendous therapeutic potential of penicillin. Every patient had improved dramatically and two had been saved from almost certain death. And yet two others *had* died, a sad outcome that would undoubtedly reduce the impact of the trial on a sceptical medical profession. The fact that one had died because the treatment had been stopped too early, and the other from an unavoidable complication, would not convert a partial success into a resounding triumph. In August 1941, the Oxford workers published their paper 'Further Observations on Penicillin' in *The Lancet*.[11] The authors were Abraham, Chain, Fletcher, Florey, Gardner, Heatley and Margaret Jennings. The paper began with a detailed account, which had not before been published, of the technique developed for the culture of the mould on the largest scale possible in an academic laboratory, and of the extraction, purification and testing of penicillin. The development of resistance by certain bacteria was described. The biological experiments followed, including the effect of penicillin on living tissues, leucocytes and other cells, and on animal tissues *in vivo*. Various routes of administration were described – including intrathecal injection (that is, into the spinal fluid) in five rabbits without any ill-effect, a point that will have a later interest. There followed a long section on the absorption and excretion of penicillin in rabbits, cats and human subjects. Finally there was a factual and detailed account of the therapeutic trial itself.

On the debit side of this historic achievement was the massive scale of the operation that had been needed to produce these numerically meagre results. Seven graduates, including two professors, and ten technical assistants had worked almost every day of the week and during many nights for several months in order to make enough penicillin to treat six patients for a few days each. And the groundwork had occupied eight or nine people for two years. The publication of the paper proclaimed to the medical world what penicillin could do; but could any drug, however effective, which was so difficult and expensive to make ever become generally available? This was the question that the pharmaceutical firms asked when Florey once more tried to enlist their help. It was evident to them that to produce penicillin by the methods used at the Dunn School on a commercial scale would be enormously difficult and costly. And penicillin might not live up to its clinical promise. There might be unexpected side effects or dangers. Above all, there was the possibility that it might be chemically synthesized at any moment, thus making a large investment in the cumbersome culture process obsolete almost overnight – Fleming had already stressed this point. So although the Wellcome organization, Boots, ICI, the Lister Institute, Kemball–Bishop and, unknown to Oxford, Parke, Davis, all showed some interest, none made any serious attempts to start production. Though the Oxford results were acclaimed by the medical press there was no appreciation beyond Florey's circle that a new era in medicine was about to dawn.

Surely however, there must have been a very important exception to this last statement. In all the many accounts of Fleming's life and career he has been portrayed as a man with a burning conviction that his precious penicillin, after years of fruitless struggle on his part and neglect by his colleagues, would one day become a therapeutic triumph. Now that, in 1941, his hopes, supposedly so often disappointed in the past, seemed about to be realized, one might have thought that a delighted Fleming would have been a frequent visitor to Oxford and a powerful champion in the campaign to promote further development. In fact, he seems to have remained relatively unmoved and inactive. This attitude may have several explanations. He may have felt that what was being done by the Oxford workers was their business, and that since they had not consulted him at the beginning he was under no obligation to help when they needed all the support they could get. There is no evidence that Florey asked Fleming for support, but equally there is no evidence that he offered it.

Another reason for Fleming's lack of enthusiasm would be his appreciation of the enormous difficulty and expense of preparing penicillin by existing methods. In his letter to Florey of 15 November 1940, and in his various lectures at that time, he stressed that penicillin would only become a better therapeutic agent than the sulphonamides if the chemists could purify and synthesize it. And, from subsequent events, it is clear that Fleming, even then, did not really appreciate the therapeutic potential of the substance that he himself had discovered. Other people's results are never as convincing as one's own. 'Seeing is believing' is an old saying, expressing a fundamental truth, and Almroth Wright's contention that belief is an emotional and not a logical reaction simply restates it. Fleming did not really 'believe' in penicillin until, in August 1942, he saw its power with his own eyes. Then, as will be related, he became galvanized into action.

After the publication of the Oxford paper in August 1941, Fleming did, however, take some steps to emphasize his rights in penicillin. On the 30th of that month the *British Medical Journal* published an editorial article on the promising clinical results in Oxford. It began by describing Fleming's original discovery, but suggested that the great therapeutic possibilities of penicillin, being demonstrated in Oxford, had been previously unrecognized. Fleming replied in a letter dated 1 September, to the Editor of the *BMJ* which was published on 13 September. In this, Fleming refuted the suggestion that he had not recognized the therapeutic value of penicillin. He referred to his demonstration of the lack of toxicity for leucocytes and living tissues that distinguished it from all other available antiseptics, and quoted the conclusion in his first paper:

'It is suggested that it may be an efficient antiseptic for application to, or injection into, areas infected with penicillin-sensitive microbes.'

He also quoted the sentence in his paper to the *British Dental Journal* of 1931:

'Penicillin is valuable to us at present in the isolation of certain microbes, but it is quite likely that it, or a chemical of similar nature, will be used in the treatment of septic wounds.'

He then went on to say that the Oxford workers had made a great advance by producing penicillin in a dry state, which 'enabled a clinical trial to be made which has more than justified the suggestions I made ten or more years ago'.[12]

Fleming seemed to be implying that he had anticipated the systemic use of penicillin, given by injection as it had been given in Oxford, and this implication was to be taken up by his colleagues and biographers. But another, and quite valid contention would be that his writings and his doings between 1929 and 1941 indicate that he had thought of penicillin only as a useful laboratory reagent and as a possibly useful local antiseptic. The reader must judge for himself between these two conflicting views.

Following these exchanges in the medical press there was a small flurry of interest in the newspapers.[13] The *Daily Herald* described Fleming's discovery, and how seven doctors in Oxford had used it on seven patients. The *Listener*, too, under the heading, 'A Vital Discovery', paid tribute to Fleming and a group of workers at Oxford. The *Evening News* carried the Fleming story. *Tit-Bits*, under the heading, 'The Cure that Came in Through the Window', described the original discovery and how chemists were put to work and the product was tried on patients in an Oxford Hospital. *Smith's Weekly* produced another variant of the Fleming story – he found the mould on a piece of cheese. It was all very good copy, and the papers that took it up made the best of it. Fleming was naturally the central character, and though the work in Oxford was mentioned – but not the names of the workers – the reader was left with the impression that he was directing what was being done there. Apart from these few newspaper articles, and some better-informed ones in such professional journals as the *Nursing Times*, *Pharmaceutical Journal* and *Veterinary Record*, there was very little general or even medical interest.

In the meantime Fleming had been living the busy, precarious – even dangerous – life of all those Londoners doing essential work in a city under bombardment. In November 1940 the house in Danvers Street had been hit by incendiary bombs while Alec and Sareen were dining out, and they returned to find their home full of firemen and flooded by water. They were given refuge by their old friend Dr D. M. Pryce at Rickmansworth. In March 1941 they moved back into their Danvers Street flat, but only a month later a land-mine exploded close by, and did extensive damage. Alec, Sareen, Robert and one of his cousins, and Elizabeth, Sareen's twin sister who lived in the upper part of the house, were all sleeping there at the time, and were half-buried by collapsing ceilings and blown-in windows, though not injured. The Fleming family, bombed-out for the second time in four months, then went to live with Alec's brother Robert at Radlett.

A few months later there was a more permanent solution to their housing problem. Dr V. D. Allison, who had worked with Fleming on lysozyme, was then a Home Office scientist. He had been posted to Cardiff, and he offered his old chief the use of his house in Highgate 'for the duration'.[14] Alec accepted gratefully, and immediately began to improve Allison's garden which in later years revealed the unexpected and growing wonders of the work of his green fingers. It was a happy arrangement, because Allison had to make periodic official visits to London, and was then a welcome guest in his own house. Fleming was often on night duty at St Mary's and Allison would sometimes share this with him, helping with the laboratory work, sleeping in the basement dormitory and joining the convivial relaxation at the Fountains Abbey across the road that Alec so much enjoyed.

In June 1941, with the first clinical trial of penicillin completed, Florey decided that a second and larger one would be needed before its tremendous value could be demonstrated to the world. Again he sought commercial help but he finally concluded that the chances of finding it in Britain were so small that he must turn to the United States. He had influential friends there, notably the officials of the Rockefeller Foundation who agreed to pay the costs of an extended visit by himself and a colleague. Professor John Fulton of Yale University was another powerful friend. Florey and Fulton had been Rhodes Scholars at Magdalen College, Oxford, and it was with the Fulton family that the Florey children, evacuated from Oxford, were living. And there was Dr A. N. Richards, with whom Florey had worked in 1925, who was, in 1941, Chairman of the US Medical Research Committee. For his companion on what was to prove a most arduous tour of exposition and persuasion, Florey chose Norman Heatley, which did not please Chain. They arrived in New York on 2 July, and spent the Independence Day holiday with the Fultons, during which John Fulton telephoned all over the United States making useful contacts for the tour that would occupy Florey and Heatley for three months.

A fruitful visit was to Dr Charles Thom, of the Department of Agriculture, the famous mycologist who had first identified Fleming's mould. Thom was a realist who calculated from Florey's own figures that 2,000 litres of mould filtrate would be needed to treat one case of severe sepsis. This implied the use, not of existing pharmaceutical-scale methods, but those of a brewery. So Thom arranged for Florey and Heatley to be passed on to the Bureau of Agricultural Chemistry, which had a large fermentation research laboratory at Peoria, Illinois, where a team was working on the production of useful chemicals by brewing techniques. Here, Florey was able to persuade Dr R. D. Coghill, head of the Fermentation Division, to undertake a pilot project beginning with the large-scale cultivation of the mould they had brought from Oxford. Coghill assigned a brilliant fermentation chemist, Dr A. J. Moyer, to the project, with Heatley as his collaborator. While they settled down to work, Florey began his visits to the pharmaceutical firms which might be interested in commercial production. He needed enough penicillin to treat 100 patients in a second clinical trial. He had very little success, even in the form of interest, and he disliked his role intensely. He was, he said 'made to feel like a carpet-bag salesman trying to promote a crazy idea for some ulterior motive'. But in the end and after many rebuffs and disappointments, his efforts did stimulate the large-scale production of penicillin in America – but not, as it happened, for use in another Oxford trial.

Even before Florey and Heatley arrived in America, there had been some desultory interest in penicillin on the part of a few drug firms as a result of the work by Raistrick and by R. D. Reid. Foremost among these was Merck, where, encouraged by their consultant, Professor S. A. Waksman of Rutgers University, a penicillin culture process had been started in the autumn of 1940, though it seems only to have produced about nine litres of culture filtrate.[15] Lederle too, were doing some experiments, and Parke, Davis at Detroit were engaged 'not very seriously' in a small programme. But nothing of any tangible, clinical use had come out of these tentative efforts at production. Florey's energetic intervention encouraged a response in the firms already inclined to be interested, and Merck, Pfizer, Squibb and Lederle eventually took positive and effective action.

Meanwhile, in Peoria, Moyer and Heatley had their production process running, and Moyer had already made improvements. The most significant was the use of corn-steep liquor in the culture medium, which led to a ten-fold increase in the penicillin content of the filtrate. Later, penicillin production was transformed by the deep fermentation technique (analogous to the production of lager beer) which allowed culture in tanks holding thousands of litres, instead of in thousands of small separate vessels. Florey, in his efforts to activate the drug companies, had appealed to his old friend Dr A. N. Richards. He, as Chairman of the Medical Research Committee, had informed the four companies reported by Florey to be interested, that penicillin production might become a matter of national importance, with Government funds available, and they then agreed to co-ordinate their efforts. Since the production process at Peoria (a Government, not a commercial laboratory) was running well, it was agreed that Heatley should transfer to Merck's factory at Rahway, New Jersey, to help to get commercial production going. This he did on 29 November 1941, and from that point development was rapid. But on 7 December the Japanese attacked Pearl Harbor, America was at war, and penicillin production had become in truth a matter of national importance. The Americans had realized very clearly its potential value in the treatment of battle casualties.

Before these developments, Florey had returned to Oxford at the end of September. He found that production had suffered during Heatley's absence, and some time had to be spent in restoring it, with Dr A. G. Sanders being promoted to take charge. The mission to America had indeed set a vast machine in motion, and its accelerating operation would, in a few months, be producing penicillin on a scale hundreds and then thousands of times greater than that of the little Oxford 'factory'. Florey had hoped for enough penicillin for a second and larger clinical trial in Oxford. But America's entry into the war changed the prospect completely. There was now official enthusiasm for penicillin production in America, but for America. The supplies hoped for in Oxford did not arrive, and

Florey found himself in as bad a position as before – in fact in a worse one, since he was without Heatley. But his tough character and unshakeable determination prevailed, and he simply set out to scale up, yet again, the Dunn School process. Adapting the large animal house that Dreyer's lavish designs had made suitable for the accommodation of an elephant, and using yet more dairy equipment, steam-heated dust-bins as stills, domestic baths as reservoirs, and unused bookracks from the Bodleian Library to support the culture vessels, Sanders constructed what was to be for the next two years the largest penicillin extraction plant in Britain.

Some commercial help did come Oxford's way during 1942. Small consignments of penicillin began to arrive in January from a pilot plant set up by ICI, and in September 1942, 200 gallons of crude mould filtrate were sent to Oxford by Kemball–Bishop and Co., the first batch of a regular weekly consignment. This small East London firm, at the instigation of Sir Robert Robinson, had for months been carrying out experiments on culturing the mould in a factory subjected to repeated air raids and bomb damage, and they made this contribution to the Oxford work entirely at their own expense. It was a contribution that added very significantly to the stocks of a more purified penicillin that were building up in Oxford.

On the Crest of the Wave

During 1942 the output of penicillin from the Dunn School plant, with small commercial contributions, became enough for a second clinical trial. Charles Fletcher had left Oxford, so Dr Ethel Florey, Howard Florey's wife, took on the exacting task of choosing, treating and recording the cases. In this trial 15 patients with serious infection were treated systemically, and all but one recovered completely from conditions that would previously have been thought hopeless. The one exception was a case of bacterial endocarditis in which the microbe became resistant to penicillin, and the patient died.

Knowing that their supplies of penicillin were limited, the Floreys then undertook a study of its value as a local antiseptic. In 22 cases of acute mastoid infection the cavity, after being opened surgically, was closed immediately around a tube through which penicillin irrigation was carried out. In 19 cases the infection was cured and healing complete within ten days. Eye infections were clearly suitable for penicillin irrigation and excellent results were obtained in 87 out of 89 cases. Chronic wound sinuses were also treated by irrigation and in 9 out of 11 cases openings that had been discharging pus for months or even years healed within a few days. Finally 50 cases of septic fingers, hands and wounds were treated locally by penicillin, with far more rapid resolution than usual. In March 1943, Ethel and Howard Florey published in *The Lancet* the results in 189 cases.[1] These could leave no doubt that penicillin was an antibacterial agent of unprecedented value – in fact the 'miracle drug' that the lay press would soon proclaim it to be. But the closing lines of their paper emphasized the main barrier still to be overcome. 'Penicillin is as yet available in only the smallest quantities – no applications for it should be made either to the authors or to ICI (Dyestuffs) Ltd for supplies.'

In fact, one such application had been made and willingly granted. This was from Alexander Fleming, and the occasion marked his active re-entry into the penicillin field after an interval of about twelve years. In June 1942, Mr Harry Lambert, of the optical firm of J. and R. Fleming became ill with what seemed to be influenza.[2] During the next three weeks he became worse, with signs of meningitis. At Robert Fleming's request, Fleming arranged for the sick man to be admitted to St Mary's Hospital, where he was treated unsuccessfully with sulphonamides for another three weeks. Fleming was recalled from holiday on 1 August, because the patient seemed to be dying. No organisms had been found to account for his condition, but Fleming succeeded in isolating a streptococcus from his cerebro-spinal fluid, and found that it was sensitive to penicillin. Almost as a last resort, therefore, he decided to try penicillin. But he *had* no therapeutic penicillin, and he had never used it systemically. So he appealed to Florey in Oxford, telephoning him on 5 August. Florey at once gave Fleming all the penicillin he had, but accounts differ on exactly how it was conveyed to St Mary's. One states that it was rushed by army despatch rider that night, but as the same source names the patient as Sir Montague Norman, Governor of the Bank of England, it must be suspect.[3] A more likely version has it that Florey simply took the penicillin himself by train from Oxford to Paddington, and explained to Fleming how to use it.

Fleming began injections on 6 August, and continued them for seven days. Within twenty-four hours of the first the patient improved and his temperature fell. But the signs of brain infection persisted, and Fleming found that no penicillin was passing from the blood into the cerebro-spinal spaces where the streptococci still lurked. He telephoned to Florey, suggesting that the penicillin should be injected intrathecally. Florey replied that penicillin had never been given by this route in man, and that he would try it on an animal. Fleming, however, did not wait for the results of this experiment and, with considerable courage, gave his patient an intrathecal injection of penicillin on 13 August followed by four similar injections during the next seven days. There was, almost immediately, a dramatic improvement. All the patient's symptoms disappeared, he was up and about by 28 August, and walked out of hospital completely cured on 9 September.

It was just as well that Fleming did not wait for the results of Florey's experiment, because the animal he injected (said by some authors to have been a cat) died an hour or two afterwards, and knowledge of this might have dissuaded Fleming from making what proved to be a life-saving innovation. In fact, Florey's laboratory notebook records the intrathecal injection of penicillin into a rabbit, with quickly fatal results, on 13 August.[4] It is strange that the animal did die, because, as mentioned on p. 187, five rabbits had received penicillin by this route in 1941 with no ill-effects. By arrangement with Fleming the case of Harry Lambert was included in the Oxford trial results published in March 1943. Fleming, too, published a more detailed account in October 1943.[5] Each thanked the other in both publications.

Harry Lambert's miraculous recovery brought home to all who had witnessed it at St Mary's the tremendous possibilities of penicillin, and they became ardent converts. It may seem strange to include Fleming himself among these converts, because it is popularly supposed that it was his lone voice that had been proclaiming the faith in the medical wilderness for the past twelve years. But his intense activity after this personal therapeutic triumph compared with his lack of action before it strongly suggests that, until he saw with his own eyes what penicillin could do, he had no sincere conviction of its power. Having been convinced, he acted. Even before his patient was out of hospital Fleming went to see Sir Andrew Duncan, Minister of Supply, a fellow member of the Ayrshire Society, to persuade him of the need for Government help in promoting penicillin production. Sir Andrew, clearly impressed, sent for Sir Cecil Weir, Director General of Equipment, saying (according to Maurois):

'Fleming has been talking to me about penicillin. He believes, and so do I, that it offers immense possibilities for the treatment of wounds and of numerous diseases. I want you to do everything you can to organise its production on a great scale.'[6]

Sir Cecil Weir acted promptly. He called a conference, which met on 25 September 1943, at Portland House. Weir himself was in the chair, and the members attending included Fleming, Raistrick, Florey, and representatives of a number of commercial firms, who agreed that they would share their information and research results in the interest of rapid production. Florey, who had more practical knowledge of such production than anyone else present, was able to describe the work at Oxford, and the supplies already being received from ICI and Kemball–Bishop. Glaxo, too, were establishing a production unit in a disused cheese factory at Aylesbury, using a scaled-up version of the Oxford process. So Fleming's intervention added the weight of official approval to a movement that had already begun.[7] And the main result of the conference, the establishment of a Penicillin Committee, of which Sir Henry Dale was to become Chairman, undoubtedly helped to co-ordinate the commercial production of penicillin in Britain and to control its distribution.

It was a 'miracle-cure' rather similar to that of Harry Lambert that convinced American doctors and officials of the power of penicillin. In March, 1942, Mrs Ogden Miller, the 33-year-old wife of the Yale University Director of Athletics, became gravely ill. She developed streptococcal septicaemia following a miscarriage, and failed to respond to sulphonamides. For four weeks her temperature swung between 103° and 106° every day, until her physician, Dr Bumstead, despaired of her life. Then he suddenly remembered a conversation with Professor John Fulton, who happened to be another of his patients, in which Fulton had told him of Florey's visit, and his remarkable results with something called penicillin. Bumstead appealed to Fulton to try to obtain penicillin for Mrs Miller. Fulton at once contacted Norman Heatley at Merck, in Rahway. Heatley had to refer him to his Medical Director, who in turn told Fulton that clinical use of the little penicillin they had could only be sanctioned by Dr A. N. Richards. Fulton ran Richards to earth in Washington, only to be told that penicillin was now controlled by the Committee on Chemotherapy. Undaunted, Fulton tracked down its Chairman, Dr Perrin Long, who gave the required authorization for Heatley to send 5.5 g of penicillin to Dr Bumstead.[8]

With advice from Heatley, Bumstead began penicillin injections on Saturday, 14 March, and what happened then is described by Fulton in his diary:

'This week the hospital has been very excited because of the extraordinary results that have followed the first clinical trial of Howard Florey's penicillin. I mentioned last week the case of Mrs Ogden Miller, who for four weeks had been going down hill with what appeared, on the basis of all previous experience, to be a fatal haemolytic streptococcus septicaemia. By 9 a.m. Sunday her temperature was normal for the first time in 4 weeks. She has eaten several enormous meals – also for the first time in 4 weeks. It really looks as if Florey had made a ten-strike of the first water, and I am glad that we have had an opportunity to make the first clinical trial of the American extract here.'[9]

Mrs Miller's recovery was both rapid and complete. It will be noted that Fulton referred to Howard Florey – as well he might.

Mrs Miller's case was indeed important because it served as an emotional catalyst. Naturally, there was a good deal of national satisfaction that a moribund woman had been saved by a new drug produced in an American factory. The public press made much of what one paper called the 'giant germ killer', and pressure for more rapid commercial production mounted. When, following the disastrous fire at the Coconut Grove night club in Boston in January 1943, Merck rushed a supply of penicillin to treat the dreadfully burned victims, it was an acknowledgement of its effectiveness in such cases. This had indeed already been proved by the work of Flight-Lieutenant D.C. Bodenham of the RAF in Britain, who had started treating severely burned airmen in June 1942 with small amounts of penicillin provided by Florey.[10]

In America, as the speed of production increased, and more penicillin became available for desperate civilian cases, the newspapers reported with increasing frequency the dramatic stories of patients 'snatched from death by miracle drug'. And in most of these accounts there is expressed a deep gratitude to its original discoverer, Alexander Fleming. The story of the growth of American penicillin production need not be told in detail. Briefly, in 1942, three companies were in the lead, Merck, Squibb and Pfizer, who had agreed (with some reservation) to share their technical advances, of which the development of the deep fermentation process was the most important. In 1942, the best penicillin preparations contained about 0.5 million units per g. Mrs Ogden Miller and Mr Harry Lambert had each needed about 5 g of penicillin, so that the effective treatment of one case of severe sepsis would require about 2.5 million units. By June 1943, penicillin production in the USA had reached 425 million units per month – enough to treat 170 cases. By 6 June 1944 (D-day), it had risen to 100,000 million per month, enough to treat 40,000 cases, that is, all the battle casualties of the Allied invasion of Europe. And in June 1945, US production was 646,000 million units per month, enough to treat over a quarter of a million patients.[11]

By contrast, production in Britain was lagging sadly. During 1942 the only penicillin available for clinical use came from Florey's department, supplemented by 5 g from ICI in March, 5 g from Merck in April (the only American contribution to him resulting from Florey's visit to the USA), and from September a regular weekly supply of crude mould filtrate from Kemball–Bishop. Following the great success of the second Oxford trial, and the official initiative of the Penicillin Committee, ICI increased their output to 20 million units per month, Glaxo to 40 million, and Wellcome were also entering the field. Though this output, even when added to that of Oxford, was only a small fraction of the current American production, it was enough to allow Florey and Cairns to begin a trial on infected war wounds in North Africa in May 1943, though in most cases by local application to conserve supplies.

The results of this trial convinced the War Office. But what impressed the local commanders in North Africa most was the fact that one or two injections of penicillin could cure gonorrhoea within twelve hours. This disease was causing more casualties in North Africa than the enemy. With the invasion of Sicily soon to be launched, the number of men *hors-de-combat* with gonorrhoea was seriously depleting the troops. Thus the limited supplies of penicillin presented the Army authorities with a dilemma. General Poole, Director of Pathology, explained it to Florey and Cairns. Was it better to use the penicillin to restore the 'invalids' to their units, or keep it in reserve for the inevitable battle casualties? Florey and Cairns wanted the penicillin to be restricted to the treatment of wounds, which still needed further research. Besides, they argued, what would be said at home if it became known that the precious drug had been given to scallywags who had brought their trouble on themselves, and denied to wounded heroes?

General Poole was unable to solve this puzzle, and appealed to higher authority. It seems that his appeal finally landed on Churchill's desk, and the Prime Minister wrote in the margin of the minute in his famous green ink: 'This valuable drug must on no account be wasted. It must be used to the best military advantage.' When Poole received this Delphic directive, he interpreted 'best military advantage' as meaning the rapid restoration to fighting fitness of the troops needed for the impending battles. He told Florey that, with the written authority of the Prime Minister, penicillin was to be used to treat the gonorrhoea cases, and so several thousand men were able to rejoin their units.[12] In the event, it was the new American supplies of penicillin that made up the deficit when the casualties mounted in Italy.

Apart from his approach to Sir Andrew Duncan, and his subsequent membership of the Penicillin Committee, Alec Fleming had taken no personal part in the production or the clinical use of penicillin. It was Florey and Cairns in North Africa who worked out its most efficient use in battle casualties, and it was Florey and Sanders who went to Russia in January 1944, to give the medical authorities there a sample of penicillin and tell them what it could do. It was shortly before this visit that Churchill, returning from the Tehran Conference, fell ill with pneumonia in Tunis. Major Pulvertaft, the pathologist at the Military Hospital in Cairo, was consulted and suggested that he should be treated with penicillin. But Lord Moran, who was with Churchill as his personal physician, would not hear of it. He had, he said, no experience of penicillin, and insisted on sulphonamide treatment. This, as it happened, was very effective and Churchill soon recovered.[13] But there grew up the myth that his life had been saved by penicillin which, in one version, had been brought and administered by Fleming in person. Fleming by this time was coming on to the stage of the developing drama of penicillin as seen by the general public, and soon he would occupy it to the almost total exclusion of the other legitimate actors. To trace this transformation of a supposedly shy little Scottish bacteriologist into a world hero, one must go back to August 1942, when, in the first case in which he had ever injected penicillin, he saved Harry Lambert from otherwise certain death.

Though the equally dramatic results obtained in Oxford during the previous months had attracted almost no publicity, news of the miraculous cure at St Mary's soon leaked into Fleet Street. On 27 August 1942, a leading article in *The Times*, headed 'Penicillium' drew attention to a remarkable new therapeutic substance and, without mentioning names, referred to work in Oxford. There were articles, too, in the *News Chronicle* on the 28th, and in the *Sunday Express* of the 30th, in which the new drug was said to be '100 times more powerful than M and B'. Again no names were mentioned. Then, on the 31st, Sir Almroth Wright's famous letter appeared in *The Times*:

'Sir,
    In the leading article on penicillin in your issue yesterday you refrained from putting the laurel wreath for this discovery round anyone's brow. I would, with your permission, supplement your article by pointing out that, on the principle *palmam qui meruit ferat* it should be decreed to Professor Alexander Fleming of this research laboratory. For he is the discoverer of penicillin and was the author also of the original suggestion that this substance might prove to have important applications in medicine.'

On the morning of the appearance of this letter reporters besieged St Mary's seeking Fleming. They succeeded to the extent that the account of an interview with him appeared in the *Evening Standard* that day, and similar articles in a number of national newspapers on 1 and 2 September.

These described Fleming's original discovery and something of his life and work. The Scottish papers made much of his upbringing at Darvel. None mentioned Florey, though the *Daily Mail* referred to development work 'by research chemists in Oxford'.

But on 1 September a letter from Sir Robert Robinson appeared in *The Times*. In this he drew attention to the work in Oxford and wrote that if Fleming deserved a laurel wreath, 'a bouquet at least, and a handsome one, should be presented to Professor H. W. Florey'. Thereupon reporters descended on the Dunn School to interview Florey. But Florey refused to see them, and told his secretary to send them away. Not surprisingly, the gentlemen of the press resented their fruitless journey and cavalier treatment, and since their living depended on making good stories out of important current events, they went back to London and a warmer welcome at St Mary's.

Florey's perhaps unwise handling of the press was the result of several factors. He had a strong personal dislike of publicity. Then there was the general aversion of almost all doctors to becoming involved in press publicity that might be construed as professional advertising – the General Medical Council, in fact, could strike a doctor's name off the Register for indulging in it. And Florey remembered the disastrous effect of publicity on the career of his predecessor at the Dunn School, Professor Georges Dreyer. He, like Dreyer, would be inundated by heartrending appeals that he could not meet if it became widely known that his department had a life-saving drug. So Florey not only sent the reporters away with empty notebooks, he told all members of the Dunn School staff to give no information whatever to the press. Professor Gardner, perhaps wiser in the ways of the world, thought that Florey's attitude was wrong and that the Oxford team would come to regret it. He knew that St Mary's had a good claim to a share of the credit for penicillin, and that they would exploit it to the full.

All voluntary hospitals (until 1948) relied on donations to pay their running expenses. It should be remembered that St Mary's had had a harder struggle than most, and had been on the verge of financial collapse more than once. Publicity of the right sort was essential to keep the funds flowing in, and it had been actively sought by every Dean and Hospital Secretary who had held office since 1854. Certainly the story of penicillin, which had actually been discovered and used there, was world publicity of the most profitable kind. Moreover, Sir Almroth Wright had throughout his career used the public press to his own advantage. Publicity for penicillin would thus enhance the reputation of the hospital, Sir Almroth Wright and his department and, of course, Alexander Fleming, a member of his staff.

Fleming's first reactions to this burst of limelight may be gathered from his letters to Florey at this time.[14] In the first, dated 29 August, he wrote (presumably about Wright's letter to *The Times*): 'You will have noticed in the Times some very undesirable press publicity. I have done my best to stop this sort of thing, but I was not asked about this particular case.' And on 2 September he wrote 'I was very glad to see Robinson's letter in the Times this morning. Although my work started you off on the penicillin hunt, it was you who have made it a practical proposition, and it is good that you should get the credit. You are lucky in Oxford to be out of range of reporters. They are a persistent lot, and I have not been able to dodge them completely . . .'

On 7 September, after the appearance of a dozen or more articles and interviews, he wrote to Florey: 'You cannot deplore the personal element which has crept into penicillin more than I do, and for the moment I am the sufferer.' He then went on to list the various newspapers and periodicals whose reporters he was trying to avoid, and ended: 'I do hope that the people who matter (the others do not count) do not think that we are in opposition. I will certainly do what I can to dispel the idea.'

Meanwhile, what was becoming a veritable press campaign on the penicillin theme was rapidly developing, and the plot of the story – which was certainly exciting enough to need little embellishment – was beginning to portray Fleming as the main hero. Newspapers all over the country told of his astonishing discovery, and of his romantic climb from poverty in the Ayrshire hills to scientific eminence. The *News Chronicle* of 5 September named him 'Man of the Week' with a photograph and a long article on his life and career, mentioning that 'a little band of scientists of several nationalities' were working to extract his penicillin. The *Illustrated London News* a few days later devoted a full page to photographs of Fleming and his laboratory, and to a description of his discovery which was 'being developed in Oxford'. Similar articles and photographs appeared in many newspapers and periodicals. The Irish papers made much of Sareen's family connections, and the Scottish ones of the Ayrshire background. And so it went on. During the next few months literally hundreds of articles in the same vein appeared in the English language press throughout the world. In almost none of these were the Oxford workers named, and if their work was mentioned at all, the impression was given that it was being done under Fleming's direction. Even the first clinical trial was often credited to Fleming as, for example, in the 'Marching On' news broadcast on 15 October 1942, by the BBC.

At first these stories were true as far as they went – they merely omitted or played down the work done in Oxford. The poor farmer's boy who had to walk barefoot to school through the wild Ayrshire hills and struggle to gain an education is a fairly authentic picture and one to grip the imagination. So is the picture of his academic brilliance, his amazing discoveries and the indifference of his colleagues to their importance. But what was not true was the picture of this lone pioneer struggling for years to produce penicillin himself, and to persuade chemists to help him, and then finally triumphing and saving the lives of his patients. Yet this was the picture that was conveyed – by implication at first, and later quite specifically.

As may be imagined, all this was not received with favour in Oxford. Florey at first took the attitude that the opinion of the general public swayed for the moment by sensational articles in the lay press did not matter. But when this publicity grew to the point at which even Florey's scientific friends began to ask him what had happened to all *his* work on penicillin, he was forced to pay more attention to the situation. And his Dunn School colleagues were becoming restive. Gardner had foreseen the consequences when Florey had dismissed reporters so abruptly. There would have to be, he had realized, a focus for the public gratitude for the gift of penicillin, and it was natural that one name rather than several should become that focal point. Florey would never have allowed his name to exclude those of the people who had worked with him. But there was a limit beyond which he could not allow the belittling of their work to grow without a protest.

On 11 December 1942, Florey made his protest to Sir Henry Dale, President of the Royal Society. Florey had been elected a Fellow in March 1941, mainly on the merits of the work that he had done before turning to penicillin, and became a member of the Council in November 1942. He wrote to Dale as follows:

'As you know, there has been a lot of most undesirable publicity in the newspapers and press generally about penicillin. I have taken a firm line here and said there was to be nothing whatever done in the matter of interviews with the press or in any other way. Gardner, I know, thinks that I have been rather wrong about this. I have had a letter from Fleming in which he assures me he was endeavouring to do the same and I accepted that at its face value and thought that this newspaper publicity would cease. I have now quite good evidence, from the Director General of the BBC in fact, and also indirectly from some people at St Mary's that Fleming is doing his best to see [that] the whole subject is presented as having been foreseen and worked out by Fleming and that we in this department just did a few final flourishes. You can see what I mean in the article published in "Britain" today, complete with photographs of Fleming and so on. This steady propaganda seems to be having its effect even on scientific people, in that several have now said to us "But I thought you had done something on penicillin too." '[15]

Florey then went on to ask Dale's advice on the possible publication of an article setting out the true facts of the work done by the Oxford team, and by Fleming. Dale replied at once. He pointed out that the appearance at that particular time of any publication in which Florey refuted statements attributed to Fleming would create a serious difficulty for the Royal Society. Fleming was, yet again, a candidate for election. Any public dispute between a member of Council and a candidate just when the

Sectional Committees were making their choices would be bound to prejudice their impartiality.[16]

As a result of this argument, or rather, directive, from Dale, Florey did nothing. Inaction was foreign to his nature and in this case it was doubly hard to bear since he could tell no one among his disgruntled colleagues in Oxford the reason for it. So his team felt that he was allowing the credit due to them to slip into other hands without even a protest. And, to complete the episode, Fleming was duly elected as one of the fifteen new Fellows of the Royal Society in March 1943.

To become an FRS is a coveted honour for any scientist. So Alec Fleming had won a high distinction, and he was proud and delighted. There was a ceremony in honour of this event at St Mary's, at which he was presented with an eighteenth-century silver salver donated by his colleagues and students. There was an eloquent and flattering speech by Dr Handfield Jones, to which Fleming had to reply. Though he was later to become so accustomed to such occasions that speeches flowed easily, on this one he was nervous and did rather badly. He had intended to use an apt quotation from Burns, but forgot its context and used it anything but aptly – to his own confusion and the affectionate amusement of his audience, as Maurois describes.[17] Fleming had had to wait a very long time for his election – over twenty years in fact. And it might be reflected that, if the therapeutic power of penicillin had not been proved by Florey and his team in Oxford, Fleming might never have been elected at all. He was already 62-years-old in 1943.

During the rest of that year Fleming rode on the crest of a wave of public acclaim and adulation. Maurois writes:

'He was overwhelmed by a mounting tide of letters. His telephone rang from morn till night. Ministers, Generals, newspapers of every country were continually asking for him. He was a bit surprised, at times amused, but on the whole enjoyed it all, and made a point of insisting on the part played by Florey and Chain.'[18]

On available evidence, this last statement seems to be true. In the surviving scripts of his lectures, talks and articles he did stress the importance of the work done at Oxford, and he never claimed to have done more than he had done. Always he emphasized the accidental nature of his discovery and explained that its development involved chemical work beyond his own abilities. He did, however, give the impression that he had handed on the problem to expert chemists who had then failed to make headway and were thus responsible for the twelve-year delay in the appearance of penicillin as a therapeutic agent. This impression, as we have seen in chapter 14, is rather a distorted one.

But the main trouble was that the newspapers themselves distorted what Fleming told them. Penicillin in 1942, was very good news, and there were national reasons for making the best of it. Most news in those days was bad

– a chronicle of disaster after disaster from the war zones. Singapore had fallen. The Japanese were victorious everywhere in South-east Asia, the greatest ships in the Royal Navy, the 'Hood', 'Prince of Wales' and 'Repulse', had been sunk, the Russian Army had been beaten back for 1,000 miles to the Volga by the Germans, and Rommel was within 50 miles of Alexandria. It is little wonder that the Ministry of Information gave every encouragement to newspapers to print the good news about penicillin. And it is little wonder that St Mary's Hospital, with Churchill's physician, Lord Moran as its Dean, and Lord Beaverbrook as its most influential patron, should direct as much as possible of the public attention to the work done there by Fleming. Fleming was the man the public wanted to hear about, and it was to everyone's advantage (except that of the Oxford workers) that the public should get what it wanted.

So, what Fleming himself called the 'Fleming Myth', grew and flourished. The accounts that make up the picture of his achievements, the press cuttings of which fill four large volumes in the Florey Archives at the Royal Society,[19] have little or nothing to say about the work in Oxford. One writer, who felt it necessary to explain why penicillin was measured in 'Oxford Units', did so by stating that Fleming's 'clinic' happened to be in Oxford.[20] Only a very small number of articles gave true and balanced accounts of the real struggle to produce penicillin.

Fleming's reaction to public mis-statements about himself was an amused detachment. He made no attempt to deny or correct them. Indeed, he positively enjoyed them, an attitude perhaps characteristic of his peculiar sense of humour. He carefully preserved the cuttings in a book labelled 'Fleming Myth',[21] enjoyed retailing them to his friends, and might even pin up the choicest examples on the departmental notice board. Two of these (out of scores) might be quoted: Under the heading 'Thank you, Luftwaffe', the *Evening Standard* of 3 March 1943, with a fine disregard for chronology (among other things), carried the story that, during the blitz, a bomb fell on Paddington Station. This blew a cloud of mouldy dust through Fleming's laboratory window, which killed the germs in his test tubes and revealed to him the amazing properties of the mould.

A second flight of fancy comes from an unidentified provincial newspaper quoted by the *St. Mary's Hospital Gazette* of 1945.[22] In this account Fleming was said to be so busy that he never had time for proper meals but ate cheese sandwiches in his laboratory. In consequence, he became run-down, and suffered from boils. One day he noticed that the cheese he was eating was mouldy. At the same time he noticed that a painful boil on the back of his neck had disappeared. The great scientist put these two things together, and discovered penicillin in the mouldy cheese.

By mid-1943, clinical trials of penicillin were expanding in America as production increased, and the press there was devoting more and more space to the patients 'snatched from death' by the still-rare drug, often under conditions of high drama. In most accounts Fleming features as the prime benefactor, with such headings as 'Thank you Doctor Fleming'. Then, in that year, a major discovery was made that was to enhance his credit to an even greater degree. Mahoney and his colleagues at the Staten Island Hospital, New York, found that penicillin can cure syphilis.[23] An eight-day course of injections would apparently defeat a disease that had taken or devastated the lives of millions, and for which Salvarsan had proved to be only a partial and rather dangerous remedy. Though in a proportion of early cases treated with penicillin relapses did occur, adequate dosage has virtually abolished the terrible dangers of syphilitic infection. It is interesting to remember that Fleming's professional career began with his invention of an improved test for syphilis, and was then enhanced by his skill in treating it with Salvarsan. Finally, he was to be hailed as the ultimate victor of the dreaded pox – the scourge of mankind for centuries.

If the steadily mounting public acclaim for Fleming caused continued irritation in Oxford, it did not produce any overt breach between him and Florey. At a discussion on penicillin at the Royal Society of Medicine on 9 November 1943, they shared the same platform and each paid generous tribute to the other in their reference to past work. And in a press report of this meeting in the *Recorder*, the headline was 'Two Great Men of Penicillin' – almost the first instance of equal tributes to Florey and Fleming. When the American Pharmaceutical Manufacturers' Association met in New York on 13 December 1943, it was announced that their annual award was to go to Fleming and Florey jointly, for their work on penicillin. To mark this auspicious occasion Major-General Norman T. Kirk, Surgeon-General of the us Army, broadcast from Washington an address in praise of Fleming and Florey, and Fleming, in London, broadcast a reply on behalf of them both. But, again, this more equal sharing of the honours was nullified by the press. It was Fleming who featured in the wide coverage given by the newspapers to the awards and the broadcasts.

The publicity crescendo continued as 1943 became 1944. On 12 December the *Sunday Express* devoted a whole page to 'Professor Fleming and the Wonderful Thing he has given the world.' On the 18th *Illustrated* published a four-page article with colour photographs on 'Penicillin. The Complete Story of the Wonder Drug' in which Fleming was given all the credit for its discovery, development and clinical use. And on the same day the *Daily Herald* had a large, close-up picture of Fleming and the caption 'These are the eyes that saw a miracle.' In January, the *Sunday Pictorial*, the *Sphere* and *Picture Post* – which named Fleming as 'Man of the Year' – all carried long illustrated articles. Then, in an interview with him published in the *Daily Mail* on 11 February, there was the first mention of money. ' "New Drug Earns Me Nothing", Penicillin Man Explains.' 'I have never had a penny out of it', Fleming told the reporter, who also discovered that his salary was less than £1,000 a year.

This struck many readers as being an extraordinary situation. For some it was evidence of Fleming's altruism, which led him to make a wonderful gift to the world with no thought of financial reward. For others it was evidence of the injustice of the medical system, which denied to doctors a share in the vast profits to be made from the commercial exploitation of their discoveries. The matter became a public issue. On 15 May, the American magazine *Time*, which appeared with Fleming's picture on its front cover (an internationally prized recognition), took up his lack of financial reward for penicillin. The response from its readers was immediate, and the magazine collected $2,720 in contributions within a few days, which it sent to Fleming together with a free subscription for *Time* for the rest of his life.

The fact that Fleming made no attempt to profit financially from a discovery that later earned countless millions of pounds for its commercial exploiters has been made much of by those who have written about him. This is a perfectly valid picture, but in reality Fleming was never in a position to have made much money out of penicillin even if he had wanted to. When Professor Gordon Stewart, a distinguished expert on penicillin wrote, in 1979, 'after all, it was Fleming who refused to apply for a patent on penicillin'[24] he was voicing the popular impression that Fleming had an option which he altruistically refused to exercise. In fact, he probably had no such option. Under the British patent law current when he made his discovery (a law that had not been simplified by five Acts of Parliament between 1883 and 1928), a claim relating to a medicine 'cannot be made for the substance itself except when prepared or produced by the special methods or processes of manufacture described and claimed'. Fleming did not invent penicillin, it is a natural substance. Nor did he invent any novel methods or processes for its manufacture, he merely used existing ones. The use of mould products for treating infection was not new – there were many published accounts of similar usage. But even if Fleming had had an option to patent penicillin, it would not have occurred to him to exercise it in those prewar days in Britain. The only 'doctors' who patented medicines were the quacks, who often did very well financially. But no reputable, registered medical practitioner or medical scientist would jeopardize his professional status by joining in such dubious practices. It surely never occurred to Almroth Wright, for example, to patent his vaccines. It was, however, considered ethical – only just – for these vaccines to be advertised and sold by Parke, Davis, and for the Inoculation Department (not individual doctors) to receive a share of the profits. This was about as close to the commercial wind as a practising doctor could sail, and Wright had less regard than most for the ethics of Harley Street that did not suit him. Yet it was considered perfectly ethical for doctors to charge high fees for injecting these vaccines into private patients.

It was just before Florey's visit to the United States in 1941 that the question of patenting some parts of the Oxford process did come up. And it was Florey (not Fleming of course) who considered this proposal, took advice, and refused to implement it. The matter had been raised by Chain. As the son of a German industrial chemist he knew far more about the cut-throat tactics of commercial exploitation than did the Oxford academics. He knew that there were two good reasons for patenting a useful invention. The first and obvious one is that its manufacture then brings in royalties which in the present case could be a useful source of research funds for the Dunn School. The second, less obvious reason, is that if an inventor does not patent his invention, some one else may do so, and the inventor will then find himself having to pay royalties if he manufactures his own invention. Chain urged these reasons on Florey, particularly since Florey was about to tell the American drug firms how to manufacture penicillin.

The idea of patenting was unfamiliar and rather repugnant to Florey, but he agreed to take advice from the two most influential men in British scientific medicine, Sir Edward Mellanby and Sir Henry Dale. Both were adamant in their view that patenting would be entirely unethical. Then he had to tell Chain of his decision, and face the most furious disagreement of their partnership. Chain announced that he would see Mellanby himself, but the interview was a humiliating defeat for him.[25] Mellanby, at his overbearingly worst, told Chain that if he persisted in 'money grubbing' he would have no scientific future in Britain. Chain, as a refugee was vulnerable, and Mellanby could make or break even established British medical research workers. So Chain gave up the struggle. Florey went to America and in due course American individuals and pharmaceutical firms took out patents covering most of the important processes of penicillin manufacture. One of the first in the field was Dr A. J. Moyer, with whom Norman Heatley had worked in Peoria. Chain had been proved right, but it was little comfort to him, and he left Oxford soon after the war. And it was a serious blow to British drug firms, when at last they began large-scale penicillin production, to discover that they had to pay royalties to the owners of American patents. It was mainly this experience that led to the creation of the British National Research Development Corporation, to which patents on the inventions of academic research can be assigned, and which can ensure their proper commercial development and protection.

It was against this unfortunate background that Florey found the public sympathy for Fleming's lack of financial reward for penicillin particularly galling. This, and the still mounting publicity that surrounded him and St Mary's Hospital, finally drove Florey to make another protest, this time to Mellanby. On 19 June 1944, he wrote as follows:[26]

'It has long been a source of irritation to us all here to witness the unscrupulous campaign carried on from St Mary's calmly to credit Fleming with all the work done here. I have sufficient evidence of one sort and another that this is a deliberate and clever campaign. My policy has been never to interview the Press or allow them to get any information from us even by telephone . . . In contrast, Fleming has been interviewed apparently without cease, photographed, etc. with the upshot that he is being put over as the 'discoverer of penicillin' (which is true) with the implication that he did all the work leading to the discovery of its chemotherapeutic properties (which is not true) . . .

'You, of course, know how dishonest this is and might reply "why worry?" (But) my colleagues here feel things are going much too far and, while for the most part do not want publicity or special credit for themselves, are getting quite naturally restive at seeing so much of their work going to glorify and even financially enrich someone else . . . I have been emboldened to write to you by the fact that during last week several people – some non-scientists – have asked me if there wasn't something a bit peculiar about the propaganda, and one of them, who is in a good position to know, lays a good deal of it at Lord Moran's door.'

Florey then went on to ask Mellanby if it would be possible for the Medical Research Council to issue a public statement setting out the true facts of the work on penicillin. He felt that the Council was 'the only body likely to have the slightest influence on the Mary's propaganda'.

But Florey got no practical help and only moral comfort from Mellanby. After a meeting in London, he wrote to Florey:[27]

'I was glad to have the conversation with you the other day about the difficult position in which you and your colleagues in Oxford find yourselves, owing to the unusual attitude Fleming has taken up in response to the public acclamation of penicillin discoveries.

'I want to assure you in writing, as I did orally, that I think the reticence as regards press interviews and the fairness and even generosity in apportioning credit to Fleming of all in your laboratory have been excellent and above criticism . . . You need have no doubt whatever in your mind that scientific men, in this country at least, and doubtless most of them in other countries, have appraised the situation correctly and know that, from the point of view of scientific merit, your work and that of your colleagues stands on a much higher level than that of Fleming.

'I realise how irritating your position must be, if you are at all affected by what appears in the public press, but you can be quite certain that this is an ephemeral reaction which means little or nothing, and the only appreciation which is worth bothering about is that of your scientific peers. In time, even the public will realise that in the development of this story of penicillin the thing that has mattered most has been the persistent and highly meritorious work of your laboratory.'

Mellanby was probably right not to involve the Medical Research Council in a public wrangle about credit, which would have brought discredit on all concerned. But in other respects his judgement can now be seen to have been wrong, as it had been throughout the Oxford work on penicillin. He had been niggardly in his original support for the project, rather pettishly censorious when Florey was driven to seek Rockefeller money, and quite wrong in opposing Chain's wish to apply for patents. And in the present context his judgement has been proved wrong, because the 'ephemeral reaction which means little or nothing' has flourished for forty years and has meant perpetual world fame for one man and public obscurity for the other. Such is the power of the Press.

The World Hero

In 1944, with the tide of war running strongly in favour of the Western Powers, the spirit of optimism was reborn in Britain. The hard-won and brilliantly planned Normandy invasion established the Second Front in June and as the inevitable casualties began to arrive in England, the effectiveness of penicillin in the treatment of wounds astonished medical officers. Fleming, with his vivid memories of wound infection in the 1914–18 war, saw with amazement the lack of sepsis among men within two or three days of being wounded. 'They didn't even have raised temperatures,' he said.[1] And civilians, too, were being treated. Doctors and patients alike were increasingly grateful, because they remembered only too well the dreadful results of sepsis from which they were now being delivered. The homage paid by the press to Fleming began to lead to honours of a more permanent kind.

In May 1944, Fleming had been elected a Fellow of the Royal College of Physicians – a purely professional honour, but a considerable one. In the July Honours List, his name featured as one of the new Knights Bachelor. This made the headline news, and the fact that Howard Florey was similarly honoured tended to be relegated to the small-type lists. Fleming's friends and colleagues were delighted, and a celebration party was planned to take place at St Mary's when he returned from the investiture. He was a little disappointed that, for security reasons, the King conducted the ceremony in the rather drab surroundings of the basement in Buckingham Palace.

When Fleming returned to St Mary's he went up to the departmental library, where Wright was presiding over the usual tea party. Then there occurred a curious little incident described by Dr Howard Hughes.[2] Wright said nothing to Fleming as he took his seat, and there was dead silence for two or three minutes. Then Wright, turning his back on Fleming, began a discourse to the rest of the party on chemotherapy as a heresy that would stifle genuine research. When he had exhausted the topic – and himself – Craxton, the departmental secretary asked Wright to sign some papers. Wright waved him away. 'Don't bother me with such trivial things,' he said, 'Doctor Fleming will deal with them.' So the newly-created knight took the papers, and went without a word to deal with them.

Perhaps Wright had simply been in a bad mood, but his boorish treatment of his old friend and colleague on this day of celebration must indicate an underlying taint of jealousy. Wright went home early that day, and the ensuing party was a great success.

Other honours began to come in the second half of 1944 – the John Scott Medal and Prize of the City Guild of Philadelphia, the Charles Mickle Fellowship of the University of Toronto, and the Robert Campbell Medal of the Ulster Medical Society. A more ephemeral one was the unauthorized announcement of the Nobel Prize by the Press. On 17 October 1944, the *Daily Mail* carried the headline 'Nobel Prize For Fleming Of Penicillin', and continued:

'Sir Alexander Fleming, who once said he had never made a penny out of the discovery of his wonder drug, penicillin, is likely to receive this year's Nobel Prize for Medicine, amounting to £8,500. There has been no distribution of this Nobel Prize since 1939, and some of the accumulated funds may be used to reward Sir Alexander's close collaborator, Professor H. W. Florey, who was knighted with Sir Alexander for the part he played in the discovery.'

Similar statements, but without the reference to Florey, appeared in newspapers all over the world. Particularly in America, Fleming's name made the headlines, and his picture appeared as 'The Nobel Prizeman'. Then, at the end of October, it was officially announced from Stockholm that the Nobel Prize had been awarded to the Americans, Joseph Erlanger and Herbert Gasser, for their work in neurophysiology. So the bubble burst, but Fleming had received a great deal of publicity.

The public misinformation seems to have started in Switzerland. It is reasonable to suppose that penicillin must have been at the top of the list of important medical advances and that, because of the scientific isolation imposed by the war, the Swedish assessors had had little time to decide exactly what had been achieved, and by whom. Fleming's name had dominated the popular story, and it has been said that the Committee had been about to award the Prize to Fleming alone, when enquiries brought the Oxford work to light and delayed the decision.[3] This, however, is speculation. The facts are that no Nobel Prize for Medicine was awarded in 1944, and that a year later it was divided equally between Fleming, Florey and Chain.

Early in 1945, Fleming was elected President of the newly-founded Society of General Microbiology, though he had not been the first choice. He referred to this in his Presidential Address: 'Other and more disting-uished members were asked to assume this presidency, but they were sufficiently strong-minded to refuse it. But, true to the Scottish tradition never to refuse anything, when it came to my turn, I accepted.'[4] Though the words were facetious they were, in fact, a statement of his real attitude. Fleming seems hardly ever to have refused any proferred honour, or invitation.

The spring of 1945 brought, for the Western Powers, a joyful and victorious end to the war in Europe – it was not until 6 August that the mushroom cloud over Hiroshima cast a shadow that has darkened the world ever since. With the defeat of Japan, there was a lifting of the wartime ban on the publication of work on penicillin in the USA, and the tremendous advances that had been made there were revealed.

One of these had been the perfection of the deep-fermentation method, in which continuous culture of the mould took place in vats holding tens of thousands of gallons of liquid. The second advance had been the development of a strain of mould that produced far more penicillin than Fleming's original one. Despite an assiduous search, none of the moulds collected from all corners of the world by obliging members of Air Transport Command were any better than Fleming's, but then the winner of all time was found almost on the doorstep of the man who had been searching the world, Dr Kenneth Raper, of the Peoria Laboratories. He had a local helper, Miss Mary Hunt, who was so enthusiastic in producing anything showing signs of decay that she became known as 'Mouldy Mary'. One day in 1943 she produced a piece of rotting cantaloup melon. Raper tested the mould on it – as he had done for thousands of other samples – and to his astonishment found that it produced far more penicillin than the standard strain of *P. notatum*. The new mould was identified as a *P. crysogenum*, and further work isolated a sub-strain that produced 150 units per ml of culture filtrate as compared with the 25 units currently achieved commercially and the 2 units per ml of the original Oxford process.[5]

Dr Demerec and others at the Carnegie Institute induced further mutations by exposing the spores to X-rays and ultra-violet light, and produced the Q-176 strain which gave nearly 1,000 units per ml. As a result, penicillin production in the USA rose to 645,000 million units per month, and the cost fell from about $200 per million units in 1944 to $6 in 1945.[6] If the antibiotic era had begun to dawn in Oxford in 1941 when the first six patients to be treated consumed the total production of about two million units, 1945 saw the full light of the new day.

Penicillin was not, of course, unlimited in its scope. There were still bacterial killers such as the tubercle bacillus, against which it was powerless. This stimulated efforts to discover new antibiotics. The first of these was developed by Professor S. A. Waksman, of Rutgers University, who set out to find antibiotics (his own word) among the antibacterial substances produced by the *Streptomyces* moulds in soil. In 1944 he announced the production of streptomycin from cultures of *S. griseus*, and showed that it was active against many organisms unaffected by penicillin.[7] Among these was the tubercle bacillus, and the development of a specific therapy based on a combination of streptomycin with other drugs has virtually eliminated the 'white plague' that had killed or incapacitated millions of mainly young people every year. Thereafter, dozens of new antibiotics have been developed, each with its own 'spectrum' of target organisms, and an advantageous lack of side-effects in patients who may be, or may become, allergic to penicillin.

The structure of the penicillin molecule had been studied intensively both in England and America during the war. Abraham and Chain, in Oxford, had come to the conclusion that its nucleus was 'a thiazolidine ring fused to a beta-lactam ring'.[8] Similar conclusions had been reached in America, and it emerged that there were at least four different sorts of natural penicillin depending on variations in the side chain. The precise molecular configuration was determined by Dr Dorothy Hodgkin by X-ray crystallography in Oxford in 1945.[9] But the hopes that such knowledge might lead to the commercial chemical synthesis of penicillin have not yet been fulfilled, though it was achieved on a laboratory scale by Sheehan.[10] There are, however, semi-synthetic penicillins with greater antibacterial versatility, and less liability to cause allergic reactions. But the virus diseases have remained undefeated by the antibiotics, and the advances that have been made have been mostly along the lines beloved by Almroth Wright. It is prophylactic vaccination that has provided protection against smallpox, rabies, yellow fever, typhus, poliomyelitis and measles, among other diseases.

In the immediate postwar years, when the world had to come to terms with the price of military victory, the virtual conquest of bacterial disease seemed to be an unalloyed bounty from heaven, manna in the form of the mould that fell on to Fleming's culture plate. And, just as any spectacular military or political enterprise tends to be identified – rightly or wrongly – with some outstanding individual, so Alexander Fleming became identified with the antibiotic revolution. It did not matter to the general public that many before him had tried and failed in almost exactly the same way that he had tried – and failed. Nor that it was the others who had come after him who had tried and brilliantly succeeded. It was Fleming who had discovered and preserved the 'miracle-mould', and every advance in the widening field of antibiotics focused yet more grateful publicity on the man who had made it all possible. 'Thank You, Fleming' was the headline expression of the emotion felt by millions who had been delivered from the dangers and misery of diseases now becoming only grim memories. They had all read about him in their newspapers – his name had become a household word. Now they wanted to see and hear him.

Fleming himself, still unaware of the heights to which his public fame would carry him, was readjusting his life to the return of peace. The Danvers Street house was repaired, and Alec, Sareen, and her sister Elizabeth, returned to live there, with young Robert, who had become a medical student at St Mary's. Dr Allison found that Alec's green-fingered exercises in his garden during the Fleming's occupation of his Highgate house produced some floral surprises. Not all such innovations were appreciated by those who accepted Alec's help. His brother Robert's wife, Ida, had a conspicuous rock garden at their Radlett house, and was grateful when Alec produced some seedlings which, he said, would become a rare addition to her prized alpines. He planted them himself, and on every visit went to see how they were doing. In due course it became obvious that Ida's rock garden was bearing a fine crop of common cabbages. Robert writes: 'She pretended to be very angry but in fact had from the first suspected that Alec's serious manner meant that he was up to one of his tricks.'

The Dhoon, too, came back into the Fleming's occupation. It had been let during the war to air-force officers. The garden had become a wilderness, and the house suffered from five years of neglect and careless damage. Sareen, already exhausted by her years of voluntary work in an army canteen, found that the task of restoring her homes and garden taxed her strength to the limit. Her son, Robert, believes that the deterioration in her health that became obvious later, dates from this period of strain and effort.[11]

One of the problems of those days was the difficulty of travel. Petrol was rationed and visits by rail to Barton Mills were inconvenient. Alec devised a partial solution. He bought a large shed from the Pegrams, set it up close to the house and equipped it as a private laboratory. He could then spend longer periods at The Dhoon, since he could bring some of his work there from St Mary's. The 'Little Lab', as he called it, became a favourite work place, perhaps recalling the primitive but efficient laboratory at Boulogne. The shed is there today in the grounds at The Dhoon, but it has become a garden room. The walls, however, are still decorated by the coloured prints of British birds collected by Alec and his son Robert.

In May 1945, Alec Fleming began what might be called his public life. On the 2nd, one of the London City Companies made him an Honorary Freeman, and in his speech of thanks he recalled his days as a junior clerk running errands between the great offices and City institutions. On the 17th the Borough of Paddington also made him an Honorary Freeman, and a few days later he left for an extended tour of the United States and Canada organized by the British Council. Before leaving, he was interviewed for the BBC by Bebe Daniels. She arrived by appointment at his department at St Mary's

'expecting twenty-four secretaries, eight guards and I don't know what else. Actually, the only person I saw was a technician in a white overall in one of the corridors. I asked him "Where shall I find Sir Alexander Fleming?" "At the end of the passage – he's making tea." I found him with his sleeves rolled up making tea over a bunsen burner. "Would you like a cup?" he asked me.'[12]

Bebe Daniels' experience, which astonished her beyond measure, was typical of that of any visitor who dared to overcome his awe and seek out the great man. The contrast between the expectation and the reality, so startling at first, almost always ended by captivating the visitor. It can be said here that fame – even the much greater fame that was to come to him – did nothing to spoil Fleming's simple, down-to-earth manner and his interest in ordinary people and things. The one change as his public commitments grew was an increased affability. He smiled more often and seldom greeted visitors with an intimidating silence.

Fleming embarked on the 'Aquitania' for New York, and on 24 May, in mid-voyage, he gave a lecture on the discovery of penicillin to his fellow-passengers. He was beginning to tailor such lectures to fit non-medical audiences who did not know a staphylococcus from a stephanotis. He arrived in New York to a civic reception, cheering crowds and a police motorcycle escort. John Cameron, of the British Mission, took charge of him during a tour that lasted for two months. The itinerary was crowded with lectures, functions at universities, scientific and medical institutions, and visits to commercial firms producing penicillin. There were press conferences, interviews and radio broadcasts, including a nation-wide broadcast of a dramatized story of his life, with Ronald Colman playing the part of Fleming and the real Fleming introducing it.[13]

The British authorities felt that all this was excellent propaganda. Dr Hugh Clegg, Editor of the *British Medical Journal*, wrote later:

'I have the impression that few people realize what a magnificent ambassador for Britain Fleming was when he went abroad. Modest to the point of shyness, by no means an orator on public occasions, he impressed those he met with his simplicity and essential humility. With it all was a naive schoolboy delight in simple pleasures.'[14]

After receiving Honorary Degrees at Princeton and Pennsylvania Universities, Fleming was the guest of honour at a grand dinner given by the American Association of Penicillin Producers at the Waldorf Astoria Hotel, New York on 25 June. The President of the Association, in his speech of introduction, reminded his audience of the healing power of the Pool of Bethesda after the angel had troubled the waters:

'Certainly it was an angel who moved the spirit of Sir Alexander Fleming when he saw, for the first time the effect produced on a bacterial culture by a wandering mould, for the pool thus troubled has cured not one sick man but myriads of sick men.'

Fleming, in his reply, also referred to the chance that had blown the mould on to his culture plate (in other speeches he suggested that it had come through the window, and even more specifically perhaps from the Fountains Abbey public house). But he emphasized the need to seize such gifts from the gods, to recognize the unusual and follow it up. Referring to the development of penicillin he said:

'We all owe a lot to Florey, Chain and their co-workers. They did not initiate penicillin but they put it on the map as an effective drug. They gave you the essential extraction process and they furnished the immediate stimulus to all of you who are now producing penicillin on a large scale. Team work here was amply justified.'[15]

But, as Fleming often said on such occasions, it was the individual worker, and not always the best equipped one, who made the discoveries. The place of team work was in their development. There was, he thought, too much reverence for team work and organization in America. When he was shown the Pfizer laboratories at Brooklyn he said, 'I could never have discovered penicillin here. Everything is much too clean and tidy.' And on another occasion when T. S. Carswell, of the Commercial Solvents Corporation, asked him why he had not developed penicillin during the prewar years, Fleming retorted, 'Why didn't you? You had all the data and all the facilities.'[16]

At the climax of the occasion at the Waldorf Astoria, the Penicillin Producers handed Fleming a cheque for $100,000, as a personal gift, to which they had all contributed. Fleming protested that he could not possibly accept such a sum for himself, and asked that the money should be used as a research fund in his department at St Mary's. The matter of his lack of personal financial reward for penicillin – which was already earning millions for its manufacturers – never ceased to mystify the profit-conscious Americans. John Smith, head of the Pfizer laboratories said to Fleming, 'Why have you never touched the royalties which could have enabled you and yours to live as a man should live who has rendered such services to humanity?' Fleming replied, 'It never occurred to me.'[17] This conversation, which was widely quoted, strengthened the view that Fleming was so unworldly that he had simply forgotten to claim what was legitimately his. In fact, Fleming had no patent rights and therefore no royalties.

On 28 June, Harvard University conferred an honorary degree on Fleming. Many old friends who had worked at St Mary's and even at Boulogne with him were there, and also six thousand people in Harvard Yard. When he rose to reply to the official speeches the whole audience rose too, cheering and clapping for several minutes. When he could make himself heard, he spoke once more about chance, the destiny that had made him a doctor and not a farmer or a businessman, that had made St Mary's his medical school and Sir Almroth Wright his teacher, and that had sent the mould to settle on his culture plate. It was a speech that he was to make in very similar terms on scores of similar occasions all over the world. Its main theme was the need to create the sorts of conditions in which things can happen – apparently accidentally – and never to neglect unusual happenings. 'Do not clutter up the mind too much with precedents and be prepared to accept such good fortune as the gods offer.'[18]

Not surprisingly, Fleming's constant references to the importance of luck – or destiny – in his career suggested to the more mystical of his American listeners that he had been an instrument tuned to a Divine Purpose. One old lady was reported to have spoken to him in such terms, to which Fleming replied, 'I can only suppose that God wanted penicillin, and that was why he created Alexander Fleming.' Fleming did not deny this report when someone showed it to him – but then he never did deny such things. The fact that he did not include it in 'The Fleming Myth' collection suggests, to Maurois, that it was true.

Occasionally, Fleming's patience with the reporters constantly at his heels showed signs of strain. One morning, emerging from his hotel bedroom, he found two reporters ready to pounce. As they went with him down the corridor, one said, 'We'd like to know what a great scientist thinks about before breakfast. What are you thinking now?' Fleming looked grave and said: 'As a matter of fact, I'm thinking about a very important problem . . .' Out came the notebooks. 'I'm trying to decide whether to have one egg for breakfast or two.'[19]

While visiting Yale University Fleming met Mrs Ogden Miller, the first patient in America to be saved from death by penicillin. It had been made possible by the intervention of Florey's friend, John Fulton, and the collaboration of Norman Heatley, then working at Merck, who provided the material. Since it was Mrs Miller's apparently miraculous recovery that had convinced the Americans of the power of penicillin, the meeting between Fleming, the discoverer, and Mrs Miller, the living proof of its effectiveness, was something of an historic occasion. The Press made the most of it, and published pictures of them standing side by side. But the reports quoted a remark by Fleming that gave great offence in Oxford. He claimed Mrs Miller as 'my most important patient'.[20] It was made, perhaps, in an unguarded moment and during a happy exchange of mutual congratulations. But it was a Freudian slip that revealed Fleming's possessive attitude towards the clinical use of penicillin. All patients cured by it were, in this sense, *his* patients, and this view was indeed accepted by the growing host of his grateful admirers.

Perhaps the most magnificent of the formal occasions at which Fleming was honoured was the annual dinner of the Variety Clubs of America, at which he was presented with their Humanitarian Award. According to the press reports, over 250 'Cabinet, Senate and Diplomatic notables' sat down to a sumptuous dinner at the Mayflower Hotel, Washington, on 25 July. Fleming, the guest of honour, was praised in speech after speech. President Truman, regretting his inability to attend (because of business in Potsdam), sent a letter to be read in his absence, and also a representative in the person of Secretary of the Treasury, Vinson. Vinson in his speech made the extraordinary statement that Fleming had twice saved the life of Winston Churchill. The first occasion, he said, was when they were boys. Winston had got into difficulties while swimming and would have drowned if he had not been rescued by another boy who turned out to be Alexander Fleming. The second arose when Churchill, desperately ill with pneumonia in Cairo, was saved by the penicillin provided by Fleming.[21]

Neither story, of course, had a grain of truth in it, and the tale of the rescue from drowning is particularly absurd since Churchill was seven years older than Fleming. Fleming made no attempt to correct the distinguished speaker – indeed, he could hardly have done so without causing offence. Nor did he ever deny the stories later. When asked about the Churchill story – it was even said that the grateful family had paid for his education – his evasive reply was 'What does Churchill say?' And when told that the story had been retailed from the pulpit during a sermon, Fleming said 'Then it must be true!'[22]

During the course of the Variety Clubs' Dinner, Fleming was presented with the award, a handsome silver plaque and a cheque for $1,000. When the famous guests had departed, some of the members decided to have a peaceful nightcap in a private room. Then, in the words of a press report, 'there was a knock at the door and they opened it to the gently unassuming award-winner, Sir Alexander, who stood clutching his plaque and said shyly that he wanted to tell them all what a good time he had had. He came in and sat talking with them until five in the morning.'[23]

There is no doubt that Fleming, almost totally aphasic in the ordinary way, could expand wonderfully on convivial occasions. For example, on his many transatlantic crossings by liner, he would sit talking and drinking into the small hours so that the wives of his cronies complained that their husbands were half-asleep all day. And when he was elected an Honorary Member of the Savage Club, his inaugural after-dinner speech went on for so long that most of the members had drifted away to the bar before he had finished. One remarked, 'A nice, modest little man, but what a *talker*.'[24] None of Fleming's laboratory associates would have recognized this hidden facet of his character.

Fleming's tour of the United States and Canada lasted for two months. It was a constant succession of reception committees, celebrations, honours, speeches. At Oklahoma his arrival was delayed and the reception committee, including the State Governor, waited patiently at the airport for nearly two hours. Then they greeted him warmly, and a Scottish pipe band played in his honour. Fleming seemed to take it all in his stride, but he did confess to a friend that, before some particularly grand occasion, he 'got that scared rabbit feeling'. But he clearly felt that he was doing a public duty and, equally clearly, enjoyed much of it. Wherever he went in America – and it was the same in every country he was to visit – people came up to him with tears of gratitude in their eyes to thank him for saving the lives of themselves or some loved one.

Fleming returned to England at the end of August 1945, loaded with honours, medals and presents, and the good wishes of millions of people who had seen him, heard him speak, or listened to the radio broadcasts by or about him. During June, while he had been away, St Mary's Hospital had staged its great Centenary celebrations and appeal. These had been planned by a committee set up in April 1944, under the Chairmanship of General Sir Hubert Gough. One of their first acts was to appoint a Press Officer, Mr Curnock, and the wide publicity that the Centenary received is a tribute to his energy and inventiveness. The target for the appeal was £2,000,000.

The festivities began on 27 June 1945 with a gala performance in the Albert Hall by the London Symphony Orchestra and Yehudi Menuhin, followed by a Grand Ball at the Dorchester Hotel. Next day the Queen visited the hospital, where she saw a splendidly mounted exhibition illustrating the discovery, manufacture and use of penicillin at St Mary's and the special 'penicillin wards' where patients were receiving the life-saving treatment. In his broadcast on 1 July, Lord Moran stressed Wright's work on typhoid vaccine and Fleming's on penicillin, saying that these two doctors working in one laboratory at St Mary's Hospital had saved more lives in the armies in the field than anyone else in the world.

Among the many novelties devised by the promoters of the Centenary was the famous 'Penicillin train'. This was provided, and paid for, by the Great Western Railway. These were two exhibition coaches displaying the penicillin story, and coaches accommodating the St Mary's students and nurses who acted as demonstrators. The train toured the GWR network, for two months, stopping at each of the major towns, including Oxford. It then visited the major cities of Britain.[25] Though a great publicity success, and despite the glamour of penicillin, the appeal was financially disappointing. Expenses were high, the war only just ending, and eventually the Hospital received less than £200,000 – a tenth of the target figure.

On 3 September 1945 Fleming flew to Paris as the guest of the French Government. There were the usual high officials to greet him and about fifty journalists, all anxious for his first words and photographs. But none of these people knew him by sight and, overlooking the inconspicuous little man among the other passengers descending the gangway, most of the journalists began to move in on a tall, impressive figure who fitted their idea of what a great scientist should look like. A few sought confirmation from Fleming himself: 'Is that man the great Professor Fleming?' they asked him. Fleming afterwards maintained that he knew so little French, that he misunderstood the question and, thinking that they meant himself, nodded vigorously. At once the whole pack of reporters fell on the impressive stranger, and Fleming was able to meet one or two old friends unimpeded. But knowing Alec's brand of humour, it is more likely that he deliberately misled the journalists and threw a fellow passenger to the wolves. If so, then this episode might explain the description of Fleming in newspaper articles at about that time, as a tall, dark man with a deep, commanding voice and an Oxford accent.

The mistake, however, was soon discovered and Fleming was engulfed by his admirers. There was a great reception in the Le Bourget air terminal, and he had to make a radio broadcast. Then lunch at the Ritz, a reception at the Académie de Médecine where he was made an Honorary Member, with cheering crowds in the streets. Next day there was a tour of the Louvre, personally conducted by the Director, lunch at the Foreign Office, with long speeches. At four-thirty Fleming was received by General de Gaulle, who created him a Commander of the Legion of Honour, hung the medal round his neck and kissed him on both cheeks. There followed an official dinner, and in one of the speeches, Georges Duhamel, the Chairman, said that Fleming had gone further than Pasteur. Fleming, in his reply, said modestly, 'But for Pasteur, I should be nothing.'

On the following day there was a reception at the Pasteur Institute, an official lunch, during which Fleming was presented with the Pasteur Medal, a visit to the Hospital for Sick Children and a reception at the Hôtel de Ville, at which the President of the Académie des Sciences made him an honorary member. On 8 September he flew back to London. The itinerary of this brief visit as described by Maurois is typical of the many such occasions at which Fleming was to receive lavish hospitality, civic and national honours in Sweden, Denmark, Belgium and Italy during the next few months. The visit to Belgium, in November 1945, was noteworthy because Fleming received three honorary degrees in two days, these being at Brussels, Louvain and Liège. In Louvain, the other recipients, Churchill and Montgomery, were unable to attend. Fleming deplored this in his speech. He would have been able to listen to a general and a politician, and little would have been expected of him, a simple laboratory worker who played with microbes. There were, he went on, many rules in such play, but with experience, it was very pleasant to break the rules and find something that nobody else had thought of. These words, about breaking rules, have formed the basis for a theory about Fleming's discovery of penicillin that will be discussed in Chapter 21.

The visit to Italy, at about this time, included Fleming's second meeting with the Pope (he was to have several) and visits to British military hospitals. Professor A. L. Stalker, then a junior army pathologist, recalls one occasion:

'I was told to expect a VIP in the lab. Fleming appeared with a considerable entourage of "brass" – who looked magnificent compared with Fleming. He came into the laboratory corridor and was introduced. He was reminded by a high-ranking officer that the schedule allowed him five minutes. He told his party to wait in the corridor as labs could be dangerous places. We went into the bacteriology section, drew up chairs and he said to forget the time limit. We went over a lot of routine plates and he chatted freely ... he gave me a lot of tips about the "Heath-Robinson" use of glass and sealing wax. He seemed to take a roguish pleasure in the thought of the "brass" having to wait.'[26]

Let them wait – he was enjoying himself.

When Fleming returned to London he had some stories for the Chelsea Arts Club. In one provincial French town, he told them, the Mayor had explained in his official speech that their guest was being honoured because he had cured the *whole population* of venereal disease! And in another, a worthy citizen had said to him: 'Thanks to you, I can have gonorrhoea on Monday, be cured on Wednesday, and ready for a fresh attack on Friday.'[27] Dr Martinez Alonso, in Spain, wrote:

'The wages of sin are now negligible. A few shots of penicillin put you on your feet (or in whatever position you may want) in no time, and you can start all over again. If the road back from sin is paved with nothing more lethal or painful than a couple of million units of Sir Alexander's discovery, why not indulge?'[28]

But behind this ribaldry there was a grim reality. Venereal diseases, by no means always self-inflicted, had brought life-long suffering and early death to countless millions. Some idea of the scale can be got from the 1980 World Health Organization figures, which show that 200 million new cases of gonorrhoea and 40 million of syphilis are being reported every year.[29] Penicillin and other antibiotics can cure these like magic, though they do not prevent re-infection. When penicillin treatment first appeared for these diseases the gratitude was therefore enormous, and it was all directed to Fleming. It reached its peak among the Latin peoples, not necessarily because they were the most afflicted, but because they were less inhibited in expressing their thanks. This most potent source of Fleming's popularity is not much stressed by his biographers. He took it all in his stride. He had, after all, been treating syphilis since 1910, and grateful sinners were no novelty.

On 25 October Fleming received a telegram from Stockholm announcing that he was to share the 1945 Nobel Prize for Medicine. This was tremendous news, a confirmation of the highest award that world science can bestow. But, though the equal division of the prize between himself, Florey and Chain was a surprise to the general public, Fleming's name once more dominated the headlines in the world's newspapers, and in most his co-recipients were only briefly mentioned at the tail-ends of the articles.

Fleming, Florey and Chain received their prizes from the King of Sweden at the elaborate ceremony in Stockholm on 10 December. Fleming had arrived there on the 6th, and had three days of public engagements. Of the actual prize-giving he wrote: 'Full evening dress and decorations at 4.30 p.m. Then with a fanfare of trumpets we were ushered onto a platform and sitting before us were the whole of the Royal Family and thousands of the audience.' There was a programme of music, song, and speeches, and then the King presented the prizes. Next there was a banquet for about seven hundred guests (Fleming sat next to the Crown Princess), and speeches from the winners. Fleming spoke about Fortune. After the banquet the Grand Ball, and on the following day the new Laureates each delivered a lecture at the University and then dined with the King at the palace. Fleming recorded: 'Early to bed it should have been, but when we got back to our hotel we adjourned to the bar and drank Swedish beer for a long time. Among us was an Argentine woman poet* who got a Nobel Prize but could not stand up to the drink.'[30] Alec Fleming's iron constitution easily stood such strains.

There are suggestions that Fleming's fame grew faster abroad than in his own country. It is true that the British scientific establishment was not as lavish in its awards of honours as were the foreign academies. Though his name was known to everyone in Britain through the popular press, Fleming seems to have felt that this was not quite enough. When he received the Freedom of Darvel on 26 October 1946, he expressed this feeling, half-humorously, in his speech. The Provost of Darvel, he said, had only come to hear of him when visiting Cairo where he (Fleming) had a 'certain notoriety'. In consequence, the Provost had come back to propose that the Burgh should honour him. 'This gave me very great pleasure,' said Fleming. 'It was the first time I knew that I had been noticed since I left Darvel.'[31]

In fact, Fleming did receive a good deal of official recognition in Britain. He had Honorary Degrees from Durham (1945), Belfast (1946), St Andrews (1947), London (1948), Bristol (1949) and Edinburgh (1953). He also became a Freeman of Paddington (1945) and Chelsea (1949), and of several City Guilds and Companies. The Royal Colleges of Surgeons and Physicians, and the Royal Society of Medicine all awarded him their gold medals. That of the Royal College of Surgeons was a rare honour, having been conferred only twenty times in 144 years. It was presented to Fleming at a dinner on 14 November 1946, attended by members of the Royal Family and the Prime Minister. As soon as the speeches were over, Fleming said to his friend, Dr G. E. Breen, 'Come on, let's go and have a game of snooker at the club' – meaning of course, his beloved Chelsea Arts Club. According to Breen 'the irruption of Fleming in full rig, with the Legion of Honour round his neck and a multitude of decorations flapping from his coat, into the club had the effect of a bomb-shell. That however, did not prevent us from having our game, and it was the small hours of the morning before we left.'[32] This little story illustrates the streak of showmanship that underlay Fleming's outward modesty. He could surely have removed his orders and decorations before arriving at the club if he had wished to avoid astonishing its members.

* The lady in question was, in fact, Chilean.

An episode at Belfast, where he had come to give a lecture, illustrates his public status. After giving it, he was driven to the station to catch the boat-train for Larne. Then, with not much time in hand, he found that he had left his lantern slides at the University. The chauffeur was sent back to fetch them, and the importance of the matter explained to the station master. So the train simply waited until the slides arrived, and the many other passengers, worried about missing the boat, caused some confusion until they too realized who was involved. During all this time Fleming, completely composed, sat quietly reading in the corner of his compartment.[33] No doubt the boat too, was delayed, and the train from Stranraer, but the great Fleming had his slides.

In 1946, Sir Almroth Wright, then aged eighty-five, retired as titular Principal of the 'Institute of Pathology' and *de facto* Director of the Inoculation Department. The question of his successor, which he had managed to keep in doubt for so many years now had to be settled. Fleming's position had become unrivalled and he was appointed without opposition. Wright's retirement, and Fleming's elevation, actually made very little difference. While Fleming was in America in 1945 Wright had appointed sectional heads with administrative authority, thus forestalling any changes that his successor might have wished to make.

Fleming, on becoming Principal, had merely inherited a title. Nothing changed. John Freeman continued his studies on allergy and looked after the routine bacteriology. Newcomb remained as Professor of Pathology, with D. M. Pryce as Reader, and Fleming himself as Professor of Bacteriology, with W. H. Hughes as Reader. A number of junior appointments were filled by young men eager to acquire training and 'do research'. But if they expected Fleming – popularly supposed to be a medical scientist on a par with Pasteur – to lead them into new realms, they were disappointed. The St Mary's Institute did not, as Florey's department in Oxford did, become an internationally famous centre for research into new antibiotics and into new approaches to the problem of immunity. Wright had been a pioneer in clinical immunology thirty years before. Now the subject had moved far beyond him and his whole team. Penicillin had been born in his department, but had lain dormant until revived in Oxford. Fleming was sixty-five when he became Principal, and much of his time was spent on his very full public life. He was content to allow the Institute to move, with decreasing momentum, along the lines laid down by its founder.

Fleming still enjoyed working at his bench. But he had not moved with the times. He had not even kept up with the research on penicillin being done by young recruits in his own laboratory. Professor Derek Rowley writes:[34]

'In the ten years that I worked as a research assistant with him (from 1945) I never had a serious talk about a research programme. After a short time . . . I decided to work on the mode of action of penicillin and to use the relatively new techniques of isotope labelling with ^{35}S, to follow the attachment of penicillin to the sensitive bacteria. He encouraged me in this, but never really understood it. Once, when I went to his room to show him some results which I felt particularly excited about, he listened to me and looked up from his microscope, saying: "Are ye enjoying yoursel, laddie?" To which I replied, enthusiastically "Yes, indeed!" "Well, awa wi ye then, and let me enjoy mesel, too," said Fleming.'

Rowley ends his letter:

'I liked Fleming and found him an upright and honest man, difficult to relate to, but loyal and even friendly. He helped me when I was just a beginner at a time when most great and eminent men would have sent me packing, and for that kindness, I will always remember him with gratitude.'

These extracts illustrate the two aspects of Fleming at that time, as a scientist and a man. World fame and his new authority made no difference to his attitude to his work or to his personal relations. He had always been popular; now, as an acknowledged genius unspoilt by fame, he inspired affection and even a sort of adoration.

In November 1946, Fleming took part in the commemoration in France of the fiftieth anniversary of Pasteur's death. In the course of these, the eminent delegates were taken by special train to Dôle, in the Jura, to visit Pasteur's birthplace. Dr W. E. van Heyningen was sitting alone with Fleming in a compartment when in came four or five of the French students who were acting as couriers. Van Heyningen writes:

'When they recognized Fleming, they all sat down on the floor, and one of the girls said to Flem: "Here we are, literally sitting at your feet, because you are one of the greatest scientists of all time. Speak to us. Tell us of your plans for the future." Flem didn't exactly tell the students what he was currently doing (which wasn't much), only that what he was doing was more interesting than what he had done in the past. He was not in the least embarrassed, or pompous – just his usual self. He enjoyed their attitude of veneration, but without the least hint of pride. He collected such experiences and his honours and decorations, as a schoolboy collects stamps, and was delighted by rare acquisitions.'[35]

In April 1947, Fleming was lecturing in Vienna, and on the 30th of that month Almroth Wright died. Fleming was profoundly grieved by the loss of the truly great man who had been his master, teacher and friend for over forty years. Wright had stamped his personality and his ways of thought and working on every member of his staff. Fleming had felt this influence as strongly as anyone and yet, with his independence of character, he had pursued his own lines of research.

Ronald Hare paints a movingly human picture of Wright:

'May, then, we leave him, as I did, one evening in 1930, when he was nearly seventy years old. I had, for some reason, to stay late at the laboratory in the November of that year. Everyone else except Wright and myself had gone home. He was, as usual, in his corner, oblivious of everything, the rain and the darkness outside, the buses in Praed Street, the fact that it was long past dinner time, that the fire had gone out and the room was getting cold. Presently, my work finished, I switched off my light, and turned off the bunsen. Wright hated one to say good night, so I crept out of the laboratory. Once outside in the corridor, I could still see him through the glass doors, with the leonine head and its snow-white hair, the wing collar that he invariably wore, the hunched shoulders and the large, ungainly hands battling away with pipettes, slides, teats, and the other tools of his trade, still trying to find, with all the obstinacy of his nature the *experimentum crucis*, as he called it, that would set all our minds at rest about immunity *in vitro*.'[36]

With Wright's death Fleming was, for the first time since he qualified in 1906, his own master. But he could hardly have been expected to change the character of Wright's old department, even if he had wished to do so. Its name, however, changed. It became the Wright–Fleming Institute.

The Last Act

Fleming's fame attracted applications from many young graduates anxious to work in his laboratory. Established posts were strictly limited, but there was room for a few research workers who had their own means of support. One of those to obtain such a niche, in October 1946, was to prove remarkable. To begin with, Dr Voureka was a woman, and if Almroth Wright had still been Principal no such feminine invasion would have occurred. In the second place, she was a vital and very attractive young woman – Hare refers to her as 'an Athenian Goddess'[1] – and she had more than a professional impact on the monastic calm of Wright's old department.

Dr Amalia Voureka was the daughter of Dr Coutsouris, a Greek physician who had practised in Constantinople until he fled to Athens on the outbreak of war in 1914. Amalia, born in 1912, became a medical student in Athens, and, after qualifying, married a young architect, Manoli Voureka. During the Second World War both were active members of the Greek resistance, suffered terms of imprisonment, and lost their house and possessions. After the war, Amalia began to pick up the threads of her medical career. She had separated from her husband, and had no family or professional ties in Greece. So she applied for a British Council bursary saying, on the advice of her old professor, that she wished to study in Fleming's laboratory. Her application was granted, and Fleming agreed to take her for an initial period of six months.

Dr Voureka described to Maurois the awe with which she first approached the great scientist. And how astonished she was to find in a tiny office a small, modest, kindly man whose 'extraordinary eyes seemed to radiate vitality, intelligence and humanity'.[2] Fleming, having suggested allergy as a subject for study – which did not appeal to her – then invited her to work with him. This both delighted and alarmed her, but she soon settled down to learn all the famous Wright–Fleming tricks of technique.

During the first few months of her appointment Wright appeared at intervals in the laboratory. For her part, she regarded him as a sort of prehistoric mammoth, huge in bulk and belonging to the long-past world of Pasteur, and Ehrlich. For his part, he deplored the fact that a woman was working in the laboratory, and until his death a few months later, his influence was such that she was not allowed to take her meals with the staff. Fleming however, strongly approved of his new recruit. He obtained an extension of her bursary for a further six months, and when this was up, appointed her as the first holder of a research scholarship endowed by one of his wealthy American admirers, Ben May. Thus, Amalia Voureka remained in Fleming's laboratory for four years.

Meanwhile much of Fleming's time was spent in travel, public appearances and the receipt of honours. In April 1948, there was a visit to Paris to receive the Honorary Membership of the Académie Septentrionale, in May to Austria for an Honorary Degree, and to Paris again for sittings for the sculptor, Baron, who had been commissioned by the French mint to design a portrait medal for public issue. At the end of May, after returning to receive an Honorary Degree from London University, Alec, with Sareen, set off for a tour of Spain. This had been largely arranged by Professor Florencio Bustinza of Madrid, an eminent plant physiologist who had become one of Fleming's most ardent, and certainly most eloquent, admirers.

Bustinza had become interested in penicillin during the war, when Dr E. M. Alonso made broadcasts in Spanish from English scripts prepared by Fleming.[3] Bustinza obtained a culture of Fleming's mould, made some bacteriological observations and a study of all the available published work. He then wrote a book, *De Pasteur à Fleming*, a history of antibacterial agents, which he dedicated to Fleming. Fleming wrote to thank him in the spring of 1945, and the contemplation of the great man's handwriting had a profound effect on the Spanish scientist. He describes this in his later book, *Diez años de Amistad con Sir Alexander Fleming*, in words translated as follows:

'His writing, clear, elegant like a drawing, impressed me greatly; in it I could see order, beauty, exactitude, rectitude, logic, bounty, modesty, generosity, good taste, artistic leanings, extraordinary penetration, serenity and mental harmony; to sum up, his spiritual aristocracy. If only I could see Fleming myself, to hear from his lips the story of his discovery and emotions, and to know intimately him whom I admired for his genius!'[4]

During the autumn of 1945, Bustinza was able to achieve this longed-for meeting. His first impressions of Fleming are typical of the impact that he made on his admirers, particularly the foreign ones. Bustinza described the thoughts of such great men as Pasteur, Koch, Behring, Metchnikoff that filled his mind as he entered St Mary's. He found Fleming waiting for him in his laboratory.

'He greeted me cordially and said "Take your coat off." He himself took my coat, hung it up and invited me to sit down. At last my wishes were fulfilled – to see him face to face, examine him, catch his gestures, listen to his voice, perceive his emotions and receive his teaching. He was rather short, of athletic appearance, healthy and vigorous-looking, broad-shouldered, deep-chested, with vigorous hands, a broad, intelligent forehead and thick eye brows. His eyes were blue, transparently clear. He had a penetrating gaze, but at the same time it was soft, serene and expressive. His hair was silver grey. He had a sebaceous cyst between his eyebrows, and his nose was slightly deformed. He was correctly dressed; his gestures are harmonious, noble. He speaks softly, slowly, calmly. He has an air of distinction, sweetness, bounty, sincerity which, together with his enchanting modesty and simplicity captivate me immediately.'[5]

And Bustinza remained an ardent devotee until his own death in 1982. Thus, to arrange the triumphal visit of his hero to Spain in 1948 gave him the greatest joy.

Alec and Sareen arrived at Barcelona, as guests of the Mayor, on 26 May, to be met by the usual dignitaries. Next day there was a formal visit to the Cathedral, and as Fleming walked in the procession along the Rambla de las Flores he received a tremendous ovation from the crowds lining the route; and the flower-sellers, in a spontaneous gesture, threw their roses and carnations on the ground in front of him. There followed ten days and nights of receptions, presentations, fiestas, galas, banquets and ceremonies. At a football match, between Ireland and Spain, the 20,000 spectators rose and cheered wildly when the Flemings took their places in the seats of honour. Fleming recorded in his diary 'Mass hysteria'. He had much the same reception at a bull-fight, and before a gala performance of Mendelssohn's *Elijah*. He gave several lectures, opened a new Research Department, unveiled a stone commemorating his visit to Barcelona, and received various honours. His last lecture at the University was entitled 'Success', but before he could begin, the students' choir sang a hymn of praise in Latin verses composed in honour of Fleming, 'the victor of disease and the protector of humanity'. And in his speech at the final gala banquet, he confessed that he had been overwhelmed by these spontaneous ovations from the general public.

From Barcelona the Flemings went to Seville, which seemed determined to give an even more lavish welcome. There were visits to Córdoba, and to Jerez de la Frontera, where the Mayor drove with them in an open carriage through streets lined by cheering crowds. At the famous wine cellars, Fleming was shown the huge casks signed by Nelson, Wellington, Pitt and other British heroes. Then he was invited to sign a cask himself, and when he had done so remarked that his signature was much better written than any of the others. He had been taught to write in Scotland![6]

In the monastery of Montserrat, Fleming was entertained to lunch in total silence, an experience that was clearly to his taste. Before leaving he presented the Prior with a medallion containing a culture of *P. notatum*. Fleming had perfected a technique for growing organisms on discs of paper, which could then be fixed by formalin, and mounted between sheets of glass for permanent display. He had used this technique to mount decorative colonies of his mould between two little discs of glass enclosed in a gold or tortoise-shell rim, to create the sort of locket or medallion worn by Victorian ladies. He made these things with his own hands and usual skill, and gave them as presents to particularly favoured people. They have remained in perfect condition to this day and have become extremely valuable as collector's pieces.

Then, on 11 June, there came the visit to Madrid. Alec and Sareen were met by the Minister for Education, the Mayor of Madrid, the Dean of the Faculty of Science and a host of distinguished officials. They were conducted to the Ritz Hotel, where a suite of rooms awaited them as honoured guests of the city. Bustinza, now in personal charge, explained the almost crushing list of engagements he had prepared, and to his relief Fleming seemed happy to comply. After visiting Bustinza's own laboratories and the Anglo-American Hospital, Fleming delivered the first of his official lectures. This was at the British Institute, and the subject (once more) was 'Success'. Since he was to give this lecture with suitable variations according to location, on many subsequent occasions, a brief summary might be appropriate.

Success might be defined, he said, as the achievement of an ambition. Those who wanted wealth, power or fame often achieved it at the expense of others. But in medicine success did not harm other people, it was usually a pure gain for the community. And it was not always the best-known doctors who were really the most successful. Many a country doctor had, by his kindness, gentleness and sympathy, achieved more than the most famous leaders of his profession. He was loved by his community, and this meant more than wealth or fame. As regards research success, he had no special formula. The key was hard work, careful observation, clear thinking, enthusiasm, and good luck. Chance had played a large part in his discovery of penicillin. Thus one should never neglect an unusual happening, one can never know if Fortune may be offering one of her prizes.[7]

After what Bustinza described as his 'magnificent discourse', there was a party at the British Institute followed by a banquet given by the Duke of Alba, and finally – beginning at 11.30 p.m. – a grand ball.

During the few remaining hours of the night, Sareen became ill, and in the morning she was feverish. Two doctors gave advice, and a nurse was engaged to look after her. But Fleming had a day full of official functions, and these had to be kept. While Sareen remained in bed, Fleming went to the University to receive an Honorary Degree. He was met by the Rector, the Dean, the Minister of Education and the whole governing Body of the University. Inside the Great Hall were packed as many of the most distinguished people as the place would hold, and many more waited outside. There were speeches by the Minister and the Secretary of Faculties. Bustinza read the citation, which emphasized the patience, perseverance, sacrifice and altruism of Fleming's work during forty-two years. The Dean then invested Fleming with the gown, blue hat, ring, and gloves of the

Doctorate of Natural Science, and gave him the official embrace.

Fleming, thus equipped and fortified, mounted the rostrum and delivered his speech. At the end, he began to describe his hobby of playing with coloured microbes, and the pictures he liked to create with them. From this he passed to the technique for preserving cultures on paper and, descending from the rostrum, invested the Rector with one of his *Penicillium* medallions. Not to be outdone, the Minister for Education invested Fleming with the sash and Grand Cross of the Order of Alfonso X. All these manoeuvres were greeted with 'thunderous salvos of applause!'[8]

There followed an official banquet at the Rectorate, a visit to the Conservatory of Scientific Investigation and, at 7.30 p.m., a public lecture at the Teatro Español, where Fleming received an ovation not only from the audience but from the crowds waiting outside to see him arrive and depart. He departed, in fact, for the Ritz, where Sareen was still ill in bed. But he himself had only just time to change his clothes and go at 10 p.m. to the banquet being given in his honour by the Marquis of Valdavia.

Meanwhile the Flemings' suite at the hotel was becoming filled by presents from grateful admirers. Bustinza helped Alec to acknowledge as many as possible, but these tributes continued to pour in during the three-day stay, and the suite had to be cleared of them each evening to make room for the next consignments. While Sareen stayed in bed under these scarcely restful conditions, Alec was busy signing autographs, books and photographs from 7.30 to 10 a.m., before setting off on his day's engagements. There was a visit to the Prado, personally conducted by the Director, a visit to Toledo, and a splendid banquet at the family mansion of Don Gregorio Marañon, a writer and scientist famous in Spain. Fleming clearly impressed him, and he later wrote:

'God selected him to carry out the greatest miracle which humanity has ever seen. If I were asked who has been the most important person in the history of medicine, the science and art of relieving suffering, and in his example of seriousness of purpose, I think I would answer without hesitation – Fleming.'[9]

Returning to Madrid in the evening, Fleming had just time to prepare for the ceremony at the Royal Academy of Medicine, where he was to be made a Member of Honour. Then it was back to the hotel to change into evening dress for the gala in his honour at the Parque del Retiro. Fleming was ready before the car that was to take him there arrived, and while they were waiting in the hotel vestibule, he suggested to Bustinza that they should amuse themselves by pitching coins into the central circle of the patterned floor. This they did for some time – Spanish punctuality being what it is – and Bustinza, amazed by Fleming's skill, lost the game heavily. The gala itself was spectacular. The illuminations were splendid, there was music, dancing, an elaborate ballet and sumptuous refreshments.

On 14 June the Flemings left Madrid for home. Sareen was still feeling ill, but was well enough to travel. With them went crates of the presents that had been showered on them during the almost unbelievably enthusiastic reception in Spain, and the many who had come to see them off watched with sadness until their plane was out of sight.[10]

Sareen must have been thankful to get back to the relative peace of her own home. Vigorous and fit until the end of the war, her health had been progressively deteriorating. At first she was proud and pleased to go with Alec to his public functions, to sit beside him on the platforms, and attend the banquets and receptions. But as she began to feel unwell these affairs became a burden and then an ordeal. She was unable to respond with her usual vivacity, and aware that she must appear awkward and ill-at-ease. There were even comments on this in the press, which increased her distress. Finally, after her collapse in Madrid, she gave up the struggle, and Alec had to go on with his unrelenting public life without her. The exact nature of her illness is not clear. Parkinson's disease – a slowly progressive nervous degeneration – is mentioned in some accounts. There were also signs of mental changes. For years she had been the powerhouse of Alec's domestic life to an extent that he seems not to have realized. She had run two houses and a large garden with great efficiency, entertained widely and was an admirable hostess. Alec's fame, which at first delighted her, finally overwhelmed her.

At the Wright–Fleming Institute there were changes. The National Health Service had been created in 1948, and the whole status of the voluntary hospitals had altered. Now, no longer dependent on their own funds, they were maintained by the State but had lost their freedom. Teaching hospitals such as St Mary's, retained some autonomy through their Boards of Governors, and their links with the University. The Wright–Fleming Institute kept its research funds and endowments, but its incorporation into the Medical School, and its service commitments to the hospital, kept it on a tighter rein. Fleming was then aged sixty-seven, and under the University Regulations he had to retire as Professor of Bacteriology. The new Professor was Dr Robert Cruickshank, a distinguished Scottish bacteriologist. But Fleming remained as Principal of the Institute – it had retained enough autonomy to allow this.

In March 1949 Fleming received the Freedom of the Borough of Chelsea, an honour that greatly pleased him. In his speech he said that Prime Ministers are soon forgotten but great artists, never. Chelsea must cherish its artists. The occasion was marred by Sareen's worsening illness. Howard Hughes, a friend and colleague, described it as 'a painful disease of the spine that was quite incurable, and which also affected her mind'.[11] Fleming was desolate during this distressing time, but he had a programme of public appearances that he fulfilled faithfully. Sareen was, for a time, in the private wing of St Mary's Hospital, and then in a nursing home run by Dr G. W. B. James, the senior physician for mental diseases.[12]

In June 1949, Fleming went to Rome for a meeting of the Pontifical

Academy of Sciences, of which he had been a member since 1946. He had a week of engagements there, of which one was an audience with the Pope, who presented him with the Papal Medal. When Fleming returned to St Mary's Hughes asked him how his meeting with the Pope had gone. Fleming replied:

'Fine. He is a nice little man. He sat on one side of the fireplace, and I sat on the other, and we talked a bit. Then he pulled this [medal] out of his pocket and gave it to me. Not to be outdone, I gave him one of mine.'[13]

This, of course, was one of Fleming's *Penicillium* medallions, now among the Vatican treasures. Fleming, apparently, had no covenanting scruples about thus adding to the riches of the Devil's Apostle and the New Babylon.

Within a few days of his return from Rome, Fleming was embarking on the *Queen Elizabeth* for New York. On 30 June he was received by President Truman at the White House, and then went to Oklahoma as guest of the city, to inaugurate the Oklahoma Foundation for Medical Research. In his speech he stressed the importance of the individual worker who may do his best research without lavish equipment. 'I have known research workers reduced to impotence by apparatus so fine and elaborate that they spend all their time playing with it.' He illustrated the point by describing the discoveries made by Pasteur, Almroth Wright and himself, 'in little back rooms' with the simplest of apparatus. And of the marble palace (a description, presumably, of the new Foundation he was inaugurating) he said, 'If the worker wins, the palace becomes . . . an ordinary laboratory. If the palace wins, he is lost.'[14]

During his stay he was made an Honorary Chief of the Kiowa Tribe of Indians, being invested in a magnificent feathered headdress. There followed visits to pharmaceutical firms producing penicillin, and meetings with celebrities. When he was asked, by friends, how he got on with such people as popes, presidents and film stars, he would say: 'They're just ordinary folk like you and me – but sometimes they're a bit conceited, and then they're not so interesting.'[15]

From the United States, Fleming went to Italy to attend a Medical Congress and to receive the Freedom of the City of Verona, on 28 July. Then he returned to London. It was a sad home-coming. Sareen was worse, and it was clear that the end was near. She died on 28 October 1949. Fleming was grief-stricken. She had been the mainstay of his home life and a constant support to him in his professional career for thirty-four years, and her death left him emotionally helpless. In the laboratory he became even more silent, and he seemed to have aged by twenty years. For the first time the door of his room remained shut. At home, in Danvers Street, he felt his loss the most acutely. Robert, completing his medical studies at St Mary's, was often away. There was a housekeeper, Mrs Marshall, who looked after Alec and Robert, and also Elizabeth, who lived in the upper part of the house. Elizabeth had been a sad person since the death of her husband, John Fleming, and suffered from episodes of acute depression. She took her meals with Alec and Robert, but did little to dispel the gloom. It is not surprising that Alec spent most of his evenings at the Club, and weekends with his brother Robert at Radlett. He could not face lonely visits to The Dhoon.

In the laboratory, however, he slowly began to regain his enthusiasm. Dr Amalia Voureka was still working with him, and her vitality was infectious. Together, they were studying the bacillus, *Proteus vulgaris*, an organism remarkable for its motility by means of flagellae – long, incredibly fine filaments that propel it like the oars of an ancient galley. Then Dr Voureka discovered that the movement was stimulated by light – an interesting and original observation that delighted Fleming. He devised demonstrations to astonish people, and between them they published a paper in the *Journal of General Microbiology*,[16] and Dr Voureka contributed a note to *The Lancet*.

Amalia Voureka spoke several languages, and she soon became Fleming's interpreter during the many visits of foreigners to his laboratory. She also translated the lectures that he gave abroad, for subsequent publication. Fleming spoke no languages other than English and Ayrshire Scots, and all his public speaking abroad had been in English. When necessary there was an interpreter, and Fleming rather enjoyed this, as he felt less nervous when the audience could not understand what he was saying, and he himself could not understand the interpretation.

In March 1950, Fleming went to the United States for a lecture tour lasting a month, in June to Milan to lecture on antibiotics, in July to Dublin to receive an Honorary Degree, and in August to Rio de Janeiro to attend the International Congress of Microbiology, where he demonstrated the mobility of *Proteus*. There were 500 delegates at this Congress, and in the course of it they all attended a special service in the Cathedral. No one knew when to stand or sit during the elaborate ritual, but Fleming, who was in the front pew, evidently did and all those behind him took their cue from him. Later, when someone asked him how he knew the right thing to do, he replied 'I didn't. I just stood up when I particularly wanted to see what was happening. I'm rather short, you know.'[17] Dr Gladys Hobby, of Pfizer, who had been assigned to look after Fleming, records that everywhere he went he was recognized from his photographs and in the shops the proprietors offered to give him anything he fancied.

From Brazil, Fleming went to Rome where he had yet another audience with the Pope, and then to Brussels to speak in honour of the eightieth birthday of Jules Bordet – one of the great bacteriologists. For the first time he spoke in French, Amalia having translated his speech for him, and coached him in its proper pronunciation. She was beginning to become more than a laboratory colleague. He took her as his guest to banquets and receptions, and when working at St Mary's he drove her to her home each evening on his way to Chelsea. With her, it seems, he was even becoming talkative. But while he was away in Stockholm in December, she went back to Greece for a holiday, and there she was offered an important post in an Athens hospital. No immediate decision was required of her, and in the meantime she returned to work with Fleming.

In the Spring of 1951, Fleming went to Pakistan as a delegate of a UNESCO congress. But, as usual, his visit became a personal triumphant tour. He was asked to make speeches and public appearances. He was taken to the Afghan frontier, to mosques and rose gardens; he was garlanded with flowers, loaded with presents and photographed riding on a camel. In Lahore, when he boarded his plane for England, the pipes and drums of the Pakistan Army Medical Corps were there to send him off with 'Hieland Laddie' and 'Auld Lang Syne'.[18]

In June he asked Amalia Voureka to spend a weekend with him at The Dhoon. It was her first visit there, and she was enchanted by the house, the river and the country around. She had decided to accept the post in Athens, and her time in England would soon be over. Fleming planned to spend the summer at The Dhoon, and suggested that she should stay there too. When she objected that she still had work to finish, he pointed out that she could do this in the little laboratory in the garden. So they spent a few days putting it in order, and she fetched what she needed from St Mary's, and started work. But it was not all work. Alec took her on the river, to local parties and auction sales, and clearly enjoyed her company. Mrs Marshall, his housekeeper, remarked to Amalia that he seemed a totally different person since she had come to stay. But if Amalia had any inclination to make this stay a permanent one, Alec gave no indication of his own feelings. He was, as always, incapable of putting emotions into words. Sareen, during her illness, had once said to her friend, Mrs Allison, that she thought she was dying. 'You can't die,' Vera Allison said. 'What would Alec do without you?' 'Oh, he'd marry again,' said Sareen 'but the woman would have to do the proposing!'[19]

In September, Alec and Amalia returned to London, but were still much in each other's company. She went to meals at Danvers Street, met his family, and was introduced to all his old haunts – except, of course, the Chelsea Arts Club. At a preview at the Royal Academy there was a portrait of him by John Wheatley, which Amalia much admired. Alec, without her knowledge, arranged with the artist to buy it for her, and have it sent to Greece. For Amalia was, indeed, leaving for Athens on 14 December. Her last evening was spent with him at the Caledonian Club, where they drank champagne. She left next day, with very mixed feelings. There was a telegram from him waiting for her in Athens bringing good wishes and remembrances, and he wrote four letters to her during the next two weeks, saying how much they all missed her. But, at the end of the month there was a final letter – 'We still miss you, but we shall get used to it.' And that seemed to be the end of a strange, tentative encounter. Alec was, after all, seventy years old, and Amalia only thirty-eight.

Fleming, according to his friends, did not get used to Amalia's absence, and lost much of his zest for his social life. He began to find official parties dull, and during a Royal Society soirée suggested to a friend, Dr D. J. Fyffe, that they should leave early. They went to Fyffe's home, drank champagne and ate bacon and eggs. The Fyffes twitted Fleming on the number of his foreign decorations. Fleming suddenly became serious. All this grandeur, he said, had come much too late in his life, and he was too old to learn the social graces and enjoy it.[20] It did not occur to him, perhaps, that if the 'grandeur' had come much earlier, when he was still actively working, he would have been unable, or unwilling, to spend so much of his time in travel and receiving honours and adulation. Without such distractions Florey's work had gone from strength to strength, but he was seventeen years younger than Fleming.

In October 1951, Fleming had received an invitation that surprised even him. This was a telegram asking if he would accept nomination as Rector of Edinburgh University. Although ready to accept almost any such challenge, he felt on this occasion that he needed the approval of the St Mary's authorities. So he consulted Lord McGowan, Chairman of St Mary's Medical School Council, and got his support before accepting. He knew that this would involve him in high-spirited pranks in which academic dignity could be blown to the winds. The students of Edinburgh University elected their Rector for a term of three years, usually from nominees ranging from comedians and entertainers to distinguished public figures. The current Rector was that most engaging comic actor, Alistair Sim. The election itself was an excuse for elaborate plots, counter-plots and kidnapping by the supporters of rival candidates, and extravagant and even violent campaigns as the actual election day approached. The post itself was honorary, and carried little authority, except the nominal Chairmanship of the University Court.

Fleming's most serious rival in the contest was the Aga Khan, whose immense wealth might have been a tangible asset to the University. But the hundreds of posters bearing the single word 'Fleming' that appeared all over Edinburgh won the day, and Alec was elected by a large majority. He was installed as Rector on 19 February 1952, and he had, of course, to deliver the inaugural address. By tradition this was made as difficult as possible for the speaker by a continuous background of shouting, whistles and even the release of pigeons or chickens from the gallery. Fleming, however, was given a respectful hearing. His address was on the subject of 'Success'. He used, as before, the examples of Pasteur, Lister, Almroth

Wright and his own good fortune in discovering penicillin. And, to suit this Scottish occasion, he pointed out that Robert Burns, who had never earned more than £50 per year, had universal immortality while millionaires and rulers of nations are forgotten. After this oration, Fleming was carried shoulder high by cheering students to the Union.[21] (See Plate 6b.)

During the summer of 1952, Fleming went to Lausanne and then to Geneva for a meeting of the World Health Organization. There he learned that the World Medical Association was to meet in Athens in October, and volunteered to represent UNESCO there. He arrived in Athens at 3 a.m. on 7 October, his plane having been delayed. But Amalia Voureka and a group of friends were there to greet him as he came down the gangway. She was to be his guide and interpreter. The official reason for his visit proved to be only a minor item, in what became a month-long triumphal tour of Greece. His first lecture at the University of Athens was attended by the Prime Minister, the Archbishop and so great a crowd of important people that many could not get into the hall. Crowds waited outside, and villagers from miles around had come into Athens hoping for a glimpse of the great man.

Fleming's tour of Greece, with Amalia as his constant companion, included Salonika, where he received an Honorary Degree and the Freedom of the City, Kastoria where he became an Honorary Citizen, Corinth, Epidaurus, Mycenae, Olympia and Delphi. Much of the travelling was done in an official car with a police escort of motor cycles. In every town *en route* Fleming was fêted and feasted. On his return to Athens, there was a private luncheon with the King and Queen, during which Fleming presented Her Majesty with one of his penicillin medallions. He received the Freedom of the City and its Gold Medal at a solemn ceremony at the City Hall.

On 9 November, the eve of his departure from Greece, Alec and Amalia had what seemed to her to be a melancholy dinner together. She thought that perhaps she would never see her 'master' again. Then, as he was leaving, he muttered something that she did not hear. After a few moments he said, 'You haven't answered me?' 'But what did you say?' said Amalia. 'I said, "will you marry me?"' Amalia replied, simply, 'Yes.'

Though their engagement was a fact, Fleming said nothing about it when he returned to England. He wrote to Amalia every day. He suggested that they should marry at the end of June, after he had visited India, Cuba, and the United States as he was committed to do. Amalia insisted that the wedding should be earlier, before the American visit, as soon as Alec got back from India. Fleming thus had to warn some close friends in America: 'It may be that I shall be able to introduce you to a new wife, but please don't say anything about this to anyone.'

His visit to India as a member of the World Health Delegation in January 1953, was to study Indian medical services. There was serious work to be done by the delegation during their two-month visit, but their tour became a triumphal progress for just one of their number, Alexander Fleming. His colleagues were astonished by the adoration shown to him by the crowds in Bombay and Madras, he was deluged with presents and invitations to speak, and the halls were not big enough to hold those who wanted to hear him. During this visit, he attended a lecture by Aneurin Bevan, who had already introduced the National Health Service in Britain. Bevan spoke, as always, with his persuasive Welsh eloquence, on Social Medicine. But his audience had recognized Fleming and shouted for him to speak too. So Fleming, who personally deplored the National Health Service, stood up and said that he was reluctant to follow such a fine orator as Bevan. 'I am no orator,' he said, 'I can only give you facts. Orators draw on their imagination.' He then went on to describe his discovery of penicillin, and was given a tumultuous ovation. Bevan, whose meeting it was supposed to have been, was submerged by the tide of hunters for Fleming's autograph.[22]

Returning to London, Fleming went to meet Amalia, who flew from Athens to join him on 3 April. If she had expected the sort of demonstrative welcome that she had given him at 3 a.m. at the Athens airport, she was disappointed and dismayed. Fleming had brought his sister-in-law Elizabeth, and they both stood motionless and expressionless as she hurried towards them. Later, Amalia was to learn that Fleming adopted this stony expression when he was most deeply moved, but at that moment she was chilled and doubtful of the future. In fact, Fleming was delighted to see her, and immediately made arrangements for their wedding. They obtained their marriage licence on the following day and, with care to prevent the news leaking out, the wedding was fixed for 9 April. Alec had told none of his friends – except Bustinza, who had written asking for Amalia's address in Greece. Fleming replied 'She is no longer there, but if you want to write to her, this address will do. We are to be married next week.'[23] He went to the Chelsea Arts Club as usual on the eve of his wedding and, just before leaving said, 'I probably won't be here tomorrow – I may have to change my habits.'

For once, Fleming had managed to avoid publicity, and the newspapers only learned of his remarriage after it had taken place. The civil ceremony was at the Chelsea Register Office, followed by a religious service at the Greek Orthodox Church in Moscow Road, to which a few relatives and close friends came. There was then a small party at Claridge's Hotel where the newly-married couple spent a week before setting out for Cuba.

The visit to Cuba, like all Fleming's foreign tours, was an immense personal success. Dr Margarita Tamargo, who had worked with him at St Mary's and adored him, was his official guide and interpreter, as Amalia had been for him in Greece. She supervised their accommodation, changing it from the British Embassy, which Amalia found too hot, to a sumptuous hotel overlooking the sea. She arranged the time-table and the transport for the crowded itinerary with great efficiency. Fleming delivered the lectures expected of him, was made an Honorary Member of eight Cuban learned academies and societies, an Honorary Professor of the University of Havana, Grand Commander of the Order of Carlos Findlay and holder of the Grand Cross of Honor and Merit. All these events involved the usual ceremonies, speeches and banquets. Fleming enjoyed them the more because Amalia did too. Her knowledge of languages and medical science were a great support to him. The visit ended with three days of relaxation at a private seaside villa, where they could swim and fish with no official commitments. Alec seemed as physically active and tireless as ever, often reducing his far younger companions to exhaustion.

After Cuba there was New York and the start of another of Alec's lecture tours. Amalia continued to be astonished by his resilience. Besides his lectures in New York, Duluth, Saint Paul, Rochester, the Mayo Clinic and Boston (where he gave the Shattuck Lecture on 21 May), he attended receptions, luncheons, dinner parties, banquets, and gave press conferences and radio and television interviews. Even during a three-day fishing 'holiday' he was prepared to visit and lecture at local hospitals. 'People seem anxious to see me,' he said, 'and I hate to disappoint them.' On these foreign tours Fleming seemed relaxed, expansive and friendly. He remained simple and modest in manner, but the unsmiling taciturnity interpreted as shyness in Britain seemed to have vanished.

Returning to London at the end of June 1953 the Flemings began their domestic married life at Danvers Street. In the mornings they drove to St Mary's, where they worked together during the day. In the evenings, Fleming would drop Amalia at the flat, and go on to the club. There he would play his games of snooker until ten minutes to seven, when he would go home to change for the evening's engagements. He emphasized to Amalia the extent to which he had revolutionized his habits. In the old days, he said, he never got home from the club before 7.30. Now it was 7. They went out every night, or else entertained at home. Hardly ever did they have an evening alone. At the weekends they went to The Dhoon, where the garden was flourishing and the house filled by guests and relations. As always, Alec's bizarre games dominated the routine and, to Amalia, he seemed to be growing younger and happier with every passing month.

In the autumn of 1953, they went to Rome for an international congress. During their stay they saw a good deal of Sir Ernst Chain, who had become Director of a department at the Istituto Superiore di Sanità, and with whom Fleming had become friendly during his frequent visits to Rome. Fleming was shown the large penicillin factory established by Squibb outside Rome, and Bustinza, who was with him, records his boyish delight at the immense results of his chance observation in 1928, with factories costing millions of pounds springing up in every civilized country in the world. The congress ended with an audience with the Pope at the Castel Gandolfo. This was, for Fleming, a familiar experience, his fifth papal reception.

After a visit to Athens, the Flemings returned to London. Alec was due to make the opening speech at an important congress in Nice on 28 October. On the 21st, he woke up at about 4 a.m. with a high fever and symptoms suggesting to him that he had lobar pneumonia – an acute illness then common but now rare. Tests at St Mary's confirmed his own diagnosis, and his doctors proposed that they should treat him with one of the new antibiotics. But Fleming insisted on having his own penicillin. He claimed that he felt very much better within two hours of the first dose, and he was indeed dramatically improved in twelve hours. But he would have to stay in bed for several days, and there was no question of going to Nice. Amalia telephoned to the organizers of the congress, who were dismayed that their star personality would be absent. They then asked Amalia herself to go to the congress and present her husband's address. She was at first reluctant, but Alec persuaded her to accept.

So Amalia flew to Nice, and was the centre of attention. Everyone wanted to know how the great Sir Alexander was, and the local journalists got hold of the story, which reappeared in the London Press. Reporters even tried to see Fleming in bed, to which attempts he replied, 'Can't a chap even be ill in peace?' In Nice, Amalia presented his speech in her fluent French, and was loaded with congratulations and flowers. She returned next day to find Alec well on the way to recovery. But he gave up smoking from that time. Previously he was seldom seen without a cigarette dangling from his lips, even while working at his microscope. According to his technician he often smoked sixty cigarettes a day.[24] But, having decided that the habit was a bad one, he simply gave it up. During his short convalescence he received a present from Nice, an album, beautifully bound in green leather, containing the signatures of hundreds of delegates to the congress and inscribed: 'Touched by the grace of your ambassadress, we add our gratitude as doctors to the universal homage.'

In mid-November, and before he was really fit, Fleming went to Edinburgh to officiate at the installation of the Duke of Edinburgh as Chancellor of the University. Then he returned to London to make preparations for an extended tour of the United States, Canada, Mexico and Brazil. This was in response to an invitation from the American Academy of General Practice, and Pfizer were contributing to the expenses, including a personal allowance of $5,000.[25] There were to be lectures and functions in many cities, and radio and television interviews. The tour, which began in February 1954, lasted about four months. It took Alec and Amalia to Washington, Bethesda, Cleveland, Salt Lake City, the Grand Canyon and many other places of interest. Alec collected an

Honorary Degree from the University of Utah, an Honorary Membership of the American Academy of General Practice, the Award of Merit of the University of Louisville, and was commissioned a Kentucky Colonel. In Canada, as a respite from official engagements, they were able to spend a few days with Robert Fleming's daughter in Ontario. Then to Mexico, and finally Brazil, where Fleming received an Honorary Degree, the Freedom of the City and of the State of San Paulo, and honorary membership of eight Brazilian academies.

The Flemings returned to London just in time for the celebration at St Mary's, on 29 May, of the 25th anniversary of the publication of the famous paper on penicillin. The Duke of Edinburgh presided at this function, and presented to Fleming a pair of silver soup tureens that had been subscribed for by the St Mary's staff. The Duke remarked, in his speech, that soup tureens seemed an appropriate present to commemorate experiments mainly done in meat broth.[26]

Meanwhile, Bustinza was active in the creation of a much larger and more permanent memorial in Spain. One of the leading citizens of Gijón had instituted a public subscription for a monument to Fleming to be erected in his town. A sum of 500,000 pesetas was raised, an architect and a sculptor engaged and a monumental garden was planned with an ornamental pool and a bust of Fleming on a 15-foot plinth. Bustinza was commissioned with obtaining his approval, and also suitable photographs from which the sculptor could work.[27] Fleming sent the required photographs and promised to be present at the unveiling ceremony. Sadly, however, this did not take place until after his death.

There were other tributes of the sort that are not often made during the lifetime of the subject. For example, in St James's Church, Paddington, there was a stained-glass window depicting Fleming at his bench. When someone remarked that it was odd to have a memorial window while one was still alive, Fleming replied that time would soon put that right.[28] And there was a stone let into the wall outside the door of the little room that had once been his laboratory, which was inscribed: 'This plaque com-memorates the discovery in this room of penicillin by Sir Alexander Fleming in September 1928, to the glory of God and immeasurable benefit to mankind.' But on occasions Fleming objected to such memorials. In November 1948, a Hollywood film company had wanted to make a film of his life, with a script by Boris Sokaloff. But Fleming refused to co-operate. 'It might be all right after I am dead. Now, I'm still trying to do a job of work.'[29]

He took the same line with people wanting to write his biography. He did not object to articles about himself in magazines and newspapers – in fact he enjoyed their inaccuracies. But when an established writer, L. J. Ludovici, told him in 1952 that he would like to write a full-length biography, Fleming at first refused to allow it. Then he relented, but on the condition (so he supposed) that the book would not be published until after his death. He therefore gave Ludovici the material he wanted, and put him in touch with relatives, colleagues and friends. Thereafter, the progress of this book seems to have escaped Fleming's attention. Nevertheless it was written, and a copy of the manuscript sent to Fleming for his approval. Fleming either did not receive this, or was too busy to deal with it, and Ludovici, hearing nothing, took Fleming's silence for tacit approval. He also had not understood Fleming's stipulation that publication must be after his death.[30]

Ludovici's biography, *Fleming, Discoverer of Penicillin*, was published in 1953 while Alec and Amalia were in Greece. Immediately, Robert Fleming, acting for Alec, tried to get the book withdrawn, but without success. In the end, Alec was not greatly displeased with the very flattering picture of himself and his work that it presents, and he was quite willing to autograph copies for friends. Being the only full-length biography to appear during Fleming's lifetime, the book has the advantage of first-hand information from the subject himself.

After a visit from Bustinza during July – described in loving detail in his own book – the Flemings spent the summer of 1954 at The Dhoon, where life regained much of the original tranquillity of the previous thirty years. Alec's enthusiasm for the garden and any sort of game seemed unflagging, and Amalia began to believe him to be indestructible. Then, in November, they went on what proved to be a memorable tour of the Bordeaux vineyards, as guests of the Dean of the University and the Mayor of the city. On 15 November, after lunching with the Mayor of Bordeaux until 4 p.m., Fleming received the Freedom of the City, and then went to the University to receive an Honorary Degree. The day ended with an official banquet. It had been a brief, crowded but enjoyable foreign visit, and it proved to be the last that Fleming was to make.

In January 1955 Fleming resigned as Principal of the Institute, but retained his own laboratory there. He was nearly 74-years-old – long past the retiring age becoming accepted for medical and university appointments. Wright had been a law unto himself, but such independence was dying out. At a valedictory dinner given at St Mary's, Fleming said in his speech, 'I am not leaving the hospital. This is not goodbye, I shall be here for years, so don't think that you are getting rid of me.'[31] But in February he was ill again, though only, it was supposed, with influenza. It seemed to Amalia that he never quite recovered his usual vitality, though he was soon up and about, and working every day in his laboratory. There was another foreign trip being planned, due to start on 17 March. This was to Istanbul, Ankara, Beirut and Greece. Amalia was eager to go and thought that the change from cold, damp London to the sunny Middle East would do him good.

Alec himself seems to have had less enthusiasm for this tour. 'You really want us to go?' he said one day to Amalia, 'I shall probably catch typhoid and die.' So Amalia insisted that he should have an anti-typhoid injection – which he must have had on many previous occasions. But Alec kept on putting off the necessary visit to the inoculation clinic at St Mary's to have his TAB vaccination.

On Saturday, 5 March, the Flemings drove to The Dhoon to see the gardener about the spring and summer plans. At midnight there was a telephone call for Alec from London. When he came back to Amalia he said, 'That was the police. Our flat has been burgled.' He seemed quite unperturbed, had not even asked what had been stolen. But they went back to Danvers Street early next morning to discover what had happened.

The burglars had broken through the front door into the flat during the previous evening, clearly with the knowledge that the Flemings were away for the weekend. They had found the safe containing all Fleming's gold medals and priceless decorations, but made no attempt to open it. Instead, after ransacking the flat they had carried the safe out of the house to a handcart that they had brought with them, but made so much noise in the process that they roused the neighbours. Windows were opened, there were shouts of alarm, and the thieves fled, leaving the safe in the street. They had, however, taken some jewellery of Amalia's, including a seal of great sentimental value, and an expensive camera. These things were never recovered.

Although Alec himself had lost none of his personal treasures and seemed quite unmoved by the incident, Robert Fleming believed that he was deeply distressed, as Amalia most obviously was, and that 'if any event hastened his end, it was this'.[32] That an attempt should be made to rob the man who was universally regarded as the greatest of all public benefactors was shocking to everyone.

Fleming, however, had one consolation that delighted him, the arrival from Oklahoma of a new toy. This was the stereoscopic projector that would allow him to screen the pictures he had taken with the special camera given to him there. The 3-D projector was a great success, and Fleming spent much of that week in playing with it. He demonstrated it at St Mary's, and on Thursday 10 March telephoned to his brother Robert to arrange for a family demonstration at Danvers Street. On that day, too, he finally had his anti-typhoid injection, but only because the doctor from the inoculation clinic tracked Fleming to his laboratory and gave it to him there.

That evening, Fleming went to the Chelsea Arts Club, as usual. His friends thought that he was in good form and said so. 'I've never felt better in my life,' he replied. From the club, he fetched Amalia from the flat and they went on to a dinner-party. When they got back, Alec's son Robert came in with his fiancée, and there was a showing of the stereoscopic pictures. Amalia records that she herself was 'dropping with fatigue' but that Alec was in high spirits, despite a sore arm following the injection. It might be mentioned that TAB vaccination often causes some fever, and that those receiving it are advised to take things quietly and avoid alcohol for a day or so.

Next morning Friday 11 March, Fleming awoke apparently in good health and spirits. He had the prospect of what Amalia called a heavy but pleasant day ahead of him, including a luncheon-party at the Savoy, and dinner with Eleanor Roosevelt and Douglas Fairbanks Junior. But when he came out of the bathroom he looked so pale that Amalia was alarmed. He had, he said, vomited, and still felt sick. Despite his protests, she telephoned their doctor, who said that he would come around in about an hour. Fleming took some bicarbonate of soda and went back to bed. Amalia went to get dressed, and heard the telephone ring. Alec took the call, and she heard him say 'No urgency whatever – see your other patients first.' Dr Hunt had telephoned to ask if he should drop his appointments and come round at once.

When she came back into the bedroom, Alec was lying down, apparently quite peacefully. She asked if he thought that he was having a reaction to the vaccine. 'No,' he said. 'I'm covered in cold sweat, and I don't know why I've got this pain in my chest.' 'Is it your heart?' said Amalia, panic-stricken.

'It's not the heart,' he replied, 'it's going down the oesophagus to the stomach.' His voice was quite calm, but he seemed to be puzzled. Then his head fell forward and he was dead. As the subsequent autopsy showed, he had died of a massive coronary thrombosis.

The news circled the world within hours. Messages of sympathy poured in to Danvers Street and to St Mary's from the highest and the humblest in many lands – from the British Royal Family, Churchill, the Papal Nuncio, the King and Queen of Greece and from the hundreds of friends Fleming had made at home and abroad. In Spain the flower-sellers in Barcelona laid bunches of roses and carnations at the foot of the stone commemorating his visit to their city. Don Gregorio Marañon, the scientist and writer said solemnly: 'We can be sure that at this moment he is sitting on the right hand of God the Father.'[33] In Greece, a motorist driving from Athens to Delphi was puzzled by the flags at half-mast in village after village. At Arachova he stopped and asked an old man the reason for the mourning. 'Have you not heard?' said the man in surprise. 'Fleming died yesterday.'[34]

Fleming's body was cremated. Curiously, he had said, while he and Amalia were driving up to London from The Dhoon after the burglary, that he would like to be cremated, his first mention of any such wish. At the urgent request of a California sculptor, who had a commission for a statue of Fleming, a death mask had been made and Bustinza, who had come to London for the funeral, and to help Amalia, was able to obtain a copy.[35]

On the invitation of the Dean, Fleming's ashes were interred in the crypt of St Paul's Cathedral. The ceremony was held on March 18, at noon. Enormous crowds had gathered around the cathedral and on the route to be taken by the cortège, and traffic police had cleared the way. Inside the cathedral was the large congregation of leading medical and academic men, representatives of scores of different universities, embassies, societies, academies, pharmaceutical organizations, and hundreds of Fleming's personal friends. St Mary's was represented by almost the total strength of the hospital and school staff, the medical students and as many nurses as could be spared from their duties. There was an impressive service conducted by the Dean.

After the alabaster casket containing the ashes had been interred in the crypt, Professor C. A. Pannett, Fleming's close friend for over fifty years, gave the address. In the course of this he said, of Fleming's discovery of penicillin:

'On that early autumn morning how far it was from our thoughts that we were in the presence of one of the greatest men of the century and that one day a large crowd would be gathered together in this beautiful cathedral to mourn the death of one acclaimed by the whole world as a scientific genius, and to do homage to his memory. Tributes to his greatness have poured in from far and wide, for it is generally recognized that by his work he has saved more lives and relieved more suffering than any other living man, perhaps more than any man who has ever lived . . . Looking back on his career, we find woven into the web of his life a number of apparently irrelevant chance events without one of which it would probably not have reached its climax. His choice of a profession, his selection of a medical school, his deviation into bacteriology, his meeting with Almroth Wright, the nature of the work he did with him, the chance fall of a tear, the chance fall of a mould, all these events were surely not due to mere chance. We can almost see the finger of God pointed to the direction his career should take at every turn.'[36]

In the crypt, Fleming's ashes lie beneath a stone in the floor inscribed, simply, with his initials – A.F. Close by, in the wall, a commemorative plaque was unveiled by Amalia a year after Alec's death. It is of marble from the Grecian quarry that, more than two thousand years ago, provided the building stones of the Parthenon. The inscription on the plaque and the designs depicting the thistle of Scotland and the fleur-de-lys of St Mary's were the work of Dyson-Smith, the sculptor friend of Alec's and a fellow-member of the Chelsea Arts Club. The memorial is close to those of Nelson and Wren.

There are very many other memorials to Fleming. Almost every newspaper and certainly every medical periodical in the world printed obituary tributes. Streets and squares in scores of cities are named after him. There are statues and portraits. In Britain, besides the memorials in St Paul's Cathedral and St James's Church, Paddington, there is a bust in Chelsea Town Hall, the Memorial Garden at Darvel, the little monument at Lochfield Farm, and commemorative plaques outside No. 20, Danvers Street, and The Dhoon. The enormous headquarters building of the

Department of Health and Social Security in London is Alexander Fleming House, and many research institutes in different parts of the world also bear his name. Even the moon is not outside the orbit of his fame. One of its craters is called after him.[37]

Myths and Mysteries

Any simple account of the events of Fleming's life raises obvious questions. The story involves mysteries that are real ones, and apparent mysteries that are no more than myths. The time has now come to examine some of these, and if one or two mysteries remain unsolved, at least the strangeness of the truth can be distinguished from the lesser strangeness of fiction.

Let us begin with a technical mystery. Just how did the discovery of penicillin – possibly the most momentous in the history of medicine – actually come about? On the face of it, it seems simple enough. Everyone knows that penicillin destroys germs, and Fleming saw staphylococci being destroyed around a mould growing on one of his culture plates. His published account suggests that what happened was this: first, he had grown the germs until they formed colonies, and then left the plate on the bench to be examined 'from time to time'; next, during one of these examinations, a mould fell onto the surface of the plate, and grew; finally, some time later, he noticed that, around this mould, the colonies 'were obviously undergoing lysis'. But in the first experiment to be recorded in his notebook, we find that he had reversed this sequence. First he grew the mould for five days at room temperature, and then sowed staphylococci near to it, putting the plate in the incubator to grow them into colonies. And these colonies failed to grow within about 3 cm of the mould. The reason for the change in technique was that he had found that he could not reproduce his original observation by implanting a mould among existing staphylococcal colonies and letting it grow at room temperature. Though the mould might grow, the colonies remained visibly unchanged. Hughes writes that if Fleming needed to reproduce the appearance of his original plate for demonstration purposes 'he had to "fake" it by growing the mould first (giving it plenty of time to produce penicillin) and then planting the staphylococci.'[1] The mould would have been grown at room temperature, and the staphylococci at 37°C, because these are the temperatures at which each grows best.

If Fleming was puzzled by this failure to reproduce the phenomenon as described in his paper he made no note of it. But other people discovered the puzzle for themselves. D. B. Colquhoun, in a paper published in 1975,[2] writes that he found, in 1929, that Fleming's mould implanted among staphylococci either refused to grow or, if it did, had no visible effect on their colonies. And in 1955 he found that inhibition of staphylococci only occurred if the mould had been grown first. Margaret Jennings, working with Florey, had a similar experience, published in 1944 and found that penicillin itself did not lyse staphylococcal colonies.[3] But it was Ronald Hare who made the most extensive study of the problem, published in his book *The Birth of Penicillin* in 1970. This led him to conclude that it is almost impossible to 'discover' penicillin in the way that Fleming seemed to describe in his published paper.[4] (See Plate 2b and c.)

It was not until 1940, when penicillin was becoming of intense interest, that its mode of action began to be understood. In that year, A. D. Gardner, working with Florey, watched through his microscope the behaviour of bacteria in the presence of penicillin. The adult cells seemed to be unaffected. But when they divided, the young cells became abnormally swollen and transparent and finally burst.[5] This effect was explained by the work of Park and Strominger, reported in 1957.[6] They found that penicillin blocks the synthesis of compounds needed by young bacteria to build their cell walls. Penicillin, in fact, does not kill adult bacteria; it produces a fatal defect in succeeding generations. Hence the delayed action observed by Fleming.

The mode of action of penicillin thus explains why its discovery could not have involved the sequence of events suggested by Fleming's description. At room temperature the grown colonies of staphylococci on his plate would have consisted largely of adult, quiescent cells impervious to the action of penicillin. A mould alighting among them and producing penicillin would not have changed their appearance and there would have been nothing of interest for him to see. It is an almost inescapable conclusion that the mould must have grown *before* the staphylococci, in order to produce what he did see. But how could this have happened?

Colquhoun has suggested that the mould colony *was* there, and producing penicillin, when Fleming seeded the plate with staphylococci and then, presumably, incubated it. The objection to this theory is that Fleming – a first-class bacteriologist – must surely have seen it, and would not have used a mouldy plate. But Colquhoun suggests further that Fleming, having noticed the mould colony, seeded his staphylococci nevertheless just to see what would happen. Colquhoun supports his idea by quoting what Fleming had said in a speech in Louvain, in 1945:

'I play with microbes. There are, of course, many rules in this play . . . but when you have acquired knowledge and experience it is very pleasant to break the rules and to be able to find something that nobody had thought of . . .'

It is true that Fleming liked breaking established rules in any game and that, when telling Bustinza about his work on penicillin, he said 'I was just playing.'[7] But if Fleming had deliberately broken the unwritten rule against inoculating mouldy plates, why did he not say so in his paper?

The most plausible explanation is that given by Hare in *The Birth of Penicillin*. His basic assumption is that Fleming, having sown his plate with staphylococci, did not incubate it but left it on the bench, where it was contaminated by a mould spore. The omission of incubation, which might have been by accident or design, is essential to Hare's thesis because he suggests that what happened next depended on the weather. If the plate remained cool for several days the mould would grow and produce penicillin while the staphylococci would remain dormant. If there was then a hot spell, the staphylococci would grow into normal colonies, except for those in the penicillin zone, which would either not grow at all, or would form colonies that lysed. The picture would then be as Fleming described it, and Hare was able to reproduce it exactly by following this temperature sequence experimentally. He then obtained records of the 1928 summer temperatures in London.[8] These showed that, after a heat-wave in mid-July, there was a cold spell from 27 July to 6 August, with maximum temperatures between 16° and 20°C, followed by a warm spell with temperatures reaching 25° or 26°.

Hare quotes evidence that Fleming's penicillin plate was among a batch that he had sown before leaving for The Dhoon at the end of July, and that these plates remained on his bench during August while he was away on holiday. Thus the conditions required by his theory would have been fulfilled. Any contaminating mould would have grown until August 6, and only after that date would the staphylococci have had enough heat to grow. It is not known with certainty when Fleming next saw the plate but from an entry in his notebook, Hare deduces that Fleming returned from The Dhoon on September 3.

Where the mould came from is a matter of dispute. La Touche, the mycologist working in the room below Fleming's, had none of the usual facilities for preventing spores becoming airborne, and one of the moulds he later supplied to Fleming seemed identical to the original penicillin producer.[9] So the mould probably came from La Touche, through Fleming's ever-open door, rather than from the richly contaminated air of Praed Street through his seldom-opened window. Even the window is in dispute. Hare maintains that it was hardly possible to open it. Allison says that it could be opened at the top by cords and pulleys, and remembers that, on hot days, it was.[10] But whether it came through the window or the door the important point is that the mould did, in fact, arrive; just as the weather was, in fact, at first cool and then warm.

Though the chance events required by Hare's theory are by no means unlikely ones, the whole chain of chance events involved in the discovery has an almost unbelievable improbability. Let us list them in the order required for the final result to occur. First, Fleming inoculates a plate with staphylococci and it happens to become contaminated with a rare, penicillin-producing strain of mould. Second, he happens not to incubate this plate. Third, he leaves it on his bench undisturbed while he is away on holiday. Fourth, the weather during this period is at first cold and then warm. Fifth, Fleming examines the plate, sees nothing interesting and discards it, but by chance, it escapes immersion in lysol. Sixth, Pryce happens to visit Fleming's room, and Fleming decides to show him some of the many plates that had piled up on the bench. Seventh, Fleming happens to pick the discarded penicillin plate out of the tray of lysol (in which it should have been immersed), and on a second inspection sees something interesting.

It is hardly possible to calculate the odds against the occurrence of such a sequence of accidents. At a rough guess they might be of the same order as those against drawing, in the right order, the winners of seven consecutive horse races from a hat containing the names of *all* the runners. But, applied retrospectively to an actual happening, such speculations are academic. What has happened has happened – whatever the chances against it might have been.

What might be called Bustinza's theory almost transcends probability.[11] He maintains that Fleming discovered penicillin exactly as described in his paper, and that no one has the right to dispute this. It is true that lysis of grown colonies by penicillin *can* occur, though only with certain rare strains of staphylococci, and with penicillin concentrations kept between very narrow limits. Fleming demonstrated such lysis in 1945, but by an elaborate culture technique that bore no resemblance to his original, essentially simple, one.[12] Bustinza, in fact, assumes the chance occurrence of an extra set of events so unlikely to have happened that his theory is hardly tenable.

There is therefore no definitive solution to the mystery, only theories, plausible and implausible. Fleming himself never clarified the matter, and he probably did not know precisely the history of the one plate among the many that he had left on the bench. It seems to have had no identifying marks, and there is no record of when it was made or when it was examined.

As if the chances against Fleming discovering penicillin were not enough, one has to add yet another improbable antecedent, his discovery of lysozyme. It was his interest in lysozyme that prepared his mind and eye for the chance gift of the penicillin plate. Moreover, it was the resemblance to lysozyme in Fleming's *description* that attracted Chain's attention when he read the penicillin paper. Lysozyme, therefore, prepared the way not only for Fleming's discovery of penicillin, but for the work in Oxford that established its value.

The discovery of lysozyme is a sort of 'déjà vu' mirror-image of the discovery of penicillin. With penicillin we have a rare antibacterial agent acting on a very common microbe. With lysozyme we have a widely occurring antibacterial agent revealed by the chance contamination of a plate by a very rare bacterium. The origin of this *Micrococcus lysodeikticus* is even more obscure than that of Fleming's mould. Allison suggests that it floated in from Praed Street, and states that neither he nor Fleming had ever come across the microbe before or since. The popular myth, that Fleming discovered lysozyme when a drip from his nose happened to fall on a culture plate, leaves the main mystery unsolved. How was it that the culture plate also happened to be covered by colonies of *M. lysodeikticus*? However they arrived, Fleming was extremely lucky to have had two such rare and important visitors as his mould spore and his *M. lysodeikticus*. Or, perhaps, we should say that the world was lucky that such chances were given to Fleming, the man with the eye to notice them and the mind to grasp their significance.

In dealing with the ten-year period during which penicillin remained simply a laboratory reagent, Fleming's biographers have found themselves in difficulties. They all insist that he was convinced from the first that penicillin was of prime therapeutic importance. But if he had such a conviction, then he would have had a moral duty to fight to get this discovery developed, just as Wright had fought for his anti-typhoid vaccine. In order to avoid the charge that Fleming must have lacked the courage of his conviction, because nothing did develop, most of his biographers have pictured him faced by insurmountable difficulties. These ranged from his own shyness and modesty, which prevented him from pushing forward his discovery, to the very real technical difficulty of extracting and purifying penicillin.

If Fleming failed to interest his colleagues in penicillin as a therapeutic agent, was this really due to shyness and modesty? He published twenty-seven papers and lectures between 1930 and 1940, and in many it would have been appropriate to express his faith in its potential clinical value. His lecture on 'The Intravenous Use of Germicides' in 1931, for example, would have given an excellent opportunity, but he did not even mention penicillin and predicted that mercurial compounds had the best chance of proving effective. Apart from the speculation in his 1929 paper on penicillin, he made only one other reference to a possible therapeutic future for it in all his publications to 1940. In the paper to the *British Dental Journal* in 1931 he remarked: 'It is quite likely that it [penicillin] or a chemical of similar nature, will be used in the treatment of septic wounds.' This solitary prediction, embedded in his numerous writings on antibacterial therapy, is hardly evidence of a strong desire to promote penicillin as a potential therapeutic agent, even allowing for the restraints of modesty.

Maurois portrayed an actual hostility to Fleming's work on penicillin.

He writes, for example, of 'the strangely superior and sullen attitude of his listeners', when Fleming gave his paper on penicillin at the Medical Research Club, and states that 'the icy reaction to something which he knew to be of capital importance appalled him'.[13] This is a novelist's dramatic imagination running away with the facts. Fleming was a popular member of the Medical Research Club, but a bad lecturer. His audience might have looked blank while he told them about the use of a strange mould to favour the growth of the influenza bacillus because they were not sure what he was talking about, not because they were hostile to a revolutionary discovery.

The supposed antagonism of Wright to the penicillin work is emphasized by some biographers. Maurois states: 'More especially was the atmosphere hostile in Wright's department,' and that 'All Wright's instincts were up in arms against penicillin.'[14] Wright, it is true, believed that the way to defeat bacterial disease lay through natural immunity and not antiseptics. Penicillin, as demonstrated by Fleming, was an antiseptic and thus suspect, despite its lack of toxicity. Wright was properly doubtful of its therapeutic value on the evidence produced by Fleming, and objected to the inclusion of a speculation on this point in Fleming's paper. But this seems to have been the only clash between them on the penicillin subject. Fleming, as a professor, head of his laboratory, and Assistant Director of the Inoculation Department, did not need Wright's approval to do his own chosen research. Wright, nearing seventy years of age, was more interested in his philosophy than in the research being done by his staff. His supposed abhorrence of chemotherapy had not prevented the active work on Salvarsan done by Fleming and Colebrook in his department before 1914, nor that on the sulphonamides done by Fleming and others there after 1935. And he was quick enough to claim publicly for his department the credit for penicillin in 1942 when it had been shown in Oxford to be a therapeutic winner.

From Fleming's writings it seems that the St Mary's clinicians were hardly enthusiastic about his few attempts to use penicillin as a local antiseptic on their patients. He complained that they never seemed to have any suitable cases, except when he had no penicillin.[15] The Inoculation Department had produced experimental treatments so often and with so little success that the clinicians were rather tired of such innovations. Mould juice, the latest of these, must have seemed particularly unattractive. But apathy can be overcome by persuasion, and Fleming was not particularly persuasive. It would, for example, have been relatively easy to try penicillin in eye infections, particularly since his assistant, Ridley, was an ophthalmologist. Success would have been probable, and would have attracted favourable attention.

The mystery that has puzzled medical writers on Fleming's work has been his omission of the sort of animal protection test that established the value of penicillin for the first time in 1940, in Oxford. Why did not Fleming, in 1929, infect a mouse with lethal streptococci or pneumococci and then attempt to save its life by injecting penicillin? The success of such an experiment might have stimulated in 1929 the research and development that took place in 1940. It was after the Oxford animal experiments, for example, that Parke, Davis wrote to Fleming, on their own initiative, asking him to put them in touch with Florey.

Various explanations for this apparently strange omission have been given. It has been suggested that animal experiments were discouraged in the Inoculation Department because Wright believed that their results were misleading. But Fleming did inject animals with penicillin to see if it was toxic. Why not others to see if it was effective? He used animal experiments in his work on combined vaccine and sulphonamide therapy in 1938, so that there was no overriding taboo on animal work in the Inoculation Department.

Chain and others have suggested that Fleming did not do the protection test because he did not think of it.[16] He thought of penicillin only as a local antiseptic, and the possibility that it might work throughout the body when given intravenously did not, according to this view, occur to him. But there are objections to this argument. Fleming had used Salvarsan extensively, and he had discussed the systemic use of other chemical antiseptics. And why, if he had no thought of using penicillin in this way, did he test its toxicity by injecting it intravenously, and measure its survival time in the bloodstream?

Another popular explanation is that Fleming believed that his preparations of penicillin were too crude to be effective in protection tests. But, without doing the experiment, how could he have known this? He did know that it was harmless, even when injected in relatively large volumes. From the figures published by Fleming and from Oxford, it can be calculated that injectable amounts of Fleming's mould juice contained enough penicillin to have protected mice from lethal bacteria.[17] And Ridley and Craddock could have supplied extracts five or ten times stronger. With so much at stake, it might be thought that the experiment was at least worth trying.

With no evidence of its potential therapeutic value to offer, Fleming was not in a position to persuade professional biochemists that the purification of penicillin would be medically worthwhile though Parke, Davis might well have helped him if he had asked them to. Yet most writers on the subject, even Fleming himself, have blamed unsuccessful biochemical collaborators for his failure to establish its therapeutic value. The fallacy in this argument is obvious. Fleming could have obtained the evidence of its value from his own penicillin preparations, without advanced biochemical purification techniques. It was natural, however, that he should want to isolate the active principle of his mould juice. Having little biochemical knowledge himself, he set Ridley and Craddock to work on the problem, and they made far more progress than he reported in his paper. They cannot be said to have failed. They did not stop because they could go no further, but because Fleming wished them to take up other work in his laboratory.

Fleming, in his later writings, gave the impression that he had handed the problem of penicillin to leading biochemists outside St Mary's, and that their failure to solve it had blocked his own progress. For example, he wrote in 1946, 'I had failed to advance further for the want of adequate chemical help. Raistrick and his associates had lacked bacteriological co-operation so the problem of the effective concentration of penicillin remained unsolved.'[18] Several authorities have stated that Fleming initiated Raistrick's chemical work on penicillin. But as already mentioned in Chapter 14, this was not the case. (See p. 141.)

It seems that Fleming did mention penicillin as a chemical problem to two biochemists, Dr Harold King of the Medical Research Council and Professor H. Berry of the School of Pharmacy.[19] They did nothing active in the matter, nor does Fleming seem to have made any efforts to persuade them. In fact, the best chemical work, before that in Oxford, was done by Dr Lewis Holt in Fleming's own laboratory in 1934. Fleming did little to encourage this, never referred to it in his publications, and may not have been aware of what Holt achieved. Holt stopped because he was supposed to be working with Wright, and only part-time with Fleming, and that on staphylococcal toxoid.

One of the difficulties that is supposed to have defeated these early attempts to extract penicillin was its lack of stability. Fleming showed in his 1929 paper that his mould juice lost half its activity when kept at room temperature for a week but he goes on to say, rather vaguely, that at the slightly acid pH of 6.8 'it is much more stable'. Craddock's notes show that such acid solutions kept at 0°C retain most of their activity for several weeks. And the Oxford penicillin standards were kept in liquid form, remaining unchanged for months. This being so, the often-quoted statement that it was the timely introduction of freeze-drying that had made the Oxford work successful is a myth – or, rather, two myths. Firstly, though freeze-drying did provide a stable, solid preparation of penicillin, lack of stability of liquid preparations had not been a major difficulty. Secondly, freeze-drying was a technique that had been available for biological material since 1935. It was, therefore, neither new, nor necessary at the time of the Oxford work.

Looking back over these tentative biochemical investigations one can see that the suggestion that they had failed and were thus responsible for Fleming's own lack of progress is unfair to those involved in them. Ridley, Craddock, Raistrick, Lovell, Clutterbuck and Holt had not failed to achieve some therapeutically important goal defined by Fleming – they had simply stopped what they were doing because there seemed to be no practical reason to go further.

Though yet other reasons for Fleming's inability to develop penicillin have been advanced, they are less convincing than those already discussed. None, in fact, is wholly convincing, and some are contradictory. When a number of conflicting theories co-exist, any point on which they all agree is the one most likely to be wrong.* The one common assumption made by all those who have tried to explain Fleming's lack of success was that he was convinced of the immense potential value of his discovery and did his best to establish this against odds that proved too great for him. But is this basic assumption justified? Factual evidence given in Chapter 13 suggests that Fleming had good reason – and reason commanded deep respect in Wright's department – to believe that penicillin would be useless as a systemic antibiotic, and might not even be much good as a local antiseptic.

Though he never published or referred to the experiments done in 1929 which pointed to such a conclusion, he did no others that contradicted them, and one must assume that he accepted their validity. Thus, Fleming must have supposed that, since penicillin disappeared from the blood-stream long before it would have had time to kill infecting bacteria, it would be useless to give it by injection. Even as a local antiseptic, though it had the advantage of being non-toxic, it seemed to be inactivated by serum, and it could not penetrate the tissues. As Hare, who has been responsible for bringing these experiments to light, points out,[21] their results were very like those Fleming had obtained with the chemical antiseptic, flavine, which he had proved to be virtually useless in the treatment of infected wounds. He probably supposed, therefore, that penicillin would be no better and was, into the bargain, a nuisance to prepare and keep.

If one accepts that, by April 1929, Fleming had no reason to believe in any great therapeutic future for penicillin, then all that followed – or, rather, failed to follow – can be seen in a new light. It would be sensible, not morally reprehensible, to turn to other things. He did not do the animal protection test because he had reason to believe that it would be a waste of time. He did not encourage Ridley and Craddock, or Holt, to spend more time on their chemical experiments because he was no longer interested in the results, and he had no incentive to badger other biochemists to take up the problem. There were no quarrels with Wright over penicillin because it was not an issue. And it was not modesty but a lack of conviction that kept Fleming silent on the therapeutic possibilities of penicillin for over ten years.

The familiar story of Fleming's ten-year struggle to develop penicillin

---

* Dr D. L. Cowen has been kind enough to refer to this principle as 'Macfarlane's law'.[20] But the author cannot claim complete originality, since it emerged during a casual conversation with a now-anonymous colleague at a now-forgotten International Congress.

against technical, professional and personal difficulties is a myth, and the mystery of his supposed failure dissolves. It was, in any case, a difficult myth to create convincingly. There was almost no factual evidence to support it, apart from an occasional remark about penicillin made by Fleming to a few colleagues and remembered by them twenty years later when Ludovici and Maurois were dredging for material that would fill in a blank part of their picture. Imagination supplied other details. Maurois, for example, writes that Fleming during that period 'seemed to be suffering from some secret sorrow', masked by his brevity of speech and dry humour.[22] The reader infers that the secret sorrow was the rejection of a great discovery by the rest of the world. Ludovici in his biography heads the chapter dealing with those years 'The Evil of Waiting', while Hughes calls his corresponding chapter 'The Period of Failure and Neglect'.

In reality, the 1930s were a busy and enjoyable time for Alec Fleming, both professionally and personally. The planning and building of the new laboratory was an exciting and rewarding interest. The discovery of penicillin had provided him with a most valuable reagent in his main routine occupation, the production of vaccines, and he had been quick to apply it in this way. It was this application that he stressed in his talk to the Medical Research Club in February, 1929; in his first paper on the subject in May of that year; in a paper with I. H. Maclean, in 1930; in a paper in 1932 on penicillin and tellurite, and in a number of lectures, including one at the Second International Congress of Microbiology in London in 1936. Penicillin favoured the selective culturing of the acne, influenza, and whooping cough bacilli. Fleming directed Craddock to this work in preference to his attempts with Ridley to purify penicillin. Crude penicillin was, in fact, perfectly satisfactory for the selective culture of these three organisms in the production of vaccines, and so it was itself produced for this purpose in weekly batches.

The survival of the Inoculation Department as a self-financing institution depended on the production of vaccines, and this in turn depended on Fleming's expertise and meticulous supervision. When the sulphonamides emerged, it became clear that their success might seriously diminish the demand for vaccines. Fleming countered this threat by advancing theoretical arguments, backed by animal and *in vitro* experiments, suggesting that vaccines would enhance the effect of sulphonamides, since it was the antibodies and phagocytes that actually killed organisms damaged by chemotherapy. He followed this line energetically, publishing three papers on it in 1939, and making it the subject of his communication at the Third International Congress of Microbiology in New York. During the next two years he continued to advocate this combined therapy in published lectures, maintaining that chemotherapy had increased the importance of vaccines, even while the therapeutic possibilities of penicillin were being convincingly demonstrated in Oxford.

When it became quite obvious that penicillin was proving itself as a systemic antibacterial agent of unparalleled power, Fleming changed his stance. He reported the results of his own *in vitro* tests on the Oxford material, found them superior to the sulphonamides, and began to predict that, if penicillin could be synthesized, it would supersede them. And, by quoting the two predictions he had made, one in his 1929 paper, and one in the paper for the *British Dental Journal*, he was able to claim that he had always been aware of the potential therapeutic value of penicillin.[23] Though it would seem that these two predictions referred to a possible local use of penicillin, many subsequent writers have interpreted them as referring to its systemic injection. This view seems to be unsupported, not only by the actual wording of Fleming's pronouncements, but by the course of events.

We might turn now to the mystery of the newspaper campaign that, between 1942 and 1945 made Fleming one of the most famous men in the world. There is no doubt of its reality, or its scale – cuttings from the English-language papers alone fill four large volumes, each holding several hundred items. It might be claimed that this was only to be expected, since penicillin was a tremendous discovery and Fleming the discoverer. But, in 1942 when the campaign began, penicillin had been used only in a very few cases and was available only in Oxford. The medical world had not had time to accept it as a tremendous discovery. A second point is that original makers of discoveries seldom achieve fame as widely and promptly as Fleming did. The sulphonamides, for example had proved to be a life-saving medical advance greater than any before it, but how many non-medical people can name the discoverer? More often it is the developers of some important innovation who become better known than the original discoverers or inventors – Marconi, for example, compared to Hertz; the Curies as compared with Becquerel; James Watt as compared with Savery.

It is not surprising that the Oxford workers, who had developed penicillin and proved its value, should come to believe that the publicity and praise lavished on Fleming was somehow contrived. Florey certainly believed this, though it had been his own treatment of the press that had begun the public eclipse of the Oxford work. In his letters to Mellanby and Dale he writes bitterly of an unscrupulous and dishonest campaign designed to credit Fleming and St Mary's with work actually done in Oxford. He seems to blame Fleming himself for consenting to be interviewed and photographed, and for claiming that the Oxford work had merely confirmed his own researches on penicillin. Florey also blamed the St Mary's publicity organization and suspected that Lord Moran was behind its operations. In some respects Florey was probably right, in others, in particular where Fleming was concerned, probably wrong.

The campaign certainly began from St Mary's, because Wright's letter to

The Times was the spark that started the conflagration, and there is evidence to suggest that the fuel had been carefully arranged. The letter was written on 28 August 1942 (a Friday) and appeared on the morning of Monday 31 August. Miss Audrey Russell, of the BBC, was sent to St Mary's to interview Fleming but, though she arrived at 10 a.m., she found other journalists already coming away armed with a prepared statement from a 'hospital spokesman'.[24] There were to be no personal interviews with Fleming – the attitude of the General Medical Council on such 'advertising' was well-known – but nevertheless an interview with Fleming appeared that afternoon in Beaverbrook's *Evening Standard*. (Miss Russell finally intercepted Fleming at about 6 p.m., and persuaded him to come with her to the BBC to make a broadcast.) It would seem that the press was alerted in advance to the publication of Wright's letter, and that the St Mary's authorities had prepared themselves for the reaction. They had everything to gain, because favourable publicity brought the prestige and financial contributions on which St Mary's depended for survival. Penicillin was a gift of pure gold, to be displayed on the open market as often and as widely as possible. All those responsible for the public relations of St Mary's, from Lord Moran downwards, would have been failing in their duty if they had not exploited it to the full.

Inevitably, Fleming became the centre of this campaign, whether he liked it or not. It seems from his letter to Florey dated 29 August that he knew what was coming and deplored it. He had to submit to being 'built up' – like a present-day pop star or politician – as the larger-than-life genius who had turned a common mould into the miracle drug that would save millions. But Florey was wrong when he supposed that Fleming deliberately took credit for work done in Oxford. There is no evidence that he ever claimed to have done more than he really did and, during that period, he paid generous tribute to the Oxford achievement in lectures and speeches. The trouble came from false statements made in the media that did give him credit for work really done in Oxford. Though this trouble was compounded by Fleming's curious attitude of detachment which allowed him to let such statements go uncorrected, his integrity as a scientist never allowed him to make such statements himself.

The people who kept the publicity moving to the point at which the world-wide triumph of penicillin itself provided the motive power were not confined to St Mary's. The whole of Britain needed good news in 1942, and the news of penicillin was good enough to dispel some of the gloom of war. The Ministry of Information must have accepted and used it with gratitude, and St Mary's had the backing not just of Lord Moran but of the whole British propaganda machine. Moran was in a strong position to play an active part in promoting the interests of St Mary's, for which he felt a passionate attachment. He had Churchill's friendship and confidence. He had personal friends among the press barons. But if one is looking for a really powerful promoter of Fleming's personal interests, one must look to one of the press barons himself.

After Fleming's death in 1955, Lord Beaverbrook wrote as follows:

'The man of genius is often an egotist. When – as sometimes happens – he is modest and simple, the world is liable to undervalue what he has done. Sir Alexander Fleming was a genius of this rare kind . . . during his life in his own land recognition of his genius was grudging . . . I became indignant on his behalf. I was anxious that justice should be done to this great pioneer. It seemed to me that it was a duty laid on me as the proprietor of newspapers in Britain, the country which gained a measure of reflected glory on account of Fleming's immense achievement.'[25]

When the son of a Scottish–Canadian Presbyterian minister feels that a duty has been laid on him, he is apt to feel morally bound to discharge it. When he is also the owner of several national newspapers one might expect him to do this through the medium ready to hand. One need look no further for Fleming's press agent.

The point that must have struck those with an interest in Fleming's personality is the contradiction between the extreme shyness from which he is supposed to have suffered and his apparently willing acceptance of a blaze of limelight that would have daunted a professional showman. Though at first he does seem to have been a little daunted, he soon came to enjoy his role as a world-renowned public figure. He was not compelled to accept all of the honours showered upon him – the 25 honorary degrees, 26 medals, 18 prizes, 13 decorations, the freedoms of 15 cities and boroughs or the honorary membership of 89 academies and societies. Most of these awards entailed travel, personal appearances and speeches. He gave over fifty public lectures on his discovery and an unrecorded number of speeches at every sort of formal occasion. For nearly ten years these activities were a major occupation.

Travel in those days was relatively slow – most of Fleming's many crossings of the Atlantic were by sea – and few doctors or scientists travelled to more than an occasional foreign congress. By modern standards it may not seem as startling as it did then that Fleming went to the United States five times, Brazil twice, India twice and several times to almost every country in Western Europe. But by any standard it is remarkable that he seems to have been received at least five times by the Pope.

To a really shy person, such a life would have been almost intolerable. The prospect of being the centre of attention of thousands of people, of having to deliver speeches and lectures with the audience and the newsmen hanging on every word, to sit through formal banquets and ceremonies as the guest of honour, would be a form of purgatory. Yet Fleming seems actually to have enjoyed all this. He said so himself, and those who observed him in action were sure of it. Sir Landsborough Thomson of the Medical Research Council wrote,

'When the work of Florey and his colleagues eventually brought penicillin as a boon to mankind, Fleming rightly received his share of public acclaim and the many honours this brought. He thoroughly enjoyed – and why not? – this late phase of his working life, and he travelled widely to receive honorary degrees and other awards. Once, in Spain, when he was walking in procession from the graduation ceremony to a bullfight, members of the crowd fell to their knees to kiss the hem of his latest colourful robe – he later resented a cynical suggestion that he had been mistaken for a new cardinal!'[26]

There have been attempts to explain the puzzling metamorphosis of the man noted for his almost painful shyness. It has been supposed, for example, that he was acting from a sense of duty and putting a very brave face on it. The duty was to St Mary's, the medical profession generally, and as an ambassador for Britain. And there was also a duty to his public, the people who genuinely wanted to see and hear him. He certainly did make every effort to live up to the theatrical tradition that 'the show must go on'. But, in general, if he acted from a sense of duty, it seems not to have been a very unpleasant experience. The simplest explanation is that Fleming's shyness was more apparent than real – that it was, in fact, another of the Fleming myths.

The *Oxford English Dictionary* defines shyness as 'avoiding observation, uneasy in company, bashful, coy, elusive'. From what we have seen of Fleming's personal life none of these definitions seem to fit. Far from avoiding company, he actively sought it. He had joined in every sort of social activity provided by his medical school, the London Scottish Regiment, and the many clubs of which he was a member. He enjoyed entertaining and being entertained, and organizing parties and his eccentric games and amusements. Even at work he disliked being alone and objected to having a room to himself. The door of his laboratory was always open, inviting visitors, and when they did not come, he went on visits of his own.

He was certainly neither bashful nor coy. He was quite prepared to make public appearances in almost any capacity, professional or otherwise, and even to play the fool. In hospital amateur dramatics he was happy to appear in female roles, and at the Chelsea Arts Ball he would dress up as a little girl or in any bizarre costume and enjoy himself. More formal and solemn occasions did not perturb him. For example, he had been a Freemason from his student days at St Mary's, and he rose through the degrees to become Grand Warden of the United Grand Lodge of England.

One person who has denied Fleming's shyness is Sir Ernst Chain, who wrote:

'According to Maurois, Fleming was too shy to tell people about his discovery and failed to raise sufficiently the interest of chemists or biochemists in the isolation of penicillin. It is my considered view that this story is a myth ... I knew (Fleming) sufficiently well to say with certainty that he was anything but shy ... he was a taciturn Scot, and small talk in any form did not come easily to him. He was oligophasic.'[27]

Fleming, in short, liked being with people, working with them, playing with them, but not talking to them. As we have seen, his favourite crony at the Chelsea Arts Club, Vivian Pitchforth, was totally deaf. With him he could enjoy games and companionship with no need for conversation. He seldom expressed his feelings in any way. He never laughed and rarely smiled. Pitchforth writes:

'He always seemed to me a dour little Scot. Though he did enjoy a joke and you knew he was enjoying it, nothing changed in his face, cigarette hanging from his lips. You knew he was smiling but couldn't for the life of you find which part of his face showed it.'[28]

Fleming seemed quite imperturbable. He never showed anger or raised his voice, and seldom became involved in any emotional departmental or domestic issue. He was kind, considerate and fair in dealings with his staff. Mrs Buckley, his secretary, wrote that the worst that she had ever heard him say about anyone was 'He's a funny sort of chap.' He was always calm in a crisis. During the blitz he seemed oblivious of the bombs. One day when he was dictating letters, the spotters on the roof gave the warning to take cover from an approaching buzz bomb. But Fleming went on dictating while the noise of the engine grew louder and louder, and his secretary's hand shook so much that she could hardly write. Then came the sudden, ominous silence, followed by a thunderous explosion that shook the whole building. Fleming looked up and said 'Duck'.[29]

Fleming, if not shy in the accepted sense, was certainly unusually reserved. As with anyone who does not or cannot express his feelings, it is difficult to know what and how deep any such feeling may be. But people who habitually repress strong emotions usually show signs of psychological strain. Fleming showed no such signs. He seemed to lead a relaxed, enjoyable life, taking things as they came without friction or fuss, and suffering none of the restless urges of ambition that make life uncomfortable. He seems, in fact, to have been a well-balanced, rather unemotional man with a youthful capacity for enjoying simple things and with considerable reserves of both physical and psychological stamina.

The final mystery is that of Fleming's world-wide personal popularity. Until Florey and his team had proved the value of penicillin, no one had supposed Fleming to be of heroic stature either as a scientist or as a personality. But when his world fame led to a flood of invitations to show himself in public he duly did so and acquired a popularity on a global scale that few of the most charismatic stars in the worlds of entertainment, religion, sport or politics have come near to equalling. Who else in those days could have drawn the crowds of people of all ages and classes who turned out to cheer Fleming in the USA, France, Italy, Spain, Greece, Mexico, Brazil, Cuba, India and Pakistan? Fleming, surely the least charismatic of personalities, won the hearts of almost everyone wherever he went.

It might be tempting to argue that it was penicillin, and not Fleming himself, that had generated this adulation. This would not be true. It was indeed Fleming himself who inspired personal affection and admiration. Yet he was certainly no orator, he did not look particularly distinguished, and he did not project a powerful personality. What, then, made thousands of his admirers behave on many occasions in a manner that he himself described as mass hysteria? The answer seems to lie in just those qualities that one would expect to be the reverse of stimulating.

At that time, in the immediate postwar years, ordinary people were sick of dictators, politicians and military leaders, and they feared the scientists who could bring themselves to make atom bombs and poison gases. All these self-important characters had brought death and destruction. What greater contrast could there have been in Fleming? He had given them life and health, freely and without thought of reward. He was the perfect example of the selfless, beneficent healer. Everyone, wherever he went, knew already of the miraculous gift of penicillin, and something of his humble origin and scientific triumphs. When they actually saw, not a dominating, alarming figure, but a simple, modest little man, they went wild with gratitude and affection.

One might close, perhaps, with a word on this modesty of Fleming's. This was real enough; Fleming had the essential humility of the true scientist, and he never lost it. He did not boast about his achievements, or overestimate their significance. He had little desire for personal or professional advancement, but when these came his way he did not become in the least pompous. He used to refer to himself as a simple bacteriologist, and as a kind of Victorian naturalist with a modern microscope.[30] This view of his own attainments underestimates his very great powers of observation. He would always stress the role of chance in his discoveries of lysozyme and penicillin. Again and again he had to say to grateful admirers: 'I did not invent penicillin. Nature did that. I only discovered it by accident.' They did not believe him. They were sure that he had worked it all out, but was simply too modest to admit his true genius.

A Personal Assessment

Again and again, in the years that have followed the Oxford work on penicillin, Fleming has been hailed as a genius, a great scientist and a great man. Can we now, unbiased by the dazzling brilliance of the antibiotic revolution, assess the validity of these judgements?

The word 'genius' is overworked and ill-defined. 'What does it take to be a genius?' asked W. H. Hughes of Fleming, showing him the double-page article in the *Daily Mirror* that placed him firmly in that category. 'You've got to be lucky,' said Fleming, laconic as ever.[1] 'You've got to be lucky twice,' said Chain when asked the same question. They were hardly serious answers. Luck may favour the fulfilment of genius, but it is no part of the quality itself.

One of the least satisfactory definitions is also the most widely quoted: 'Genius is an infinite capacity for taking pains' seems to be a rewording of de Buffon's 'Le génie n'est qu'une grande aptitude à la patience.' Again, this capacity may be an important factor in the successful expression of genius – it may be necessary but it is certainly not sufficient.

Thomas Edison was nearer the mark when he defined genius as 'One per cent inspiration and ninety-nine per cent perspiration', though it is hardly possible to plot these two components on the same scale. It is the application of inspiration that confirms genius. Inspiration *in vacuo* is futile – it has to be given form in words, or art, or some practical endeavour, to become a reality. And it is this process of 'realization' that can be more or less arduous. No one can be in any doubt that Mozart and Brahms were both geniuses. Mozart wrote forty-one symphonies and twenty-seven piano concertos before he died at the age of thirty-five. Brahms worked for twenty years on his first symphony. For Mozart, music flowed with the effortless clarity of a spring of sparkling water; for Brahms a symphony had to be built with the monumental precision of Roman architecture. They illustrate two kinds of musical inspiration but there can be geniuses in any medium: what is needed is the mysterious aptitude that sets one high above the common herd, and the determination to use it. The range can be quite narrow. Some mathematical geniuses are mentally deficient in other ways.

If Fleming was a genius, then it was presumably as a scientist. He has been compared to Newton, Galileo and Pasteur, but the comparison reveals a confusion of thought. The discovery of penicillin may have been more important to suffering humanity than the discovery that the gravitational pull between two bodies varies directly as the product of their masses and inversely as the square of the distance between them. But this does not imply that Fleming was the intellectual equal of the author of the *Principia*. The means by which Fleming achieved what he did are of a different order.

Fleming, when talking about the lessons to be learned from his success, always stressed the need to be on the look-out for the unusual. It was acute, unbiased observation that led to his discoveries. Alexander Haddow wrote, after Fleming's death, that his mind would *pounce* on the one odd happening that would prove to be significant.[2] Most adults are unobservant because they tend to see only what they have been taught to expect. The totally unexpected is often disguised, by a sort of optical illusion, to conform to the familiar. Fleming had retained the unblinkered observancy of his Ayrshire childhood, when every natural event was interesting and had a hidden meaning to be discovered. So he had two great aptitudes – the power to see what was really there and the more mysterious flair for distinguishing between the important and the trivial – whether, in fact, what he was seeing was the tip of a vast, submerged iceberg or merely a passing ice-floe. But to compare him to Newton, Galileo or Pasteur is to enter another dimension of thought. For these men it was the *usual* – not the unusual – that was a source of wonder and inspiration.

The incident of Newton's apple may have been a myth, but the fact of gravitation, which we all normally take for granted, was for Newton a mystery to be woven into the laws of motion expounded in the *Principia*. The familiar swinging of a pendulum and the daily passage of the sun across the sky were not beyond Galileo's questing spirit and literally heretical conclusions. The starting point for Pasteur's life-long exploration of the world of 'the infinitely small' was the mundane process of fermentation, one that had been used with skill but without much thought for millennia. What emerged from his exploration was the whole concept of bacterial disease, and the foundation for immunology. When Georges Duhamel said in a public speech that Fleming had gone further than Pasteur, what did he mean? That Fleming had simply taken Pasteur's work on the therapeutic use of antibiosis a stage further? Or that Fleming was the greater scientist? Many people seemed to have accepted the latter meaning.

To rank Fleming with such towering scientific geniuses is a symptom of the mass hysteria that he had noted himself and surely did not take seriously. It is a comparison that is actually unfair to Fleming. It inevitably exposes the fact that he did not possess the vision that sees familiar things in a new light and transforms the world, or the brilliant wide-ranging originality that transcends doctrine and dogma. To have to stress this is unfair because Fleming has his own position in science, and to put him in a false one is to invite criticism. No one would criticize a scientist because he is not a second Newton, Pasteur or Einstein unless he is wrongly claimed to be so.

Within his own sphere, Fleming had a kind of genius. It must be said at once that this sphere was very limited – he had no great interest in the wider issues of science. Fleming's genius was essentially practical, and its expression was through technical inventions that were neat, extremely clever and beautifully executed. His germ paintings are a good example of this aptitude and also of his ability to take immense trouble when he wished to. Inevitably, writers who persist in regarding Fleming as an intellectual giant, have found in these miniature masterpieces an endearing descent from the stratosphere of higher thought to the level of human play. This attitude is quite wrong. Fleming's natural level was indeed play, and if he ever ascended into the stratosphere of higher thought there are no signs of it. 'I play with microbes' – his often repeated description of his work – was literally true. Most of his research was a game to him and indeed most of his enjoyment came from games of all kinds. His germ paintings involved bacteriological skills of the highest order. They depended on the isolation of bacteria that would produce a range of bright colours, the study of their cultural needs, and then the construction of a picture within a 4-inch circle in which all the colours would appear only after a period of incubation. The pictures themselves were marvellously executed. Union Jacks and Grenadier Guardsmen were hardly of artistic merit, but the little dancing ballerinas, gardens of brightly coloured flowers, and tiny land-scapes, including a picture of The Dhoon, would have been charming even if painted in normal pigments. Fleming became, incidentally, quite an accomplished watercolour painter, though Pitchforth, the artist, wrote that he had little aesthetic feeling.[3] But if anyone doubts the amount of skill, time, and effort needed to produce one of the germ paintings, let him try it for himself.

Fleming's germ paintings were a by-product of his skill as a bacteriolog-ist and his love of playing. One of his lines of research was the development of selective culture media that would favour the growth of one particular organism and discourage all others. Penicillin was a valuable addition to his range of such selective 'weed-killers', and he would demonstrate this range by setting up a series of plates, on each of which only one out of a mixture of organisms would grow. But, to emphasize the point, he would contrive that the selected germ grew in the form of its own initial letters – in fact, signed its name. He did much the same trick in demonstrating the different sources of lysozyme. He would, for example, write the words 'Egg' or 'Tears' on the agar surface of a plate using egg-white solution or extract of tears, and then cover the surface with a thin film of melted agar.

When this had set, he sowed the plate thickly with M. *lysodeikticus*. After incubation, the words would stand out as clear areas against the background of unlysed colonies.

Fleming did such things to please and amuse himself, and to please and astonish others. He did equally clever things in the more serious pursuit of his researches. For example, the layer of solidified vaseline on the top of a culture mixture in a test-tube allowed him to measure the volume of gas generated by the mixture which raised the plug like a piston. It was by this means that he showed that carbolic, by destroying the antibacterial power of normal blood serum, actually promotes the growth of the gas gangrene organisms. And his 'artificial wound' – a test-tube with hollow spikes like the prickles of a hedgehog – enabled him to prove that antiseptics cannot reach the microbes in such narrow channels which must also exist in a real wound. The main outlets for his technical ability and inventiveness were the systems of capillary glass tubes used in Wright's work on phagocytes, serum, opsonins, and microbes in which a single drop of blood or other fluid would suffice for the most complex reactions to be carried out. These tiny systems were, in fact, laboratories in miniature. They had begun with Wright, who wrote a whole book about the technique,[4] but they were carried much further by Fleming.

It has often been said that it was Fleming's powers of observation that put him in a class of his own. The argument runs that hundreds of bacteriologists had to deal with mouldy plates and infected throat swabs every day of their working lives, but it was only Fleming who rightly interpreted the signs that must have been there for all to see. No one would deny that Fleming was very observant, or that some bacteriologists are less so, but to suppose that Fleming noticed two striking and important things that everyong else had repeatedly missed is quite wrong.

In observing the action of lysozyme, Fleming made an original and important discovery. It seems that no one before him had seen and recorded lysozyme in action. But this was not due to lack of observation, it was due to lack of opportunity. Thousands of throat swabs were cultured every day in hospital laboratories and, while it can be said that almost all must have contained lysozyme, this did not cause visible lysis of the organisms that grew, simply because it was only those resistant to lysozyme that *could* grow. M. *lysodeikticus* is so susceptible to lysozyme that it dissolves in a few minutes. It was a chance visitor to Fleming's laboratory that happened to grow on a plate and advertise itself – and lysozyme – by dissolving visibly in the vicinity of a drop of mucus. It is a very rare organism. Neither Fleming nor Allison had ever met with it before or afterwards in nature, nor have a number of clinical bacteriologists questioned by the author. Its chance arrival on a plate where mucus was being cultured was a stroke of pure fortune. It is the only organism that reacts with the lysozyme in mucus so rapidly that the results are obvious to the eye. It is highly unlikely that such a set of chance circumstances would have occurred very often – if at all – in the experience of other hospital bacteriologists.

The discovery of penicillin is quite different. Bacteriologists are often confronted by moulds growing among their cultures and scores of workers before Fleming had observed, as he did, that some moulds inhibit bacterial growth. Not only did they make the observation, many of them set out to extract the antibacterial substance, to use it therapeutically, and some did the animal protection tests that Fleming did not attempt. These predecessors of his were less fortunate than Fleming because the moulds they were working with – mostly *P. glaucum* – were relatively very poor producers of antibacterial subtances. Fleming's rare strain of *P. notatum* was far more active than any used by Burdon-Sanderson, Lister, Tiberio, Duchesne and many others from 1870 onwards. If any one of these had been lucky enough to have been visited by the mould that alighted on Fleming's plate in 1928, they too would have discovered penicillin and might possibly have taken it further than he did.

If we concede that Fleming had a certain technical genius, can we accept him as a great scientist? Popular opinion would certainly do so, and this is easy to understand. Einstein's greatness is universally acknowledged, even by people with no comprehension of the theory of relativity – they simply accept the verdict of experts. Fleming's greatness seems to be endorsed by a similar verdict, and penicillin is not an abstruse theory but a self-evident fact. Since most people believe that this immense advance was due largely, or even solely, to Fleming's personal qualities, it is not surprising that he is firmly established in the scientific pantheon and is likely to stay there. We must be allowed, however, to look beneath the surface of this popular image to discover its substance. We would expect to find a record of original and important research extending over a period of years, and achieved through personal qualities of the highest order. And, in Fleming's case, we must project ourselves back in time to the first half of this century, when medical science was simpler, less dependent on advanced technology and more dependent on the individual worker.

The recognition of greatness in a scientist comes first from professional colleagues who know the field in which he works. They would base their judgement on a number of points. The most obvious is the success of his research, as measured by the importance of personal contributions to knowledge or of practical advances. But another consideration is the way in which these are achieved. Some discoveries follow patient exploration, others are made by pure accident. A scientist cannot expect much credit for an accident, but his recognition of its potential importance and the use to which he puts his discovery reveal his qualities.

The qualities that lead to success need definition. One is originality. Research moves at a variable pace. For a time it may be clogged by accumulated facts apparently without pattern. Then may come what is popularly called a 'breakthrough', the result of a flash of insight that gives meaning to the previous jumble, or the invention of some technique that throws new light and transforms the picture. Usually such innovations come from the imaginative originality of an individual – not from a team or a committee. But inventions and hypotheses begin as ideas which have to be given substance and rigorous testing by experiment. However brilliant and attractive, if they fail the test they must be scrapped or modified. Here there is a sometimes fatal temptation for the creator to keep his brainchild alive by misinterpreting or disregarding the brute facts that should lead him to despatch it. So, among the qualities of a great scientist should be a ruthless objectivity, particularly towards his own ideas, and with it the ability to design and carry out just those properly controlled experiments that will test those ideas and lead him on to new ones.

There is another gift that contributes to scientific success. This is a sense of direction in research. Lines of investigation often branch as they are followed, presenting enticing diversions. Which is the main and which the most profitable route? Which are the blind alleys? Some scientists – Florey was one – have a positive flair for choosing the paths that lead on and out into widening fields. And with this there should be a breadth of vision, the ability to recognize and exploit the new territories revealed.

Finally, there is the matter of dedication. There is no room for the dilettante, however talented, in the top rank. Becoming a great scientist is hard work. Exceptional energy is needed, almost all to be channelled into the one absorbing subject of research. The energy is emotional in origin. For some, it comes from the irresistible urge to explore, to discover, to be the first to reveal some natural wonder. For others it is insatiable curiosity or the intense intellectual satisfaction of solving problems. Personal ambition can be a factor – fame and occasionally fortune are tangible rewards. A genuine desire to benefit humanity and its environment can be a powerful motive. But, whatever its source, dedication is essential for a scientist to achieve greatness. It not only drives him, it inspires others. It attracts collaborators, followers and students. Whether he intends it or not, a great scientist will usually find himself the leader of a research school moulded by his own personality.

Admitting that only a paragon could have all these qualities, can we now examine those possessed by the two main scientific characters in this book, Almroth Wright and Alexander Fleming? There is no doubt that Wright had many of the attributes of a great scientist. He had a flood of original ideas. Though he was not the discoverer of the principle of vaccination, he developed it, fought for it and achieved its application. Prophylactic vaccination was his great practical success. His field was the then new one of immunology and he added much to what was known about it. He founded the first clinical research laboratory in Britain, and collected his famous band of talented and devoted disciples. But he had serious faults. He was so convinced of the inherent truth of his ideas that he refused to abandon them or listen to any criticism when facts did not support them. He stuck obstinately to his faith in therapeutic vaccination because he relied on highly artificial experiments *in vitro* and disregarded the plain truth of clinical failure. The work on opsonins which occupied so much of his own time and that of his team, proved to be a blind alley. Can a man with such faults be a great scientist? The answer, in Wright's case, is a qualified 'yes'.

What can we say of Fleming in this context? Let us leave for the moment, the issue of his two great discoveries, and consider the research that had occupied most of his time. For about twenty-five years he worked on antiseptics, following the line dictated by Wright. We have seen that he used clever new techniques, but the work itself has a pedestrian gait. Fleming had a battery of routine tests that he applied to every new antiseptic as it was produced by the chemists. He seems never to have produced one himself – until he discovered penicillin. He tested this in the same way, finding it superior to other antiseptics in important ways, but inferior in others. The work on antiseptics was largely negative, in the sense that his tests led him to the conclusion that none would be clinically effective. A positive result was that, by discrediting existing antiseptics, Fleming unconsciously helped to pave the way for chemotherapy.

When chemotherapy became established in 1936, Fleming confirmed that sulphonamides prevented the growth of bacteria but did not kill them, and he observed that, in his slide-cells, it was the leucocytes that killed bacteria maimed by the drug. He then supposed that stimulating the phagocytes by vaccination might increase the effectiveness of chemotherapy. Fleming put this idea to the test by animal experiments that seemed to prove the point, and he published several papers and lectures on this subject between 1939 and 1941, strongly advocating combined vaccine and chemotherapy. But his campaign did not lead to a clinical trial, probably because vaccine therapy needed six days to produce an effect and because, by 1941, the penicillin work in Oxford was already attracting attention.

We come now to one of Fleming's accidental discoveries, lysozyme, and to a research that lasted for about six years. The bacteriological work was impeccable; the charting of the natural sources of lysozyme was a process of arduous and far-ranging collection. But chemical work on the nature and mode of action of lysozyme was beyond Fleming's technical resources, and though he believed it to be an enzyme, he did not prove it. (The proof came, in fact, from Florey's laboratory in 1938.) Fleming's interest in lysozyme was sustained by his belief that it was an important part of the natural defence of living things against bacterial attack. To the objection that most pathogenic bacteria are resistant to lysozyme, he argued that it was just those organisms that had developed this resistance that had been able to become pathogenic. But he did no experiments to support this idea, and Florey's work on lysozyme seemed to suggest that its presence or absence in certain animals made no difference to their natural immunity to infection.

Probably because of these uncertainties about the significance of lysozyme, Fleming's work on it attracted little attention during his lifetime. Yet, as a piece of scientific research, it shows him at his best. It should be mentioned, however, that he had a most able and active collaborator in Allison, who has not received, from writers obsessively preoccupied with Fleming, as much credit as he deserves.

Fleming's work on penicillin began well, and along the lines of his research on lysozyme. He quickly collected a list of sensitive organisms including, of course, many important pathogens. Once more the bacteriological work was admirable and, apart from adding a few more organisms to Fleming's list, later workers could not improve on it. But on the natural distribution of penicillin-producing moulds, Fleming did little. He collected a small number of different species and found no antibacterial activity except in one, which may have been identical with his original strain.

Fleming did few experiments on the mode of action of penicillin. He discovered that it took over four hours to kill bacteria, and put it in his class of 'slow-acting' antiseptics. Though he had watched through his microscope the effect of lysozyme on bacteria, he did not do this with penicillin, and it was Gardner in Oxford who observed in 1941 its dramatic effect on dividing organisms. The experiments on the extraction of penicillin were carried out by Ridley and Craddock, obviously at Fleming's suggestion, but equally obviously without much interest on his part. Indeed, it is clear that he was unaware of all that had been achieved, and was not inclined to prolong the work.

Fleming recognized at once that penicillin might be a useful antiseptic. Unlike all those that he had tested before, he found it to be non-toxic. Against this was its slow action, its apparently rapid destruction by blood serum, and its inability to penetrate the tissues – theoretical arguments against clinical effectiveness. But despite this, Fleming did try it locally in a small number of septic cases, and the results seemed to confirm his theoretical doubts.

To the possibility that penicillin might be an effective antibacterial agent when given by injection, Fleming had similar theoretical objections. He and Craddock had found that penicillin injected into the bloodstream of a rabbit disappeared within thirty minutes. Such rapid destruction coupled with such slow action seemed to him to be conclusive – or so one must assume. How else can one explain the fact that Fleming did not do the crucial animal protection tests? The alternative would be a lack of initiative inexcusable in a supposedly great scientist.

As noted in Chapter 21, Fleming's most sustained work on penicillin was its application in selective culture techniques, and for many years it was produced in regular weekly batches for this purpose. Penicillin is valuable in the isolation of certain organisms that are otherwise difficult to obtain in pure culture, and had a general application in clinical bacteriology. But its special interest for Fleming was its value in the preparation of vaccines.

Fleming's scientific contributions, then, consist of a prolonged study of antiseptics, a number of ingenious bacteriological techniques, and two major discoveries – lysozyme and penicillin. With this record, should he be classed as a great scientist? Very many people would say 'yes' but only because they now know that lysozyme has become of considerable scientific interest (though its importance in the animal economy is still in doubt) and that penicillin therapy is probably the greatest single medical advance of all time. This, once more, reveals a confusion of thought. What, in fact, did Fleming actually *do* as a scientist in making and developing these discoveries?

The discoveries themselves which are, after all, Fleming's main contributions, were both made entirely by accident and not by carefully planned and executed design such as that which revealed, for example, the double helix of DNA. If he cannot be given the credit for the accidents, he should be granted the keen eye that observed them and the prepared mind that appreciated their interest. There is doubtful credit in the clutter of old cultures and the haphazard conditions in which he liked to work, since it was an environment entirely favourable to accidents – as he himself often stressed.[5] For the rest, we have already seen that, in the development of his discoveries, Fleming did some good work on lysozyme and very little on penicillin. Indeed, it may be said here that, had it been lysozyme and not penicillin that became a therapeutic triumph, Fleming would have been the more deserving of his world fame.

We may turn now to Fleming's personal qualities as a scientist. We have seen that he was inventive and ingenious, but his clever tricks seem to have had no more than a local importance in the Inoculation Department; they were not widely adopted and they led to no startling new discoveries. As regards original ideas, Fleming seems to have had few of his own, and to distrust those of others. Perhaps it was Wright's incessant theorizing and philosophizing that drove Fleming's independent spirit in the opposite direction. He expressed little interest in the wider aspects of science and none in its philosophy. Though he had an excellent brain, a retentive memory, and a logical approach to his research, he used these qualities within a very narrow compass. Only in his work on lysozyme did he broaden his vision to include a view of its possible evolutionary importance. As an experimentalist, he was a technical genius and many of his experiments were beautifully contrived. But he seems to have been limited to the small-scale *in vitro* methods that were the foundation of Wright's own work. This work was based on the assumption that what happens in test-tubes also happens in the living body – an assumption that might be valid if human beings and animals were made of glass. And the doctrine – also derived from Wright – that a single experiment is sufficient to establish a principle, seems to have led Fleming to conclude that penicillin could have little therapeutic value.

What of Fleming's dedication as a research worker? Here he really seems to have lacked the emotional urge that drives a man to devote all his time and energy to some longed-for objective. Wright drove himself and all his helpers almost to the limits of mental and physical exhaustion. When Wright slackened in old age, everyone in his department, including Fleming, slackened too. Fleming then led an easy-going life, with regular 9 a.m. to 5 p.m. hours in the laboratory, evenings at his club, week-ends in the country, long holidays and many interests outside his work. He had no obvious personal ambition. His motivation in his laboratory, as he said himself, was a love of playing with microbes and new techniques, and he was a collector of anything strange or unusual – an observant bacteriological naturalist. No one could call him dedicated in the intense uncomfortable way in which Wright had been dedicated. If Fleming had realized in 1929 just how important penicillin actually was, it is possible that he might have been fired with the sort of energy and determination that finally proved the point in Oxford in 1940. But that we shall never know.

For a contemporary judgement of his scientific merits, we can appeal to some of Fleming's colleagues for an expert opinion. The most careful and searching examination of his work came from the selection committees of the Royal Society that, between 1923 and 1943, considered him for election. On eleven different occasions these committees assessed Fleming's work and decided that it was not as good as that of the candidates they finally selected. There can be no question of a personal bias because, as the years went by, the membership of the committees changed several times. The inescapable conclusion is that Fleming's work failed eleven times to pass the test because it really was not good enough. Not all Fellows of the Royal Society are of equal scientific standing, but it must be almost impossible for a truly great scientist to have failed so often to be elected. It might be argued that some artists, thinkers and scientists have been so far ahead of their times that their work is misunderstood and unappreciated by their contemporaries. But there is nothing to suggest that Fleming comes into this category.

Fleming's final election to the Royal Society was, like his Nobel Prize, retrospective – awarded for something done years before and developed elsewhere. Though these awards were undoubtedly fitting tributes to a discovery later proved to be a great one, they raise a curious situation. If they were not justified in 1929, what had happened since then to justify them years later? The answer, of course, is the Oxford work that had proved the importance of penicillin, and the newspaper campaign that had given so much credit to Fleming. But did these happenings enhance in any way the value of what he had really done? Such doubts entered Fleming's own mind – he was honest as well as modest. Dr W. E. van Heyningen, a distinguished bacteriological chemist, was Secretary of the Society of General Microbiology when Fleming was President, and came to know him well. He writes:[6]

'He (Fleming) told me often that he didn't deserve the Nobel Prize, and I had to bite my teeth not to agree with him. He wasn't putting on an act, he really meant it, at least around 1945/6. At the same time he would tell me that he couldn't help enjoying all his undeserved fame, and I liked him for that. I don't know whether he took a different line with laymen, but if he'd have liked to pretend to be a great scientist with me and other of his scientific colleagues, he had the sense to know that none of us were any more impressed by him than he was himself. He was a perfectly competent President of the SGM.'

'Was Fleming a great man?' wrote Professor Robert Cruickshank after Fleming's death, and he tries to answer his own question.

'To casual colleagues he appeared an ordinary kind of man with perhaps no great personality, even in his fame. But he had great intellectual ability and capacity for work, observation, technical ingenuity and skill. Some kind of intuitive instinct showed him the kind of thing likely to lead to great results. In this respect I believe he had greatness, and in his capacity for getting things done without fuss or bother.'[7]

This tribute is less than whole-hearted, and we have reason to doubt the 'intuitive instinct' that directed Fleming to great results. But we should first try to decide what we mean by a 'great man'. Lord Acton, having pronounced on corruption by power, continues bleakly, 'Great men are almost always bad men'. Acton was writing in the context of worldly power and, in this sense, Fleming does not qualify for greatness since he was neither powerful nor bad. Personal greatness is difficult of definition and means different things to different people. It must be distinguished from executive greatness; for example a great politician may be surprisingly small-minded. Personal greatness is generally a matter of strength of character and mental stature, which seem almost automatically to command respect. This is a tribute to the man himself, not to his worldly position. But it often follows that great men do achieve great things and high positions. Tending to be natural leaders, they are to be found as heads of great organisations. Equally, many great men in history have preferred seclusion and even the hermit's cave.

Fleming was not born great, neither did he achieve greatness in his professional life. But he certainly had the trappings of greatness thrust upon him in 1945, at the age of sixty-four. It was an experience that revealed a quite unexpected strength of character, because his incessant public appearances must have been a daunting ordeal. And their obvious success must have been due to the projection of an admirable personality. A trained actor could have achieved the same result, perhaps, but Fleming had to rely on an inherent personal quality. In his perambulations as a world hero Fleming was, indeed, a great man.

In his ordinary life, however, Fleming showed little evidence of this *persona*. Van Heyningen writes: 'Flem, as we called him, was a nice old josser, completely harmless and unpretentious. He had a pawky Scots manner which I think was put on a bit.' Here one might a little extend a view of Fleming's personality. He was universally popular because he was easy-going, modest, uncritical and gregarious. Though he seems to have had few intimate friends, those who were closest felt a real affection for him. In the days of his fame his unchanged simplicity and modesty inspired a kind of adoration among scientific hero-worshippers. The pawky sense of humour – not uncommon among Scots – was one of Fleming's characteristics, and there was the usual hint of malice in the mischief. He had, in his make-up, something of the *Till Eulenspiegel* portrayed by Richard Strauss. Fleming enjoyed sowing a little confusion and he probably derived some amusement from the discomfort in Oxford occasioned by his own world fame. But, however likeable he may have been, he did not fit the standard image of the 'Great Man'.

Fleming did not become a powerful scientific personality in Britain. Though he succeeded Wright as Principal of the Institute of Pathology, it was almost an automatic appointment and he left no individual stamp on its character. Wright had done that, and his influence, though diminishing, remained during Fleming's lifetime. Colonel Parkes, Secretary of St Mary's, in an article in the *Daily Telegraph* in 1959, wrote: 'Unhappily he [Fleming] never built up around him a group of young men who would continue what he had begun.'[8] What exactly these young men would have continued is beside the point. The fact is that Fleming was not the sort of person to found a school, and he had no original attitude to research or teaching that would inspire its creation.

That Fleming did not attain a position in the British scientific establishment to match his status as a world hero has several explanations. One is that he had no such ambition, and people in high places have usually got there through their own efforts. Another is that despite his success as a guest of honour and recipient of awards on countless foreign occasions he really did not have the commanding presence and the social and political acumen needed by presidents of august bodies, or chairmen of important official committees. A third reason is that the leading scientists in this country (though not in others) knew very well what Fleming had actually done, and they had not accepted his popular image uncritically. It is significant that the Royal Society did not award him any of the medals given annually for outstanding scientific work. Nor did it elect him to serve on any of its committees, or to its Council.

This and similar instances of an apparently deliberate slighting by the British establishment of the man regarded by the world at large as a hero, incensed many of Fleming's influential friends, including Lord Beaverbrook. Why had Fleming not received a peerage, the Order of Merit and a National Memorial? Colonel Parkes voiced a common view when he wrote

'Professional jealousy can be a most brutal and terrifying phenomenon, and on occasions Fleming had to meet more than his share. From his country he received a knighthood while much greater honours were conferred on members of the medical profession during his life time.'[9]

It is, incidentally, difficult to see how merely professional jealousy could have influenced the award of national honours in which the facts of merit are judged at the highest level. The charge of professional jealousy is probably aimed at the Oxford team who, with good reason, felt that Fleming had received much of the credit that belonged to them. Astonishingly, Fleming's protagonists took the opposite view that it was Oxford that had claimed too much. W. H. Hughes, for example, writes in his book on Fleming: 'There has for many years been a plaque in the memorial rose garden outside the (Oxford) Physic Garden which credits Florey and Chain with the entire discovery.'[10] In reality the inscription on this plaque is as follows: 'This rose garden was given in honour of the research workers in this university who discovered the clinical importance of penicillin. For saving of life, relief of suffering and inspiration to further research all mankind is in their debt. Those who did the work were: E. P. Abraham, E. Chain, C. M. Fletcher, H. W. Florey, M. E. Florey, A. D. Gardner, N. G. Heatley, M. A. Jennings, J. Orr-Ewing, A. G. Sanders.'

The inscription is a true statement of fact, to which exception can only be taken by those who do not know the facts. That there are many in this position is demonstrated by the question so often asked by visitors to Oxford who, when shown this memorial, say 'But why is Fleming's name not mentioned? Surely it was he who did all this work?'

Florey, ten years after Fleming's death, received a life peerage and the Order of Merit. These were tributes not only to his work on penicillin, but to a life-time of important research on many other subjects; to his founding of the best school of experimental pathology in the world; to his presidency of the Royal Society which brought a new vitality to a centuries-old institution; and to his part in the founding of the Australian National University. During the years that Fleming was travelling to receive his foreign honours, Florey, seventeen years younger, was directing the researches that have yielded new antibiotics, new knowledge of their chemistry and tremendous advances in the field of immunology.

Harry Dowling has written: 'Perhaps Fleming unwittingly did Florey and the Oxford group a favor by monopolizing the lime-light.'[11] Florey, in fact, had been given time, without distractions, to complete the work that made him a great scientist, and which had already made Fleming a world hero.

Sources

The main sources of unpublished material are as follows:

1. The *Alexander Fleming Papers* collected and deposited by Lady (Amalia) Fleming at the British Library, British Museum. They are available in the Student's Room, Department of Manuscripts. There is a list of subjects, but no detailed catalogue. The material consists of correspondence, scripts of lectures and speeches, laboratory notebooks, journals, biographical material and other papers, contained in 120 parcels, designated Add. Mss. and numbered 56106 to 56225.

2. *Sir Alexander Fleming* by Robert Fleming (Sir Alexander's brother), a typescript of 117 pages describing their early and family life. It also contains a list, compiled by Lady Fleming, of 189 honours, medals, decorations and major prizes awarded to Sir Alexander. A copy is available to the public in the Reference Library, the Dick Institute, Kilmarnock.

3. A manuscript list, in the author's possession, compiled by the late Professor F. Bustinza, of 110 publications by Fleming, additional to the published list of 85 publications compiled by Leonard Colebrook (ref. 3.7). This manuscript will, in due course, be added to the Fleming Papers at the British Library.

4. Personal letters to the author from members of the Fleming family and from Sir Alexander's surviving friends, colleagues, and students.

5. Personal notes of interviews with Dr Robert Fleming (son), Mr Angus Fleming (nephew), the late Dr V. D. Allison (collaborator and friend), Professor Ronald Hare (colleague and historian of the work on penicillin) and members and former members of the staff of St Mary's Hospital.

6. The Florey Archives at the Royal Society, Carlton House Terrace, London. These are designated 98 HF, followed by Box or Volume number, file number, and item number. There is a complete catalogue. Access to this material requires Lady Florey's permission.

7. Records of the Medical Research Council, Park Crescent, London.

8. A manuscript copy of an essay, as yet untitled, by Professor Ronald Hare on the scientific work of Alexander Fleming, intended for publication in *Medical History*. This was very kindly sent by Professor Hare to the author for his use in the present book.

References

References to published material follow the usual form. For scientific papers, the title of the journal, suitably abbreviated, is followed by the volume number, initial page number, and year (in brackets). For unpublished material, details of the locations are given under the heading 'Sources' on the previous page.

CHAPTER I

1 Paterson, James. *History of the County of Ayr*. John Dick, Ayr. (1847)
2 Donaldson, Gordon. *Scotland. Church and nation through sixteen centuries*. Scottish Academic Press, Edinburgh (1960), pp. 93–103; also Woodburn, John. *A history of Darvel*. Walker and Connell Ltd, Darvel (1967), p. 21
3 Woodburn, John. p. 8
4 *Ibid.* p. 6
5 *Ibid.* p. 31

CHAPTER 2

1 Fleming, Robert. *Sir Alexander Fleming*. Typescript book (1955). Available at the Dick Institute, Kilmarnock. p. 4
2 Stirling, Marion. Letter. Br. Lib. Add. MSS 56222
3 'The Story of Kilmarnock Academy' in *The Gold Berry*. Standard Printing Co., Kilmarnock (Christmas Number, 1910), pp. 22–41
4 Kilmarnock Academy records. Personal examination, September, 1980
5 Gray, William. Letter to the author, 28 March 1981

CHAPTER 3

1 Boswell, James. *Life of Johnson*. ed. J. W. Croker. John Murray, London (1876), p. 145
2 *Ibid.* p. 269
3 *History of the London Scottish*. Hadden Best and Co., Ipswich (1967)
4 Fleming, Robert (ref. 2.1), p. 57
5 *The Plays of J. M. Barrie*. ed. A. E. Wilson. Hodder and Stoughton, London (1942), p. 682
6 Chapman, J. V. (Assoc. Dean, College of Preceptors), Letter to the author, December 1980
7 Colebrook, Leonard. *Alexander Fleming. Biogr. Mem. Fellows R. Soc. Lond.* vol. 2, p. 117 (1956)
8 *Ibid.*
9 Newhouse, Dr Muriel. Personal communication, December 1982
10 Bulpin, J. (Secretary, the London Scottish Regiment). Letter to the author, 28 July 1980
11 Ritchie, Anthony. Letter. Br. Lib. Add. MSS 56214

12 Maurois, André. *The life of Sir Alexander Fleming*. Jonathan Cape, London (1959), p. 35
13 Fleming, Alexander. Speech, 18 June 1945. Br. Lib. Add. MSS 56122

CHAPTER 4

1 Cope, Zachary. *The history of St. Mary's Hospital Medical School*. Heinemann, London (1954)
2 Clunn, H. P. *The face of London. The record of a century's changes and developments*. Simpkin Marshall, London (1937), p. 388
3 Burdon-Sanderson, Lady, Haldane, J. S. and Haldane, E. S. *A memoir of John Burdon-Sanderson*. Clarendon Press, Oxford (1911)
4 Burdon-Sanderson, J. Appendix 5 in *The 13th report of the Medical Officer of the Privy Council, 1870*. HM Stationery Office, London (1871), pp. 56–66. Quoted by Selwyn, S. *J. Antimicrobial Chemotherapy*, vol. 5, p. 249 (1979)
5 (a) Lister, J. *Commonplace books*. Royal College of Surgeons, London (1871), vol. 1. pp. 31–45; (b) Lister, J. *Letters to Arthur Lister* (1872). Cited by Fraser-Moodie, W. *Proc. R. Soc. Med.*, vol. 64, p. 87 (1971)
6 Cope, Z. (ref. 4.1) p. 41
7 Gordon, A. *A treatise on the epidemic puerperal fever of Aberdeen*. G. G. and J. Robinson, London (1795)
8 Godlee, R. J. *Lord Lister*. Macmillan, London (1917), p. 162
9 Pickering, George. *Creative malady*. George Allen and Unwin, London (1974), pp. 122–64

CHAPTER 5

1 Cardew, Dr P. N. (Photographic Dept, St Mary's Hospital Medical School). Contemporary photograph. Personal communication, December 1982
2 Cope, Z. (ref. 4.1) p. 100
3 Fleming, Robert. (ref. 2.1) p. 42
4 Pannett, C. A. Letter. Br. Lib. Add. MSS 56218
5 Fleming, A. Application for post of Casualty House-surgeon, St Mary's Hospital. 1908. Br. Lib. Add. MSS 56162
6 Cope, Z. (ref. 4.1) p. 179
7 *Plarr's lives of Fellows of the Royal College of Surgeons of England*. R. Coll. Surg. Lond. (1930), vol. 2, p. 434
8 Hughes, W. Howard. *Alexander Fleming and penicillin*. Priory Press, London (1974), p. 14

CHAPTER 6

1 Colebrook, Leonard. *Almroth Wright*. William Heinemann Medical Books, London (1954), p. 40
2 Chick, Harriette, Hume, Margaret, and Macfarlane, Marjorie. *War on disease*. André Deutsch, London (1971), p. 37
3 Wright, A. E. *British Medical Journal*, vol. 2, p. 223 (1893)
4 Wright, A. E. *Alethetropic Logic*. William Heinemann, London (1953)
5 Wright, A. E. *Br. Med. J.*, vol. 2, p. 57 (1894)
6 Macfarlane, R. G. In *Human blood coagulation, haemostasis and thrombosis*. ed. Rosemary Biggs. Blackwell Scientific Publications, Oxford (1972), pp. 1–31
7 Colebrook, L. (ref. 6.1) p. 30
8 *Ibid*. p. 38

CHAPTER 7

1 Colebrook, L. (ref. 6.1) p. 3
2 *Ibid.* p. 47
3 Cope, Z. (ref. 4.1) p. 217
4 Wright, A. E. *The world's greatest problem. Liverpool Daily Post*, 30 August 1905
5 Colebrook, L. (ref. 6.1) p. 55
6 Colebrook, L. *Almroth Edward Wright. Obit. Not. Fellows R. Soc.*, vol. 6, p. 297 (1948)
7 Wright, A. E. *The technique of the teat and capillary glass tube.* Constable, London (1912)
8 (a) Cope, Z. (ref. 4.1) pp. 103–5; (b) Colebrook, L. (ref. 6.1) p. 176
9 Parke, Davis and Co. *Pharmacal Notes*, vol. 9, No. 2 (1908), p. 35. *Catalogue* (1911–12), pp. 215–17
10 Hare, Ronald. *The birth of penicillin.* George Allen and Unwin, London (1970), p. 62
11 Colebrook, L. (ref. 6.1) p. 240

CHAPTER 8

1 Wright, A. E., Douglas, S. R., Freeman, J., Wells, J. H., and Fleming, A. *Lancet*, vol. 2, p. 1217 (1907)
2 Fleming, A. *St. Mary's Hosp. Gaz.*, vol. 15, pp. 67–9 and 72–7 (1909)
3 Fleming, R. (ref. 2.1) p. 47
4 Fleming, A. *Lancet*, vol. 1, p. 1512 (1909); *Br. Med. J.*, vol. 2, p. 984 (1909); *Trans. Med. Soc. Lond.*, vol. 33, p. 91 (1910)
5 Kettle, Prof. E. H. Personal communication c. 1934
6 Hughes, W. H. (ref. 5.8) p. 30
7 Fleming, A. and Colebrook, L. *Lancet*, vol. 1, p. 1631 (1911)
8 Davis, Mrs M. B. Letter. Br. Lib. Add. MSS 56216
9 Maurois, A. (ref. 3.12) p. 76
10 Hancock, T. H. H. 'Club history. An introductory note on the background of the founding of the club.' *Chelsea Arts Club Year Book* (1978), p. 4. 'The Chelsea Arts Club in retrospect.' *Ibid.* (1979), p. 10
11 Ludovici, L. J. *Fleming, discoverer of penicillin.* Andrew Dakers, London (1952). Science Book Club ed., p. 54
12 Maurois, A. (ref. 3.12) p. 77
13 Colebrook, L. (ref. 6.1) p. 194
14 Wright, A. E. (ref. 6.4) pp. 222–33
15 Colebrook, L. (ref. 6.1) p. 238
16 Wright, A. E. *Militant hysteria.* Letter to the Editor of *The Times*, 28 March 1912
17 Moran, Lord. *Annual address by the President*, Royal College of Physicians of London (1948), pp. 7–8
18 Colebrook, L. (ref. 6.1) p. 5

CHAPTER 9

1 Maurois, A. (ref. 3.12) p. 79
2 Fleming, R. (ref. 2.1) p. 51
3 Colebrook, L. (ref. 6.1) p. 70
4 *Ibid.* p. 42
5 Pringle, J. *Phil. Trans.*, vol. 46, p. 480 (1750)

6 Fraenkel, G. J. in *Infection in surgery*. ed. J. M. Watts *et al*. Churchill Livingstone, London (1981), pp. 29–37
7 Colebrook, L. (ref. 6.1) p. 72
8 Claydon, William. Letter. Br. Lib. Add. MSS 56214
9 Fleming, A. *Lancet*, vol. 2, pp. 376 and 638 (1915)
10 Colebrook, L. (ref. 6.1) p. 74
11 *Ibid*. p. 73
12 Wright, A. E. *Br. Med. J.*, vol. 2, pp. 629, 670, 717 (1915)
13 Cheyne, W. W. *Br. J. Surg.*, vol. 3, p. 427 (1915–16)
14 Wright, A. E. *Lancet*, vol. 2, p. 503 (1916)
15 Fleming, A. and Porteous, A. B. *Lancet*, vol. 1, p. 973 (1919)
16 Wright, A. E. (ref. 6.4) pp. 321–2

CHAPTER 10

1 Keith, Norman. Letter. Br. Lib. Add. MSS 56216
2 See ref. 9.15
3 Allison, Mrs V. D. Personal communication (1981)
4 *Report on the pandemic of influenza, 1918–19*. Ministry of Health, London (1920)
5 Fleming, A. and Clemenger, F. J. *Lancet*, vol. 2, p. 869 (1919)
6 Fleming, Dr Robert. Letter to author, 7 January 1981. See also Fleming, R. (ref. 2.1) p. 4
7 Fleming, Dr Robert. Personal communication, 4 October 1980
8 Hare, R. (ref. 7.10) p. 35
9 Colebrook, L. (ref. 6.1) p. 253
10 Hare, R. (ref. 7.10) p. 36
11 *Ibid*. p. 58
12 Fleming, A. Notebook, 21 November 1921. Br. Lib. Add. MSS 56154
13 Macfarlane, Gwyn. *Howard Florey*. Oxford University Press (1979), p. 304
14 Allison, V. D. *Ulster Med. J.*, vol. 43, p. 89 (1974)
15 Allison, Dr V. D. Letter to author, 18 March 1982
16 Dale, H. H. Letter. Br. Lib. Add. MSS 56219

CHAPTER 11

1 Fleming, A. *Proc. R. Soc.* B, vol. 93, p. 306 (1922)
2 Allison, V. D. (ref. 10.14)
3 Dowd, J. H. Cartoon, *Punch* (June 28 1922)
4 Fleming, A. Notebook, 12 January 1922. Br. Lib. Add. MSS 56154
5 Fleming, A. Notebook, 16 February 1922. Br. Lib. Add. MSS 56155
6 Royal Society records
7 Fleming, A. *Proc. R. Soc.* B, vol. 93, p. 306 (1922)
8 Hare, Prof. R. Letter to author, 17 May 1980
9 Colebrook, L. (ref. 6.1) p. 240
10 Colebrook, L. (ref. 3.7) p. 125
11 Allison, V. D. (ref. 10.14)
12 Fleming, A. and Allison, V. D. *Proc. R. Soc.* B, vol. 94, p. 142 (1922)
13 Fleming, A. *Lancet*, vol. 1, p. 217 (1929)
14 Fleming, A. and Allison, V. D. *Lancet*, vol. 1, p. 1303 (1924)
15 Wright, A. E., Colebrook, L. and Storer, E. J. *Lancet*, vol. 1, pp. 365, 417, 473 (1923)
16 Fleming, A. *Proc. R. Soc.* B, vol. 96, p. 171 (1924)
17 *Ibid.*

18 Fleming, A. and Allison, V. D. *Br. J. Exp. Path.*, vol. 8, p. 214 (1927)
19 Fleming, A. (ref. 11.13)
20 Fleming, A. *Proc. R. Soc. Med.*, vol. 26 (sect. of path.), 1 (1932)
21 Fleming, A. and Allison, V. D. (ref. 11.14)
22 Muir, R. and Ritchie, J. *Manual of bacteriology.* Oxford University Press (1932), p. 234
23 (Footnote). *Lysozyme.* Osserman, E. F., Canfield, R. E. and Beychok, S., eds. Academic Press, New York (1974), pp. 1–641
24 Moran, Lord. *The anatomy of courage.* Constable, London (1945)
25 Fleming, A. and Allison, V. D. *Br. J. Exp. Path.*, vol. 3, p. 252 (1922)
26 Cope, Z. (ref. 4.1) p. 108
27 Fleming, Dr Donald. Letter to author, 9 November 1980
28 Hare, R. (ref. 7.10) p. 57
29 Allison, V. D. (ref. 10.14)
30 Pitchforth, Vivian and Hancock, T. H. H. Letters to author, August 1980

CHAPTER 12

 1 Fleming, A. *Br. J. Exp. Path.*, vol. 10, p. 226 (1929)
 2 Fleming, A. In *A system of bacteriology in relation to medicine.* Medical Research Council, London (1929), vol. 2, pp. 11–26
 3 (a) Hare, R. (ref. 7.10) pp. 93–100. (b) Craddock, S. R. Notebook. Br. Lib. Add. MSS 56224
 4 Fleming, A. Penicillin plate. Br. Lib. Add. MSS 56209
 5 Fleming, A. Notebook. Br. Lib. Add. MSS 56162, pp. 13–86
 6 Fleming, A. (ref. 12.1) p. 232
 7 Hare, R. *Med. History*, vol. 26, p. 1 (1982), p. 15
 8 *Ibid.* p. 5
 9 *Ibid.* pp. 7–18, and (ref. 7.10) pp. 93–104
10 *Ibid.* p. 8
11 Fleming, A. *J. Path. Bact.*, vol. 35, p. 831 (1932)

CHAPTER 13

 1 Fleming, A. (ref. 12.1) p. 229
 2 Fleming, A. (ref. 12.5) pp. 20 and 42
 3 Fleming, A. (ref. 12.1) p. 232
 4 Hare, R. (ref. 12.7) p. 15
 5 *Ibid.* pp. 14–15
 6 Hare, R. (ref. 7.10) p. 90
 7 Fleming, A. (ref. 12.5) p. 34
 8 Maurois, A. (ref. 3.12) p. 133
 9 Craddock, S. R. (ref. 12.3b), 2 April 1929
10 Rogers, K. Letter. Br. Lib. Add. MSS 56214
11 Dale, H. H. Letter. Br. Lib. Add. MSS 56219
12 Maurois, A. (ref. 3.12) p. 137
13 Papacostas, G. and Gaté, J. *Les associations microbiennes.* Doin et Cie., Paris (1928)
14 Burdon-Sanderson, J. (ref. 4.4)
15 Lister, J. (ref. 4.5a)
16 Lister, J. (ref. 4.5b)
17 Fraser-Moodie, W. *Proc. R. Soc. Med.*, vol. 64, p. 87 (1971)
18 Pasteur, L. and Joubert, J. F. C. *R. Acad. Sci. Paris*, vol. 85, p. 101 (1877)
19 Garré, C. *Korresp. Bl. schweiz Ärz.*, vol. 17, 385 (1887)
20 Tiberio, V. *Annali d'Ig. sper. Roma.*, vol. 5, p. 91 (1895)

21 Meneces, A. N. T. Letter to *The Times*, London, 21 July 1977

CHAPTER 14

 1 Fleming. A. (ref. 12.11)
 2 Fleming, A. *Proc. R. Soc. Med.*, vol. 34, p. 342 (1941)
 3 Fleming, A. *Harben Lectures. J. Roy. Inst. Publ. Hlth.*, vol. 8, pp. 36, 63, 93 (1945)
 4 Fleming, A. *Proc. R. Soc. Med.*, vol. 24, p. 808 (1931)
 5 Fleming, A. *Brit. Dental J.*, vol. 52, ii, p. 105 (1931)
 6 Fleming, A. (ref. 11.20)
 7 Fleming, A. (ref. 12.11)
 8 Royal Society records
 9 Hare, R. (ref. 12.7) p. 10
10 Fleming, A. Letter. Roy. Soc. archives, 98HF, 35, 12, 25
11 Birkinshaw, J. H. *Harold Raistrick. Biogr. Mem. Fellows R. Soc.*, vol. 18, p. 489 (1972)
12 Maurois, A. (ref. 3.12) p. 127
13 Curteis, Ian. *Sir Alexander Fleming*. BBC 2 Biography broadcast, 4 January 1972
14 Craddock, S. R. (ref. 12.3b), 20 February 1929
15 Masters, David. *Miracle drug*. Eyre and Spottiswoode, London (1946), p. 53
16 Clutterbuck, P. W., Lovell, R. and Raistrick, H. *Biochem. J.*, vol. 26, p. 1907 (1932)
17 Masters, D. (ref. 14.15) p. 56
18 Taylor, A. J. P. *Beaverbrook*. Hamish Hamilton, London (1972), pp. 258–9
19 Bunker, H. J. Letter. Br. Lib. Add. MSS 56214
20 Hare, R. Essay on the scientific work of Alexander Fleming. To be published in *Medical History*
21 Hughes, W. H. (ref. 5.8) p. 73
22 Hare, R. (ref. 7.10) p. 103
23 Fleming, A. and Petrie, G. F. *Recent advances in serum and vaccine therapy*. Churchill, London (1934)
24 Fleming, A. *Practitioner*, vol. 133, p. 537 (1934)
25 Fleming, A. Diary. Br. Lib. Add. MSS 56184
26 Allison, V. D. (ref. 10.14)
27 Hare, R. (ref. 7.10) p. 147
28 Domagk, G. *Deut. Med. Woch.*, vol. 61, p. 250 (1935)
29 Hare, R. (ref. 7.10) p. 139
30 Fleming, A. Notebook. Br. Lib. Add. MSS 56172, 23 October 1936
31 Fleming, A., Maclean, I. H. and Rogers, K. B. *Lancet*, vol. 1, p. 562 (1939)
32 Fleming, A. *Proc. R. Soc. Med.*, vol. 32, p. 911 (1939)
33 Fleming, A. *3rd Int. Cong. Microbiol., New York (1939). Abstracts* (1940), p. 587
34 Fleming, A. *Proc. R. Soc. Med.*, vol. 34, p. 342 (1941)
35 Fleming, R. (ref. 2.1) p. 62
36 Masters, D. (ref. 14.15) p. 63
37 Maurois, A. (ref. 3.12) p. 144
38 Ludovici, L. J. (ref. 8.11) p. 123
39 Fleming, Dr Robert. Personal communication, 4 October 1980
40 Willcox, Gerald. Letter. Br. Lib. Add. MSS 56218
41 Ludovici, L. J. (ref. 8.11) pp. 131–2

CHAPTER 15

1 Florey, H. W. Notebook. R. Soc. archives, 98HF, 2, 17 January 1929
2 Macfarlane, Gwyn. *Howard Florey. The making of a great scientist.* Oxford University Press, Oxford (1979)
3 Sherrington, C. S. *Man on his nature.* Cambridge University Press, Cambridge (1940)
4 Sherrington, C. S. *The assaying of Brabantius and other verse.* Oxford University Press, Oxford (1925)
5 Goldsworthy, N. E. and Florey, H. W. *Br. J. Exp. Path.*, vol. 11, p. 192 (1930)
6 Fleming, A. (ref. 11.20)
7 Florey, H. W. *et al. Antibiotics.* Oxford University Press, Oxford (1949) p. 634

CHAPTER 16

1 Douglas, S. R. *Georges Dreyer. Obit. Not. Fellows R. Soc.*, vol. 1, p. 569 (1932–5)
2 Abraham, E. P. and Robinson, R. *Nature*, London, vol. 140, p. 24 (1937)
3 Blake, C. C. F., Koenig, D. F., Mair, G. A., North, A. C. T., Phillips, D. C. and Sarma, V. R. *Nature*, London, vol. 206, p. 757 (1965)
4 Epstein, L. A. and Chain, E. B. *Br. J. Exp. Path.*, vol. 21, p. 339 (1940)
5 Florey, H. W. Grant application, Jan., 1939. Med. Res. Council archives, London. File 1752, Vol. 1
6 Florey, H. W. Letter to E. Mellanby, 6 September 1939. Loc. cit.
7 Mellanby, E. Letter to H. W. Florey, 8 September 1939. Loc. cit.
8 Florey, H. W. Application to Rockefeller Foundation, 20 November 1939, Sir William Dunn School of Pathology archives, Oxford
9 Florey, H. W. and Abraham, E. P. *J. History Med.*, vol. 3, p. 302 (1951)
10 Clarke, H. T., Johnson, J. R. and Robinson, R. *The Chemistry of Penicillin.* Pergamon Press, NJ (1949)
11 Chain, E., Florey, H. W., Gardner, A. D., Heatley, N. G., Jennings, M.A., Orr-Ewing, J. and Sanders, A. G. *Lancet*, vol. 2, p. 226 (1940)
12 Chain, E. *J. R. Coll. Phycns.* Lond., vol. 6, p. 103 (1972), p. 115
13 Chain, E. *et al.* (ref. 16.11)

CHAPTER 17

1 Heatley, N. G. Personal diary, 15 July 1940
2 Florey–Mellanby correspondence (1940). Loc. cit. (ref. 16.5)
3 Curteis, Ian (ref. 14.13)
4 Buckley, Mrs Helen. Letter. Br. Lib. Add. MSS 56219
5 Fleming, A. *Br. Med. J.*, vol. 2, p. 715 (1940)
6 Fleming, A. Letter to H. W. Florey, 15 November 1940. R. Soc. archives, Lond. 98HF 35. 12
7 White, Stanley. Letter to A. Fleming, 29 November 1940. Br. Lib. Add. MSS 56113
8 Howitt, R. M. and Everitt, S. F. Letters to author, March, 1981
9 (a) Dawson, M. H., Hobby, G. L., Meyer, K. and Chaffee, E. *J. Clin. Invest.*, vol. 20, p. 434 (1941). (b) Bickel, Lennard, *Rise up to life.* Angus and Robertson, London (1972), p. 124
10 Bickel, Lennard. Loc. cit. p. 121
11 Abraham, E. P., Chain, E. B., Fletcher, C. M., Gardner, A. D., Heatley, N. G., Jennings, M. A. and Florey, H. W. *Lancet*, vol. 2, p. 177 (1941)
12 (a) Annotation. *Br. Med. J.*, vol. 2, p. 310 (1941). (b) Fleming, A., Loc. cit. p. 386

13 Press references: *Daily Herald*, 4 September 1941; *Listener*, 9 October 1941; *Tit-Bits*, 21 November 1941; *Smith's Weekly*, 29 November 1941; *Nursing Times*, 4 October 1941; *Pharmaceutical Journal*, 25 October 1941; *Veterinary Record*, 4 October 1941

14 Allison, V. D. (ref. 10.14)

15 Helfand, W. H., Woodruff, H. B., Coleman, K. M. H. and Cowen, D. L. In *The history of antibiotics*. ed. J. Parascandola. American Institute of the History of Pharmacy, Wisconsin (1980), p. 32

CHAPTER 18

1 Florey, M. E. and Florey, H. W. *Lancet*, vol. 1, p. 387 (1943)

2 Fleming, Robert (ref. 2.1) p. 64. Case notes: Br. Lib. Add. MSS 56183

3 BBC Radio 4 broadcast, 5 August 1981

4 Florey, H. W. Notebook, 13 August 1942. R. Soc archives, Lond., 98HF. 9

5 Fleming, A. *Lancet*, vol. 2, p. 434 (1943)

6 Maurois, A. (ref. 3.12) p. 183

7 Wilson, David. *Penicillin in perspective*. Faber and Faber, London (1976), p. 217

8 Dohrmann, G. J. *Surg. Neurol.*, vol. 3, p. 227 (1975)

9 Fulton, J. Diary, vol. 18 (1942). Quoted by Dohrmann (ref. 18.8)

10 Bodenham, D. C. *Lancet*, vol. 2, p. 725 (1943), and *Proc. R. Soc. Med.*, vol. 37, p. 105 (1943)

11 Helfand *et al.* (ref. 17.15) pp. 50–51

12 Howie, J. *Br. Med. J.*, vol. 2, p. 1631 (1979)

13 Bickel, L. (ref. 17.9b) p. 211

14 Fleming, A. Letter to H. W. Florey, 29 August 1942. R. Soc. archives, Lond. 98HF. 35. 12

15 Florey, H. W. Letter to H. H. Dale, 11 December 1942. Loc. cit. 98HF. 38. 3. 1

16 Dale, H. H. Letter to H. W. Florey, 17 December 1942. Loc. cit. 98HF. 38. 3. 2

17 MacLeod, D. Letter. Br. Lib. Add. MSS 56218. See also Maurois (ref. 3.12), p. 190

18 Maurois, A. (ref. 3.12) p. 188

19 Penicillin press – cuttings. R. Soc. archives, Lond. 98HF. 49: Vol. 1,2. 50: Vol. 1,2

20 *Illustrated*, 18 December 1943

21 Hughes, W. H. (ref. 5.8) p. 88

22 *St. Mary's Hosp. Gaz.*, vol. 51, p. 114 (1945)

23 Mahoney, J. F., Arnold, R. C. and Harris, A. *Vener. Dis. Inform.*, vol. 24, p. 355 (1943)

24 Stewart, G. T. Letter to Editor, *Glasgow Herald*, 7 July 1979

25 Chain, E. B. Personal communication, 1978

26 Florey, H. W. Letter to E. Mellanby, 19 June 1944. Roy. Soc. archives. 98HF. 36. 4. 107

27 Mellanby, E. Letter to H. W. Florey, 30 June 1944. Loc. cit. 98HF. 36. 4. 108

CHAPTER 19

1 Fleming, A. Reported in *Glasgow Evening News*, 27 July 1944

2 Hughes, W. H. (ref. 5.8) p. 82. See also Maurois, A. (ref. 3.12) p. 197

3 a) Sheehan, J. C. *The Enchanted Ring*. MIT Press, Cambridge, Mass. (1982), p. 28. b) pp. 123–60

4 Fleming, A. Br. Lib. Add. MSS 56122. See also Maurois, A. (ref. 3.12) p. 199

5 Wilson, D. (ref. 18.7) pp. 199–203

6 Coghill, R. and Koch, R. S. *Chemical and Engineering News*, vol. 23, pp. 2310–2316 (1943); also Wilson, D. (ref. 18.7) p. 203

7 Schatz, A., Bugie, E. and Waksman, S. A. *Proc. Soc. Exp. Biol. Med.*, vol. 55, p. 66 (1944)

8 Abraham, E. P., Chain, E. B., Baker, W. and Robinson, R. 'Pen 103'. 23 October 1943. A classified and restricted report. See Sheehan, J. C. (ref. 19.3) p. 114

9 Hodgkin, Dorothy Crowfoot. See *The Chemistry of Penicillin*. eds. Clarke, H. T., Johnson, J. R. and Robinson, R. Princeton University Press (1949), p. 310

10 Sheehan, J. C. (ref. 19.3b)

11 Fleming, Dr Robert. Letter to author, 7 January 1981

12 Maurois, A. (ref. 3.12) p. 200

13 Fleming, R. (ref. 2.1) p. 75

14 Clegg, Hugh. Letter quoted by Maurois, A. (ref. 3.12) p. 199

15 Fleming, A. Speech. Br. Lib. Add. MSS 56122. See also A. N. Richards' letter. 56215

16 Carswell, T. S. Letter. Br. Lib. Add. MSS 56218

17 Maurois, A. (ref. 3.12) p. 202

18 Fleming, A. Speech. Br. Lib. Add. MSS 56122

19 Cameron, J. Letter. Br. Lib. Add. MSS 56218

20 Fleming, A. Reported in *New Haven Register*, 11 March 1962

21 Vinson, Sec. US Treas. Reported in unidentified US press cutting, 26 July 1945. R. Soc. archives. 98HF. 50. Vol. 2. See also Walter Winchell, *Philadelphia Inquirer*, 17 July 1945 98HF. 50. Vol. 2

22 Fleming, Mr Angus. Personal communication, 2 October 1980

23 Ludovici, L. J. (ref. 8.11) p. 205

24 Williams, L. Letter. Br. Lib. Add. MSS 56214

25 *St. Mary's Hosp. Gaz.*, vol. 51, pp. 120–21 (1945)

26 Stalker, Prof. A. L. Letter to author, 3 December 1981

27 (a) Hancock, Mr T. H. H. Letter to author, 16 June 1980
   (b) Lovell, Prof. R. R. H. Letter to author, 29 August 1980

28 Alonso, E. Martinez. *The adventures of a doctor*. Robert Hale, London (1962), p. 164

29 Alder, M. W. *J. R. Soc. Med.*, vol. 75, p. 4 (1982)

30 Fleming, A. Letter to John Cameron. Maurois. (ref. 3.12) p. 212

31 Fleming, A. Speech. Maurois. (ref. 3.12) p. 212

32 Breen, G. E. Letter. Br. Lib. Add. MSS 56216

33 Thomson, Lady. Letter. Br. Lib. Add. MSS 56218

34 Rowley, Prof. D. Letter to author, 8 July 1981

35 Heyningen, Dr W. E. van. Letter to author, 3 August 1980

36 Hare, Ronald, *St. Mary's Hosp. Gaz.*, vol. 68, p. 4 (1962)

CHAPTER 20

1 Hare, Prof. Ronald. Letter to author, 17 May 1980

2 Maurois, A. (ref. 3.12) p. 223

3 Alonso, E. M. (ref. 19.28) p. 164

4 Bustinza, Florencio. *Diez años de amistad con Sir Alexander Fleming*. Editorial M.A.S. Madrid (1961), p. 56

5 *Ibid*. p. 59

6 *Ibid*. p. 87

7 *Ibid*. pp. 89–90

8 *Ibid*. p. 98

9 *Ibid*. p. 107

10 *Ibid.* p. 114
11 Hughes, W. H. (ref. 5.8) p. 86
12 Hunt, Mrs B. Personal communication, 6 October 1981
13 Hughes, W. H. (ref. 5.8) p. 85
14 Fleming, A. Speech. Maurois. (ref. 3.12) p. 232
15 Maurois. (ref. 3.12) p. 209
16 Fleming, A., Voureka, A., Kramer, I. R. H. and Hughes, W. H. *J. Gen. Microbiol.*, vol. 4, p. 257 (1950)
17 Hobby, Gladys. Brit. Lib. Add. MSS 56218
18 Ross, Sandy. Loc. cit. above
19 Allison, Mrs V. Personal communication, 30 September 1981
20 Maurois. (ref. 3.12) p. 246
21 Hughes, W. H. (ref. 5.8) p. 84
22 Maurois, A. (ref. 3.12) p. 256
23 Fleming, A. Letter to Bustinza. (ref. 20.4) p. 150
24 Stratful, D. Letter. Br. Lib. Add. MSS 56221
25 Pfizer. Letter. Br. Lib. Add. MSS 56215
26 Maurois, A. (ref. 3.12) p. 266
27 Bustinza, F. (ref. 20.4) p. 162
28 Parkes, Col W. *Daily Telegraph*, 4 May 1959
29 Sokaloff, Boris. Letter, 2 November 1948. Br. Lib. Add. MSS 56110
30 Fleming, Robert. (ref. 2.1) pp. 92–3, and Ludovici, L. J. Letter to author, 24 August 1981
31 Hunt, Dr Thomas. Letter. Br. Lib. Add. MSS 56220
32 Fleming, Robert. (ref. 2.1) p. 94
33 Bustinza, F. (ref. 20.4) p. 107
34 Papadopoulou, A. Letter to Editor. *Girton Review.* Easter, 1955
35 Bustinza, F. (ref. 20.4) pp. 215–19
36 Pannett, C. A. *St. Mary's Hosp. Gaz.*, vol. 61, p. 73 (1955). See also Maurois, A. (ref. 3.12) pp. 274–5
37 Moore, Patrick. *'The moon'.* Mitchell Beazley and the Royal Astronomical Society, London (1982), p. 78

CHAPTER 21

 1 Hughes, W. H. (ref. 5.8) p. 51
 2 Colquhoun, D. B. *World Med.*, 29 January 1975, pp. 41–3
 3 Florey, W. H. *et al.* (ref. 15.7) p. 1152
 4 Hare, R. (ref. 7.10) pp. 66–70
 5 Gardner, A. D. *Nature*, Lond., vol. 146, p. 837 (1940)
 6 Park, J. T. and Strominger, J. L. *Science*, vol. 125, p. 99 (1957)
 7 Bustinza, F. (ref. 20.4) p. 181
 8 Hare, R. (ref. 7.10) p. 77
 9 Hare, R. (ref. 12.7) p. 5
10 Allison, Dr V. D. Personal communication, 30 September 1981
11 Bustinza, F. Letter to Dr Norman Heatley, 22 September 1981
12 Fleming, A. In *Penicillin.* ed. A. Fleming. Butterworth, London (1946), p. 9
13 Maurois, A. (ref. 3.12) pp. 136, 137
14 *Ibid.* p. 154
15 Fleming, A. (ref. 14.3) p. 42
16 Chain, E. B. In *The history of antibiotics.* (ref. 17.15) p. 18
17 Chain, E. B. (ref. 16.12) p. 115
18 Fleming, A. (ref. 21.12) p. 14

19 Berry, Prof. H. Letter. Br. Lib. Add. MSS 56218. Stewart, Prof. G. Letter to author, 24 July 1979

20 Cowen, D. L. *Bull. History Med.*, vol. 54, p. 608 (1980)

21 Hare, R. (ref. 12.7) p. 16

22 Maurois, A. (ref. 3.12) p. 156

23 Fleming, A. *Br. Med. Bull.*, vol. 2, p. 4 (1944). p. 5 quotes refs. (14.5) and (12.1)

24 Russell, Miss Audrey. Letter to author, 13 August 1982. Letter to R. Hare (ref. 14.20)

25 Beaverbrook, Lord. Statement, 5 June 1956. Br. Lib. Add. MSS 56217

26 Thomson, A. Landsborough. *Half a century of medical research.* HM Stationery Office, London (1975), Vol. 2, p. 55

27 Chain, E. B. In *The history of antibiotics.* (ref. 17.15) p. 17

28 Pitchforth, Vivian. Letter to author, June 1980

29 Buckley, Mrs H. Letter. Br. Lib. Add. MSS 56219

30 Hughes, W. H. (ref. 5.8) p. 71

CHAPTER 22

1 Hughes, W. H. (ref. 5.8) p. 88

2 Haddow, Prof. A. Quoted by Maurois, A. (ref. 3.12) p. 279

3 Pitchforth, Vivian (ref. 21.28)

4 Wright, A. E. (ref. 7.7)

5 Rogers, K. Letter. Br. Lib. Add. MSS 56214. Allison, V. D. (ref. 10.14)

6 Heyningen, Dr W. E. van. Letter to author, 3 August 1980

7 Cruickshank, Robert. Letter. Br. Lib. Add. MSS 56219

8 Parkes, Col W. (ref. 20.28)

9 *Ibid.*

10 Hughes, W. H. (ref. 5.8) p. 71

11 Dowling, Harry. *Fighting infection: conquests of the twentieth century.* Harvard University Press, Cambridge, Mass. (1977), p. 136

Fleming's Honours

Quoted from *Sir Alexander Fleming* by his brother Robert (ref. 2.1), by permission of Mr Angus Fleming.

1902	Senior Open Entrance Scholarship in Natural Science, St Mary's Hospital Medical School.
1902-06	Almost all class prizes and scholarships at St Mary's Hospital Medical School.
1903	Medal, Swimming Club, London Scottish Regiment Volunteers.
1906	Licentiate Royal College of Physicians. Member Royal College of Surgeons, 26 July.
	Medal, Rifle Competition.
1908	M.B., B.S.(London). Gold Medal.
	Cheadle Gold Medal in Clinical Medicine, St Mary's Hospital.
	Medal, The Daily Telegraph Rifle Competition.
1909	Fellow of the Royal College of Surgeons of England, June.
	Territorial Force Efficiency Medal.
1914	Monthly Medal, West Middlesex Golf Club.
1919	Hunterian Professor, Royal College of Surgeons of England.
	Assistant Director of the Inoculation Department at St Mary's Hospital, 7 July.
1928	Professor of Bacteriology, London University, at St Mary's Hospital Medical School, 18 July.
1929	Arris and Gale Lecturer, Royal College of Surgeons.
1932	President of the Section of Pathology, Royal Society of Medicine.
1941	William Julius Mickle Fellowship, University of London.
	President of Comparative Medicine, Royal Society of Medicine.
1943	Fellow of the Royal Society, 11 March.
	Award of Distinction of American Pharmaceutical Manufacturers Association, 13 December.
1944	Foreign Associate of Royal Physiographic Society of Lund, Sweden, 8 March.
	Fellow of the Royal College of Physicians, 21 May.
	Knight Bachelor, 4 July
	John Scott Medal and Prize – City Guild of Philadelphia, 21 July.
	Charles Mickle Fellowship, University of Toronto, 10 December.
	First Lister Memorial Lecturer, Society of Chemical Industry.
	Robert Campbell Orator (Medal). Ulster Medical Society.
1945	Honorary Freeman and Liveryman of the Dyers' Company of the City of London, 2 May.
	Honorary Freeman of the Borough of Paddington, 17 May.
	Honorary D.Sc. University of Princeton, 13 June.
	Honorary D.Sc. University of Pennsylvania, 18 June.
	Honorary D.Sc. University of Harvard, 28 June.
	Honorary Fellow Medical Chirurgical Society, Montreal, 19 July.

Cameron Prize in Practical Therapeutics, University of Edinburgh, 11 July.
Humanitarian Award, Variety Clubs of America, 25 July.
Médaille d'honneur de service de Santé Militaire, France, 31 August.
Commander of the Order of Public Health, France, 5 September.
Louis Pasteur Medal (Institut Pasteur), 6 September.
Commander of the Legion of Honour, France, 18 September.
Doctor Honoris Causa of Medicine and Surgery, University of Rome, 18 September.
Doctor Honoris Causa of Medicine, University of Brussels, 6 October.
Nobel Laureate in Physiology and Medicine, 25 October.
Honorary Member of the Philadelphia College of Pharmacy and Science, 5 November.
Jydsk Medicinsk Selskab, Alresmedlem, 18 November.
Doctor Honoris Causa of Medicine, University of Louvain, 30 November.
Doctor Honoris Causa, University of Paris, M.D. 15 December.
Medal of Honour, Canadian Pharmaceutical Manufacturers.
President of the Society for General Microbiology.
Honorary D.Sc. University of Durham.
Honorary Member, Royal Society of New Zealand.
Doctor Honoris Causa of Medicine, University of Liège.
Medal of the City of Liège.
Moxon Medal, Royal College of Physicians.
Corresponding Member of the Société Nationale des Sciences naturelles et Mathématiques de Cherbourg.
Honorary Member of Royal Medical Society, Edinburgh.
Honorary Fellow of Jutland Medical Society.
Cutter Lecturer, Harvard University.
Associé Etranger, Académie de Médecine, Paris.
Honorary Member of the Society of American Bacteriologists.
Hebra. Dec. Fac. Med. Virdobonensis. Sir Alexander Fleming gratio amino.
Honorary Award of the Schroeder Foundation.

1946   Correspondent Member of Academy of Sciences – Institute of France, 11 February.
Member of Pontifical Academy of Sciences, 12 March.
Honorary Professor, University of Brazil, 10 April.
Fellow of the Eingelige Danski Videnskabernes Selskab (Royal Danish Academy of Sciences and Letters), 12 April.
Honorary Member, Academia de Medicina, Buenos Aires, 6 June.
Honorary Member of Pathological Section, Royal Society of Medicine, 2 July.
Honorary D.Sc. University of Dublin, 3 July.
Honorary M.D. University of Athens, 6 July.
Honorary Doctor of Science, Queen's University, Belfast, 10 July.
Honorary Member, College of Surgeons, Brazil, 5 September.
Honorary Member of Academy of Medicine, Turin, 4 October.
Freedom of Burgh of Darvel, 26 October.
Gold Medal, Royal College of Surgeons of England, 14 November.
Honorary Fellow of Institute of Medical Laboratory Technology.
"Harben" Gold Medal, Royal Institute of Public Health and Hygiene.
Knight of Mark Twain.

Honorary Member of the Philadelphia College of Pharmacy and
Science.
Honorary Fellow of Royal College of Physicians, Edinburgh.
Medal in Therapeutics, Worhipful Society of Apothecaries, London.
Albert Gold Medal. Royal Society of Arts.
Foreign Honorary Member of Royal Academy of Medicine, Brussels.
Honorary President, Centre of Information and Study of Antibiotics,
Milan.
Honorary Member of Academy of Medicine, Brazil.
Honorary Member, Medical Society of Lombardy.
Honorary Member, Shut-Ins Association of America.

1947   Citation of the Order of the Purple Heart, U.S.A. 11 May.
Honorary Fellow, Greek Surgical Society, 26 May.
Gold Medal, Royal Society of Medicine, 17 June.
Honorary LL.D., St Andrew's University, 4 September.
Member Lynceorum Academia, Rome, 5 October.
Medal for Merit, U.S.A. 13 October.
Corresponding Member, Société Philomathique, Paris.
Honorary Member, the Wiener Gesellschaft der Aerzte.
Honorary Fellow, Royal Society of Edinburgh.
Fellow of the Académie Septentrionale, France.

1948   Member of the Athenaeum, 19 January.
Doctor Honoris Causa Medicine, Graz, 3 May.
Honorary D.Sc. University of London, 26 May.
Honorary Member, Royal Academy of Medicine, Barcelona, 3 June.
President of Honor, Sociedad Médica de Hospitales, Sevilla, 5 June.
Honorary Member, Sociedad Español de Higiene, 8 June.
Honorary Member, Royal Academy of Medicine, Seville, 8 June.
Honorary Member, Ateneo, Seville, 8 June.
Grand Cross of Alphonso (X), el Sabio, Spain, 11 June.
Honorary D.Sc. Madrid, 12 June.
Honorary Member, Royal Academy of Medicine, Madrid, 13 June.
Professor Emeritus of Bacteriology in the University of London, 1
October.
Gold Medal, Royal Academy of Medicine, Seville.
Addingham Medal.

1949   Honorary Freeman of the Borough of Chelsea, 16 March.
Honorary Member, Instituto Brasileiro de História da Medicina,
17 May.
Actonian Prize, July.
Freeman of the City of Verona, Italy, 28 July.
Grand Cross of the Order of Phoenix, Greece, 16 September.
Honorary D.Sc. Bristol University, 19 October.
Honorary Life Membership 4-H Clubs, U.S.A.
Honorary Member Future Farmers' Association, U.S.A.
Chief Doy-Gei-Taun (Maker of Great Medicine), Honorary Member
Kiowa Tribe, U.S.A.
'Grand Croix' Order of Chypre.
Past Grand Warden, United Grand Lodge of England.
Permanent Honorary Member of the Caledonian Club.
Honorary Member, Savage Club.
Honorary Member, Società per lo Studio delle Malattie Infettive e
Parasitarie, Italy.

1950   Honorary D.Sc. The National University of Ireland, 3 July.
        Honorary Member, National Society for the Prevention of Blindness,
            21 July.
        Gold Medal, American College of Chest Physicians.
1951   Member, Reale Accademia Internazionale del Parnaso, 16 February.
        Honorary Member of the Pakistan Medical Association, 8 April.
        Honorary Member, National Institute of Sciences of India.
        Sir Devaprasad Sarvadhikary Gold Medal (University of Calcutta).
        Lord Rector, University of Edinburgh.
1952   Cross of Officer of Merito Insigni. Belgian National Foundation of
            Charity, 12 May.
        Doctor Honoris Causa in Medicine, University of Salonika, 8 October.
        Honorary Member of the Greek Paediatricians Society, 10 October.
        Honorary Citizen of the City of Salonika, Greece, 16 October.
        Honorary President, Medical Society of Salonika, Greece, 22 October.
        Gold Medal of Athens, 31 October.
        Foreign Member of the Academy of Athens, October.
        Honorary President of the Greek Society of Microbiology and Hygiene,
            7 November.
        Honorary Citizen of Athens, 31 October.
        Honorary Member of almost all Medical Societies in Greece.
        Honorary Citizen of Kastoria.
        Honorary Member, Société Française de Biologie Médicale.
        Foreign Member, Royal Netherlands Academy of Sciences and Letters.
1953   Honorary Member, Societas Medica Havaniensis, 5 February.
        Honorary Member, Cuban Society of Clinical Pathology (Laboratorios
            Clínicos) 10 April.
        Honorary Member, Royal Society of British Sculptors, 16 April.
        Honorary Member, Cuban Good Neighbour Foundation, 20 April.
        Honorary Member, National Pharmaceutical College of Cuba,
            21 April.
        Honorary Member de la Assoc. de Estudiantes de Med., University La
            Habana, 23 April.
        Grand Cross, Orden de Honor y Mérito of Cuban Red Cross, 23 April.
        Grand Commander, Order of Carlos Finlay, 23 April.
        Honorary Professor of the University of Habana, 28 April.
        Honorary Member, Colegio Médico Nacional de Cuba, 28 April.
        Honorary Member, National College of Pharmacists, Cuba.
        Grand Lodge Medal for Distinguished Achievement, (Grand Lodge of
            Free and Accepted Masons of the State of New Jersey) 5 May.
        Honorary Member, Academia de Letras José de Alencar, Brazil, 7 June.
        Honorary Member, Botanical Society of Cuba, 29 September.
        Honorary Member, Brazilian Association of Ex-Combatants,
            24 October.
        Doctor Honoris Causa in Law, University of Edinburgh, November.
        Honorary Member, Copenhagen Medical Society.
        Honorary Citizen of Mikonos, Greece.
1954   Foreign Associate, l'Académie des sciences de l'Institut de France,
            15 February.
        D.Sc. University of Utah, 27 March.
        Honorary Member, American Academy of General Practice, March.
        Commissioned Kentucky Colonel, 7 April.
        Award for Merit, University of Louisville, 13 April.

Honorary Member, Medical Society Ribeirão Prêto, 4 May.
Honorary Member, Academy of Medicine, São Paulo, 10 May.
Citizen of City of São Paulo, 11 May.
Ordem Do Estilingue (Order of the Catapult), Ribeirão Prêto, 11 May.
Citizen of Ribeirão Prêto, 11 May.
Honorary Member of Centro Académico XXV de Janeiro, 13 May.
Doctor Honoris Causa, University of São Paulo, 13 May.
Honorary Member, Medical Association of Santos, 14 May.
Honorary Member, Escuela Paulista Medicina, May.
Honorary Fellow, Royal Society of Medicine, 20 July.
Citizen of State of São Paulo.
Honorary Member, Academy of Pharmacology and Odontology, São
  Paulo.
Honorary Member, Central Academy Pereira Barretto.
Citation from University of São Paulo.
Citizen of Honour, Town of Bordeaux, 15 November.
Doctor Honoris Causa, University of Bordeaux, 15 November.
Freeman of the Company of Barbers of London, 7 December.
Vice-President Emeritus of the Royal Sanitary Institute.
Commander of 'Compagnons du Bontemps Médoc.'
Jurade du St. Emilion.
Honorary Member of the Alpha Omega Alpha of the University of
  Oklahoma.
Honorary Member of the Brazilian Association of Ex-Combatants.
Diploma, Fédération Internationale des Arts des Lettres et des Sciences.
1955 Doctor Honoris Causa Veterinary Medicine, University of Vienna,
      10 March.

Fleming's Main Scientific Papers

From a list compiled by L. Colebrook (ref. 3.7). A supplementary manuscript list of minor items compiled by the late Professor F. Bustinza is in the author's possession and will be deposited with the Fleming papers in the British Library.

1908 (With L. NOON.) The accuracy of opsonic estimations. *Lancet*, vol. 1, p. 1203
      Some observations on the opsonic index, with especial reference to the accuracy of the method and to some of the sources of error. *The Practitioner*, vol. 80, p. 607
1909 On the aetiology of acne vulgaris and its treatment by vaccines. *Lancet*, vol. 1, p. 1035
      A simple method of serum diagnosis of syphilis. *Lancet*, vol. 1, p. 1512
1910 Contribution to debate on vaccine therapy. *Proc. R. Soc. Med.*, vol. 3, p. 137
1911 (With L. COLEBROOK.) On the use of salvarsan in the treatment of syphilis. *Lancet*, vol. 1, p. 1631
1915 On the bacteriology of septic wounds. *Lancet*, vol. 2, p. 638
      Some notes on the bacteriology of gas gangrene. *Lancet*, vol. 2, p. 376
1917 (With S. R. DOUGLAS & L. COLEBROOK.) On the question of bacterial symbiosis in wound infections. *Lancet*, vol. 1, p. 604
      (With S. R. DOUGLAS & L. COLEBROOK.) On skin grafting. A plea for its more extensive application. *Lancet*, vol. 2, p. 5
      The physiological and antiseptic action of flavine (with some observations on the testing of antiseptics). *Lancet*, vol. 2, p. 341
      (With S. R. DOUGLAS & L. COLEBROOK.) On the growth of anaerobic bacilli in fluid media under apparently aerobic conditions. *Lancet*, vol. 2, p. 530
1918 (With A. E. WRIGHT.) Further observations on acidaemia in gas gangrene and on conditions which favour the growth of its infective agent in the blood fluids. *Lancet*, vol. 1, p. 205
      (With S. R. DOUGLAS & L. COLEBROOK.) A case of rat-bite fever. *Lancet*, vol. 1, p. 253
      (With A. E. WRIGHT & L. COLEBROOK.) The conditions under which the sterilization of wounds by physiological agency can be obtained. *Lancet*, vol. 1, p. 831
1919 On some simply prepared culture media for *B. influenzae*. *Lancet*, vol. 1, p. 138
      (With A. B. PORTEOUS.) Blood transfusion by the citrate method. *Lancet*, vol. 1, p. 973
      (With A. B. PORTEOUS.) On streptococcal infections of septic wounds at a base hospital. *Lancet*, vol. 2, p. 49
      (With F. J. CLEMENGER.) An experimental research into the specificity of the agglutinins produced by Pfeiffer's bacillus. *Lancet*, vol. 2, p. 869

The action of chemical and physiological antiseptics in a septic wound. *Br. J. Surg.*, vol. 7, p. 99

1920 A simple method of recording automatically the gas produced by bacteria in culture, and the oxygen absorbed by aerobic gas-forming bacteria. *Br. J. Exp. Path.*, vol. 1, p. 66

1921 (With S. R. DOUGLAS.) On the antigenic properties of acetone-extracted bacteria. *Br. J. Exp. Path.*, vol. 2, p. 131

1922 On a remarkable bacteriolytic substance found in secretions and tissues. *Proc. R. Soc.* B, vol. 93, p. 306
       (With V. D. ALLISON.) Further observations on a bacteriolytic element found in tissues and secretions. *Proc. R. Soc.* B, vol. 94, p. 142
       (With V. D. ALLISON.) Observations on a bacteriolytic substance (Lysozyme) found in secretions and tissues. *Br. J. Exp. Path.*, vol. 3, p. 252

1924 A comparison of the activities of antiseptics on bacteria and leucocytes. *Proc. R. Soc.* B, vol. 96, p. 171
       On the accuracy of measurement of small volumes of fluid with a capillary pipette. *Br. J. Exp. Path.* vol. 5, p. 148
       (With V. D. ALLISON.) On the antibacterial power of egg-white. *Lancet*, vol. 1, p. 1303

1925 (With V. D. ALLISON.) On the specificity of the proteins of human tears. *Br. J. Exp. Path.*, vol. 6, p. 87

1926 On the effect of variations of the salt content of blood on its bactericidal power *in vitro* and *in vivo*. *Br. J. Exp. Path.*, vol. 7, p. 274
       A simple method of removing leucocytes from blood. *Br. J. Exp. Path.*, vol. 7, p. 281

1927 On Wright's centrifuge method of estimating phagocytosis and the rate of opsonisation of bacteria by normal serum. *Br. J. Exp. Path.*, vol. 8, p. 50
       (With V. D. ALLISON.) On the development of strains of bacteria resistant to Lysozyme action and the relation of Lysozyme action to intracellular digestion. *Br. J. Exp. Path.*, vol. 8, p. 214

1928 On the influence of temperature on the rate of agglutination of bacteria. *Br. J. Exp. Path.*, vol. 9, p. 231
       The bactericidal power of human blood and some methods of altering it. *Proc. R. Soc. Med.*, vol. 21, p. 25

1929 On the antibacterial action of cultures of a *Penicillium*, with special reference to their use in the isolation of *B. influenzae*. *Br. J. Exp. Path.*, vol. 10, p. 226
       The Staphylococci. A section of *A system of bacteriology in relation to medicine*. Med. Res. Council, London, vol. 2
       The Arris and Gale Lecture on 'Lysozyme—a bacteriolytic ferment found normally in tissues and secretions.' *Lancet*, vol. 1, p. 217

1930 (With I. H. MACLEAN.) On the occurrence of influenza bacilli in the mouths of normal people. *Br. J. Exp. Path.*, vol. 11, p. 127

1931 The intravenous use of germicides. *Proc. R. Soc. Med.*, vol. 24, p. 808
       Some problems in the use of antiseptics. *Br. Dental J.*, vol. 52, p. 105

1932 Lysozyme. *Proc. R. Soc. Med.*, Section of Path., vol. 26, p. 1
       The trend of modern research in bacteriology. *J. State Med.*, vol. 41, p. 559
       On the specific antibacterial properties of penicillin and potassium tellurite—incorporating a method of demonstrating some bacterial antagonisms. *J. Path. and Bact.*, vol. 35, p. 831

1934 Recent advances in vaccine therapy. *The Practitioner*, vol. 133, p. 537

1936 In Memoriam—Stewart Rankin Douglas. *J. Path. and Bact.*, vol. 42, p. 515

The growth of micro-organisms on paper. *Report of Second International Congress of Microbiology*, London, p. 552

1938 The treatment of pneumonia. *Br. Med. J.*, vol. 2, p. 37

The antibacterial action in vitro of 2-*p*-aminobenzene sulphonamide pyridine on pneumococci and streptococci. *Lancet*, vol. 2, p. 74

The antibacterial power of the blood of patients receiving 2-*p*-aminobenzene sulphonamide pyridine. *Lancet*, vol. 2, p. 564

1939 (With I. H. MACLEAN & K. B. ROGERS.) M and B 693 and pneumococci. *Lancet*, vol. 1, p. 562

Serum and vaccine therapy in combination with sulphanilamide and M and B 693. *Proc. R. Soc. Med.*, vol. 32, p. 911

Recent advances in vaccine therapy. *Br. Med. J.*, vol. 2, p. 99

1940 Antiseptic and chemotherapy. *Proc. R. Soc. Med.* (Section of Odontology), vol. 33, p. 127

The effect of antiseptics on wounds. *Proc. R. Soc. Med.*, vol. 33, p. 487

Observations on the bacteriostatic action of sulphanilamide and M and B 693 and on the influence thereon of bacteria and peptone. *J. Path. and Bact.*, vol. 50, p. 69

(With M. Y. YOUNG.) The inhibitory action of potassium tellurite on coliform bacteria. *J. Path. and Bact.*, vol. 51, p. 29

Chemotherapy for war wounds: comparisons and combinations. *Br. Med. J.*, vol. 2, p. 715

1941 A pneumococcus which required CO_2 for its growth. *Lancet*, vol. 1, p. 110

Chemotherapy and wound infection. *Proc. R. Soc. Med.*, vol. 34, p. 342

Some uses of nigrosin in bacteriology. *J. Path. and Bact.*, vol. 53, p. 293

1942 A simple method of using penicillin, tellurite and gentian violet for differential culture. *Br. Med. J.*, vol. 1, p. 547

In vitro tests of penicillin potency. *Lancet*, vol. 1, p. 732

1943 Active immunity. General considerations. *Proc. R. Soc. Med.*, vol. 36, p. 145

Streptococcal meningitis treated with penicillin. *Lancet*, vol. 2, p. 434

The use of paper and cellophane discs for the preparation of museum specimens of mould cultures. *Proc. Linn. Soc. Lond.*, vol. 155, p. 5

1944 The discovery of penicillin. *Br. Med. Bull.*, vol. 2, p. 4

Penicillin for selective culture and for demonstrating bacterial inhibitions. *Br. Med. Bull.*, vol. 2, p. 7

Penicillin. The Robert Campbell Oration. *Ulster Med. J.*, vol. 13, p. 95

Micro-methods of estimating penicillin in blood serum. *Lancet*, vol. 2, p. 620

(With M. Y. YOUNG, J. SUCHET & A. J. E. ROWE.) Penicillin content of blood serum after various doses of penicillin by various routes. *Lancet*, vol. 2, p. 621

1945 The Lister Memorial Lecture on Antiseptics. *Chem & Ind.* 20 Jan., p. 18

The Harben Lectures, on penicillin, its discovery, development and uses in the field of medicine and surgery. *J. Roy. Inst. Publ. Hlth.*, vol. 8, pp. 36, 63, 93

The Nobel Lecture on Penicillin. Stockholm, December 1945

1947 (With C. SMITH.) Estimation of penicillin in serum. Use of glucose, phenol red and serum water. *Lancet*, vol. 1, p. 401

Louis Pasteur. *Br. Med. J.*, vol. 1, p. 517

Sir Almroth Wright. *Br. Med. J.*, vol. 1, p. 646

(With J. R. MAY & A. E. VOUREKA.) Some problems in the titration of Streptomycin. *Br. Med. J.*, vol. 1, p. 627

The role of penicillin in surgical practice. *J. Int. Chir.*, vol. 7, p. 184

(With E. W. Fish.) Influence of penicillin on the coagulation of the blood with especial reference to certain dental operations. *Br. Med. J.*, vol. 2, p. 242

1949 (With W. H. Hughes & J. R. Kramer.) Morphological changes in some bacteria grown in presence of penicillin. *J. Gen. Microbiol.*, vol. 3, p. xxiii

1950 (With A. Voureka, I. R. H. Kramer & W. H. Hughes.) The morphology and motility of Proteus vulgaris and other organisms cultured in the presence of penicillin. *J. Gen. Microbiol.*, vol. 4, p. 257

Further observations on the motility of Proteus vulgaris grown on penicillin agar. *J. Gen. Microbiol.*, vol. 4, p. 457

1951 (With A. C. Ogilvie.) Syringe needles and mass inoculation technique. *Br. Med. J.*, vol. 1, p. 543

1953 The Shattuck Lecture. Twentieth-century changes in the treatment of septic infections. *New England J. Med.*, vol. 248, p. 1037

Index

Note: bacteria are entered under their common names with, in brackets, the specific names used by Fleming.